Tim Bowden is a writer and broadcaster with the Australian Broadcasting Corporation. He shares Neil Davis's Tasmanian origins, and was an ABC correspondent based in Singapore from 1965 to 1967. In recent years he has specialised in radio documentaries based on oral history techniques, including a twenty-four-part series on the Australian colonial experience in Papua New Guinea *(Taim Bilong Masta)*, and a sixteen-part series on Australian prisoners of war of the Japanese in World War II *(POW: Australians Under Nippon)*. He is the co-author of a book *Changi Photographer — George Aspinall's Record of Captivity*.

A long-time friend and colleague of Neil Davis, he persuaded him to collaborate on this biography in 1984. He is married with two children, and lives in Sydney.

ONE
CROWDED
HOUR

NEIL DAVIS
*Combat Cameraman
1934-1985*

TIM BOWDEN

An imprint of HarperCollins*Publishers*

AN ANGUS & ROBERTSON BOOK
An imprint of HarperCollinsPublishers

First published in hardback in 1987 by William Collins Pty Ltd,
Reprinted in 1987 (twice)
Published in Imprint paperback in 1988
Reprinted 1988 (three times), 1989 (three times), 1990

This edition published in 1991 by
CollinsAngus&Robertson Publishers Pty Limited (ACN 009 913 517)
A division of HarperCollinsPublishers (Australia) Pty Limited
Unit 4, Eden Park, 31 Waterloo Road, North Ryde
NSW 2113, Australia

William Collins Publishers Ltd
31 View Road, Glenfield, Auckland 10, New Zealand

Angus & Robertson (UK)
77-85 Fulham Palace Road, London W6 8JB, United Kingdom

National Library of Australia
Cataloguing-in-Publication data:

Bowden, Tim, 1937 –
  One crowded hour

  ISBN 0 207 16947 0.

  1. Davis, Neil, 1934-1985. 2. Journalists – Australia –
  Biography. 3. Journalists – Asia, Southeastern –
  Biography. 4. Vietnamese Conflict, 1961-1975 –
  Journalists. 5. War photographers – Biography. I. Title.

070'.92'4

Typeset in Century by Setrite Typesetters Ltd, Hong Kong
Printed by Globe Press Pty Ltd, Brunswick, Vic.

16   15   14   13   12
95   94   93   92   91

Contents

Acknowledgments

Originally, Neil Davis and I planned to collaborate on his biography. The loss of the principal source before the manuscript had begun to take shape necessitated heavy reliance on Neil's many friends for their recollections, photographs and unstinted help and support to produce this biography. The list that follows is by no means complete, but includes people and organisations to whom I owe a special debt of gratitude.

Neil's widow Julie has been totally supportive, making available all his papers and work diaries, which will form the basis of the Neil Davis Memorial Collection at the Australian War Memorial in Canberra. Neil Davis's sister Barbara Newitt and her husband Doug, Neil Davis's brother Darrel and his wife Lyn provided family photographs and letters, and Peter 'Twilight' Donnelly, Malcolm French and the late Jack Thwaites helped with details of Neil's Tasmanian career.

NBC News and Visnews Ltd, for whom Neil Davis worked for most of his professional life, have not only given permission for stills from his footage to be used, but have made available scripts and records. Thanks also to the *Far Eastern Economic Review* for permission to quote articles written by Neil Davis for the magazine from Phnom Penh in 1974 and 1975. David Bradbury made available a print of *Frontline* to select stills and provided full transcripts of all his original interviews.

I am particularly grateful to Gary Burns, who allowed me to question him about the events of 9 September in Bangkok only weeks after he had dragged the body of his dying friend from under the guns of the Thai tanks. Jim Gerrand and Bill Pinwill were generous with recollections, photographs and continuing advice about the Cambodian days.

Correspondents past and present, in Australia and overseas, wrote or taped their reminiscences of Neil Davis. Bruce MacDonell personally delivered diaries and papers from his Bangkok apartment. Special thanks to Donald Wise, Geoff Leach, Paul Lockyer, Richard Palfreyman, Don Simmons, John Tulloh, David Brill, Russell Spurr, Denis Warner, Kate Webb, Pat Burgess, Athol Meyer, Derek Davies, Brian Barron, Jim Revitt, Tom Aspell, Jack Langguth, John McBeth, Derek McKendry, Jim Bennett, Tony Ferguson, Peter Hollinshead, Willy Phua, Ian MacIntosh, Rodney Tasker, Yosep (Joe) Lee, Jack Cahill, David Phillips, Jim Laurie, Derek Williams, Philip Koch, Al Dawson, John Milne, Stuart Inder, Peter Barnett and Nora Bonney.

Hank Nelson and Gavan Daws gave essential and continuing editorial advice on structure and content. Jacqueline Kent edited the manuscript with great competence and cheerfulness.

Ros Bowden found herself once again a single parent in company with a cranky lodger while the manuscript was being compiled.

Foreword

Sound, sound the clarion, fill the fife,
Throughout the sensual world proclaim,
One crowded hour of glorious life
Is worth an age without a name.

By Thomas Osbert Mordaunt (1730—1809), written during
the Seven Years' War of 1756—1763

Neil Davis wrote the last two lines of Mordaunt's verse in
the flyleaf of every work diary he kept in Southeast Asia
from 1964 to 1985. He told me it was his motto, and summed
up his philosophy.

A burst of shrapnel in a Bangkok street ended his remarkable run of crowded hours on 9 September 1985.

His work diaries have been invaluable in charting the
movements and major stories covered by Davis, the bravest
and most distinguished Australian news cinecameraman
and war correspondent since Damien Parer. These diaries
were hand-carried out of Phnom Penh days before the city
fell to the Communist Khmer Rouge troops in April 1975.
All his other records, notebooks, scripts and personal
records and effects were lost. But these diaries say nothing
about the persona of Neil Davis, the boy from Sorell,
Tasmania, who made the big time, the compulsively competitive likable larrikin who always had the crowd on his
side, the sensitive student of other cultures, the sensualist
and relentless lover, perpetrator of wild wagers, confidant
of leading Asian political figures, seemingly fearless war
correspondent and the man acknowledged and liked by his
peers (no mean achievement in the cut-throat arena of
international journalism) as one of the best in the business.

Yet Davis, outwardly gregarious and friendly, revealed

very little to anyone about his intimate thoughts and motivations. This biography has drawn from taped interviews with Neil Davis and his own taped and written reminiscences. Friends and colleagues have been generous with their contributions. Some of the most revealing glimpses of the inner Neil Davis come from a complete record of letters he wrote to his Aunt Lillian Davis, a former World War I nurse who lived in Tasmania.

Journalists, saturated with a constant overdose of human suffering and despair during war and natural disasters, construct a carapace of cynicism and black humour. So did Neil Davis, but many of his journalist friends did not know of the commitment of his modest savings to Vietnamese and Cambodian orphanages, and of his personal help to refugees — particularly to mothers of the 'children of the dust', the Amerasians of Vietnam.

His work diaries, however, do reveal some remarkable statistics about his astonishing stamina and courage as a war correspondent. In Cambodia, in 1973, he covered twenty-eight combat incidents in one month. During sustained periods in the field in Vietnam, he filmed combat for three days out of every four.

Like many rookie war correspondents arriving in Vietnam in the mid- and late 1960s, I received the Davis treatment — an informed backgrounding on the current situation, information on negotiating the bureaucratic difficulties of becoming accredited with the Americans and the South Vietnamese; I learned how to get copy, tapes or film shipped out of the country, change money and, most importantly, how to gain battlefield experience without being killed the first time out.

Completing Neil Davis's biography in the absence of the principal source has been at first a painful and, as I went on, a personally rewarding experience. As I began to collate the surprising amount of source material available, it became clear that *One Crowded Hour* would be more than the chronicle of the life of a remarkable man. It is also a journey through significant events in recent Asian history.

If Neil Davis is reincarnated — and he admired Buddhist teachings — he will probably be a Cambodian. Forced to leave Phnom Penh in 1975 when the Communist Khmer Rouge forces so brutally took over, he maintained a passionate involvement and interest in that country and its people. The Cambodians believe that when a soldier dies bravely in battle, death comes not as the Grim Reaper, but in the form of a laughing and beautiful woman.

Neil Davis's friend and colleague Gary Burns confirms that he was always very philosophical about death. 'We always said to him, "If she's a lady, then you probably know her."'

Tim Bowden
Sydney, 1987

1

The
Quiet Australian

I wasn't afraid of being killed, but I really didn't want
to be wounded and lie out there with a gut full of
shrapnel — I'd seen a lot of wounded soldiers die like
that, and I didn't care for it at all.

Neil Davis

On the morning of 9 September 1985, I began to write
the opening chapter of a biography of Neil Davis. The
Tasmanian-born cine-cameraman and war correspondent
had been sending me tapes of reminiscences to swell
a growing pile of tapes and transcripts. But I had a sudden, almost panicky desire to make a start — the process
of research and collection can go on too long.

The irony of beginning his life story on the day he died
would have amused Neil Davis if he ever could have known.
He liked those crazy, fateful coincidences. He would have
told the story with gusto over a drink in the Grand Prix Bar
in Patpong Road, Bangkok: 'That bloody Bowden. Bastard
was actually writing my epitaph when I copped it!' I was,
too.

I typed the heading 'ATTITUDES TO FATE AND DEATH' and
turned to the many hours of tape we had recorded over the
previous two years to find the quotes I wanted.

*I did become addicted to combat after experiencing
my first three years of frontline action in Vietnam. It
was exhilarating, much the same as playing a good
hard game of football, or catching the big fish. It was
testing your skill and faculties, physical and mental,
against a given situation or an opponent.*

*It is a time of heightened perception. I was never
afraid in action . . . I was apprehensive many times
and very excited, but when I got used to it, I used to
look forward to combat.*

The soft, distinctive voice of this quiet Australian paused,
and continued:

*There's the oft-repeated thing, 'Any man who says
he's not afraid is a fool'. But I think fear means that you
can't handle things, that you lie down and whimper or
something. I felt very confident I could handle any
situation, partly because I developed an extra sense,
instinct if you like, which wild animals have and which
we have lost in our so-called civilised life.*

*You will see a dog react to certain situations and
wonder if it had a premonition. That's what becomes
addictive, and it was exhilarating, like going into
overdrive on a car. On occasions I have instinctively
dropped to the ground before a shot was fired.*

But not on the morning of 9 September 1985. Thai coups
were not uncommon but were a damned nuisance when
you were just about to go on holidays. Cursing the Thais'
abominable sense of timing, Davis, resplendent in the bright
red socks he had taken to wearing on all occasions, pulled
on a pair of dark green pants and lighter green shirt and
began the methodical checking of his camera gear.

Neil Davis had filmed combat in the Indo-China war for
eleven years from 1964 and had recorded and witnessed

extraordinary events. He worked for the British international newsfilm company Visnews and later for the American television network NBC. Unlike most other Western cine-cameramen, he had consistently filmed the fighting efforts of the Vietnamese and Cambodian soldiers. His viewfinder had framed their pain, anguish and action and begun the process of projecting it to the world.

After the fall of Saigon, which he stayed to film, he had continued to cover Asia for NBC, adding Africa and the Middle East to his areas of operation. I had known him in Tasmania and had worked with him in Southeast Asia during the mid-1960s. Our paths had diverged, but I nourished a long-term plan to write his biography.

Neil Davis was a byword among foreign correspondents, universally liked in a competitive profession not without intense personal jealousies. Tall, blond and always looking ten years younger than his real age, he won the Singapore-based Visnews job in 1963. He moved from the cold wind-swept beauty of Tasmania to base himself in the smaller, fully tropical island of Singapore. It was the beginning of a passionate love affair with Asia and its people. He sent his first film out of Saigon in April 1964 when American Secretary of State Dean Rusk toured allegedly Viet Cong-controlled areas of the Mekong Delta region. It was almost as though the Vietnam war had been waiting for Neil Davis to arrive, although he was no lover of violence.

When you are in danger of losing your life, all pretensions are stripped away. Irritating little facets to a person's character don't matter any more; it's what kind of human being he is, and whether he does his job. When I was with Vietnamese and Cambodian soldiers I found a feeling of comradeship and sympathy that even extended across the line to the other side, even in the most desperate frontline situations. I found that very rewarding.

He lost count of the number of times he was wounded — more than twenty, but only six of those he considered serious.

People have sometimes said to me, 'What does it feel like to be a living legend?' I know that behind my back, not to my face, I have been called Suicide Davis or Death Wish Davis. The 'death wish' tag has stayed with me. One of my great friends, Jim Bennett, an American television correspondent, once put people to rights on that one. I was not present at the time when he said, 'Well, he hasn't got a death wish, and that's easily proven. He's still alive.'

. . .

It was 9.30 a.m. in Sydney, 6.30 a.m. in Bangkok.

There were tanks in the streets. Cursing the rebels' timing and thinking wistfully of his now-delayed holiday in Vanuatu, New Zealand and Australia, Davis shouldered his camera gear and teamed up with his soundman, Bill Latch. Latch, an American married to a Thai, had been taking his daughter to school when he saw the tanks and raised the news alert. If this job had not come up, Davis had planned to go to the Cambodian border that day to meet An Veng, his former Cambodian soundman and driver in Phnom Penh. An Veng had managed to get out to a refugee camp after ten desperate years under the Pol Pot and Vietnamese regimes. It would have been an emotional reunion.

News of a Thai coup was not enough to get Davis's adrenalin pumping. Somewhat seasonal in character, they were generally relatively bloodless affairs, with the losers rather sportingly being allowed to fly out of the country (returning discreetly some time later). Davis and Latch teamed up with the Bangkok-based Visnews cameraman, Gary Burns, also an Australian, and his Thai soundman Daeng Kariah.

Neil Davis had become a victim of changing technology.

He had always worked by himself in dangerous situations, not only because he was a natural loner, but because he did not want the responsibility of making life-and-death decisions for others. In Vietnam he filmed combat with a cassette tape recorder strapped to his waist and a compact hand-held Bell and Howell spring-loaded camera. For less hectic sound-on-film work, he shouldered his CP 16 Commag sound-on-film camera and managed his own sound. But the switch to videotape had put the clock back in his terms. For the last six years of his reporting life he needed a soundman to shoulder the heavy battery and cassette pack, linked to the nine-kilogram camera by a video cable.

Working independently, Gary Burns and Neil Davis took shots of tanks in the streets. They met at the rebel-held First Division radio station compound in Phitsanuloke Road. As the dissidents continued to broadcast from inside, tanks assembled in the road outside. The newsmen filmed loyalist Thai soldiers setting up machine-gun nests. Then in a lull, Bangkok's morning peak-hour traffic took over again, with the usual parade of taxis, Honda motorbikes, trucks and bicycles weaving their way between the tanks and the radio station.

The two crews decided to send back their early coverage tape cassettes by taxi to their offices, and Davis cadged his traditional cigarette from Burns (it was a ritual that he never bought his own). They sent one of the drivers to buy Cokes and munched some breakfast bananas while they watched the cluster of tanks and about twenty soldiers on the other side of the road.

According to Gary Burns, there was no sign of any danger, when, 'Suddenly a machine gun opened up, firing at the radio station directly behind us. We grabbed our gear, and the first inclination was to run. Unfortunately, my soundman ran the wrong way, to the left, which took us right in front of three of the tanks. In hindsight, if we'd run to the right we would have been clear of the tanks and the soldiers very quickly.'

Davis stayed beside two telephone booths to film the outbreak of firing. Taking what cover he could behind a small metal telephone junction box, Burns looked along the road to see Davis up on one knee and filming. 'I thought, oh, shit, if he's filming, I've got to film. I switched the camera on and poked it out from behind the telephone junction box, but I was still behind cover. Davis was out in the open for at least a minute and a half before the tanks opened up with their cannons.'

During the brief lull before the tanks opened up, Davis and Latch ran over to join the Visnews crew behind the metal junction box. Then all hell broke loose as machine guns, tank cannons and automatic weapons fired at the radio station. The four men, yoked in pairs with camera gear and cables, were desperate for cover, crammed in behind the junction box which was barely a metre high.

'They were firing directly into the gate and the wall behind us,' says Burns.

It was utter pandemonium. The street filled with smoke and the sound tapes were saturated with cannon and machine-gun fire. Gary Burns noticed blood on Davis's arm as he tried to pull him closer in behind the small metal box.

'Jesus, you're hit,' he said.

'No, I'm all right, I'm all right,' said Davis, and showed his arm. It was just a scratch.

An unbelieving Gary Burns saw Davis preparing to film again, even though machine-gun bullets and cannon shells were screaming overhead and exploding against the wall behind them. Burns says, 'I could feel him there, he was lying across the lower half of my body. I had Bill Latch on the other side of me, which as it turned out, meant that I was perfectly protected and they copped the shrapnel.

'The firing was so intense I felt certain we were all going to die. I was lying there trying to get through the cracks in the pavement . . . you want to return to mother earth. I felt some close rounds come in, and we all shook and shuddered. I didn't feel Neil hit.'

There was a brief lull, and the newsmen started screaming to the tank crews to let them get out. But the firing started again, and continued for another five minutes — it seemed longer. Another pause, and this time one of the soldiers on the nearest tank signalled them to get away quickly. Gary Burns said to Davis, 'Come on, mate, let's get out of here.'

He says, 'I half pushed Neil, and he rolled over. His head just lolled back in front of me, his eyes rolled back, and he was quite obviously dead. I went to pull him back, and it was like one of those horror things. His whole side just opened up and spilled on to the pavement . . . he'd been virtually cut in half by shrapnel.'

Stark footage, soon to flash around the world, relayed what may be termed the ultimate television story. Always the complete professional, Neil Davis had filmed his own death. His head, astonishingly almost in focus, appeared in front of his own lens. Then as Gary Burns began to pull him away, at enormous personal risk, Davis's running camera tilted over on its side. His mortally wounded soundman Bill Latch, hit in the stomach and legs, was filmed desperately crawling away as Gary Burns attempted to rescue Davis's body. His still rolling camera also showed tank cannons still inexplicably firing, seemingly at them. Other cameras showed the ghastly blood trail from Davis's terrible wounds staining the ground as he was dragged along. They are searing images.

It was 10.30 a.m. in Bangkok. In Sydney, not knowing what had happened, I continued running through the tapes in which Neil Davis described his own attitudes to fate and death.

Some of my friends have categorised me as being foolhardy, suicidal. But I believe myself to be a methodical and careful person — admittedly with a streak of impetuousness at time — but I think most people have that. Perhaps there is a paradox here. I have a motto I picked up from somewhere. It says simply; 'One crowded hour of glorious life is worth an age without a name.'

By early evening, the television pictures had been bounced from satellites around the world. Neil Davis's death was a bigger story than the half-hearted coup he was covering.

In his shop in Dodges Ferry, a small seaside town in southern Tasmania, genial Porky McKinley was about to serve a customer with a packet of fish and chips. As he moved across to the counter, his eye was caught by the television news, and he saw his boyhood friend Neil Davis dying on a Bangkok street. He burst into tears and dropped the deep-fried food on the floor. Almost unaware of what he was doing, he picked it up, gave it to the startled customer, and locked up his shop, to come to terms with his grief.

In newsrooms throughout the world, hardened profess-ionals gasped in equivalent shock. It was impossible that the charmed Davis, that laughing cavalier of the camera, should be dead — that the man who had so often lain alongside the lady of death in the Indo-China war should have bought it in a tinpot Thai coup. While the general public stared in disbelief at its television screens, the profession mourned the passing of a very special man and colleague. Neil Davis dead! It was unthinkable.

The *New York Times* published a three-column obituary. From Tokyo, Korean cameraman Joe Lee wrote to me: 'My wife went crazy when I told her. "Why him?" she screamed. Every one of us had the same question, I think. Why now? He is the guy who escaped death so many times . . . I think as long as I remember him he is always with me and will live in my memory while I'm here.'

In Sydney, my heading 'ATTITUDES TO FATE AND DEATH' mocked me from the printed page. Even in grief I could hear Neil Davis's amused chuckle.

Of course, a sense of instinct doesn't stop a well-

aimed bullet . . . you can always be killed — unluckily killed.

Davis, who said he valued friends and friendship above everything else, was a man without enemies. Most of his many friends were Asians. In the years after the Indo-China war, he had devoted much of his time and money to helping refugees from Cambodia and Vietnam.

In Washington, New York, Sydney, London, Tokyo, Bangkok, Singapore, Hong Kong and in distant and unexpected places, journalists and friends gathered to mourn 'The Fox', as he was called in Bangkok. The orginal nickname had been 'The Old Fox', but the word 'old' seemed inappropriate. Neil Davis was actually fifty-one, although his boyish blond good looks belied his age.

Although worldwide television audiences had seen thousands of metres of his Indo-China coverage during the eleven years of war, it took David Bradbury's award-winning documentary *Frontline* to make people aware of Neil Davis and his extraordinary achievements. The film had an enormous impact on Australian, British and American audiences. *New York Times* critic John J. O'Connor wrote, 'Mr Davis is a big, gentle, soft-spoken man, making his tales and scenes of brutal destruction all the more shattering.'

Frontline highlights Neil Davis's most celebrated 'crowded hour of glorious life' — when he took his exclusive footage of the North Vietnamese tanks crashing down the gates of Saigon's presidential palace on 30 April 1975. To cover such stories, Davis had to sustain his technical and artistic skills in violent and unpredictable surroundings. Despite such actions of great skill and courage, it is the lot of the cinecameraman to be submerged beneath the impact of his own work. Essentially a modest man, this was of no great concern to Neil Davis. The opinion of his peers meant more to him than any public recognition — and he need have had no doubt about that.

2

Nala

On 4 February 1973, Neil Davis drove himself down into the Mekong Delta region south of Saigon to engineer a long-cherished scoop — to cross to the other side and film Viet Cong soldiers in the field. By sunset he was deep in 'enemy' territory, billeted with an old Vietnamese rice farmer and his family in their thatched hut. He had used his extensive Vietnamese contacts to make the switch into the Communist-controlled area.

It was not the first time Davis had lodged with Vietnamese villagers, and he was quickly accepted by the old man and his family.

> As we talked on into the night, the old man got out a bottle of basaday, a kind of rice whisky, poured a tot into a small glass, and handed it to me. I took a sip of the clear spirit, and handed it on.

Davis knew instinctively that they only had one glass, and it had to be shared.

> I knew of similar occurrences when a Westerner, unaware of the situation, had simply downed the tot in one gulp and handed the glass back, causing great embarrassment.
> I felt quite at home with those people, as I did with the

Vietnamese they were fighting on the American-backed side. The farmers were the same, there was no difference in their philosophy.

Neil Davis's empathy with the peasant farmers of Asia sprang from his own upbringing on a subsistence farm in the remote hamlet of Nala in southern Tasmania, a small cluster of farms beside a railway siding. It may seem incongruous to find connections between his own rural upbringing and the lives of Vietnamese peasant farmers, but nevertheless they existed.

I've always had sympathy with country people and whether they were rice paddy farmers or farmers in the mountains, their attitudes didn't differ much from those of my father and the people who lived in and around Nala. There is the same basic acceptance of life and death, the phenomena of good and bad seasons and an acceptance of the fact that you have to work hard six or seven days a week. There's also a lot of what we call homespun intelligence, which I accept and have a great regard for. There is a common bond between farming people throughout the world, whether they are up to their thighs in waterlogged paddy fields planting rice or harvesting wheat from a tractor. The philosophy is forged through the weather, the crops and the hardships which draw people who work on the land together.

It isn't just the farmers of Asia. I've been in the countryside in Britain, and I got on well with the farmers there too, because they have a similar attitude to life. That feeling for the land has helped me a great deal, and I've never felt a stranger in Asian countries. I never had to tell people that I was a farm boy myself. They sensed that and were well disposed towards me.

Neil Davis was born on St Valentine's Day, 14 February 1934. He was the youngest of four children — three boys and a girl — and picked up the enduring nickname of 'Tiny' despite growing up to be 1.83 metres tall. He was born into tough economic times.

> You were always aware of the possibilities of hardship, and the word 'depression' would come up again and again. There was also much talk of war.
>
> My father was one of twelve children, he had a twin sister, and they were the second youngest of the family. Several of his older brothers had fought in World War I, and his older sister, my Auntie Lillian, had been a nurse in Europe during the Great War.

Neil Davis's father had acquired some family land and arrived in Nala with all his possessions on a horse-drawn dray to farm in the centre block of a square of settlement. The families at Nala ran sheep and a few cows, planted out some wheat and oats and effectively lived off the land.

Although life on the farm was hard, the Davises were better off than poorer city folk during the Depression years. At least they had adequate meat and vegetables.

> It was sixty miles by road to Hobart, which had roughly one hundred thousand people at that time. The whole of Tasmania supported a population of about three hundred and thirty thousand in an island as big as Sri Lanka, or Cambodia — a country I was later to love very much.

The Davis family lived a simple life, not much different from that of the Australian pioneer settlers. There was no electricity at Nala and lighting and heating came from kerosene lamps, open fires and wood-fuelled kitchen ranges.

> We had two cows which we milked daily for fresh cream and milk. I don't remember eating butter, because we used to sell it. We ate beef dripping from the roast

joints of meat, so I didn't feel deprived by not having butter. We never went short of food. My mother baked bread and there were always vegetables, which we grew, and fruits in season like apples and pears and sometimes peaches. There were lots and lots of potatoes, and we didn't go short of mutton because the Nala families killed a sheep once every two or three weeks and shared it.

On very rare occasions we had poultry, a rooster, or when an old laying hen was killed. Eggs were much prized. We ate them every day, and they were used for cooking. Sunday lunch was the big event of the week — we called it Sunday dinner even though it was in the middle of the day. It could be a fresh roast leg of lamb, or a shoulder, depending on each family's turn.

The Davis dwelling was typical of Tasmanian farmhouses of that time, a weatherboard structure with a corrugated iron roof and a veranda on two sides. The family lived mainly in the kitchen.

Everybody spent their time there. It was warm in the winter because of the wood stove, and the neighbours would come and chatter to Mother as she worked. The family ate there, and it was the communal room.

We did have a front sitting room, which served practically no other purpose than to house the better furniture, which we kids were not allowed to sit on. It was always, 'Don't get your boots on the furniture. Wipe your boots before you go in.' It was only used when what might be termed VIP visitors came from Hobart, or the town of Sorell where our ancestral home of Belle Vue was located. So that room was a dead loss. It was ridiculous, really; it should have been turned into a master bedroom or something for all the good it was, but every house had its front sitting room which was seldom used.

So we were short of bedrooms. My sister had to have

her own room, and my oldest brother Jimmy would have to get out of his bedroom when visitors came. My next eldest brother Darrel and I slept out on the veranda, which was enclosed at one end.

Most of the time we slept without sheets in grey army-style blankets, and during winter we used hessian wheat-bags as a bedspread and top blanket. We were quite warm, and didn't think we were deprived in any way.

One of the earliest family photographs shows Neil Davis standing barefoot in the snow at Nala. Footwear was expensive, simply because it had to be bought and was not able to be provided from the farm. There was a system of hand-me-downs for clothing, boots and shoes.

When it was snowing, we kids would want to go out and throw snowballs, build snowmen and run about. And my parents would say, 'Fine, go out and play, but take off your shoes, you're not going to be scorching around in the snow in your new shoes.' After we'd finished playing we'd come in and if the wood stove wasn't too hot, we'd open the oven door and put our chilled feet right inside to warm them up again.

The family rose early, and was in bed by 9 p.m. News of the outside world came from newspapers dropped off at the Nala railway siding twice a week. Apart from the Hobart *Mercury*, there was the popular *Smith's Weekly*, from Sydney. World news was gleaned through the His Master's Voice radio — a magnificent oblong contraption about a metre long and thirty centimetres high and deep, with a trumpet-like speaker sprouting from the top.

Neil Davis could ride a horse by the age of five, and the daredevil streak that later distinguished his career in sport and journalism was already well developed.

I rode on my father's big horse one day, and the horse got sick of me and decided to bolt for home, about three-quarters of a mile away. I remember being not too worried, because I knew the horse would pull up when it got to the front gate.

It was as fast as I'd even been on a horse, and I was enjoying it. Unfortunately a farm worker saw what was happening and did completely the wrong thing by jumping out from behind a big pine tree to try and stop the runaway. The horse pulled up dead and I went flying over its head and landed on the road. The next thing I remember was coming to inside the house with my mother's worried face looking down at me.

Davis carried a scar on his upper right arm for life. Most of his friends took it to be one of his many war wounds. It was often easier to smile modestly than go through the full story.

He enjoyed looking after the horses belonging to his Uncle Barney.

I remember being very proud of myself when I was no more than ten years old, going out and harnessing up the two big draughthorses. They were massive animals, and I could walk under their bellies almost without stooping. I had to stand on boxes to get them harnessed to a big wooden sled.

It wasn't until years later in Southeast Asia, particularly in South Vietnam, when I saw tiny Vietnamese children — probably the same age as I was but much smaller — leading the water buffaloes home after work, or washing them down in the paddy fields and feeding them, that reminded me of my earlier days on the farm. I had the same instinctive communion with those big gentle horses as the Vietnamese kids had with their buffaloes.

Neil Davis's cousin Graeme remembers telling him that he seemed to have a sixth sense and an uncanny ability to anticipate horses' behaviour as he untangled their legs from a mass of twisted chains and harness. Davis, then aged twelve, responded with a smile: 'Sixth sense? No — horsesense!'

Once a month, with luck, the family would drive into the feeder town of Oatlands on the Midlands Highway connecting northern and southern Tasmania. There, set among nineteenth-century convict-built stone cottages, was a weatherboard hall with 'Roxy Talkies' in large letters over its front entrance. Neil saw his first movies at the Roxy — silent films featuring Charlie Chaplin or Tom Mix. Sometimes there were newsreels with sound commentary.

By 1940, war in Europe was affecting southern Tasmania. Neil Davis's father, who had been a teenager and too young to go to the first war, was now too old to enlist in the second. In any case, farming was a protected occupation. He joined the Light Horse, as part of a home guard.

They carried out exercises from time to time when he would go away for a few weeks on field manoeuvres and then come back. It all seemed very dashing and exciting.

Tasmania, with its volatile eucalypt forests is, like many other parts of Australia, especially vulnerable to catastrophic bushfires. Davis's father died on Black Tuesday 1967 when ferocious firestorms devastated the southern half of the island. On Black Friday 1940, the Nala district was completely burned out and all crops were destroyed. The Davises hung on, but when Neil's grandfather died in 1941, the family moved back to the ancestral home Belle Vue at Sorell, a sleepy farming town only twenty-six kilometres east of Hobart.

3

Belle Vue

Today, a bridge over the River Derwent and two causeways across the shallow tidal estuaries of Pittwater have brought Sorell to within a few minutes' drive of Hobart. But even so, development has bypassed these small rural centres. Richmond's well-preserved Georgian stone buildings are among Tasmania's most visited tourist attractions. The main road to the east coast and the convict settlement of Port Arthur still runs through the main street of Sorell, but the district has changed little since Neil Davis was a boy. Cereal crops are still grown in neat fields, and cattle and sheep graze reflectively on lush pastures. The Davises have been farmers in the area since records were kept.

Great-grandfather Davis worked on the *Mercury* newspaper in Hobart and used to run the forty-eight kilometres home to Bream Creek east of Sorell every Friday night for the weekend. He would stop for urgently needed refreshment on the way. One fateful day, he stopped at the Gordon Highlander pub in Sorell for an ale or three after his first twenty-six kilometres, had a heart seizure and dropped dead outside the pub.

I thought it was a pretty good way to go myself, but Granny always worried I would end up like great-grandfather Davis.

In any case, the realities of death were immediately apparent to a country boy like Neil Davis. As small boys, he and his brother had found the body of an itinerant farm worker who had died of cold or natural causes under a bush.

We regarded death as a natural thing, like the birth of calves and puppies or kittens and the things that were done to animals, like cutting the tails off the lambs, or castrating the lambs.

My grandfather didn't use the dreadful knife, with clippers on one end, to tear out the lambs' testicles. He used an old pocket knife to cut open the testicle bag and would go down quickly with his head, take the testicles in his teeth and throw his head back, tearing them out at the same time.

He said that was much cleaner and safer for the lamb, and there was little or no blood.

Neil Davis's acceptance of the realities of life and death in the country were tested when he was ten years old. In 1944, his mother Marjorie died suddenly.

She had a weak heart, and one night shortly after her fortieth birthday she went out of the house to feed the poultry and didn't come back.

It got dark and we went out looking for her. My father found her and carried her in. It was a traumatic experience in the sense that my mother had just died, and I helped my father carry her body into the bedroom, but that's life in the country. Children were born in the farmhouse, and most people died there too. She wasn't the first dead person I'd seen.

I remember we called the country doctor, who was a lovely old guy. My father rang him up, and as he did so — it was about seven p.m. — remarked that 'old Andy would be drunk', and of course old Andy was drunk, but he drove out in his car and solemnly pronounced my mother not to be alive.

Whenever somebody died in the district, no matter what the time of day, word would be passed to the vicar and the local church bells would ring.

Then the people in Sorell would ask 'Who are going to be the next two?' because they were convinced that deaths always came in threes. I remember this happening many times. There would be no deaths in Sorell for say two years, and then three within a month or six weeks. People didn't think that was astounding, they just accepted that was the way things happened.

After Neil Davis's mother died, his older sister Barbara took over much of the responsibility for running Belle Vue, and his Aunt Lillian Davis assumed a larger role in his life.

She became my mother by proxy, I suppose. She was my father's oldest sister, a very capable but very tough lady. We became much closer after I was an adult, actually.

There was also the remarkable Granny Davis, with her raucous good humour and sage advice, who always spoke of England as 'home', and Sorell as 'the village'.

In many ways, Neil Davis had an idyllic boyhood, living close to nature, with senses honed keen. He believed that city dwellers lose a sense of intuition that country people retain, and he later claimed that the adrenalin and tension of frontline combat triggered a kind of sixth sense, during which heightened perception caused him to act in certain ways that on occasions saved his life.

The relationship between a sheepdog and its master demonstrated this acute, perhaps telepathic, communication.

Whole books have been written on how dogs read their masters' minds. If you see trained sheepdogs with their owners, they watch their eyes. A change of focus or eye movement tells the dog he is about to receive an order, and usually the dog knows what that will be.

My father used hand signals to direct his dog to round up sheep. For instance, if he wanted the flock rounded up he would simply wave his hand behind his back, and say something like, 'Get up around there'. Often the dog was under way, not only before he had spoken, but before he had had time to move his hand.

Every farm had three or four working dogs, but there was always one favourite. Geoff Davis, Neil's father, had a marvellous sheepdog called Jack who was quite an old dog when the family moved south to Sorell.

Jack would follow my father everywhere, and was his constant companion. When he was fifteen or sixteen years old, which is a remarkable age for a dog, he went blind and deaf, but he still had the instinct. He would sit at the front door of the house, slightly to one side, and wait. When my father came in the back door — and I don't think he could have smelt him because he was twenty or thirty metres on the other side of the house — he would always know, and would make his way stiffly down the outside path which converged with a path from the back door.

He managed to reach the junction at the same time as my father, who would reach down and pat him, and they would walk along slowly, with old Jack following blindly a pace or so behind.

One Sunday my father said almost casually that Jack would have to be destroyed. We usually went for a family walk on Sunday afternoon, and while we were away a young man from Sorell had been asked to do the job. No farmer would shoot his own dog, but a friend would do it, as an act of friendship.

Now it's pretty quiet in the countryside at any time, with almost no traffic, and only bird noises or cattle lowing. It was inevitable we would hear the gunshot that killed old Jack. And we did. My father was a very quiet man, and always kept his emotions very well under control, but I knew he was very, very much affected.

In a city, you take your dog along to the vet and he puts it down, but it is a clinical process. Jobs in the countryside have to be done by country people themselves. They hold the power of life and death, and have to exercise it.

Years later, Davis often heard the distinctive 'crack' made by a bullet fired towards him. He heard it first at Belle Vue. All the Sorell kids grew up with firearms, and were confident in their use. They shot rabbits and birds.

My father was a crack shot, but he disapproved of wanton killing. We didn't go on a wholesale slaughter, and there might not be a magpie or starling shot for months. Then we might shoot three or four in a week.

Other targets beckoned. A quince tree in the garden dangled tempting fruit from one of its branches, and Neil Davis drilled a neat hole through it with a .22 rifle from fifty metres away. He stuck a feather through it so that others could admire his marksmanship.

Once I threw a shot at something, and to my horror saw one of our cows immediately drop to its knees. I went over in fear and trepidation and found I had indeed hit it, but the bullet only clipped the leg. It hadn't shattered the bone or anything. The cow got up and continued grazing, and I never told my father or anyone else how I nearly killed or crippled a prize cow.

Cowboys and Indians was a popular game, inspired by the black-and-white movies of the day. But Neil Davis and his friends did more than shout, 'Bang bang'. Such was their confidence in their ability with .22 rifles that they would shoot in the direction of another group of kids.

We would have a little war aiming over our opponents' heads. Terrible to think back on it. There was the occasional ricochet off a rock which can go anywhere. We always broke off the engagement before there were any casualties.

I suppose all this was symptomatic of boredom. We needed more adventure than we got. Modern kids have access to television, radio, watches, cars and other paraphernalia to bring some excitement into their lives. We didn't have anything like that.

. . .

The Sorell state school provided certain excitements. Some strong characters presided over the three-roomed school building. They had to be strong because the local boys were rough diamonds who would, if given half a chance, resort to a physical challenge.

It was a test of wills, and I assure you that any sign of weakness on the part of the headmaster would have ended in a debacle for the whole school. In fact, each change of headmaster was preceded by propaganda — possibly from the Education Department, or the incoming teacher himself — of what a terribly tough person he was.

One headmaster, known as 'Killer' Cunningham, was to be replaced by 'Basher' Crawford — whose reputation had preceded him. This represented an immediate challenge to the senior boys aged from eleven to fourteen. Neil Davis and his rival Neil 'Nigger' Jones, immediately competed to be the first to try Basher Crawford and to be the first boy whom he caned.

We all lined up in the playground to have our hair and fingernails inspected and have roll call before marching off to our classrooms. Nigger Jones was a rough customer, and was intent on winning our competition.

He turned up with deliberately dirty hands, but to my relief he wasn't caned, just told to stay in after school. I thought I'd play up in the first class by talking and mucking about — it didn't take much to be caned.

As we trooped into class I realised Nigger was going to beat me to it, so I had to get in first. As I walked in the door I deliberately tripped the boy in front of me, who fell heavily right in front of Basher Crawford. In a flash he had me outside and gave me six of the best, and Nigger Jones was really pissed off. I won that one all right. I suppose I've always been very competitive.

To the day he died, Neil Davis was passionately fond of absurd wagers and physical challenges. He rarely lost.

Caning was not the ultimate deterrent at the Sorell state school — it was more of a badge of honour. The real humiliation was to be forced to sit next to a girl. Neil remembers the embarrassment and fury of being made to sit next to Marcia Iles, the prettiest girl in the school.

We were both about ten years old, I suppose. I mean, what an idyllic situation! There I was sitting next to this beautiful girl student right at the back of the class where the teacher couldn't see us . . . and I hated the whole thing and actually felt antagonistic towards poor Marcia!

It was probably the only opportunity Neil passed by.

Yet, despite the tough discipline, Neil Davis was fortunate in his choice of school. Tasmanian school inspectors were stern faultfinders, and the report for 1944 — in Killer Cunningham's era — is generous. 'An excellent tone prevails throughout the school,' commented the inspector. 'The neatness and general appearance of the pupils, many of whom come from poor homes, reflects credit on school training.'

There is an approving note about the well-cut lawns, flower beds and flourishing vegetable garden. The school library of some seven hundred volumes was used by the pupils, who were ready to discuss the subject matter of recently read books.

'Expression in written composition is fresh and natural, ideas are abundant, many have imaginative power and there is a wide vocabulary. Spelling both free and formal is particularly good throughout the school.'

Not a bad start for a future journalist and foreign correspondent.

4

No Time to
Pick the Wildflowers

From the age of ten, Neil Davis yearned to travel, but the
prospect was remote. Memories of the Depression still
weighed heavily on people, and a job and security were
high on the list of priorities.

In those days nobody made any career plans for kids,
other than to follow their fathers as bankers,
pharmacists, farmers, labourers or railway workers, or
whatever. There was an unspoken feeling that I would be
a farmer. I certainly loved the farm and the countryside,
and being in Sorell rather than in Nala was almost like
being in the metropolis.

People also spoke vaguely of my going to work in a
bank. I had a mental image of myself being forever
behind bars — and there were bars in front of bank
tellers in those days to stop people like John Dillinger
robbing banks. (As a matter of fact I was born in 1934,
the year that John Dillinger was shot down in New
York.)

I did have a yearning to do something else, and knew
if I went onto the farm I wouldn't be able to fulfil that
hope, whatever it was.

In Sorell just after the war, the Saturday night dance was
the highlight of the week. The music was usually provided

25

by the AIF band — but the name had nothing to do with the Australian Imperial Forces.

The initials stood for Amy and Ida Featherstone, two spinster ladies of indeterminate years. One played the piano and the other the drums. They were thin but happy souls and they could really thump out the tunes.

A farmer, Hughie Montgomery, played the piano on some Saturday nights, although he played in the countryside more often than in Sorell. He had star quality because he had never had a music lesson in his life. Hughie was a goggle-eyed sort of feller, and he would happily pound away on the keyboard. People would say, 'Isn't it marvellous, . . . he plays by ear.' Young as I was, I can remember thinking that he might have been better off having a few lessons.

Thursday night was an opportunity to 'go to the pictures'. Films were provided by a travelling picture show man who set up his projector in the same old weatherboard community hall that housed the dances. There were two movies, with a fifteen-minute intermission to buy icecreams from the shop, and the show ended about 11 p.m.

The first film was a shorter C- or B-grade movie, Tom Mix, Gene Autry or Roy Rogers. After the icecreams would come the full-length feature. One of the first sound-synchronised-speech films I saw was *Random Harvest*, with Ronald Colman and Greer Garson.

Apart from the celluloid magic provided by the picture show man, the wider world began to open out for Neil Davis when he left the Sorell state school for high school in the city of Hobart, a twenty-six kilometre journey by bus and ferry across the Derwent River.

Davis had topped his classes in primary school, and re-members being largely bored by the Hobart High School's

English-style education. He learned more British and American history than Australian history. Southeast Asia barely rated a mention except as a British sphere of influence. He remembered learning about the Boxer Rebellion, but only in the context of pseudo-colonialism in China.

There was no career counselling, and Neil Davis put off casual inquiries by saying he wanted to be an engineer. But he disliked mathematics, although he was proficient in that subject.

I stumbled through some French, which was enormously useful to me later because of the French colonialisation of Indo-China.

It wasn't that the teachers were bad — they were warm and caring, perhaps more so than today. It was the system.

A sudden surge of hormones to fourteen-year-old Neil Davis's pituitary gland caused an intense interest in girls that remained an enduring obsession. He had always had good marks, but once his juices started to run, he failed seven out of twelve subjects in one year.

Hobart High School, which was the only true high school in southern Tasmania at that time, was integrated, with about two hundred boys, and the same number of girls.

Although we moved to different classrooms for our lessons, we kept the same desk positions to make it easier for the teachers to remember our names.

A girl called Marie sat directly behind me — she was from a country area too. She was obviously feeling her oats, and she and I became very interested in sex. We did a lot of fiddling under the desk. We were pretty clever at it, because the teachers never caught us.

I suppose they must have known what was going on, but we were never caught while we were mucking around.

Hobart High School's most notorious ex-pupil had been Errol Flynn and students used to vie for the status of sitting at the desk in Room 11 on which he had carved his name. The headmaster in Neil Davis's day was H.V. Biggins.

I used to think Mr Biggins pompous, but he was a nice gentle man really — although he walloped me severely on one occasion, which gave me added status as it was unusual to be caned by the headmaster.

Neil Davis's happy exploration with Marie under the desk coincided with another awakening interest — competitive sport, particularly athletics and Australian Rules football. It is difficult for followers of other codes of football to appreciate the passions generated by this fast-moving game. A hard body contact sport, it is played in southeast and western Australia with two teams of eighteen. High catching (marking) leads to spectacular clashes by soaring players. Even as a schoolboy Neil Davis was good enough to qualify as a player in Sorell's senior district team. These local football teams were rugged, with rural workers and timbercutters competing. So intense was the rivalry between neighbouring towns, that the Kempton side was once banned from competition for 10 years after a footballing brawl engulfed the whole town. (An amnesty was declared by Queen Elizabeth the Second during one of her Royal Tours, but the ban held for at least five years.)

I suppose I was considered the boy wonder. I was fast, and by the time I was fifteen, I was six feet [1.83 metres] tall, but very light in build. The job I was given was the number one ruckman, which meant I leapt up to tap the ball away when it was bounced high to start the game, and followed the play wherever it went.

Bored with school (despite the below-desk fumblings with the pubescent Marie) and besotted with sport, Neil Davis set his sights on getting into the Tasmanian Schoolboys' football team. In 1948 the All States Schoolboys' Carnival was scheduled for Queensland, and he was attracted to the idea of travel outside Tasmania for the first time, as well as three weeks away from school. He made the team and had his first taste of travel. The Tasmanians did not win, but they did beat the Victorian state side, a David-and-Goliath feat that won considerable acclaim and was not repeated until the 1960s.

. . .

Back in Sorell, Neil Davis started to dabble in photography as a hobby. He was determined to get a picture of one of Sorell's eccentrics, a tall, gaunt old man named Adam Featherstone, who used to walk around the Sorell district wearing a black 'bluey' coat, a heavy woollen garment that almost reached his knees and was favoured by farmers because it was warm without being too cumbersome. Adam must have been 60 or 70 years old, and he was at least 1.9 metres tall; he always walked with his head down and his hands clasped behind his back. He was a bachelor who lived with his brother and his family in a cottage near the Anglican church in Sorell.

When I was living in Cambodia in the early 1970s I noticed that the Cambodians were very tolerant of people who would be considered crazy in Western society — they might have had some kind of psychiatric disorder, but they were absolutely harmless. In Cambodia these people were always absorbed and cared for by their own district, and they survived and were obviously much happier than they would have been in some kind of institution because they operated in familiar situations without fear.

I can recall four or five such people who lived in and around Sorell, and Adam Featherstone was one of them. I certainly never heard him utter a word, nor did I ever hear of anyone else who had. He would roam around the

back roads on the district with long loping strides,
looking neither left nor right.

The Sorell kids weren't afraid of Adam Featherstone, but
they did hold him in some awe. He was never teased or
taunted. Neil Davis was unsure of Featherstone's reaction
if he realised he was being photographed, so he thought he
had better take his picture secretly.

> I had a friend Johnny Wright, a few years older than
> me, who was a photographer, and he lent me a box
> Brownie camera. I set the camera up pretending to be
> looking elsewhere, and as old Adam walked past I
> clicked the shutter. I thought it was the scoop of the
> century to get this shot of Adam — as though I was a
> London *Times* man.

John Wright worked in the Tasmanian Government Film
Unit in Hobart and let Davis know about a vacancy on the
staff at the end of 1948. Davis was too young to leave
school, but somehow managed to do so.

He joined as an office boy, making the tea and mixing
the raw chemicals for the photographic work. He was certainly learning photography from the bottom up. Just after
the war, film was expensive and difficult to obtain and
glass plates were sometimes used as negatives. Davis recalled that flash powder was used when flashbulbs were
scarce; a fuse ignited a quantity of the powder in the instant that the lens was opened in the big speed Graphic
cameras.

To be at work on time, Neil Davis had to catch a bus
from Sorell at 7.30 a.m., and he used to run the 1.6 kilometres from Belle Vue as part of his training for football and
athletics. Not many months after he had snapped his secret
photograph of the eccentric Adam Featherstone, he was, as
usual, literally running late. He used to take a short cut
past the cemetery of the Anglican church and through a

vacant lot near Adam Featherstone's house to save a valuable few seconds. On this particular morning he saw Trooper Chilcott, the local policeman, sitting on something directly in his path. Old Adam Featherstone lay in the dry grass, obviously dead, and the policeman sat on his chest (rigor mortis having set in) writing in his notebook.

What was more bizarre was that Adam had collapsed and died while apparently digging his own grave! There was a hoe and a shovel, and the beginnings of a grave dug down to a depth of about nine inches and six and a half feet in length. Adam was a very tall man.

We believed at the time that he had had a premonition of his own death. He must have got up from his bed about midnight and started to dig. As far as I know Adam had not shown any sign of sickness, and I think a post-mortem showed he had died of a heart attack. No one in the township of Sorell thought it was strange that Adam had a premonition of his own death. Country people are more prepared to accept the supernatural or the slighly unnatural than city people are.

Being able to leave school and start work was something of a relief for Neil Davis. His eldest brother Jimmy had died when Neil was thirteen and his mother only three years before that.

My father remarried shortly before my brother died, and I was never close to my stepmother and always felt uneasy at home — so the idea of going back to the farm was not inviting. My sister Barbara had married, and my other brother Darrel had already started an apprenticeship to become a motor mechanic.

His immediate problem was how to survive as office boy in the Tasmanian Government Film Unit in Hobart on the princely salary of £2 10s a week. Jack Thwaites, the sympathetic administrator of the unit, arranged for Neil to take over the cleaning of the building.

Neil Davis had moved from Sorell to lodgings at Bellerive on the eastern shore of the Derwent River. He caught a ferry across to the city and walked to the Tasmanian Government Film Unit in North Hobart by 7.30 a.m. in time to clean the building for an hour and a half before starting work at 9 a.m. That brought in an extra 35s a week. After work, although he was too young to drink alcohol legally, he worked several nights a week as a drink waiter in a Hobart hotel.

. . .

Neil Davis also made money from sport. He became a professional footballer and a member of the eastern shore football club of Clarence. That brought in 10s per training session (twice a week) and a £1 match fee on Saturdays. The extra money was urgently needed to buy sporting gear and to finance the ferocious beer drinking that was the fashion of the day.

An eight-ounce glass of beer cost the equivalent of five cents then, and later it went up to eight cents. In other words, you could get pretty high for a dollar.

I had lots of mates to go drinking with; not only my Sorell friends, but through my work, and of course through football.

One consistent boozing and football mate was Ron Batchelor, although Batchelor eventually gave up football because he said it interfered with serious drinking. Davis joined him in many mid-week liquid lunches and evening sessions in the pub.

One of the saddest days of my life was when I arrived in South Vietnam for the first time early in 1964. There was a telegram waiting for me in Saigon with the news that Batchie had died of a liver complaint. It was caused by his drinking, of course.

Neil Davis counted himself fortunate to survive that period of heavy beer drinking, which was the accepted method of youthful exuberance and rebellion before other drugs such as marijuana offered alternatives. His boyhood friend Johnny Wright, who organised Neil's first job at the Film Unit, became an alcoholic. Davis, who would do all in his power to help a friend, made several trips back from Southeast Asia in the late 1960s to dry him out and encourage him to go into hospital voluntarily for psychiatric treatment. He stopped drinking and began work again as a cinecameraman, but he had wrecked his health during the drinking years and died in July 1974.

Neil Davis returned to Tasmania as often as possible during the years in Asia. He often spoke of the island's physical beauty and even after twenty years as a foreign correspondent with extensive travelling throughout the world, he thought he had seen few places to equal its stark beauty and areas of untouched wilderness. That wilderness is now under threat not only by logging interests, but by the island's Hydro Electric Commission seeking the last wild rivers to tame into power projects. Neil Davis spoke passionately against the HEC's role, saying it was a kind of pseudo government, slashing into all that beauty and depriving mankind and particularly Tasmanians of their heritage.

One of the things I regret is not seeing enough of Australia, and Tasmania in particular. It can be taken hypothetically or literally, I think, but I'm afraid I haven't taken enough time to pick the wildflowers.

5

Escape From the Iron Lung

The Tasmanian Government Film Unit, where Neil Davis's camera career began, occupied ramshackle premises at 79 Bathurst Street in Hobart. There was no indoor toilet, and staff had to use the little hut at the bottom of the yard.

The Unit building was only one room wide with our darkrooms and work areas spread over two storeys. There was a small office at the front with a reception counter and a storeroom and a little projection booth for the sixteen-millimetre colour films we made at the time.

We did quite a lot of still photographic work, filming diseased fruit for the Department of Agriculture and jobs like that. We had to wash the chemicals from the prints in an old wooden tub that was out in the yard.

We used the big downstairs workroom to make sound recordings and lay soundtracks for our documentary films.

(The building became a pet shop after the Film Unit moved on, and birdseed crossed the counter without a query about scratched lenses or torn sprocket holes.) Unfortunately for the film makers, the premises next to the Unit were occupied by Vince Tucker who ran a saw- and tool-sharpening business. The only window in Vince's workroom faced the Film Unit's yard and their so-called sound studio.

To get the best light to work by, Vince had his workbench right by the window, which was usually open. So we had to put up with the screech and rasp of the sharpening files at least three or four hours a day. From our yard we could see Vince, with his tongue stuck out on one side of his mouth, concentrating as he did his job.

Immediately upstairs in the same building, was the studio of an alcoholic violin teacher. This unfortunate middle-aged woman taught schoolchildren and when we walked up our back stairs to the second floor we were very close to the lessons.

Of course Vince could hear the violin teacher and her pupils upstairs and she could not fail to be aware of him. For most of the time there was a most unholy duet which seemed to go in increasing discord and mounting crescendo.

Between pupils, the music teacher used to take a few tots of the doings and by early afternoon she was well and truly drunk. She rarely ventured outside her little dilapidated apartment building, and the poor woman, I remember, had a deathly pale, flour-white face.

Over the back fence, behind the outside toilet, was a yard belonging to a Chinese family. Because they generally cooked in the open air or under a roofed shelter with no walls, mouthwatering smells would drift across, completely defeating the competing fragrance of the dunny.

It was my first experience of Chinese food, and of course during Chinese New Year or other festivals such as weddings, christenings or funerals there were always firecrackers which exploded hour after hour.

The Tasmanian Government Film Unit itself contributed to this cacophony by adding music and commentaries, which were constantly being edited and played backwards and forwards.

Harry Lloyd, the unit's veteran sound technician, had a hot temper which was usually overridden by his good humour. But sometimes the combination of the saw sharpening, wailing violins and Chinese firecrackers would get too much for Harry. He would throw open the back door and turn the volume of his machine up full bore and add a few well-chosen, colourful comments that a camel driver would be proud to have in his repertoire. The neighbours would stick stolidly to their tasks, apparently oblivious of and undaunted by Harry's efforts to drown them out.

The Film Unit's administrative officer, Jack Thwaites, (who gave Neil Davis the chance to double his wages by acting as charboy and cleaning the premises) taught Neil the rudiments of maintaining accurate records and keeping track of stock, equipment and costs. Davis's quick grasp of administrative detail stayed with him all his life. His work diaries from Asia are models of record-keeping, with details of assignments, names of people interviewed, expenses and lists of film shipments — all because of the patient tuition given by Jack Thwaites in Hobart.

He drove home to me the necessity of keeping records wherever you are. When I became bureau chief for NBC in Bangkok in 1980, head office in New York demanded that certain records be kept. I usually cut through the bullshit or ignored it and simply gave them — as I did way back in those Tasmanian days — a record of how much money we spent, the stock we had and where it went, the equipment on hand, bills for electricity, phone and telex and a list of our work output.

That applied to my life when I was running a television news agency in Southeast Asia during the Indo-China war.

For the first two years of his wage-earning life, Neil Davis did not take a photograph, but worked in the darkroom mixing photographic chemicals, processing stills, drying the prints and doing the filing. Then, in his role as office boy, he delivered the photographs to the various government departments around Hobart.

Photographic materials were still in short supply in the postwar years, and Neil Davis remembered that the Film Unit (a government department) was once rationed to a total of six flashbulbs a week. Very few photo flood bulbs (strong lights) were available either, but they tended to explode. The Unit had to learn to make do with natural light.

With film stock extremely expensive and almost unobtainable, other valuable lessons were learned. The Film Unit used to make documentaries on the amazingly tight ratio of two feet of film exposed to one foot of film actually used in the finished production. Later producers thought little of using four or even five times as much film.

The Unit was headed by an ebullient film producer, Norman Laird.

In my view, his main contribution was his neverending effort to expand the Film Unit into something greater than it was — and he succeeded.

He was variously described as being brilliant, erratic — which he certainly was — mad, a fool and a good photographer. There was always tension when Norm was around, but quite often lots of fun as well. He would make outlandish statements and challenge you to contradict him.

We made a dramatised documentary *Hard to Windward* on the Sydney-to-Hobart yacht race, and it was the first Tasmanian film to win an overseas award, the Cortina di Ampezzo Cup at the International Festival of Sporting Films in 1962.

Neil's laborious apprenticeship taught him other skills that became invaluable in combat photography — the art of making every frame of film not only usable, but framed to build up a story so that every newsclip he took became a mini-documentary.

When I started working for American television networks they would give me about ten minutes of sixteen-millimetre film and ask later, 'How much of it is usable?'

This used to puzzle me a great deal, because I might have had trouble with about twenty seconds of it due to a lighting problem, but otherwise it was *all* usable. I couldn't understand why American network cameramen would shoot ten minutes of film for a two-minute newsclip.

Of course in combat, if you film everything that moves, you will get by, but it always seemed a tremendous waste to me. But when you are really short of film, and only have two or three minutes left, it is still possible to cover the action if conserving film is second nature to you.

The impoverished Film Unit had to maintain its camera gear meticulously to stay in business — another lesson Neil Davis never forgot. He was contemptuous of cameramen who missed shots because of failed equipment and poor maintenance. He also carried his sporting instincts over to photography, particularly the importance of training and being constantly on the alert.

Whenever I drive through the countryside, my camera is beside me and I'm constantly changing the exposure in case something should happen. Maybe there'll be a plane crash, or a sudden riot, or a UFO landing, or something that demands proof on film or video. Then all I need to do is flick off the lens cap and start filming with no fumbling.

At the age of sixteen, Neil Davis lost his virginity. It was not, he said, a spectacular affair.

It happened in the girl's house and her parents were home at the time. Apart from that, the experience was not terribly memorable except that, I suppose, my sexual career was launched.

A colleague, also from Tasmania, remarked enviously that Neil always left his women on good terms, adding wistfully, 'Mine always hate my guts for evermore.'

By the age of sixteen, Neil Davis was a professional footballer, but because of the few pounds he earned, he was barred from taking part in any sport as an amateur. In his early twenties, he became a professional runner, training amateur athletes in the little spare time he had left from working, running, drinking and keeping track of his turbulent love life.

My best distance was four hundred and forty yards [400 metres] 'for fools and horses' — maybe the most lung-tearing test of endurance on the track.

Davis believed that those years of tough training and running gave him the endurance to survive the backbreaking footslogging with the South Vietnamese soldiers in the Vietnam war years.

One always has a little bit left after struggling through the rice paddies hour after hour, day after day. You are rarely as physically buggered as you think if you are in good condition to start with. As an athlete I was always at my best at the end of a race, or in the last desperate quarter of a hard footy game.

But at the age of sixteen, a passion for Australian Rules football (and drinking Tasmania's Cascade beer) dominated his life outside his working hours. His chosen football club, Clarence, was on the eastern shore of the Derwent River, and tended to be the underdog in the fiercely fought winter competitions. Later, in the midst of the Indo-China war, he wrote to his elderly Aunt Lillian seeking news of Clarence's fortunes.

They say that Australians will bet on two flies walking up a wall, and Neil was a relentless punter. He did not bet regularly on the horses, being more likely to favour unlikely contests on which he would place sizable bets. It is entirely typical that in Bangkok on the morning of 9 September 1985 — the day he died — the last thing he did before going on his last assignment was to hand his secretary an envelope addressed to Rodney Tasker, Chief Correspondent of the *Far Eastern Economic Review*, and heavily marked 'IMPORTANT'. He had bet Tasker 1000 baht ($US 50) that Australia would win the cricket Test series in England. They lost. A note with the money read, 'Lucky Tasker . . . Lucky', and was signed 'The Fox'.

Neil Davis did not often lose a bet, although his judgment in investing money was appalling. One of his first attempts to invest in real estate in Hobart ended when the legal firm concerned went broke. He and another Australian journalist bought a vineyard in South Australia in the early 1970s that grew only red wine grapes at the time when the whole nation had switched to white, and a Cambodian floating restaurant in which he had an interest sank. Absurd wagers, on the other hand, compensated to some extent.

A wager could come up at any moment. During one football game playing for Clarence, Neil took a high mark — catching the ball cleanly — which meant he could have an unhindered 'free' kick at the goal. Unfortunately he was on such an acute angle that he could barely see daylight between the posts. Not only that, he was a notoriously unrealiable goal kicker, even if he happened to be right in front.

But what Davis and some of his mates knew was that he

was particularly good (and lucky) at kicking from almost impossible angles. As he began to line up for his goal kick, he could hear a team mate, Bill 'The Ferret' Kingston, clearly getting bets down on him!

I knew that he would get about three to one on me because of the acute angle, so in order to give the Ferret more time to fix the bets, I carefully wiped the ball and delayed as long as I could. I could also see my father standing where he usually did behind the goal posts, knowing that he enjoyed watching his sons playing football. I also knew he would be aware that money was going on my chances, and that although there would be no shame if I missed, he had confidence in me.

So I came in to kick, doing everything wrong according to the purists, and made a wobbly old punt kick which sailed very uncertainly towards the big posts. At the last second, a gust of wind screwed the ball around, and it went straight through for the goal.

Well, the Ferret and I tied one on that night. Free beer always tastes best, and we had enough to drink through the night on the winnings.

There was a further triumph that night. During the beer session a raunchy debate began about who had the biggest penis in the team. Davis, who was enviably endowed in that department, backed himself, but quite good money was going on the only other contender in the phallic stakes.

Davis was quietly confident. Measurements were to be taken in the relaxed mode and an eager circle formed to watch the tape measure being applied.

Neil Davis's sense of fair play was outraged when his rival worked up a half-erection. A split second before final measurement, he dashed his glass of icy-cold Cascade beer into the crutch of the partly tumescent contender, putting things back into correct perspective. Davis won.

The cycle of betting, football, work and beery merrymaking

was rudely interrupted in 1952 when, with all other fit young Australian men aged eighteen, Davis was conscripted for compulsory military service. The first stage was three months' basic infantry training at Brighton Camp, a stark establishment on a treeless plain about thirty kilometres north of Hobart. That was followed by several years of part-time service in the Citizen Military Forces. Davis was not too concerned about being called up. The army pay during the basic training phase was £5 a week — more than he was getting at the Film Unit, but less than his total income.

I was interested to see how I would go. Just to keep the National Servicemen on their toes, they kept talking about the Korean War flaring up again. It was August — winter — when I went in, and it was hard, tough training. I enjoyed it, because it gave me an insight into the military mind, and what is expected of a soldier in the way of discipline, and I found it useful many years later when I went to Vietnam and Cambodia.

I only did guard duty once, the first night I went into camp. Christ, I never forgot it. It was freezing, and I absolutely hated guard duty, two hours on and two hours off through the night. Bugger that, I thought. The only way to get out of it was to be a good sportsman.

Neil Davis took up cross-country running, and came eighth out of the 412 competing in the battalion championship. Told that the winner of another footrace could have weekend leave, he practically flew to the winning post.

What with the boxing, running and football — as well as the infantry training — I came out of Brighton camp enormously fit. I don't think I've ever been fitter in my life.

Davis had a week's holiday before starting work again with the Tasmanian Government Film Unit. He spent the entire time riotously drunk with his Clarence Football Club mates and somehow contracted poliomyelitis. Also called infantile paralysis, the disease was epidemic in Australia and other countries in the 1950s.

It can affect any part of your body. You can be paralysed in the legs, the arms or the chest — or all over. I was immediately struck and paralysed in the chest and in my upper legs. This was particularly dangerous, because many of the deaths from polio were caused by victims being unable to use the muscles in their chest to breathe, and they would die of asphyxiation or drown in the fluid collected in their lungs.

Within days of emerging from Brighton camp as fit as he had ever been, Neil Davis was in the Vaucluse infectious diseases hospital, Hobart, fighting for his life in an iron lung.

The thing was like a greatly oversized iron coffin, and they put your whole body except your head and arms into this awful thing. It had rubber seals around your neck and arms, while a compressor pumped air in and out about sixteen times a minute. It made a dreadful sucking and hissing sound while it was helping you breathe.

You didn't stay in the iron lung all the time, but when I first went into hospital I was in a ward opposite about seven or eight of these things so you could be put in at a moment's notice.

That didn't always save people, of course, and people always seemed to be rushed into an iron lung at night. The frightening thing was you could hear this thing in the dark at night like a giant breathing . . . and of course if the patient died, the breathing stopped. That happened two or three times while I was there.

But psychologically — and I've always believed this —

I was not only convinced that I wasn't going to die but that I would be out of that hospital in a short time.

Fortunately for Davis — and this happened several times in his life at times of medical crisis — he found an outstanding doctor to treat him. Dr Douglas Parker was Tasmania's best-known orthopaedic surgeon at that time. He was a short, tubby man barely 1.5 metres tall with a superficially gruff manner.

I liked him because he was very direct, and didn't speak over or around his patients, using lots of technical terms as many doctors tend to do. Douglas Parker spoke directly to you, and he also agreed with the work being done by an Australian nurse, Sister Kenny, who believed that victims of poliomyelitis should not be kept inactive, which was the conventional treatment of the day. She urged the opposite, that patients should keep their paralysed muscles working as much as possible, while hot compresses were applied to ease pain and discomfort.

Her ideas were still considered revolutionary and I was very fortunate that Douglas Parker had been to Queensland to observe her methods, and agreed with her. Every day, we polio patients were taken down to a heated indoor swimming pool which had stainless steel bars across it. Swimming was the best exercise because you had the weight off your body, and could try swimming movements. I still had the power to grasp the bars in my hands, and the water exercises helped to keep the muscles in my chest working.

Davis was so badly paralysed that that he could not even sit up.

It was impossible, I couldn't move. If someone propped you up in a sitting position, you couldn't even lean forward. If you tried, sharp pains would go across your chest. But I was determined to get out of there so I could join my friends for the Christmas piss-ups. We always went to a lot of parties and did a lot of drinking at that time.

Davis challenged Dr Parker that he would be out of hospital within three weeks.

I was determined to be. Dr Parker was encouraging, saying that if I did everything I was told and had that attitude, I'd be out. He told me later that he didn't really think so.

I felt the swimming was helping me a lot, and it was the only exercise I could do anyway. So every night after lights out at 9 p.m. I would haul myself out of bed, and crawl along the floor of the ward — because my legs weren't working properly — and somehow get down the stairs and into the pool to exercise for a couple of extra hours.

Years later, Douglas Parker said the staff had told him about it because they were concerned, and he had replied, 'For goodness' sake, let him do it. Just make sure he doesn't drown in the pool, because psychologically it's very good for him.'

Parker set another challenge for Davis. He told him that if he could sit up in bed, draw up his kness and lean forward with his hands behind his head and touch his knees with his chin three times straight off, he could go home for Christmas. Davis knew that the last day he had to achieve this was 22 December 1952, because Parker would not come again for another five days and Christmas would be over.

I set about this with maniacal dedication so that when he came to see me on the twenty-second I tried to appear nonchalant and relaxed as I did those three pushes forward with my chin. It was excruciatingly painful, with hard, driving pain going straight through my chest. And he kept his word. I was allowed to go home and have that Christmas piss-up with my mates.

Davis's next challenge to the delighted Dr Parker was an undertaking to play football again within four months.

He encouraged me in all this madness; others said it was madness, and other doctors strongly disapproved. And four months after I came out of hospital, I did play hard competitive football. It was very painful, particularly across my chest, but I firmly believe that it was a good thing that it did hurt me.

I suppose it's fair to say that beating polio was my first big challenge. If you look at life as a series of challenges — and it is for most people, I think — you meet them by getting up and fighting. I believe most people do that, or they don't survive.

In 1969 I contracted a very bad case of recurring hepatitis in South Vietnam, which I approached with the same optimism and psychologically positive attitude. When I was wounded or in dire combat situations, I always had a positive attitude.

In my football days I was known as a battler — one who didn't give in — rather than as a brilliant player. I could sometimes pull off a spectacular feat, like taking a very high mark, but all footballers have those good days. I believe in fighting on. Life is a battle anyway, so you've got to fight on, and after a while it becomes a habit.

Overall, I'd say it's one of the best habits I've developed. I don't believe there is an alternative. I've always been an optimist over my chances of survival, under whatever circumstances.

6

Under Fire
in Tasmania

By 1954, Neil Davis had left the darkroom of the Tasmanian
Government Film Unit.

I filmed and photographed assignments ranging from
pig pens to idyllic tourist spots, sport, hydro-electric dam
construction of which there was plenty in Tasmania and
still is, and I was even the police photographer for a
while because they didn't have one.

One of my jobs was to photograph the unidentified
dead, mainly paupers or people who had died in unusual
circumstances. I'd have to go down to the government
morgue and see the pathologist Dr Campbell Duncan. He
would be there, among the bodies at his desk, sometimes
having a sandwich and a cup of tea. 'Oh, yes,' he would
say. 'I know the one you've come to photograph,' and
would fling back the sheet to reveal the body they'd
picked up overnight. Dr Duncan didn't falter in eating his
sandwiches and drinking his morning tea.

1954 was the year that Queen Elizabeth and Prince Philip
toured Australia: the first time a reigning British sovereign
had set foot on Australian soil. Davis was involved in
shooting a full-length colour film on the Queen's Tasmanian
tour.

Television did not start in mainland Australia until 1956, in time for the Olympic Games in Melbourne. The early 1950s were the era of the newsreels, screened before the main features on Friday and Saturday nights. Most Australian cities had special newsreel theatres, running news, shorts and cartoons continuously in an hour's cycle. The three main newsreel companies were Pathe, Cinesound and Fox-Movietone.

The Tasmanian Government Film Unit acquired two thirty-five millimetre cameras and became the Tasmanian representative for Fox-Movietone and Cinesound. I shot assignments for both, but not at the same time.

I found it exciting to move into newsreel work, and it taught me to be even more frugal with film, because thirty-five millimetre film was terribly expensive and the edited newsclips ran less than a minute. If it was a really interesting story it might make a minute and a half. We were expected to cover a story using only one hundred feet of film [30.5 metres] with a running time of two minutes forty seconds, although for a big story like the disastrous Hobart floods of 1960 we would shoot more footage.

I'm proud to say that most of my protégés, the people I taught to become news cinecameramen, have been Asians, and I established a great rapport with them about the need to conserve film. They understood instantly, because most of them were poor and accustomed to making the most of limited resources.

But in 1954 Neil Davis had not thought seriously about what he wanted to do with his life. That was never clear; he said he never planned more than one day ahead.

Meanwhile, life was good. He had an interesting job that took him all over Tasmania, he had a succession of girl-friends and cars, he threw himself enthusiastically into

The Davis family at Nala. From left: Geoff Davis (father), Barbara (sister), Marjorie (mother), Jimmy (elder brother), Darrel (brother), and in front Neil 'Tiny' Davis.

(Left) The redoubtable Granny Mary Davis (née Crocker) aged 85. (Right) Aunt Lillian Davis (1891-1973), who helped bring Neil Davis up after the death of his mother and remained in close touch with him through correspondence during the Indo China war.

As the No. 1 ruckman for the Tasmanian schoolboys side, Neil Davis flies high during the football carnival in Brisbane, July 1948.

Filming aerobatics from a light plane in Tasmania in 1961. *Brian Curtis*

Australian Rules football, and was chosen to represent southern Tasmania in a combined football side.

I was reported for 'unduly rough play' — which meant striking another player. He was a good friend of mine off the field actually, but that was not unusual. His name was Ron Jacobs, and he became a successful owner of hotels in tourist resorts in Tasmania.

Ron and I clashed on the field and had to face a football tribunal. We told outrageous lies which they didn't believe and I was let off lightly with a two-game suspension, but Ron lost ten weeks' play because he was a repeat offender. That, of course, elevated my status in the eyes of most of the fanatical Clarence fans.

On my very first game back, after serving my two-week suspension, I was immediately in a fracas again, and faced the tribunal again that same night. I was a bit lucky that time and the charge didn't stick. I was severely reprimanded. The fans loved it, and I guess it was relatively exciting in a routine life. We had to create these minor crises to generate adventures.

Neil Davis's remarkable love life had rather a slow start.

That was not unusual. In the 1950s in Australia, a young man and girl would say that they were 'going steady'. Or you might be asked, 'Who are you going with?' I took my girlfriends to the movies or to the Saturday night dance. Sometimes there would be a bust-up at the dance because the boys tended to drink too much and abandoned their girlfriends for their mates' company around the beer keg.

Before I left Tasmania for Asia in 1964 I was engaged to be married two, maybe three times. They were all nice girls and there was no reason why I shouldn't have married any of them. I suppose in the back of my mind was that uncertainty, a subconscious feeling that I would one day leave Tasmania and Australia, although I didn't make any serious moves to get out at that time.

Neil Davis's sister Barbara recalls that he had a row with one of his fiancées coming across the Derwent River on a ferry from Bellerive to Hobart. His girlfriend impulsively pulled the diamond engagement ring from her finger and threw it overboard. The two rushed to the rail and watched the tiny sparkle sink into the green depths, Davis's fiancée weeping bitterly at her act of dramatic folly.

In the mid-1950s, Davis tore the lateral cartilage of his right knee badly during a football match, when a very heavily built player crashed down on his leg. Cartilage operations were not common in those days, and he put it off for three years. His old medical mentor Dr Douglas Parker agreed to perform the operation and told Davis he could play football again within a few months.

I was determined to make it a lot earlier than that. It meant very sustained and painful exercises like riding a stationary bicycle in the gymnasium and forcing my stiffened leg to bend again.

During convalescence, before going back to work, I would exercise fanatically for eight hours a day. I would have gone on longer, but Dr Parker put an eight-hour limit on me. He knew there was a limit to the psychological value of this sort of dedication.

Six weeks after I had the cartilage out, I did play football and proved to myself that the best way to meet any hardship was to fight it mentally and physically. So before I ever went to Vietnam or engaged in combat, where I had to make some difficult decisions regarding my own safety in precarious situations, I had become somewhat used to facing and overcoming mental problems. You have to have strong willpower to do that and most of my friends will agree that has been one of my positive attributes, whether in war, work or sport.

Neil took up professional running in the summer months to help him recover from the operation.

One of my uncles — and best friends — Jim New was a former professional runner and footballer, and he trained me. Later on I got very interested in the technique of training runners and began some radical techniques. I believed that you shouldn't run against the clock all the time, getting faster and faster. That can destroy the morale of the athlete.

After all, what do you compete for? You compete to enjoy a physical outlet. It isn't the beginning and end of everything or the most important thing in life, but it's important to try hard, give it all you've got, and accept the result — then determine to go out and do better next time. But there's no point in running unless you enjoy the training and enjoy racing.

So I approached training runners in this vein. I'd take them down to the beach to train — not on the sand but through the water, which forces the runner to lift his legs up high in front, the classic movement for a sprinter. Also the upper body has to work harder. I did things like that and worked on the psychology of runners to relax them.

I had success with these methods, both with professionals and amateurs. In the end, I trained one of the six amateur teams and chose to coach the unfashionable Northern Suburbs team. They were mainly boys from the other side of the tracks and I liked to work with them because they had a high competitive spirit and were able to absorb the important elements of my theories on training and running.

If someone asks me, 'What would you like to do, if you were not a foreign correspondent and cameraman?' my immediate answer is that I love to train runners. I get great satisfaction out of it as a worthwhile thing to do. Often when I am jogging in Asia in the cool of the early morning, I look at other runners and think I would like to train a certain individual because he has potential. There are a lot of runners in Southeast Asia in particular who haven't lived up to their potential because they have not been coached psychologically as well as physically.

In 1961, Neil Davis left the Tasmanian Government Film Unit to become Tasmania's first staff cinecameraman for the Australian Broadcasting Commission. Although television had started on the island only the previous year, Neil Davis was already an experienced cinecameraman because of his documentary film making with the Film Unit and his news experience with Fox-Movietone and Cinesound.

Working in television wasn't a great switch for me. Of course most of the newsfilm business is pretty boring, but I still believed in doing a good job, and when people said I'd made a documentary out of a one- or two-minute newsfilm clip, I took that as a compliment.

I travelled all over Tasmania filming the opening of new roads, the first apple blossoms in spring (Tasmania was known as the Apple Isle in those days) and other pedestrian news events.

Wherever possible, however, Davis sought opportunities to push himself — and a story — to the limit. One assignment in midwinter was to film heavy snow-storm damage to Hobart's television towers, built spectacularly on the 1220 metre peak of Mount Wellington, overlooking the city.

Television on both the ABC and commercial station had gone off the air because ice had formed on top of the towers, expanded and smashed some vital transmitting equipment. It had also broken away the safety fence right at the top of the tower, more than three hundred feet [one hundred metres] up. I was not keen on heights but I was determined to force myself to climb the tower and film the damage close up.

It was windy and still freezing as I began to climb the perpendicular iron ladder which was as cold as hell on my hands. There were two guide wires behind my back, but nothing really to stop me falling right down. About a hundred feet up, I started to get a detached feeling and said to myself, 'Well, bugger it, I'll go right up,' and I did. The film wasn't all that spectacular, I might say, but there were some good views over the city.

On another day the Hobart fire brigade were testing a new safety device for rescuing people from high, burning buildings. It was a canvas belt and pulley arrangement so small you could hold it in your hands. They were giving a public demonstration from the top of a fireman's ladder a hundred and thirty feet up.

I took my camera up, strapped on the belt, put the camera on wide-angle and jumped off. I was swinging madly as I came down, so it gave a rather peculiar effect on film that produced some good shots. It certainly gave me a bit more excitement than was normal on the average news jobs for ABC television.

Neil Davis was instinctively drawn to people who tackled problems and life itself in unconventional ways. One such man was Verne Reid, who in 1961, had adapted a DH82 bi-plane (known colloquially as a Gypsy Moth) into a seaplane. When it flew, the floats looked bigger than the plane. The Gypsy Moth was wonderfully underpowered by modern standards. Tasmania lies in the path of the Roaring Forties, and violent changes of wind and weather are common. The Moth had a cruising speed of only eight-five knots and in a spanking breeze could apparently be flying backwards over the ground.

In 1962 word came through that a freighter was in diffi-culties off the Tasmanian coast and was being towed to Hobart by another freighter.

The ABC wanted to get film before the rival commercial station. I needed a plane that could not only fly very low slowly but could also land on the water while I filmed the disabled and listing freighter being towed through Storm Bay near Hobart.

Verne agreed to do it and I got some nice film. Then he landed on the water and I got some good shots of the ships steaming past from water level. But the damn plane wouldn't start, and the tide was going out, and we looked like drifting out into Storm Bay, which can be very rough indeed.

Decisions had to be made quickly. There was no paddle and the pilot obviously had to stay in the cockpit. Davis agreed to try to tow the Gypsy Moth to shore. It was August and the water was bitterly cold. Antarctica was just beyond the horizon.

Fortunately Verne had some rope and I made a rough harness, stripped off, slipped it over my shoulders and began towing the plane towards the beach. I had to swim across the current, and it seemed to take an eternity, but I did get the plane back to the beach.

By that stage, the best idea was for Davis to get his film back to Hobart by land while Verne Reid (who was also licensed to carry out repairs and maintenance on his plane) fixed the broken impulse spring in the magneto. Davis walked for eight kilometres over sand dunes and rough bushland to claim his car and he drove back to town to ensure his film was first on air. (Incidentally, in 1986 Verne Reid, who says he is 'seventy going on fifty', was still flying and operating an aerial photography company in Hobart.)

Other assignments could be hazardous for different reasons; a keen sense of humour can be dangerous for a newsman. In 1963, Davis was assigned to cover the arrival of Tasmania's new governor, Sir Charles Gairdner, who was being met at Hobart airport by the chief justice and Acting Administrator of Tasmania, Sir Stanley Burbury.

Sir Stanley had a stiff leg, which he handled very well, and which everyone knew about. However, when Sir Charles Gairdner came down the steps, it was immediately apparent that he had one too.

The next stage was to film Sir Charles meeting senior members of the Tasmanian government, escorted by Sir Stanley. They both stepped out swinging their stiff legs — I think Sir Charles Gairdner had a wooden leg — and as the third government minister in line stepped out to shake hands, we saw that he had a gammy leg too.

Things started to get really out of hand when I got to Government House to film the new governor relaxing in the grounds of his new home. We arranged to film in the superb gardens there and after a few minutes the chief justice and the governor limped into view, followed by Sir Charles Gairdner's dog — which also had a pronounced limp!

This just broke us all up; I was literally sobbing with laughter and had to stop filming. Chief Justice Sir Stanley Burbury, who had a superb sense of humour, tried to keep a straight face, but when dear old Sir Charles saw the funny side too, everything was OK.

Neil Davis came to know a remarkable man, Lloyd Jones, chief instructor of the Aero Club of southern Tasmania, who flew light aircraft over the island's then unexplored southwest region. Jones was an enthusiastic stills photographer and the first man to land a plane on the beach of inland Lake Pedder (now drowned beneath the peat-stained waters of the Lake Gordon hydro-electric power development). Mechanical failure of the single-engined Tiger Moths and Auster aircraft would have meant almost certain death in the mountains and rainforests of this unique area, and Davis flew with Lloyd Jones on many occasions.

At one stage the ABC wanted to do a film on aerobatics which interested me as a challenging film assignment. Looping the loop was simple enough, but there was one manoeuvre where you rolled off the top of the loop sideways, and then went into a controlled spin!

Flying with Lloyd Jones certainly relieved the boredom of filming canary shows and country fairs. There was no union for cinecameramen at that time, and Neil Davis joined the Australian Journalists' Association. He usually wrote the story on the film assignments he covered for television news.

That's a thing that can't be done now, because cameramen have their own union. There was no sound on film in those early days, with a reporter talking to camera. My scripts were read by the newsreader over the edited film.

By the early 1960s, Neil Davis's emotional life had become more complicated than the 'going steady' rituals of the 1950s.

Although I had been engaged to be married twice — maybe three times, I don't quite remember — I didn't really class myself as a philanderer. At the same time, I can't put myself in the category of an all-true-blue and one hundred per cent faithful type, either.

At one stage I was enamoured of a girl who worked in a hotel cocktail lounge, a very pretty girl who was the sister of a footballing friend of mine. She had been married but was separated from her husband. She was a fine girl. I thought so then, and I think so now, and she has well and truly married happily since then. But at that time, it seemed that she would possibly be divorced and we would marry.

She did sue for divorce on grounds unconnected with

me, but her husband countersued, alleging adultery with me. There was one wild incident, straight out of a B-grade movie, when he burst into her parents' house with a photographer while I was visiting. It was late at night, and he didn't find anything except pictures of me having a cup of tea with the lady in question.

What was more exciting was my friend's mother dashing out and giving the ex-husband a physical beating down the stairs of the apartment building. He was a small man, and the noise was startling.

The estranged husband knew that the attempt to name me as a co-respondent in his countersuit for divorce was bound to fail through lack of evidence, and he became obsessed with the affair and a little mad.

I was twenty-six or twenty-seven at the time and living in a private room in the back of a house owned by a pensioner couple, Mr and Mrs Blake. I'd lived in that room, on the left side of the house, for a couple of years and because a schoolteacher who occupied a rather bigger and better room on the right-hand side had left, I changed rooms a couple of weeks before my girlfriend's estranged husband had tried to photograph me *in flagrante delicto*.

A young Polish migrant named Alex had moved into my old room. He was about my age and build and also had fair hair. He had just arrived in Tasmania, and spoke very little English.

I came home one night after going to the movies and having a few beers to find signs of activity in the street and a police car just pulling out from the front of the house. My landlady Mrs Blake was still up, and I asked her what had been going on.

She said, 'Oh, someone tried to kill Alex.' I said, 'Kill Alex? Christ, what for? What could poor Alex have done? He's only just arrived in Australia.'

'Oh, I don't know,' she said. 'Anyway, somebody shot at him through the window with a shotgun.'

I realised that the assailant had seen a tall, slightly built guy silhouetted against the blind in what he thought was my room — and he'd let fly. The charge had blown the shit out of a big china light fitting hanging down from the ceiling, and Alex had been hit with a few pellets in the shoulder and the cheek. He had to spend a couple of days in hospital while they dug them out.

Mrs Blake said the police had come and there had been a disjointed story allegedly about some husband who said the person he shot had been on with his wife!

They'd caught my girlfriend's husband and charged him. I went on holiday the next day and when I came back I found my name hadn't been mentioned, and the bewildered Alex (who had only been in the country a few days) did not want to lay charges. In the end the police charged my rival with discharging a firearm to the danger of others, and he was found guilty and given a substantial fine. Luckily the really juicy stuff which could have got into the scandal sheets never came out.

So I missed out on being wounded before I had even heard of the Vietnam war.

Shortly after joining the staff of the Australian Broadcasting Commission in 1961, Neil Davis began to think about moving on from Tasmania. The aim of most other cinecameramen working in the outer states of Australia was to get to Sydney.

That wasn't my aim at all, because I didn't think Sydney would give me greater experience — in fact, I thought it might restrict me, as I was the only staff cameraman in Tasmania and had my pick of many different fields. I was looking for work in a foreign country, but not Europe or the United States. I thought vaguely of South America, Africa or Asia, but I didn't know much about Asia because of the strange British-history-oriented schooling I had had.

The United Nations advertised a cameraman's job in Uganda, but I didn't apply because I had just joined the ABC. Almost immediately after that, a job turned up which did interest me — as a cameraman in Papua New Guinea, which was still administered by Australia at that time.

The paradox was that there were two applicants from Tasmania, both from the Tasmanian Government Film Unit, and I was appointed to a panel to interview them. It was quite strange. Within a month of joining the ABC, I was sitting in judgment on my fellow-workmates of a few weeks before for the job that I really wanted myself. Another job came up as cameraman on the Woomera rocket range in central Australia with quite a good salary, but I realised it would have to be bloody good money to justify being stuck out on a rocket range in the middle of nowhere.

Davis worked for the ABC for three years before the right opportunity presented itself — that of cameraman and correspondent in Southeast Asia, based in Singapore for what was then called BCINA (British Commonwealth International Newsfilm Agency), better known shortly afterwards and today as Visnews.

It was and is the largest television newsfilm agency in the world. They work with videotape almost entirely now. But they are to the television world what Reuters and the American newsagencies Associated Press and United Press International are to the written word.

Visnews was London-based and the major shareholders were the British Broadcasting Corporation, the Australian Broadcasting Commission, Reuters and in those days, the J. Arthur Rank Corporation.

Its main aim was to cover world news without any bias. Before that, television stations throughout the world could have bought television news, but it quite often came from the American networks and naturally the coverage had a strong American emphasis.

The shareholders of Visnews wanted something different and they had been operating for about five years when they advertised for their first staff cameraman in Southeast Asia. They also believed that Australians had entrée to most of the countries in the region. A British or American cameraman would not be able to get into Indonesia, for example, which was a closed shop. Although Australia supported the newly formed state of Malaysia, we had been sympathetic towards the Indonesian revolution against Dutch colonial rule just after the war, so Australian journalists could still go into Indonesia.

It was almost certain that an Australian applicant would get the job and I knew I had a strong chance not only because of my quite extensive experience with film and news coverage but because I could write and script my own material.

Neil Davis was appointed Visnews staff cameraman in Southeast Asia at the end of 1963. He flew to Singapore to begin work during the first week of February 1964.

7

'Singapore Was a Magic Name'

Neil Davis arrived in Singapore at dusk, and as the door of the Qantas Boeing 707 opened at Paya Leba airport he breathed in the moist, spicy, crutchy, faintly decaying and profoundly exciting smell of the Southeast Asian tropics. There was a whiff of clove-scented cigarettes, and a pleasant musky odour emanated from the perspiring Asian throng at the airport terminal. Responding to the powerful sensuality of it all, Davis felt a surge of excitement verging on tumescence as he took in the sights, sounds and smells of his first Asian evening.

Singapore was a magic name for me, really. It was one of the countries — a city state — that I knew a little bit about because it had been a British colony. In 1964 it was still part of Malaysia. So I not only entered Singapore, I entered an entirely new world and with new friends, most of them Asian. This was to be my home from then on.

Singapore then was a vastly different city to today's super-efficient metropolis. Everything was new to me — the mugginess of the weather — which I liked, although Singapore can be very humid and debilitating — the street activity, noodle sellers, shoeshine boys, newspaper stands, bric-a-brac stalls and vendors of all descriptions. It seemed to me that all minor commerce was done openly and with vast good humour and very loudly, right there on the footpath, and I loved it.

I quickly became accustomed to this sort of thing in all the cities of Southeast Asia. Singapore was not unique, but for an Aussie boy, especially an islander from Tasmania, I might just as well have landed on another planet.

For the next two years I lived out of a suitcase, always in hotels. In Singapore I stayed at the famous Cockpit Hotel, a lovely converted European mansion. Today there is a new skyscraper in front of the Cockpit, but it lacks the charm, grace and ambience of the old Cockpit, one of Asia's great hotels.

I was up at dawn the day after I arrived, at 6 a.m. Singapore is virtually on the equator, less than one degree north of the line, so day and night hours are almost evenly distributed — 6 a.m. dawn, 6 p.m. dusk. That first morning I walked down Orchard Road to the ABC's office. It took me twenty minutes. I did the same thing many times thereafter, and never tired of it.

Twenty-four hours after I arrived in Singapore, I met a man who was to become a close lifelong friend, a Singaporean Chinese named Willie Phua. I had been invited out to the studios of Television Singapura, the government television station, by a Tasmanian friend, Keith Wilkes, who was working as a producer there.

TV Singapura is now a fine series of modern buildings, but in 1964 it was a complex of old weatherboard army huts. Some time later, during the live on-air screening of a production called *Campfire*, the altogether-too-realistic campfire set alight to the set, and much of the old TV Singapura went up in flames!

However, at dusk on my first full day in Singapore I joined Keith in the studio canteen, and he introduced me to Willie Phua who was a stills photographer then, just moving into TV news and documentary filming. Chinese New Year was being celebrated, so the few drinks I intended to have grew into a New Year party for the three of us. We were beer drinkers, and Singapore Tiger and Anchor beer are good, and as it was a hot and humid night we had no trouble sinking quite a few.

Around midnight, after about six solid hours of drinking, Willie insisted he would drive me home to the Cockpit which was situated on a small hill overlooking Orchard Road. Willie had to negotiate a traffic island to get around and up to the hotel. He managed to get his little Fiat sedan on to the traffic island circle, and could not get it off! That damned car kept going around and around the circle with Willie immobile at the wheel.

Every time we came opposite the road back to the Cockpit Hotel, I'd say, 'Here she is, Willie,' but round we'd go again. After ten circuits I said, 'Stop the car, Willie.' There was almost no traffic late at night in Singapore then. Willie did stop, and I got out and made my way very unsteadily up towards the hotel, every now and then looking back to check on Willie.

Each time I looked, that little blue Fiat was still going around and around in a perfect circle. Willie doesn't know what time he got home.

On 11 February 1964, Neil Davis wrote the first of a series of weekly letters to his Aunt Lillian in Tasmania; they continued until her death in 1973. Aunt Lillian was his father's eldest sister who had been a nurse in Europe during World War I. In the years following his mother's death, Davis had found her rather hard and strict, but aunt and nephew grew closer when he became an adult.

Aunt Lillian armed herself with a world map to follow his travels and during the ten years of correspondence with her nephew she came to know the major towns and cities, as well as the leaders and principal politicians of Southeast Asia. Aunt Lillian's keen and inquiring mind demanded incisive commentaries and descriptions about the personalities and politics of the region, and Neil Davis responded with literary models of observation and political analysis.

The letters provide added insights into the mind and motivations of this intensely private though outwardly gregarious man. At first though, the letters simply reveal an early fascination with the different cultures around him.

Letter to Aunt Lillian, 11 February 1964

Dear Auntie,

. . . Things here are not quite as the travel folders tell you . . . the political situation here and in the near countries is very different to what you read in the papers. Some situations which may appear explosive to Australians are generally only bluff. Others which we hear little about down there are real hotspots and are just about ready to 'go off'.

The Chinese New Year is about to commence and the place is already seething with all kinds of revel makers, black marketeers, con-men (and women) and opportunities of all kinds.

The Chinese believe they must enter the New Year free of debt. A very fine attribute — except they are having a real ball. At least one payroll grab per day, many daylight robberies, and of course at night they really cut loose. Well, they've got to pay their debts, they say . . .

I expect my first trip away from Singapore to be either North Borneo, Jakarta, or Laos . . .

The Australian Broadcasting Commission's office in Singapore included the Visnews operation at that stage. The whole ABC's Southeast Asian operation had few staff and little money: Australia was just beginning to come to terms with the geographic reality of its situation and the countries to its near north. Confrontation between Malaysia and Indonesia was more about rhetoric than action and the Vietnam war had not escalated into its long dominance of the world's headlines and radio and television news bulletins. The ABC's Singapore office was run by a notable character, Ted Shaw.

Ted Shaw was a genuine Walter Mitty character, at times irritating, but you only needed the semblance of a sense of humour to appreciate Ted. He liked a drink or two, and his greatest supporter, who followed him adoringly when he was at home, was his blue heeler cattle dog, Skippy, that he had brought from Australia. The stories Ted told about himself stretched credibility a bit.

They were mainly centred around the period 1932−34 — his golden years, presumably — and because younger people like the other ABC correspondents and myself weren't born then, we couldn't really check on him. By his own account, during that period he was an ace foreign correspondent on the European scene, where he naturally interviewed Adolf Hitler. He was at other times the middleweight boxing champion of Australia and he rode a wild brumby that only he could manage to eleven consecutive victories on major country racecourses in Queensland.

So we had a mental vision of Ted speeding around Queensland defending his middleweight title at roughly seventy kilos, then shedding fifteen kilos to ride his brumby to yet another win, putting on the weight again to defend his boxing title, and in between times zipping over to Europe to interview Hitler, Churchill, Mussolini and other world leaders.

Ted also at that time — according to Ted — wrote a book which was based on the Indian subcontinent. That seemed to be an afterthought. He spent a lot of time, it seems, with the British Raj on the Northwest Frontier.

Another of the ABC journalists in Singapore then was Tony Cane, who also came from Tasmania. Tony appeared to swallow at least some of Ted's tall tales, and said he would like to read the book allegedly based on the subcontinent. Ted said, 'Oh yes, it was called *Through the Khyber Pass*.'

Tony, a methodical fellow, went down to Singapore's big National Library to look for it and told Ted he couldn't find it. 'You're a bloody fool,' said Ted. 'Why didn't you tell me you were going down there? It's called a different name here.'

'Well, what's that?' asked Tony.

'*Life In An Indian Village*,' said Ted without a flicker or an instant's hesitation. Tony couldn't find *Life In an Indian Village* either, but he didn't tax Ted with it.

Neil Davis quickly found that his training in Tasmania as a documentary maker, newsreel and television newsfilm cameraman and scriptwriter had more than equipped him for his new job. In fact it was not nearly as difficult as he had imagined.

I had always made my own arrangements for transport and accommodation when I covered stories in Australia. The difference in Singapore was that I had to get entry visas in my passport for most of the countries of Southeast Asia. Naturally there was a language problem, which was usually overcome with goodwill and humour on both sides. I might say that a sense of humour in Asia helps a lot.

Most Asians are not inscrutable — damned if I know where that tag came from. They enjoy a good joke. In fact the most frequent criticism from Westerners is that Asians don't take things seriously enough. In every Asian language there's a phrase that means more or less, 'Never mind, it doesn't matter'. That's usually when things go wrong and nothing can be done about them. It's important not to get mad, just say, 'Never mind'. Political sides of the fence don't seem to matter. The Vietnamese Communists, for example, have a well developed sense of humour, which makes them more

like their Southeast Asian neighbours Thailand,
Singapore, Malaysia and the Philippines than their
fellow-Communists and ideological big brothers the
Russians.

I've seen Vietnamese Communists sigh somewhat
resignedly when they have to go into lengthy discussions
with the generally pretty stodgy Russkies. I find I've
spent most of my time at work and play with Asians. Of
course I had Western friends in those early days, and I
have them still — but the overwhelming majority of my
friends and acquaintances are Asians. In the Visnews
office in Singapore, for example, there were Malays,
Chinese, Indians and Eurasians, all Singaporeans and
very representative of the island itself.

Neil Davis's settling-down process was helped immeasur-
ably by meeting the first of many Asian girlfriends. Patsy
was a Singaporean, of Chinese and Indian parentage.

Patsy was relatively tall for an Asian from that region,
slim — although I must say she was a well developed
lady — and she had beautiful olive skin, flashing white
teeth, and of course raven-black hair. She was a model
who worked part-time as a hotel receptionist.

Alas, Patsy was rather scatterbrained. She just loved
dogs, and she had a German Shepherd called Sandy. One
day we were driving from Singapore to Johore Bahru,
across the causeway in Malaysia, in a little Sunbeam
Alpine I had bought. Patsy used to irritate me because
she was always on the lookout for dogs she thought
might be in danger. The dog might be halfway up a hill,
quite safe, but Patsy would make sure he wasn't going to
run in front of the car.

On this particular day she suddenly screamed out,
'Watch the dog, look out for the dog!' I hit the brakes,
skidded to the side of the road and then felt pretty silly.
The dog was at least two hundred metres ahead of us.

What was worse, it was a typical Singapore mongrel, a real survivor, and well able to look after itself. If there had been a car behind us we'd have had an accident.

I said, 'For Christ's sake, Patsy.'

'No, no,' said Patsy, 'no Christ's sake, you could have hit him.' We had been having an argument about the way she managed her finances, and I had charged her with lacking any kind of method of financially looking after herself.

'Forget the dog,' I said, 'you should keep your own affairs in order.' Of course, I was a great one to talk — but I used to talk to Patsy like that. She generally took it, but this time she said, 'I do, I do.' I knew that the modelling agency owed her money, and suggested that she had no idea how much.

Patsy indignantly pulled out a little notebook and said, 'Look, I'm owed exactly $925.70.' And there, as neat as you like, she had logged her hours, the taxi fares she had paid, and the different hourly rates for different jobs. I was stunned and immediately a new Patsy emerged before my eyes. It's a lesson I've never forgotten. You can be as dim as a two-watt lamp economically, but if you simply write things down every day you can keep your books straight. I learned that first from Jack Thwaites in the Tasmanian Government Film Unit, it was reinforced by Patsy, and I've done it ever since.

She was quite a lady, Patsy, and she had a terrific sense of humour. She told me once she posed for an advertising agent in a bikini to try out for a magazine layout. The agent, being a red-blooded man, found it got a bit too much for him when Patsy stripped down to the bikini in his office, and he came on strong.

Patsy stopped him short and said that as she was in a little bikini and he had all his clothes on, they would be rough on her body and it would be better if he got all his clothes off. Well, you can imagine he was pretty eager by this time. He threw his gear off like a mad dervish, and looked around, stark naked, to see Patsy pick up her little pile of neatly folded clothes and step gracefully into the outer office. The secretary was pretty startled, but then quietly applauded in great and silent glee as Patsy methodically dressed and left.

One of the ABC correspondents based in Singapore in 1964 was Peter Barnett, later to become the ABC's Washington correspondent during the Johnson, Nixon and Carter years from the mid-1960s until 1979. Shortly before Neil arrived in Singapore Barnett had been reporting in South Vietnam, where he had developed useful contacts with the famous Madame Nhu (the Dragon Lady), whose brother-in-law President Ngo Dinh Diem was assassinated in November 1963, shortly before President John Kennedy was himself shot. Madame Nhu's husband was the police chief, so Barnett's contacts in Saigon were very good. However, the confrontation of Indonesia and the newly formed Malaysia was a more prominent story early in 1964, with Indonesia's President Sukarno vowing to *ganyang* (crush) Malaysia. To Sukarno the stitching together of four former British territories to form a new nation to the north of his country was a neo-colonialist plot.

The problem faced by Peter Barnett and Neil Davis was to extricate themselves from Singapore and go to Borneo to cover this story. They needed Ted Shaw's permission and Ted preferred to have them in Singapore as drinking companions and as an audience for tall tales.

At that time some Indonesian troops were actually infiltrating into the Malaysian-controlled states of Sarawak and Sabah, and British troops, Gurkhas, Malaysian and even some Australian troops were in action in Borneo.

Peter Barnett knew how to handle Ted. Because he was such a contrary character, you couldn't just say that there was a good story in Borneo, because he would immediately reject that idea. After I had been in

Singapore for about a week and a half, we went searching for Ted one night around his favourite bars. We finally found him, very late at night, at the American Club.

Peter managed to turn the conversation away from Ted's cricketing, fighting and brumby riding to work and the region, and suggested that South Vietnam was the story of the day and that we should go and cover it.

Ted took a reflective sip of his Scotch and said, 'No, you're quite wrong. I was up at Phoenix Park today, and Confrontation is the story. I want you both on the first plane to Borneo in the morning.'

This, of course, was just what we wanted. Ted often used to say he'd been up at Phoenix Park, which was the centre for British military intelligence. Well, nobody went there unless they were either in intelligence or specially invited. When Ted didn't get in to the office until one p.m. or two p.m. he generally said he'd been up at Phoenix Park to consult with the intelligence experts on our behalf.

On this occasion we knew he wouldn't be 'back from Phoenix Park' the following day until early afternoon, so we had time to pack up our gear, get our tickets and by the time Ted came into the office looking for a drinking mate or two, we were on our way to Borneo, and my first Asian assignment, to cover the confrontation with Indonesia in the Borneo states of Malaysia.

8

The Last of the Fun Wars

Confrontation was a grassfire war really, military harassment but a war nevertheless. It was named and instigated by President Sukarno, the father of Indonesia's independence, to oppose the newly independent Malaysia, which included the former British North Borneo states of Sarawak and Sabah, and the tiny oil-rich Sultanate of Brunei, still a protectorate of Britain.

I don't think Sukarno's charges that Malaysia was a neo-colonialist creation propped up by Britain were entirely unfounded, but in any case he was easily contained by the efficient British Commonwealth forces, which had had a lot of experience fighting in the Malayan Emergency against the Chinese Communists which lasted officially from 1948 to 1960. Although isolated remnants of the Malayan Communist Party still exist, the British handling of the Emergency was successful.

The Indonesians were facing experienced counter-insurgency jungle fighters. Some of the finest troops you could find anywhere in the world were concentrated in Borneo at that time. There were Malaysian troops, some Australians — and of course the famous Gurkhas from Nepal, said to be the best soldiers in the world.

What action there was took place in what I call real jungle — triple-canopy impenetrable rainforest thickly coating steep hills and mountains. Later, journalists would write about the war 'in the jungles of Vietnam'. There were some heavy forests in Vietnam and some areas like the U Minh forest were rather like the Everglades of Florida, but I never saw real jungle in any part of Vietnam or Cambodia. Borneo had the real thing.

Strategically the Commonwealth troops didn't have all that hard a job, simply because there were only about nine tracks along the border with Indonesian Borneo (Kalimantan) through which opposing troops could penetrate. The most difficult part was simply being there, operating helicopters and moving troops and supplies around that impenetrable and wildly beautiful place, which was also inhabited by splendidly independent and colourful tribespeople, the Ibans and Dayaks.

For the foreign correspondent and the career soldiers in the British Army, Confrontation was the last of the fun wars. There were few shots fired in anger, and all the excitement of setting up forward jungle bases and playing soldiers in exotic country. The first story Peter Barnett and Neil Davis had to cover in March 1964 was the aftermath of an Indonesian attempt to infiltrate about a hundred troops through a low-lying swampy river complex near Tawau, on the extreme northeast coast of Sabah.

It was a ghastly place to mount a military operation, as there were few places where your feet could touch dry ground. All but a handful of the Indonesian soldiers died in the jungle before they even made it to the Sabah border, and when we arrived at Tawau, the Gurkhas were picking up five or six stragglers who were only too happy to surrender after their nightmare journey through the swamps.

I could not have had a better travelling companion

than Peter Barnett. He has a well developed sense of humour and was professionally very resourceful and innovative. He naturally had an eye for the ladies, particularly if they were well endowed between neck and waist. The Dayak and Iban girls do have one thing in common, they are big-breasted, and as a dedicated voyeur, Peter had a field day in Borneo.

The two Australians went back to Kuching and Barnett returned to Singapore for a between-assignments ration of more tall tales from Ted. Neil Davis prepared for what he later remembered as one of his most memorable journeys — up the Rejang River by longboat to visit a detachment of Gurkha troops deep in the interior near a tiny village called Belaga.

The Rejang River in Sarawak is one of the great rivers of the world. When I finally got to a place called Kapit, which is roughly two hundred miles [320 kilometres] inland, a seven-thousand-tonne freighter was docked there, which illustrates how big the river is. It is fast-flowing and rather frightening in its upper reaches, through heavy jungle country and tribal areas controlled by former headhunters who had barely had time to give up the habit.

The Ibans were the sea Dayaks and the land Dayaks did not encroach on their territory. The Ibans were the most aggressive, and they were great boat people as well. Beyond Kapit were the renowned Pelagus Rapids, and it took local experts to negotiate them. The Rejang was about a mile wide at that point, with formidable rocks jutting up from the river bed, and more just below the surface which were even more dangerous.

At one point they brought the longboat to the bank and asked me to walk a mile or two because it was too risky to have me on board. They explained that I did not know how to move my weight about in the boat — and in any case, I had my expensive camera gear and film and they were worried about that.

I walked along the river bank watching them — which was exciting enough in itself — until I came upon a wild tiger! It was a terrifying, exhilarating and exciting five seconds, seeing that tiger in the wild, the only time I ever did. He was about a hundred metres away, and looked as big as a pony.

I was terrified and knew it was no good yelling out to my escorts, who were out in the middle of the roaring rapids. If I waved to them they would just wave back. So I stood in the water, as far away from the bank as I could, waiting for that bloody animal to come on to me. There was a flash of movement and he was gone. Of course he was probably as unnerved as I was, and had well and truly pissed off.

Davis was relieved to join up with the Nepalese Gurkha troops at Belaga, and they immediately invited him to a game of volleyball.

The Gurkhas were the best disciplined soldiers I have ever seen — the most courageous and intensely loyal. If they have a fault, it is a lack of flexibility. Once committed to an action, they press on regardless. If their officer is killed, they have been known to carry on with the original plan to the point of destruction. But they were rarely placed at a disadvantage. When they were in the jungle on operations they did not smoke or talk, and moved soundlessly like cats.

Apart from rifles, they carried their *kukris*, a wicked curved knife that was hooked in a way to make it easier to decapitate an enemy. It was kept razor-sharp, and if you asked to see the *kukri* they would gladly show it, and then before sheathing it would startle you by nicking their finger and drawing blood. This was tradition — a Gurkha never draws his *kukri* without drawing blood.

After losing his sweat on the volleyball court, Davis was taken to the mess and introduced to another Ghurka tradition, their daily tot of 100 per cent overproof rum.

> It was issued in an army pannikin and seemed an enormous slug, and their method was to drink it down in one go, which I did, too. There didn't seem to be any limit to the ritual and I got enormously drunk. The next thing I knew a Gurkha orderly was standing beside my bed at five a.m. with a cup of hot strong sweet milky tea — urgently needed for my blistering hangover — and a reminder I had promised to go crocodile shooting that day.

Davis did, but it was not a happy day lurching about crocodile-infested backwaters in narrow canoes with Gurkhas obviously impervious to hangovers.

> There are many stories about the Gurkhas and their attitudes to combat, but one of the most famous actually took place in Borneo while I was there, and was told to me with great gusto by a British Gurkha officer.
> The Gurkhas were not trained as paratroopers, but were asked if they would be prepared to jump from a Hercules C130 transport aircraft into combat against the Indonesians if the need arose. The Gurkhas had the right to turn down this request because they had not been trained for this combat role.
> Now the Gurkhas usually agreed to anything, but on this occasion they provisionally rejected the plan. But the next day, one of their NCOs sought out the British officer who had made the request and said they had discussed the matter further and would be prepared to jump under certain conditions.
> 'What are they?' asked the British officer.
> The Gurkhas told him they would jump if the land was

marshy or reasonably soft with no rocky outcrops, because they were inexperienced in falling.

The British officer considered this, and said that the dropping area would almost certainly be over jungle, and there would not be any rocky outcrops, so that seemed all right. Was there anything else?

Yes, said the Gurkhas. They wanted the plane to fly as slowly as possible and no more than one hundred feet high. The British pointed out that the planes always did fly as slowly as possible when dropping troops, but to jump from one hundred feet was impossible, because the parachutes would not open in time from that height.

'Oh,' said the Gurkhas, 'that's all right, then. We'll jump with parachutes anywhere. You didn't mention parachutes before!'

Landing in a helicopter in Borneo was almost as dangerous as jumping, with or without a parachute. The few emergency landing pads were created by the ingenious method of winching men down onto sharply pointed hilltops. Finding a shelf where the ground rose less sharply than the smoke from their cooking fires, they hacked out a clearing. Next, a small bulldozer was winched down to literally flatten off the mountain top. The only other emergency landing possibility was to ditch in a river. The odds were not good.

Even where there were established landing pads at the forward bases, you had to come down through a kind of funnel between sixty- and ninety-metre trees. I flew in to these pads on quite a few occasions. The rotors used to strip leaves from the outer branches as you descended. The trouble was that once a helicopter started its controlled descent through that very restricted area, it was difficult, almost impossible, to get the power or manoeuvrability to go up until the soldiers left the aircraft.

So you were committed to landing, and if there were any enemy around, they would be able to pick you off.

It was Neil Davis's first introduction to filming a war, but he neither saw nor heard a shot fired in anger.

Letter to Aunt Lillian, 22 March 1964
Aurora Hotel,
Kuching

... I work under an entirely different system than I ever have before, but it seems to work well and I definitely prefer it. Visnews evidently has great faith in their cameraman! I get a set salary (plus allowances and certain expenses like travelling costs) but no overtime whatever — which is reasonable, as no doubt you'll agree that it would be hard to determine what time should be paid when one is in the depths of the Borneo jungle.

To get here, I merely received an instruction from London which said 'PROCEED BORNEO'. Everything else is left to me — where I go, how I travel, how long I stay, what film I take, how many films I shoot and what time (if any) I have off.

I have worked very hard here — it is generally accepted that you work hard while away, and do virtually nothing in Singapore. There is little work there, anyway. I'm up early in the morning wherever I am, as it is necessary to get an early start if you are to get anywhere that day.

A great deal of time is taken up meeting people and getting them on your side — this is perhaps the most important thing, as without their co-operation it would be impossible to work effectively. The armed forces, police officials, government officials, tribal chiefs, hotel receptionists and telephonists, the people in the various cable offices, customs and immigration people, and especially the officials of the local airlines. This is extremely important to ensure quick despatch and delivery of film, as well as being a great help in getting seats on aircraft.

Filming also relies to a great extent on who I know and what transport I can get in a hurry. When I complete each individual news item, I do a complete description of every shot I've taken, besides giving as much background scripting material as possible. This is quite often done late at night, or early in the morning. So I usually end up working fourteen to sixteen hours a day, one way or another . . .

On 4 September 1985 — only five days before he died on assignment in the streets of Bangkok — Davis taped further comments on the techniques of being a successful foreign correspondent, having long forgotten his letter to Aunt Lillian.

A journalist must know the background of the story he is covering. If he has to fly suddenly to a country having a coup d'état, he should be aware of the basic circumstances surrounding the government's fall. If you do have to go in cold — and this does happen — you have to have a game plan.

The important thing to do first is to get to the people who can help you immediately. Always carry a guidebook to Southeast Asia. It's marvellous what you can pick up about a country, climate, population, political affiliations, and short- and long-term history. There will be important practical information like whether the power system is alternating or direct current and whether they have an automatic telephone system.

As soon as you land, you start talking to people. Taxi drivers can give you succinct comments and background on the situation, so can the guy who carries your bags at the airport, the room boy at the hotel and the waiters or people at your table in the restaurant. Then of course you talk to the diplomats, local politicians and the army people — if that is relevant.

It's always useful to get down to the bars, because nobody knows the local situation better than bar girls, bartenders or street hawkers — everyone can give you information. You don't need to walk around unenlightened and ill-informed, because everyone you meet can make a contribution.

In Borneo in March 1964, Davis was confident that he had the training and ability to handle his wide-ranging international assignments. But it was nice to be reassured.

Letter to Aunt Lillian, 22 March 1964
Aurora Hotel,
Kuching

... received a telegram from London yesterday which said CONGRATS — ALL ITEMS WIDEST POSSIBLE SYNDICATION, which means to about 70 countries. It was pleasing to get this as it was a little worrying not quite knowing how the film was going to stand up on an international basis ...

Davis returned to Singapore towards the end of March and in the next few weeks covered assignments in the Philippines, Malaysia, Singapore, Thailand, South Vietnam, Laos and Cambodia. It was to be a familiar circuit, and would fill twenty-one Australian passports with his visas — about one passport a year.

Before heading off to Manila and Saigon to cover a visit by the then US Secretary of State Dean Rusk, Davis submitted his Borneo expenses to the unpredictable Ted Shaw. Ted was not overfond of paperwork, but like many an administrator in a similar situation he accepted the major claims, but homed in on anything that looked a little out of place.

Neil's expenses were usually models of accuracy and propriety, but these were early days, and he had slipped.

Ted held up an entertainment receipt from a Kuching night-club which simply stated: 'Rosette, $25.00'.

'What's this Rosette business then?' he asked belligerently.

Rosette was, in fact, the name of the dance hostess who had been assigned to Neil for the evening — standard practice in many Southeast Asian establishments. In Singapore and Malaysia the girls were called 'taxi dancers' and were hired by the hour.

Neil thought quickly. 'You know Ted,' he said, 'the French wine *rosette*?'

Ted knew everything. 'Of course I bloody well know,' he said. 'But why didn't you buy Algerian? It's cheaper!'

9

The Land of
One Million Elephants

Letter to Aunt Lillian, 13 April 1964
The Shellbourne Arms Hotel,
Manila

Just a brief letter to let you know I'm leaving Manila
earlier than expected, and going to South Vietnam before
Thailand. The United States Secretary of State Dean
Rusk is going directly there from the SEATO
conference . . .

Manila is fascinating, but completely lawless. It's just
astounding — it makes the American TV gangster films
look quite insipid. The police and troops all carry
holstered revolvers and use them frequently.

When you go to a hotel or nightclub, you see notices
asking clients to check their guns in, please! Just like
leaving your hat and coat. Some of the signs say
'weapons', which is more appropriate as the Filipinos are
very fond of using their knives . . .

Letter to Aunt Lillian, 19 April 1964
Hotel Majestic
Saigon

. . . Went down into Viet Cong country yesterday and got
some good film of Rusk in a village. This is a real hotbed
here, as the whole country is alive with guerillas and you

don't venture out after dark even in Saigon (population
2 500 000).

It is a typically French town with many treelined
avenues and sidewalk cafés . . .

Will close for the present, Auntie. Actually I'm feeling
very low at the moment. When I arrived here on Friday
there was a telegram saying that my old footballing
friend Ron Batchelor had died in Melbourne.

Letter to Aunt Lillian, 28 April 1964
Hotel Constellation,
Vientiane

Just to let you know I'm in Laos, and have been for a
week now. I got word of a coup d'état here, in South
Vietnam, so got a plane to Bangkok, an RAF transport to
Udorn in northeast Thailand, and crossed the Mekong
River into Laos. There were no planes flying, and all
communications cut off.

However a journalist friend from Manila who works
for the London *Daily Telegraph* and myself were the first
foreign pressmen into Vientiane, the capital of Laos, and
both got scoops. This is an amazing and almost
unbelievable situation, with intrigue and counter-intrigue
— all a cross between pantomime, comic opera and
tragedy. Right now things are quiet, but another coup is
imminent, I think . . .

Davis and Laos struck an instant accord. He grasped the
basic insanity of the situation there, but realised that the
lunacy had benefits.

In a way the tripartite government of left, right and
neutral did save Laos. It presented a facade of neutrality
and peace which did not exist in reality — but the
mechanics were still in place much later when the
Communists were gaining control of all Indo-China, and

Laos was handed over more or less peaceably. Many Laotians did die in the war, but it could have been genocidal.

Vientiane was one of the few capitals in the world where the United States, Russians, Chinese, East Germans, West Germans, North and South Koreans were all permitted to establish embassies, due to the tripartite government encompassing Communist, neutralist and right-wing elements.

You could visit the embassies of East and West Germany, who were both giving aid to Laos. So were Russia and the United States, of course. Meanwhile on the battlefield, the left wing fought the right wing with the Russians and Chinese supplying the left and the Americans doing the honours for the right.

In Vientiane the diplomats representing all factions went to diplomatic parties and exchanged pleasantries over cocktails together.

In the mid-1960s it was all gentlemanly and quaint, but became less so by the end of the decade. Battle- and brothel-weary war correspondents from Vietnam welcomed a periodic coup d'état in Laos as an excuse to experience the comparative tranquillity of that beautiful country.

The conflict was not very serious in the sense that few people got killed. The Laotians had an admirable sense of destiny and an extremely civilised attitude to warfare. The Communist Pathet Lao would send polite indications to the American-supported side that they were about to attack. Quite often the Communists went into a Buddhist pagoda during their assault to bring Buddha down on their side.

The defenders would predictably retreat in the face of this threat, and the Pathet Lao would announce a great victory with appropriate celebrations. There were a few shots fired, but little damage done because the disputed area had been sensibly vacated.

When the rightists wanted the territory back, they did the same in reverse. In comparison with Vietnam Laos was a very gentle land with only two or three million people and lots of elephants — it was known as the Land Of One Million Elephants. In its way it was the Switzerland of Southeast Asia.

From time to time the delicate political balance was disturbed, but a coup d'état was practically a family affair, as the Laotian leaders were all blood relatives. The right-wing coup that brought Neil to Vientiane in April 1964 was engineered by a twenty-eight-year-old, General Siho.

Prince Souphanouvong, the leader of the Pathet Lao known as the Red Prince, was at the Communist headquarters at Khang Khay. Davis decided it would be a coup of his own to interview the Communist prince. He was told officially that it was impossible, but he had become friendly with a key Laotian family one of whose sons had gone to school with General Siho. Not only that, but one of the daughters worked as a high-class maid in the home of the prime minister of the day, Prince Souvanna Phouma.

Although the coup leaders had Prince Souvanna Phouma under house arrest, he was still prime minister. To get to Pathet Lao headquarters, Neil had to get the signatures not only of the prime minister but also of the coup leader, General Siho.

The son of the Laotian family took Neil through the pouring monsoon rain and eleven checkpoints at midnight and persuaded Siho to sign the authority.

Neil had become extremely friendly with the daughter, who worked in Souvanna Phouma's house — just how friendly was never mentioned in letters to Aunt Lillian.

She smuggled me in through the scullery, and brought me face to face with the startled prime minister. In a fit of pique against the coup-makers who had him under house arrest, he, too, signed my authorisation.

The Pathet Lao honoured the paper and I was allowed to drive to Khang Khay, their headquarters. The Red Prince Souphanouvong (who was the prime minister's half-brother) looked at me sharply and asked if I was American. On hearing I was an Australian, he invited me to sit beside him. He was very jolly and friendly, and I had the first Western coverage out of Khang Khay for several years.

Foreign correspondents coming to Vientiane always stayed at the Constellation Hotel in Vientiane in those days, presided over by the urbane Maurice. Maurice always used to talk about 'going back to France', but Davis thought it unlikely he had ever been there.

He knew everybody at a very high level, so if you wanted passes to go anywhere or visa extensions, he could give you a home. And most important of all, he would convert your traveller's cheques into other currencies of the region. If he did not have cash, he would give you a note to redeem in Saigon or Phnom Penh.

Eric the German was a notable character who lived at the Constellation. He had served in the German army under Hitler and had gone on to the French Foreign Legion after the war. He seemed quite happy to be sent to Indo-China, because I think it was as far away from Germany as possible.

He was captured at Dien Bien Phu when the French were defeated there by the Viet Minh in 1954, and the North Vietnamese allowed him to stay. He married a Vietnamese girl but the Communist-controlled life was not to his taste and he and his wife moved to Laos, where he ran a small local airline doing charter work for the American Central Intelligence Agency and ferried opium and marijuana around when the occasion arose.

But Eric the German would also cart your furniture
down to Bangkok or have it shipped overseas — or even
get you some gold if you needed it. Eric could arrange to
get you anything that was going.

The watering point for off-duty journalists, spies and zestful
diplomats was the White Rose, a bar and nightclub on the
banks of the Mekong River. It was a place of considerable
charm and simplicity in 1964 and 1965.

It had a dirt floor for most of its working life. The girls
there would dance, in the later 1960s they danced topless
and smoked cigarettes while talking to you. The
cigarettes were not in their mouths.

You could meet all sorts of interesting people at the
White Rose. Some members of the American community
would be there and tucked away in the corner you'd
often find the Russians. I never did see the Red Chinese
at the White Rose.

Walking through the Vientiane market one day, Neil spotted
a shirtless, shoeless European with a Beatle haircut. He
wore only a pair of jeans and bowler hat and he sat on a
rubber groundsheet on which were little piles of white pills.
According to Donald Wise, roving correspondent for the
London *Daily Mirror*, Davis asked, 'What have you got
there, old fellow?'

'Clap pills,' replied the young man, with an English accent.

'Then I'll buy the lot,' said Davis.

The young Englishman was Tim Page. Davis took him
back to the Constellation for a meal, showed him for the
first time in his life how to take pictures with a stills camera,
and set him on the way to becoming a war photographer
'known,' said Wise, 'both for his multiple wounds and great
action pictures'.

Page went on to Saigon to share digs with Sean Flynn (a
movie actor turned photographer), son of Errol Flynn, and a

collection of other blithe spirits. They became war groupies, taking advantage of the American invitation to ride on their choppers anywhere at any time and be landed smack in the action. The trick was to jump out of the helicopter with stills cameras festooned around the torso like worry beads and blaze away.

When Page judged it right, he came back with action pictures for the front page and inner double page spread of *Life* magazine. He captured the anguish and madness of battle, the taut faces of medics ramming emergency drips into the veins of a GI with his legs blasted off and Medivac choppers hovering like demented dragonflies over the dust and debris of battle.

But it was crazy, chancy stuff. Page was peppered with shrapnel four times before being shot up — by the Americans — on a patrol boat in the South China Sea. He was slashed and punctured with 200 separate wounds. It was lucky, said his friends, that the most serious were in the head, and therefore not vital. The gangling Page seemed like an overgrown and exceedingly naughty schoolboy. To everyone's surprise, he lived through it all. He went on flashing a leering lopsided smile from his shrapnel-battered face, and tempting fate again. There was a special kind of madness about Page.

Pat Burgess, a big, tough Australian correspondent who had given weight and power to Rugby forward packs, liked Page and Sean Flynn, who had recently arrived in the area from a stint of B-grade moviemaking with Run Run Shaw's Hong Kong studios. Pat enjoyed introducing Flynn to the wonderful eccentricities of Vientiane. Their own behaviour was bizarre enough. The good citizens of Vientiane would marvel at the sight of these two Westerners hurling a heavy medicine ball at each other on the roof of the Constellation Hotel in the blinding heat of the midday sun. After more frenetic athletics, the two correspondents would climax their mad-dogs-and-Englishmen routine by jogging down the street and swimming across the Mekong River to the

Pathet Lao-controlled bank and back again.

Burgess recalls that other correspondents and Laotians would shake their heads and prophesy that they would be shot by the Communists. But they never were.

'Sean and I were buying some vegetables one day and we found a roneotyped lesson in Lao with phonetic translations. So after our Mekong swim, we'd give each other language lessons. It was basic stuff. "Hello", "Goodbye", and how to count from one to ten and onward. Then there were useful phrases like, "Aren't the mangoes green this year", or "Hello, I see your sister is pregnant again".

'After dark we would go over to the White Rose, which in those days was full of CIA types, big beefy men with crewcuts, all answering to names like Chuck or Rocky and all very knowledgeable about aircraft. The White Rose had not yet become a bordello, and still had some of its original charm and warmth.

'We'd meet up with Neil Davis, who would sit between us at the bar. Sean would look across Neil — who would keep a straight face — and say in perfect Lao, "Hello, I see your sister is pregnant again," to which I would reply, "My, aren't the mangoes green this year." Sean would then count from one to twenty, and pause meaningfully. I would respond sternly, "You are a very lazy girl — do the washing!"

'Sean would volunteer, "I have a sore finger". The Chucks and Rockys were convinced we were fluent Lao speakers, the bar girls were convulsed with laughter, and Davis was beside himself. They were good days — and a welcome change from the war in Vietnam.'

But even in Laos, the good days were numbered.

Letter to Aunt Lillian, 17 May 1964
   King's Hotel,
   Bangkok

   . . . Things in Laos are very shaky now with Chinese
Communists and Viet Minh troops (North Vietnam)

crossing the Lao border and joining forces with the Pathet Lao Communists. Managed to get down to the Plain of Jars and got some exclusive film of General Kong Le (Neutralist) as well as my film of the Pathet Lao leader Prince Souphanouvong.

In Vietnam the South Vietnamese (assisted by the Americans) are taking a real hiding, with wholesale slaughter on both sides, and many atrocities. 1700 were killed in one week just three weeks ago in South Vietnam, and some hundreds have been killed in Laos in the last few days, including the slaughter of two entire villages (women, children and animals) . . .

. . . One can't help but feel anger at the French, who brought much of their culture and fine living (for themselves) to Indo-China and precious little else; the British on the other hand really got things done, and by comparison really set their countries on the way to a reasonable standard of living.

Now America is trying her hand, and possibly doing in some ways worse than the others. Many things are being done with US dollars, but they are finding it doesn't buy loyalty, and the people tend to despise and hate them (mixed with envy) and their almighty dollar . . .

Don't know where I go from here, could be South Vietnam, Borneo, or back to Laos . . .

It would be a familiar pattern, as Davis shuttled through the region's trouble spots. Back to Singapore, over to Borneo for more Confrontation, and then on 12 July a return to Saigon and his first real taste of the reality of combat.

Letter to Aunt Lillian, 2 August 1964
Hotel Caravelle,
Saigon

. . . Things have been stepped up lately, with with the USA pouring about $2 000 000 per day into the country now, plus 'advisors' — 1600 of them, and 6000 more to come shortly. Tan Son Nhut airport in Saigon is the busiest I've ever seen — hundreds of fighters, bombers, supply and transport planes, helicopters, troop carriers, reconnaissance planes — plus of course seven or eight major commercial airlines. Usually one can count ten or twelve aircraft in the air at any time, either just taken off or waiting to land.

Military activity has been stepped up lately, they had about 250 to 300 battles last week. Two nights back the Viet Cong launched a 300-man attack on a military post near the airport — ten kilometres from the heart of Saigon! There were three bombings (hand thrown) in the city yesterday, but only four killed fortunately — about twenty injured. They were more on the mark last week when a well aimed grenade landed in a jeep and killed three American officers and their Vietnamese driver.

As I sit here now I can hear the light artillery (and see the flashes) about thirteen kilometres away on the outskirts of town. The province adjoining Saigon (about 1035 square kilometres;), is completely held by the Viet Cong, so the attacks on the southern and western city perimeters occur nightly . . .

By mid-1964, despite covering Confrontation in Borneo and the aftermath of battles on the Plain of Jars in Laos, Davis had not filmed actual combat, nor had he been under fire. But in July he headed into the Mekong River delta area south of Saigon, then the major disputed area with the Viet Cong. Some seven million people, half the population of South Vietnam, lived there. There were American military advisers active there, but no American troops. The battle was on for 'winning the hearts and minds of the people', a Maoist-sounding phrase used relentlessly by the Americans and promptly abbreviated to WHAMMO.

I was anxious to get out and see what the war was all about, and of course I had in my mind the example of

Damien Parer, the great Australian cameraman from World War II.

Nobody is ready for a combat zone except a trained soldier. I was nervous and apprehensive. I can't say I was afraid, because I had confidence in the South Vietnamese unit I was with. The battalion commander's name was Captain Long. He was in his early thirties, but he had been a field commander for ten years.

I was very inexperienced, and really didn't know what I was doing at all. I do remember one of the first things Captain Long said to me was always watch the soldiers and tread in their footsteps, a golden rule for someone as inexperienced as I was then. The other essential advice was to do exactly what the soldiers did. Hit the deck when they do, and respond to every situation with them. When they advance, stay with them. It's no good staying back, because you would then be on your own.

I was very green. I don't know how I survived those first combat experiences, really. There was a certain amount of luck, but my own National Service military training in Tasmania had made me aware of certain infantry procedures, and I quickly learned to do whatever the soldiers did. After all, they were very experienced and had looked after themselves for quite a number of years by that stage.

The reason for the 'Good King Wenceslas' advice [he told a pageboy to tread in his footsteps in the snow and he would be safe] was to avoid booby traps. In later years they would usually be mines or grenades, often American Claymore anti-personnel mines acquired and used against the makers and their allies. The Viet Cong also used fearful sharpened bamboo *punji* sticks, set in the ground. These were sometimes coated with poison, and could actually pierce the sole of an army boot. Sometimes the *punji* sticks would be set like a rabbit trap, so that you sprang a trigger and the sharpened stakes clamped onto your foot and leg.

With beginner's luck, Davis saw and filmed action on that first patrol. Two South Vietnamese soldiers triggered a booby trap mine early in the day, and died instantly. Davis filmed their bodies. He had still not heard a shot fired in anger. When it came, the *'piow'* of a bullet whining overhead was curiously familiar. He learned that day that those you hear are those you don't worry about.

> The one that gets you is the one you don't hear, of course.
> Television had done a remarkable job in preparing me. There was even a popular series at the time called *Combat* which gave a sense of what happens.

Captain Long's patrol had made contact with the Viet Cong at the end of a long, hard, hot day slogging across the wet rice paddies.

> I was very tired, and I remember thinking, God, I don't want it now, I'm not ready. Why don't they do it in the morning when I'm fresh? But that's not the way it happens. There was nothing I could do. I was up to my waist in water, bogged down in an open field. The tiny Vietnamese soldiers with me were almost up to their chests. It's hard to charge forward into an attack when you are up to your crutch in mud. Fortunately the opposition wasn't too strong and we won that engagement. Otherwise I'd have died in my first combat in a waterlogged paddy field, I suppose.
> The Vietnamese battalion commander Captain Long became one of my best friends, and three years later he told me in confidence that it had taken me that long to really understand how to take care of myself in combat.
> We made the treeline ahead where the shots had come from and trod on firm ground. During the action I saw the Liberation Front flag fluttering from a bamboo pole

over a tiny village. One of our soldiers died as we took
the village. Eight little men in black pyjamas died also,
and Captain Long presented me with the flag: 'Vee Cee
flag for remembering this day'.

There was no question that reporting the ARVN (Army of
the Republic of South Vietnam) activities was tough and
dangerous. Yet Davis preferred to go with them than to go
with other forces. It was their war, after all.

It meant a great deal to them, and they were fighting it
on their own terms. They didn't have the sophisticated
support that the Americans had, but I still thought their
activities were a truer reflection of what was really
happening in South Vietnam. After the big American
build-up in 1965, almost no foreign correspondents went
with the South Vietnamese until after the big Tet
offensive in 1968, when they started to go with the ARVN
again because the Americans were disengaging from
then on.
I went with the ARVN troops because they did the
bulk of the fighting. That was what the war was about. I
believed it was necessary to emphasise this, particularly
as they were getting almost no coverage from the rest of
the international media.
It was much more comfortable to go with the
Americans. You quite often had your own helicopter, and
fresh food and water provided every day. You weren't
guaranteed any of these things with the ARVN. You had
to drink water from the rivers using tablets to purify it,
and you ate their food, which was rice with maybe some
vegetables and a small piece of fish.

Journalist John Tulloh, who worked for Visnews during the
Vietnam years and beyond, does not agree with those who
say Davis was obsessed by the Vietnamese side of the war.

Tulloh thought he was certainly very intense about it, but he was not anti-American. Davis knew that Visnews would be getting plenty of American coverage from NBC. He wanted to ensure balance by covering the Vietnamese as well as the South Korean and Australian contributions to the war. That was how he saw his responsibility as a Visnews cameraman. His liking for Asians also had something to do with it. During the tenth anniversary commemoration of the fall of Saigon, he was interviewed from Hanoi on NBC's *Today* show and pointed out how Americans tended to overlook the South Vietnamese contribution to the war. He said he could recall only three weeks in three years when the American casualty figures had been higher than those of the South Vietnamese.

There were other practical reasons why correspondents did not go with the ARVN. With the Americans it was possible to meet copy and film deadlines more easily, and medical evacuation and treatment were instantly available. To go out with an ARVN unit could mean four or five days' footslogging, away from any possible outside help. It is not that surprising most Western correspondents and cameramen left Davis on his own.

While the so-called 'Glory Boy' correspondents would jump on American choppers in their black-market-purchased combat fatigues for a day in the field, Davis would make his own way to an ARVN unit. He was well aware that the ARVN had a bad reputation.

I never subscribed to that, anyway. People told me they were no good, they would desert me in times of stress, run away from action, and get me killed. I never did see them run away. Of course you had to select a unit you had confidence in, and if you couldn't do that, it was better not to go, because if the tension was too great, you might react in a stupid manner under stress. If you had confidence in the people you were with, then you were much more likely to be cool under fire.

Letter to Aunt Lillian, 2 August 1964
Hotel Caravelle,
Saigon

... I'll be here another week, and then I am going on to Laos again ... then to Thailand for a couple of weeks. There was a great flurry a few days ago when there were strong rumours that a coup d'état was about to take place. This was later confirmed by the Thai government, but they settled things peaceably. They usually stage bloodless coups there!

7 September 1964
Hotel Caravelle,
Saigon

... The Viet Cong exploded a bomb in this hotel last week, wrecking three floors, but miraculously killed nobody, and only injured five or six. However, ten people lost everything except the clothes they stood up in, which is very inconvenient regarding passports and money. My room was wrecked, but I lost very little — a couple of pairs of trousers, a pair of shoes, and a few odds and ends ...

After the bombing of the Caravelle Hotel, Neil moved across Lam Son Square to the older and more gracious Continental Palace Hotel. Built in the French colonial style with a terrace bar and potted palms, the Continental Palace was one of Saigon's traditional meeting places. Neil stayed there consistently during his periods in Saigon, and the staff knew him very well.

New York Times correspondent Jack Langguth recalls that while Davis had a sharp eye for the loveliest Vietnamese girls, he always treated them with great respect. He instructed the waiters at the Continental to use the same form of words when they served breakfast in his room, whichever woman was in bed with him in the morning:

'Would Mrs Davis like sugar or cream? Would Mrs Davis like some more juice?' Davis didn't want the girls embarrassed, and his thoughtfulness won many hearts.

The same waiters sometimes employed Neil's help to smooth over embarrassing moments of another kind. A former senior South Vietnamese Army officer, General Duc, who led an unsuccessful coup in 1964 in Saigon and who subsequently spent some years in jail, used to frequent the terrace bar of the Hotel Continental in the early 1970s. Imprisonment had left him mentally unstable, and he would sometimes shout and harangue the hotel guests as they sat at the terrace tables. As the waiters knew, Davis could charm the general if not into silence, then into another location for his next speech — which was generally an anti-American diatribe.

Davis had been present on 13 August 1964, the day of the general's triumph and the beginning of his destruction. Davis was wakened by the hotel switchboard operator. 'Please get up, sir. There's been a coup d'état. You will want to take pictures, right?'

Troops and tanks were deployed in Lam Son Square below, and Davis raced to the post office and then to the prime minister's office.

All the troops there seemed very friendly, and there was no shooting. It was the kind of coup I liked.

'Where have you come from?' I asked the soldiers. 'What are you doing?'

'We're from the Delta, and we've come to visit Saigon,' they answered cheerfully. Finally an officer said he thought the commanding general of Military Region Four (the Delta) had overthrown Prime Minister Nguyen Khanh and proclaimed himself the leader of the nation.

But where was the new leader? Just after one p.m. I noticed some people crowded around a radio, listening closely. 'It's the IV Corps commander,' they explained.

'He's saying that he's in charge and he's the number one man.'

Davis reached Radio Saigon just in time to catch the commander, General Duc, whom he asked, 'Do you mind telling me what's happening?'

The general replied, 'Not at all, Neil. I've just explained to our people that I've removed General Khanh. He is not a good man. We will form a new government.'

Davis spent the afternoon with General Duc, but the powerful and ambitious air force commander Nguyen Cao Ky refused to join him.

Ky was one of a clique of young officers — known later as the Young Turks — who planned to take over the leadership themselves. Duc had upset the apple cart. His coup failed, and the next morning he surrendered.

Even though he became a broken, rather pathetic figure, he still remembered me, and he would stop shouting and haranguing the crowd while we talked quietly about old times over a drink. He was a nice old man, and the waiters were fond of him too, and didn't want to call the police to have him removed.

Davis was always enormously popular, not only with the staff of the hotels in which he stayed all over Southeast Asia, but with all the street vendors and the associated throng that is always attracted to major establishments. The veteran Australian correspondent Denis Warner remembers the raffish crew of shoeshine boys, girls with flowers to sell and others who thronged around the entrance to the Continental Palace Hotel; they had been collectively adopted by Davis.

They worshipped him. One day he returned from an assignment, slightly wounded and bloody, covered in dirt and looking as if he was about to collapse.

He dropped his camera and film with the concierge and then, for the first time that his friends outside could remember, he walked up the street to a bar of disrepute. Denis Warner says that the gang outside the hotel were so shocked and concerned for him that they followed him to the bar and dragged him back to the more conventional gentility of the Continental Palace.

10

Confrontation Continues!

Letter to Aunt Lillian, 25 April 1965
  Hotel Indonesia,
  Jakarta

Received your letter a few days ago by devious means
from Singapore. As there is no communication officially
between Indonesia and Malaysia, messages, mail and
other things have to be exchanged illegally, or by a very
roundabout method . . .

  I have met President Sukarno several times and he has
promised an interview on television for me. At least he
did a few days ago, but he now intends to go to Tokyo
shortly to have talks with the Malaysian Prime Minister,
Tunku Abdul Rahman. But today he announced he has
taken over all foreign investment in Indonesia! So I
imagine the 'imperialist' press will be struggling to see
him.

  I must say with all his arrogance and Hitler-like tactics
(in some respects), he is a charming devil . . .

President Sukarno took a keen interest in the foreign press
and always moved among his guests at official functions.
He was reputed to be able to converse in at least eight
foreign languages, and in April 1965 he gave the impression
of enjoying himself hugely as he orchestrated the confron-

tation with Malaysia, and juggled the various elements of NASAKOM, a Sukarno-coined acronym to embrace within one word the nationalist, Communist and religious power groups in Indonesia.

In April 1965 Neil Davis was in Indonesia to cover the tenth Afro-Asian Conference of non-aligned nations in Bandung. The tall fair-haired Australian caught the ebullient president's eye at a reception. Sukarno had a sharp memory for names.

'Who are you?' he asked. Taken unawares, Davis answered, 'I'm an Australian,' meaning to go on and give his name. Sukarno cut him off.

'Ah, the *Australian* is a very bad newspaper.'

Davis was flummoxed. The *Australian* had been taking a very anti-Sukarno line, as had most of the press.

'No, no, Mr President,' stammered Davis. 'My name is Neil Davis and I'm an Australian, I don't work for . . .'

He might have saved his breath; Sukarno cut him off again. 'Well, you're the *Australian*', and walked off.

Davis covered events in Indonesia up to and beyond Sukarno's eventual removal from power in March 1967, and they had many conversations during that time. He relentlessly called Davis 'The *Australian*' and made the same joke about the newspaper. Of course it always drew the response he wanted.

Sukarno asked very pointed questions and encouraged frank exchanges, but in 1965 it was unwise to take too many liberties. A journalist could easily have his visa revoked and a mob could suddenly form to express its 'spontaneous' rage against any named enemy of Indonesia's sensitive nationalism. At that time the capital, Jakarta, was one enormous fetid slum of some five million people. The city's canals were open sewers in which thousands washed, drank and drew their cooking and drinking water.

There were grandiose buildings under construction but the only modern structure of any note was the Hotel Indonesia, which was a first-class hotel and an oasis amongst the chaos. President Sukarno once suddenly asked Davis, 'What do you think of Jakarta?'

Davis replied guardedly, 'Oh, it's quite an interesting city.'

'It's an awful city,' said the president. 'It's one great big dirty kampong.'

> He didn't care much for Jakarta. He had a palace there, but much preferred his second palace up in the hills of Bogor, about sixty-five kilometres away. It was a delightful place with spotted deer roaming in the grounds. He also liked to go to Bali, where he had yet another palace.

Bandung, the conference centre, was also in the mountains, a five-hour drive from Jakarta. Among the visiting leaders were China's Chou En Lai, Prince Sihanouk from Cambodia and a contingent of princes from the various factions in Laos — Prince Souvanna Phouma, and the Red Prince, his half-brother Souphanouvong. Davis was fascinated to find that North Vietnam's longtime prime minister Pham Van Dong was there and arranged to meet him.

> Pham Van Dong seemed most elated by his visit to Indonesia and I had tea with him in the North Vietnamese embassy to ask if I could have a visa for Hanoi and North Vietnam. He said of course I could — but it was over ten years after that before I got to Hanoi.

As Neil Davis and Pham Van Dong talked, a great rally of excited Indonesians gathered outside the North Vietnamese Embassy offering to fight in Vietnam against the Americans.

As an Australian citizen, Davis was allowed to enter Indonesia, which put him well ahead of his British or American journalist rivals. One of the most dramatic events of confrontation was the sacking and burning of the British embassy in Jakarta.

In Singapore, all this got a bit much for Arthur Cook of the London *Daily Mail*, who optimistically put himself on a flight from Singapore to Jakarta. Of course as soon as the Indonesians found he was British, he was boomeranged back on the next plane. If he was allowed out of the aircraft, he certainly didn't leave the airport terminal.

However, he could file with a Jakarta dateline. But Arthur got a bit carried away with the occasion and began his story: 'As I stood among the shoulder-high ruins of the burnt-out British embassy . . .'

Cook was a short, stocky man, and would not have been seen to advantage inside the shell of the three-storeyed structure. From that day, he was known in the region as 'Shoulders' Cook, or sometimes 'Shoulders High' Cook. Cook was one of the old guard of Fleet Street foreign correspondents, never shy about giving his opinion on any subject under the sun. Later, when British correspondents were allowed back into Indonesia, he was sitting alongside the pool of the Hotel Indonesia while an overweight American made numerous attempts to dive from the high board. Each time, he landed with a catastrophic crash in the water.

After a while this irritated Arthur, and he said very pompously to the American, 'If you don't know how to dive, why do you make such a fool of yourself?'

The rest of us rather favoured the American's position. He was a happy soul, doing no one any harm. There wasn't much else to do in Jakarta in those days. Not surprisingly, the American said, 'Well, why don't you show me how to do it?'

Arthur, on the wrong side of fifty and overweight, strode imperiously to the ladder and began the climb to the high board, where he turned around with his back to the water, his toes gripping the edge of the board.

I remember thinking that he seemed to have a reasonable balance — but then Arthur bullshitted about so many things. However, he suddenly sprang up, executed a faultless double somesault with pike, and entered the water with barely a ripple.

We were struck dumb. Arthur emerged from the pool with the same aplomb as he had entered, marched back to his seat and picked up his gin and tonic!

One of the group at the poolside was the Australian Broadcasting Commission's resident correspondent Philip Koch who, like Davis, came from Tasmania. (The novel *The Year of Living Dangerously* by Christopher Koch was partly based on his brother Philip's experiences.) Allegations of a Tasmanian Mafia among the correspondents of the day were hard to refute, with Koch, Davis, Tony Cane and Tim Bowden all working for the ABC at the time in Southeast Asia.

Neil Davis covered street demonstrations against the Western nations he represented and found the crowds generally good-humoured and tolerant of his presence. He did, however, develop techniques of moving to the outskirts of a mob if he felt it was looking about for a focus. Once the attention of the crowd had directed itself to throwing stones at an embassy or overturning a car or two, he would move back into the heart of the action again. Reading mob psychology was valuable training for the Buddhist street riots in Saigon the following year.

Meanwhile, President Sukarno was amusing himself by coining more acronyms, such as NEFOS, the new emerging forces (meaning countries such as Indonesia, North Vietnam and Cambodia), while Western nations such as Britain and America were dubbed OLDEFOS — old established forces.

Because President Sukarno was quite pro-Australian in his own way, I asked him once at a press conference where Australia fitted in the OLDEFOS and NEFOS scheme of things. After a pause he said triumphantly that Australia was a REFOS — recently emerged force.

Because President Sukarno was so gregarious and likable, there was a danger of overstepping the mark while talking with him. He was a vain man, always impeccably dressed in military uniform, topped with his close-fitting *pitji* cap, and very conscious of his dignity as the father of Indonesia's revolution. But he did like to joke with Westerners in perfect English or Dutch, and he often sought out the foreign correspondents. During one reception at Merdeka Palace, Davis saw Sukarno in coversation with a Western ambassador who was very short. Sukarno was about 173 centimetres tall and solidly built.

> This Western ambassador was only about five feet [152 centimetres] tall, and Sukarno towered over him. He turned away and saw me. I came out in my best Indonesian with an Australian-style joke, saying, '*Orang ketjil, zakar besar*', which means, 'Little man, but big penis'.

To Davis's intense embarrassment and alarm, Sukarno looked away impassively with absolutely no reaction. 'My God,' Davis thought, 'I've done it this time!' It was too late to take it back, and if Sukarno thought he was having the mickey taken out of him, he could well have Davis banned from the palace or even kicked out of the country. The seconds ticked by.

The delay was caused by Sukarno never having considered this particular Australian-engendered fantasy. When the penny dropped, he turned to Davis and burst into roars of laughter. The delighted president moved among his guests, repeating the line and pointing at the blissfully ignorant ambassador. With sweat still trickling down his back, Davis resolved never to risk a chancy joke with him again.

Outside the palace, in the streets of Jakarta and throughout the cities and towns of the Indonesian archipelago,
there was not much to laugh about. The economy had
collapsed with the Indonesian rupiah officially pegged at
forty-five to the US dollar, but soaring to four and five
thousand rupiahs on the black market. Inflation was running
at about six hundred per cent. As they had done in Berlin
in 1923, people were forced to carry around great wads of
paper money for simple transactions. The presses rolled
out vast quantities of pristine engraved banknotes which
were hardly worth the high-quality paper they were printed
on. One Australian correspondent papered a wall of his
Singapore apartment with Indonesian currency.

Sukarno might have fathered the Indonesian revolution,
but he was no economist. His approaches to the economy
were not without heart, but had little practical reality.
Davis felt it would have been best if this colourful and
charismatic figure had retired about 1960.

In the early 1960s Sukarno went to Bali and was lobbied
by some villagers who wanted a suspension footbridge
across a steep ravine that divided their community.

Sukarno was a bit bored by the triviality of this
grassroots politicking and asked them how much money
it would cost.

They came up with the figure of ten thousand revalued
rupiahs. Sukarno then turned to an aide and said, 'For
goodness sake, give them ten thousand rupiahs now!'

No one said 'no' to Sukarno and the official managed
to find ten thousand rupiahs, which the president handed
over to the villagers and told them to go and build their
bridge. I suppose a chit had to be put into Treasury later
to account for it, and it showed a lot of personal
concern, but it was no way to run the economy of a
country of one hundred and thirty million people.

The Indonesian economy was beyond rational salvage. Even
the foreign embassies operated on the black market. As

inflation galloped, the situation was further complicated by President Sukarno's refusal to shift the hopelessly unrealistic exchange rate. The price of petrol (which Indonesia produced from its own oil) was artificially held down at about fifteen rupiahs a gallon [4.5 litres] at the pump.

There were actually aluminium one- and five-cent coins that even the beggars spurned. They printed one-thousand-, five-thousand- and ten-thousand-rupiah notes and if you tried to pay for a tank of petrol for a big American car, you sometimes had trouble finding notes small enough.

Life in the Hotel Indonesia, that oasis of modernity in the heart of Sukarno's 'big dirty kampong', was conducted in hard currency. Correspondents could and did stand in the eighth-floor bar at the hotel holding a drink (costing US$3) and watching a petrol tanker drive by, knowing that they could have purchased every drop of gas in the tanker for the price of their dry martini. In July 1966 Neil Davis and the BBC's Anthony Lawrence drove from Jakarta across Java and by vehicular ferry to Bali — a distance of approximately 1600 kilometres. The petrol cost them US$2.

People reverted to a barter system, but that, too, fluctuated wildly. One roadside stall might charge five hundred rupiahs (about ten cents) for a cooked or live chicken, while at another town you might pay ten rupiahs — less than half a cent.

Sukarno was never without ideas on how Indonesia should be run, most of them impractical. To his credit his formulae for government did not include military dictatorship, which in effect Indonesia has now become. He paid respect to the religion of the country which was ostensibly Moslem, but that was only a surface religion to the sixty to sixty-five million people on the island of Java, which is the most heavily populated area in the

world. The people there really believe in what is best
described as Javanese mysticism. Even today, when
President Suharto [who has ruled since Sukarno was
overthrown in 1967] needs to make an important
decision, he'll go to his home village in Java and wait for
a propitious time, which is usually after midnight with
the moon in a certain phase, and take off his shoes and
walk barefoot in his garden to meditate on the problem.

Sukarno's dream of a tripartite balancing of religious, national and Communist elements sustained its most fervent
opposition from the powerful Indonesian armed forces.
They had been responsible for the liberation from the Dutch
and had been loyal to the president, as he was to them. But
the growing strength of the PKI, the Indonesian Communist
Party, under its able leader D.N. Aidit, and the president's
tolerance of it, had strained their loyalty. The three-million-
strong PKI was numerically the third biggest Communist
party in the world, following China and the Soviet Union.

Open conflict was about to break out, and nobody
knows to this day whether President Sukarno was
implicated in the attempted Communist coup d'état on
30 September 1965.

Sukarno's uncertain health might have forced the PKI to
move earlier than they had planned. The president had a
superstitious dread of going under the surgeon's knife, and
was believed to have failing kidneys and probably gallstones.
On the night of 30 September, President Sukarno was ad-
dressing a conference of technicians. During his speech he
seemed to falter and left the stage for a short time. He then
returned and finished his speech. It was later that night
that a group of army officers launched the coup.

Davis speculates that this evidence of the president's
fading health may have decided the September Thirtieth
Movement to act that night.

The Communists moved first and took into custody six of the country's leading generals, who were tortured and murdered at Halim airfield, which is now the main international airport for Jakarta.

The coup began many days and nights of long knives, during which Sukarno's fragile political balancing act imploded. Nobody knows how many hundreds of thousands of Indonesians died. Rivers literally ran with blood and the Indonesian Chinese in particular were almost decimated. Long-suppressed communal enmities were unleashed throughout the archipelago as old scores were settled alongside political differences.

Some members of the PKI were Indonesian Chinese, and I suppose the theory was that if you kill enough Chinese, you kill all the Communists. Most experts believe approximately half a million people died during the aftermath of the attempted coup.

One of the worst affected areas of Indonesia during the killing times was Bali, an island that has long seduced Westerners with its physical beauty and its apparently gentle village life. There were also fewer Chinese there than in other parts of Indonesia. Yet as many as ninety thousand out of the island's two million population were slaughtered.

In many ways the traditional life of the Balinese, based on sharing and harmony, could be described by ideologues as pure Communism. But Balinese village life is dependent on strong traditional unity. Put crudely, they either live together or die together. The expansion of the Communist PKI into this highly structured and traditional village life was disruptive, and that was intolerable to the Balinese.

In July 1966, Neil Davis and the BBC's Anthony Lawrence made their US$2 car trip through central Java to Bali. President Sukarno was still nominally in power because the new military administration of General Suharto dared not depose him. As Davis and Lawrence drove through the terraced emerald green rice paddies of central Java, they found the political climate as volatile as the distant smoking volcano cones. They were in the heart of Sukarno country and Davis filmed black-shirted youth groups loyal to him, drilling and giving fascist salutes.

When Neil Davis and Tony Lawrence took the vehicular ferry to the western tip of Bali, the first impressions were in contrast to the cold horror of the revelations to come.

> The western part is seldom visited by tourists even today. But then it was just like the storybooks said. It was late afternoon, and the men and women were returning from their work in the rice paddies.
> Bare-breasted Balinese women were wending their way along the paddy dykes, carrying baskets on their heads, with one arm held up to steady them.
> These slim-bodied but ample-breasted women were silhouetted against the early evening sky and it was one of the most beautiful sights I have ever seen.

Davis and Lawrence found the Balinese frank about the executions that had taken place. Apparently the Balinese PKI members had accepted they must die because of their role in disrupting the harmony of the Hindu-Buddhist-controlled rhythm of village life. Davis and Lawrence heard how village communities had brought the Communists before the councils of elders. They were tried immediately and found guilty. After being given time to pray in the temple, they were executed, usually by decapitation.

> One quite isolated village of some five hundred people agreed to re-enact what had happened on the night they

decided to get rid of the Communists in their midst. Balinese people are very honest, and like to explain aspects of their religion and way of life. Thirty men were tried by the council of elders.

The council acquitted four of the thirty, who were allowed to resume normal life because it was considered they had been unduly influenced, and weren't really Communists. They were freed immediately. The other twenty-six were sentenced to death and led away.

They acted it out for my camera. The condemned men were led past the village temple — it was almost dawn — and asked if they wanted to enter and pray before going on. Most did, but three or four refused. They were then taken to the place of execution, where the most venerated man of the community decapitated them with a big Balinese *kris*, a sabre-like sword.

Their wives and children were then taken in and looked after by the community and were not discriminated against in any way, because ironically the Balinese villages were genuine communes, which had practised what you might describe as 'pure' Communism for thousands of years.

Had the Indo-China war not captured his professional attention, Davis might well have tried to live in Indonesia. He was fascinated by its contrasts and there were other attractions.

In 1966 he visited the inland Balinese artistic centre of Ubud, where he became friendly with the last prince of Ubud. He also met the Filipino artist, Antonio Blanco, who had had his home and studio there for the previous twenty-five years. The Blanco house is built on a hill to the south of Ubud, overlooking a rushing mountain stream.

His daughter, Tjempaka, was absolutely the most beautiful woman I have ever seen. She was seventeen when I first saw her. If you went to Blanco's house as a family friend, the three ladies of the house stayed bare-breasted in the Balinese way.

Blanco's Balinese wife was still very beautiful at around forty years of age, and so was her younger sister-in-law. Tjempaka herself was absolutely stunning — a mixture of Filipino and Balinese. It was an amazing experience to sit around a table at the Blanco house surrounded by these glorious women. They all posed for Blanco, but his sister-in-law was his most favoured model.

Davis stayed for some days with the prince of Ubud in the crumbling beauty of his palace and temple. All Balinese buildings look immensely old because the soft stone of their construction is constantly weathering. The prince had safeguarded the interests of his people under the Dutch and Japanese, and now with the administration of an independent Indonesia. He was well educated, practical, widely travelled and an extremely gifted conversationalist. Bobby Kennedy had stayed with the prince, and had continued to correspond with him.

As I walked with him through the grounds of his palace I noticed there was a coffin on top of a bamboo frame about six metres high. This was not unusual, as some time elapses between death and the elaborate rituals of a Balinese cremation.

We were discussing Indonesia's present difficult political situation, when he waved his arm in the general direction of the coffin, and said, 'As I was saying to the old *jokorda* [prince] just before he decided to die ...'

I said, 'What do you mean, he *decided* to die?'

The prince told Neil there was nothing unusual about that in Bali. The old prince was more than ninety years old, and he decided it was time he died. One of his lifelong friends had died three weeks before, and they had promised each other that when one died, the other would follow in the same cycle, so that they could be cremated together.

Two weeks after his friend died, the old prince worked all night to complete a particular wood carving he had been working on. He called his family to him and explained that he was going to take a bath, rest and sleep. Then he carefully dressed himself in his best clothes and lay down to relax. He asked his sixteen-year-old grandson to hold his mouth closed with his hand under his chin, because the old man snored a bit, and often went to sleep with his mouth open, which was not the way he liked to be seen.

He told his grandson to leave him after he had gone to sleep. The family knew he had decided to die right then, and the grandson did as instructed, and left him resting, apparently asleep, at eight-thirty a.m.

They didn't do anything until about five p.m., and then they found that he was well and truly asleep, and called the doctor. This was unnecessary in their view, but had to be done to comply with civil law. The doctor confirmed that the old man had died at about eight-thirty that morning. Other such deaths were well documented in Bali.

After the prince had explained this to Davis, he began talking about other Balinese customs.

'See that boy over there?' he said pointing to a nine-year-old walking towards them. 'He is my grandmother. She died about the time I was born, and the boy is her reincarnation.'

Davis did not dispute either that the old prince had chosen his own time to die or that the nine-year-old boy was the prince's grandmother.

Knowledge of Indonesian or Javanese customs could help an observant correspondent-cameraman in his work. One of the first occasions on which Davis met President

Sukarno was at a garden party in the Merdeka Palace grounds in Jakarta. A heavy tropical shower came down and the president took off his shoes and walked in his bare feet on the wet grass.

He had his hands raised to the sky as though he felt the power that came from the elements — especially from the earth.

Then in 1966, Davis was present when President Sukarno — at that stage president in name only — was permitted to make a rare speech.

Sukarno bided his time until he was being filmed for international television and Radio Indonesia was broadcasting to the world. I saw him slipping his shoes off as he began to speak and began filming immediately, because I knew he was about to do something dramatic. He put his written speech to one side and declaimed dramatically in Indonesian, *'Konfronasi jalan terus!'* ('Confrontation continues!').

Well, Confrontation had well and truly ended by then, and President Suharto, the foreign minister, Adam Malik, and all the other diplomats there were appalled. But Sukarno had the platform, and he just went on.

He was an immensely likable man, despite the tragedy that he engineered for his country. During one of the last times I saw him, I took a personal photograph. I rarely carry a stills camera, but on this occasion General Suharto and President Sukarno were together. They were surrounded by news people, and Suharto was saying nothing, but stood in the background with an enigmatic smile on his face.

Sukarno was trying to be his old bombastic self. I stood up on a chair about two metres from him and called out softly *'Bapak'* [Father]. The Indonesian people called him that and he liked it. He stopped talking and looked straight at me as I took the shot.

For Davis, the photograph expressed everything that was going on at the time. Sukarno was a defeated man and he had a look of defeat in his eyes. Standing behind him with a public smile was the man who was about to take his power and position, General Suharto. Unfortunately the photograph was lost when Davis was forced to abandon all his personal effects in Phnom Penh days before the Khmer Rouge captured the city in April 1975.

The new leaders of Indonesia had to be careful with the demystification of President Sukarno, Great Leader of the Revolution. As Davis knew, black-shirted youths were drilling in his name in central and eastern Java, and his portrait had pride of place in every Indonesian home. It was done in a very Indonesian way, by keeping Sukarno out of the limelight and gradually stripping away his many titles. Davis came in and out of Indonesia during 1966 and 1967, monitoring the process with fascination. From time to time the powerless president would be allowed to speak, usually at Merdeka Palace in Jakarta, and the occasion was well covered by the foreign press.

His speeches were always memorable and he had a superb sense of theatre. He would stride briskly to the microphone, which was generally free-standing. A small, round, marble-topped table with a plate of small cakes and a glass of fruit juice was at one side. Sukarno would remove his gloves, lay them with his silver-knobbed swagger stick on the table, tap the microphone to make sure it was 'live', eye his audience keenly, and begin to speak. His voice would begin almost at a whisper, and then would become more resonant as he made his key points — often breaking into English, Dutch or German if the mood took him. He was a magnificent orator.

On one of these occasions, during the socialising after his speech, an uproar broke out among the palace security men. Someone had eaten the president's cakes! They were just four cookie-sized biscuits, but only crumbs remained on the plate.

The guards grabbed the culprit, a gangling six-foot-four freelance journalist from North America, Donald Kirk, who was looking most embarrassed with the crumbs of the President's cake clearly visible at the corners of his mouth. Kirk was bundled out and promptly barred from the Palace for good.

Kirk was effectively cut off from one of the main sources of information for international journalists. Despite the pleas of his correspondent colleagues, the ban stayed. Apparently Sukarno himself was not amused by the incident.

Finally we managed to make representations to President Sukarno again and explain that Kirk did not mean to insult him, that he was actually hungry, and that is why he had eaten the cakes.

Sukarno thought about that, and then he said, 'Well, every man can be hungry,' and relented. So Donald Kirk got back into the palace.

Inevitably he became known in the trade as Kirk the Cake Eater.

It was about this time that Davis developed his disconcerting habit of eating the flowers decorating diplomatic dinner tables. He chose less public occasions than Kirk, but would, while someone was talking to him, pull a petal from a rose or orchid and chew and swallow it with apparent gusto. He would then move on to consume the heads from the rest of the flowers.

One night he was dining at the table of the same Western ambassador who had been the butt of his joke to Sukarno regarding the relative proportions of stature and the penis. Another guest was a newsagency correspondent — let's call him Bill Miller — who was finding relief from the frenetic pressures of the Indonesian situation at that time by hitting the bottle. Miller had been alcoholically amused by a joke told earlier in the day, the punchline of which was, 'Give me a kiss and I'll tell you!'

Miller was sitting opposite the diminutive ambassador, whose sense of self-importance more than compensated for his size. His Excellency was finding Miller heavy going. To his right and out of eyeshot, Davis had just begun munching the table orchids in a distracted kind of way. For reasons not immediately apparent to her husband, the ambassador's wife was literally sobbing with laughter.

The ambassador transfixed the befuddled Miller with a laser look and said a trifle desperately, 'Mr Miller, what's your basic assessment of the strategic situation in east Java at the moment?'

Miller was miles away. He lifted his flushed face from his glass and beamed amiably at his host, 'Give me a kiss and I'll tell you!'

The most important story for foreign correspondents continued to be the fate of President Sukarno. By early 1967 demonstrations, tacitly approved by the new Suharto administration, were taking place outside Merdeka Palace calling for his arrest and trial for treason, and even for his execution.

Sukarno was rarely permitted to appear in public. But on 2 February 1967 Davis received word that the president was to be allowed to leave the palace to visit a sick friend in hospital.

The organised mobs of demonstrators were absent and while Sukarno was at the hospital, word spread among the ordinary people that he was there. He drove through a crowd at the hospital gates. As Davis filmed, a *betjak* (trishaw) driver stood up on his machine and called out '*Hidup Bung Karno*' ('Long live brother Sukarno'), and the cry was taken up by the friendly crowd.

It was clear that the daily anti-Sukarno demonstrations outside the Palace did not represent the feelings of all the people by any means.

The next day, Davis and other foreign correspondents were surprised to be invited to the palace for a press conference with Sukarno. Suharto was also there, looking uncomfortable, while the president held court as he had not done for many a day.

After a time he said casually, 'I went to see a friend of mine in hospital yesterday.' We said we had seen him.

'Oh,' he said, 'were you there when I came out?'

We said, 'Yes, we saw you.'

And he just smiled again, and said, 'Good.' He wasn't going to say any more, and we knew what he meant. He never did make that comeback, of course, but he was not averse to giving those who were about to supplant him a bit of a dig.

The actual manner of Sukarno's leaving was carefully orchestrated in March 1967, and done with some dignity. The People's Consultative Congress of Indonesia met every five years to decide policy for the next five years. All political parties, ethnic groups from the different islands, women's groups, farmers, fishermen, religious groups and the military were represented.

One unusual aspect of the Congress is that all its findings have to be unanimous. That seems an impossible condition, but the delegates enter into debate with a spirit of finally coming to unanimous decisions, and that is what they did with the President Sukarno issue.

Sukarno himself opened the People's Consultative Congress. It was a very stirring occasion, including the playing of Indonesia's magnificent national anthem. But the major issue was the President's destiny.

Letter to Aunt Lillian, 3 March 1967
Hotel Indonesia,
Jakarta

The Congress eventually were able to remove Sukarno as only Indonesians can — whilst making the wording of their communique very obscure . . .

The main thing is that the old man is finished — beaten — and it's really quite sad all round. He will keep a sort of honorary title of president, although most people are now referring to him as Bung Karno (Brother Sukarno).

Suharto is effectively President, and his first act was to make a nationwide broadcast appealing to the people to remain calm. He swore an oath that a panel of doctors had said that Sukarno was a very sick man . . .

The congress was very frank. Some speakers accused Sukarno of being a traitor and urged that he be put on trial for treason and executed. Others said that there was no evidence that he had done anything treacherous, and that he should remain as Indonesia's honoured president. The debate went on for five days, and the press was invited to hear the congress findings on 11 March 1967.

There was enormous interest. The conclusions were read out by the Congress Chairman, General Nasution. The way he phrased it, it seemed almost an afterthought that 'Dr Engineer Sukarno' as he then called him, was to retire forthwith, and that Gerneral Suharto would become acting or temporary president.

There was some confusion over Sukarno's own status, which was finally resolved by General Suharto who said that he would be treated 'as a president who is no longer in power'.

The last time I saw Sukarno was at his favourite Bogor Palace in the mountains and he was, as usual, attended by General Suharto. I think we all sensed it was the last time we would see him.

At that time the Indonesian word *'susu'* — it simply means 'milk' — was in wide use among the young men around town in Jakarta. It could mean milk, tits, or a kind of silly greeting. It obviously had sexual connotations, and it was the word of the moment — the kind of thing a boy would call out to a girl across the street.

After his last press conference in Bogor Palace, only a few days before he was ousted as president by the People's Consultative Congress, he walked down the front steps and we all crowded around him.

As he reached the door of his car to be driven to the villa nearby where he actually lived, he turned towards us as we stood on the steps, all waiting for one parting remark.

He did not let us down. He smiled and held up his hand and said *'susu'*, and everybody laughed as he got into his car and drove away.

Dr Engineer and former President Sukarno died in Jakarta under virtual house arrest on 21 June 1970.

11

A Victory
Simply to Survive

Letter to Aunt Lillian, 17 June 1965
Hotel Caravelle,
Saigon

The Government is taking some very heavy defeats, and
for the sake of morale all round they are falsifying losses
and exaggerating Communist losses. However, the
Government has suffered tremendous losses, the worst
of the war to date — it always seems possible to write
that.

I managed to get some exciting film that you should
have seen by now. I went with a relieving force by
helicopter — they put us down within twenty metres of a
Viet Cong held barracks area and I really got some great
shots. However, Government losses were extremely
heavy — about 1000 dead, and the town was abandoned,
civilians and all . . .

I've had a rather big offer from CBS (Columbia
Broadcasting System) the largest and richest radio and
TV company in the world — American, of course. They
make a tremendous profit, and to work for them is
considered the ultimate among cameramen. The money
is really good — staggering by Australian standards —
but it is by no means certain I'll take it. There are a lot of
things in this world more important than money, and a

great many things will have to be considered ...

As I am now with Visnews, I have complete freedom to go where and when I please to a great extent, and to cover stories in the way I feel is best representative of the true situation. Also I write the scripting material, which gives me great influence over the film I produce.

With CBS I would be a cameraman only — much easier in many respects, but I'm not sure I want to do just that *only* ... guess I'll be sorry whichever way I decide ...

From his earliest days in Vietnam in 1964, Neil Davis determined to film the Vietnam war from the perspective of the South Vietnamese infantryman. By doing so, he hoped to become familiar with the realities of the war in Vietnam, and although he was often a lone figure, he could give television viewers throughout the world a partial idea of what it was like to be a South Vietnamese soldier.

I didn't have strong anti-Communist leanings although a lot of my friends were on the anti-Communist side. I just thought the Vietnamese people needed to work it out for themselves, and it was the responsibility of the foreign correspondents — who are allegedly non-aligned and absolutely neutral — to report fairly and accurately.

The unfair thing was that from the time the Americans came into South Vietnam in force in 1965 until they announced a limited withdrawal in 1968, the impression given to the world was that the Americans were doing almost all of the fighting, while the inefficient and cowardly ARVN were sitting back and doing nothing.

That was not true, and the international press should accept responsibility for not telling the truth. It was inaccuracy by omission. The figures were available all the time, and clearly show that the South Vietnamese army lost at least fifty per cent more men from 1965 to

1968 than the Americans, and it was constant, week after week.

I used to follow the figures constantly, and only in three weeks in three years did the Americans have more soldiers killed than the South Vietnamese. That is why I was determined to cover the ARVN fighting effort.

At the beginning of a typical field patrol, Davis would be out on the streets of Saigon by 6.30 a.m. checking if it was sensible to leave the city from a news point of view, that there were unlikely to be street riots or a coup d'état that day. By 7.30 a.m. he was on his way to Tan Son Nhut airport, then the busiest airport in the world because of all its military traffic. Within an hour, he was on an aircraft or helicopter heading down into the Mekong Delta.

> I'd land at a small airfield and make contact with the Vietnamese commander of the area to be briefed on what the local situation was, what units were there and where they were fighting — and what areas were controlled by the Viet Cong.

Davis talked to the Vietnamese in a racy patois of French, Vietnamese and English, and a great deal of body language. He used his hands constantly when he talked to people, Asians or Westerners. Communication with Vietnamese or Cambodians was never a problem for him.

> By midday of the same day, I would most likely be in the field and I would stay with a Vietnamese unit for at least three days. There was no resupply in the field like the pizza helicopters for the American troops. They really had pizzas and icecream helicoptered out to them — which was wonderful intelligence for the Viet Cong. Apart from the helicopters buzzing around and giving away their position, they could smell the pizzas!

Some American soldiers used to walk with transistor

radios playing through earpieces — while they were allegedly on patrol in the jungle looking for the Viet Cong. Unfortunately they also carried far too much gear, at least thirty kilograms of equipment, including very heavy armoured flak jackets.

Davis was with an American patrol once going through light jungle when he heard a black American soldier scream in fear. A twig had pulled the pin on a hand grenade strung on the back of his pack. He was a dead man from that instant. As he frantically clawed around behind him, the grenade exploded, tearing him apart. He was a victim of his own arms and armour.

In contrast to the American Barnum and Bailey circus, the average Viet Cong soldier carried very little equipment. He had his weapon, a sock of rice, and his ammunition. He had no flak jacket, no helmet or big boots, and was dressed in black pyjamas with rubber Ho Chi Minh sandals on his feet, enabling him to move quickly through a countryside he knew intimately.

After three days of slogging across the paddies or through the jungle, the Americans were usually exhausted and easy prey for fresh Communist troops.

The lightly equipped South Vietnamese soldiers could cover from eight to fifteen miles [thirteen to twenty-four kilometres] in one day. The Americans would be lucky to manage four.

The Viet Cong had no respect for the Americans as soldiers. There were one or two American units — the Special Forces, for instance — who were very good, and of course they respected them. But the average American units were treated with contempt because the men had no real jungle craft or sense of survival in the field.

They used to call them 'elephants' because they would blunder around the jungle, and the Viet Cong could smell Americans literally a mile away — their toothpaste, cigarettes and shaving cream.

But the ARVN troops were also Vietnamese, and many of the soldiers were peasant boys like the Viet Cong. Sometimes it was brother against brother.

Actions speak louder than words, and in the Tet offensive of 1968, when the North Vietnamese and Viet Cong launched nationwide attacks and captured many towns and whole provinces all over the country, it was the South Vietnamese who did not break, who held on and won back that territory.

For the first time, Americans at a high level realised that the ARVN troops could do it. That was the beginning of the policy of 'Vietnamisation', but they had left it too late. Before that, they made it clear that they thought the South Vietnamese were the worst soldiers in Vietnam.

The South Vietnamese units often made camp just before sundown, but within minutes they would be off and moving again, because it was just a fake camp. They would go forward for another hour and then set an ambush for the Viet Cong or make a secret camp.

The Americans would bunch together at night and create a fortified camp with a defensive perimeter, which made them very vulnerable to mortar attacks. They used to surround themselves with Claymore anti-personnel mines, which could be set up to spray thousands of pieces of shrapnel towards an oncoming enemy. It only went in one direction.

The Viet Cong would crawl in carefully and turn the Claymores around 180 degrees, and then mount a bogus attack with lots of noise and yelling. The Americans would often detonate the mines straight back on themselves.

The Americans soon cottoned on to that little ploy, and put a tiny piece of phosphorus tape on the back of the Claymore so they could see it in the dark. Not to be outdone, the VC crawled forward as before, gently prised the tape off, and turned the mines around anyway.

There were other cunning stunts.

Quite often American forces would go into a deserted village, which would look completely normal. But there might be a plough — a typical two-handled plough — left very close to the track so that the soldiers had to walk around it. If you had a hundred soldiers walking by, there would be one who would take hold of the handles of the plough and pretend he was a farmer — and the whole thing would blow up, because it was booby-trapped.

Or they would walk into a house. Americans liked to have little souvenirs. There might be an Asian teapot on a table. A GI would lift it up, and it would blow up. This would go on and on, until they had a number of casualties before exchanging a single shot with the Communists.

Medical evacuation helicopters would be called in, usually to the village square. As the helicopters came in, the breeze created by the rotors would set off hand grenades which were positioned in the trees about three or four metres up to explode and disable the helicopters or kill or wound the people already waiting in the open area below.

There were some good American units, and the American soldier could have been just as good as any other soldier if he'd had the opportunity and the training. It wasn't the GI's fault, it was the system. The Special Forces were very good units, but even they were not allowed to do the job they were trained for, which was long-range patrols. They were ordered to train ethnic

125

mountain tribesmen in the Vietnam highlands to intercept North Vietnamese troops and supplies coming down the Ho Chi Minh trail.

Consequently they were isolated in small base camps, and could be ambushed by Communist forces instead of being allowed to roam out as small efficient fighting forces — which they had been trained to do.

In its own way, Neil's ARVN partrol was doing just that, moving deeply into Viet Cong territory and seeking contact. The general American approach was to saturate a target area with blanket bombing and artillery strikes and some-times literally bulldoze through with earth-moving equip-ment.

They didn't kill many of the enemy that way, although they did kill a lot of Vietnamese.

The Viet Cong were no less sophisticated with booby traps for their own countrymen. Davis had learned very early on to tread in the footsteps of the soldiers in front of him. He even tried to avoid brushing the foliage along the track. If he felt any entanglement around his foot or leg, he stopped immediately.

It might be a very fine piece of black or green cotton which you could hardly see, but it would set off a booby trap — a mine — suspended in the trees. Or they might simply dig a pit lined with sharpened and poisoned *punji* sticks, in the same way as they'd trap wild animals.

There were other worries, unconnected with hidden engines of war. The jungle concealed its own booby traps. A tiny snake, the krait, would come out at night and great care had to be taken. Its bite was deadly, and the ARVN medical kit had no antidotes. Pythons and boa constrictors were as frightened of the troops as the soldiers were of them, and

Crossing a river in the Mekong Delta, south of Saigon in May 1967, on patrol with South Vietnamese troops. Unlike his shorter Vietnamese comrades, Davis was able to keep his head (and gear) above water. *Peter Arnett.*

On patrol with ARVN troops in the Mekong Delta, South Vietnam, during the Communists' Spring offensive in 1972. The easy friendship he formed with Asian troops is clearly evident in this photograph.

A South Vietnamese soldier gives Davis a much needed drink from his helmet during the Spring offensive in the Mekong Delta, 1972.

stayed well away. Spiders could inflict nasty bites causing extreme nausea, but were not thought lethal.

In the highlands there was bigger game. The area had been famous for tiger hunting before the war.

On one occasion an American soldier was on night guard duty in the highlands, and was attacked by a tiger. Maybe he went to sleep — nobody knows for sure — he swears he didn't go to sleep. But a big tiger managed to approach through the deep jungle, fastened onto his shoulder, and began to drag him away.

The man screamed blue murder and pounded on the great head of the tiger with his fists, and after less than a hundred metres the tiger let him go. Maybe he wasn't as tasty as the tiger thought, but the American survived and his arm was saved, although he was badly lacerated.

There were no tigers in the Mekong Delta, but water crossings were an inevitable hazard in that low-lying area. Many of the streams were narrow but deep. Being tall, Davis could usually hold up his camera and sound gear above his head and wade through chest-high. Some of the ARVN infantrymen were about thirty centimetres shorter than he was, and would actually disappear under the water for several steps, their gear manfully held over their submerged heads.

They were country boys and used to that sort of thing, and it was quite a diversion for them. They didn't mind as long as the Viet Cong weren't putting them under fire. Then it was a different matter.

The ARVN patrols did not eat anything during the day, and breakfast was a handful of dried fruit, fish or 'jerky' — dried meat. In the evening, if they were not setting up an ambush, there might be some soup and rice eked out with weeds or some vegetables. Drinking water was from the paddies, purified with tablets.

The Vietnamese soldiers did on occasions drink the paddy water — but a Westerner never could. I always had to remember to take tablets, because you could die of thirst surrounded by paddy field water.

Davis expected action on all his patrols with the ARVN, and generally got it.

There was always contact of some kind. It depended on the area and what the intentions of the Communists were, because that governed the action. In the early stages they held to the old tried and true Communist guerilla warfare adage — attack your enemy only when you know you have the strength and upper hand.

Therefore if you were attacked while you were with a South Vietnamese unit, you knew you were at a disadvantage. And you also knew that you weren't going to get any strong air bombardment or artillery support, because you were generally well out of range of help.

Later in the war a conventional pattern developed in which the North Vietnamese army, reinforced by the Viet Cong, did attempt to take over complete areas and hold them to deny access to Allied forces. But early on, it was pure guerilla warfare.

The Viet Cong would usually attack late in the afternoon, when Neil and the ARVN troops had been walking through the paddy fields for twelve or thirteen hours. They were hot, tired and at a low ebb.

They would hit you just as the sun was going down and they could still see you and we would have a dreadful time through the night surviving. In the morning the attack would continue, but we usually managed to fight our way out of it.

The ARVN lost a lot of soldiers in these clashes. Sometimes thirty or forty per cent of a unit were casualties — they never announced the number wounded, only deaths. Sometimes their casualties would be as high as fifty and sixty per cent — totally unacceptable in a Western army, but they had to be accepted by the Vietnamese. There was no other way. Nobody was going to come and help bail them out. They were either defeated and wiped out or they got back.

On many occasions it was not a question of defeating the enemy — it was a victory simply to survive.

There were military successes. The Viet Cong had exceptions to their golden rules. Sometimes they would be caught in the advance of two battalions of ARVN troops — about a thousand men. One tactic was to leave behind small suicide units of Viet Cong to hold up the advance, while the main body withdrew and regrouped.

These small groups would hold up the ARVN advance, and die to a man. Unlike the Americans, who always telegraphed their punches in advance by blanket bombing or artillery strikes, the South Vietnamese would often move quietly into an area and take the Viet Cong unawares. Skirmishes erupted that way. But the big battles were always initiated by the Viet Cong.

Neil Davis's aim on each field trip was to centre his story on a particular character — one of the infantrymen, the radio operator or a grenade thrower.

They had specialists in the field, but they weren't really trained in these specific skills, and had to pick up their expertise as they went along. On occasions, an individual I had chosen for that kind of profile was killed during the operation.

I personalised the story to try and get over to the viewer the hardships and humanity of the Vietnamese fighting the war — that they weren't funny little animals running around, as their allies liked to depict them. I wanted to show them as compassionate people with a feeling for their fellow human beings, for their families, and for life itself — and for their own lives, even though they gave those lives courageously on many occasions.

Letter to Aunt Lillian, 10 July 1965
Orange Grove Rd,
Singapore

... It's so difficult to explain from so far away, but just because the Viet Cong are Communist doesn't naturally make them enemies of all the people. Rather it is easier to forget that one side is Communist and the other not, and look on it as a very horrible and bloody civil war, with both sides able to put up fairly convincing arguments to back them up ...

When you hear that a Government battalion has been overrun, it means about 500 men have been killed (not counting enemy losses), plus of course anyone with them. Also when you hear that a Viet Cong village has been bombed, you can imagine how many women, children and innocent people are killed in this way. Think what would be the result if Sorell (which has the same population of a small village here) was practically bombed off the face of the earth in order to get rid of the undesirable elements there ...

It's difficult to understand the different outlook the people have in Vietnam. Indeed they must, otherwise they would live in a state of perpetual hysteria ...

I told my company, Visnews, about the offer from CBS, and they sent a representative to see me here and talk about what I wanted. They said all sorts of nice things (in a letter) about how well I had done and so on, but I think they still got quite a shock when they realised that I operated here on such a relatively small scale compared to the American companies who are our strongest competitors. That we have been able to do so well in the face of all this astounded them, so much so that they immediately raised my salary by about 50 per cent and gave me virtually an open order to do as I pleased.

The outcome is that I will have a permanent apartment in Singapore at their expense . . . I will also have an office and apartment in Saigon, and authority to employ a full-time Vietnamese to take the fiddling jobs off my hands like Customs clearances and official passes which never seem to end. So all in all, things have turned out satisfactorily . . .

12

Saigon —
Pearl of the Orient

Letter to Aunt Lillian, 25 July 1965
Orange Grove Rd,
Singapore

. . . I'm afraid I'm going to be here in Singapore for a
couple of months doing nothing. I was unlucky enough
to get a bad case of hepatitis — jaundice — a couple of
weeks ago. Came down with what I thought was malaria
and stayed in bed at my hotel in Saigon for a week
feeling just terrible, unable to eat, and with a high fever. I
was being treated by a French doctor for malaria, but
last Monday some American friends got me up and took
me along to the American Naval Hospital where they
admitted me immediately with hepatitis . . .

Have regained my appetite over the last couple of
days, and am feeling much better — afraid I lost quite a
bit of weight, though. Only treatment now is lots of rest,
not too much fatty food, and no alcohol whatsoever (this
for up to one year!)

. . . One of the worst damn things with this hepatitis is
a terrible depression, which even though you realise is
one of the symptoms, it doesn't alter the fact of it much.
However, I guess it will pass as I recover . . .

It was a bad time to get sick. The war was escalating by the
day. Despite President Johnson's injection of half a million

troops into South Vietnam, the Viet Cong savaged the Allied forces. The new Visnews office needed to be established and stringer cameramen engaged. And Davis was very sick indeed.

I remember the American doctor at the military hospital in Saigon said it was the worst case of hepatitis he had seen. My whole skin was yellow, the whites of my eyes had turned golden, and when I passed water my urine was a brilliant orange, and my stool — which proved my liver wasn't working at all — was an insipid grey. The doctor spoke with some satisfaction, I might say, because he was looking forward to treating me. He was bored with battle casualties and surgery, and welcomed a medical challenge!

New York Times correspondent Jack Langguth remembers 1.83 metres of bright yellow Davis stretched out on his hospital bed looking like a giant cob of corn, but smiling through his considerable pain.

Again Davis found the right medico at the right time. Instead of the conventional 'rest and bland foods' routine, the American doctor forced him to eat fatty foods. The idea was to jolt the liver back into action.

It was absolute torture, and I used to throw up in anticipation of the fatty meals several times a day. But it worked, and after about six days I felt much better.

When Davis returned to Singapore, the conventional British treatment mentioned to Aunt Lillian was less effective, and he suffered a relapse. By October 1965 he was ordered back to Tasmania to recuperate. It was by no means certain he could ever return to Vietnam and resume his strenuous job. But he was absolutely certain that he would be back, and set about overcoming his hepatitis with the same vigour that he had attacked his polio years before.

I walked into a young doctor's surgery in Tasmania —
he fortunately had an interest in tropical medicine —
and the first thing he said was, 'Thank Christ for a sick
man!' Like the American doctor in Saigon, he was bored
and looking forward to an interesting case.

It gave me great satisfaction to overcome my medical
disabilities and I have confidence that I can overcome
any physical or mental problem that will happen to me.
I'm never beaten psychologically, whether it is a social
game of tennis, or in my work, or anything else. I will
never admit defeat — even though I've had some fairly
serious defeats, both on the tennis court and in my work.

That philosophy was put to the test immediately Davis returned to Vietnam clear of eye and with a functioning liver.
He slipped a disc, leaving him in constant pain and debilita-
tion. So that he could support his camera gear and equipment, he wore a steel-ribbed back brace on his forays into
the sweltering paddy fields and jungles of Vietnam during
most of 1966 and 1967.

It was for all the world like a woman's corset, and it
had to be strapped on tightly to be effective. It braced
my back while I carried my gear and I wore it every day I
was working. I'd take it off at night. The problem was, I
didn't know when my back might give out. But I was not
going to allow it to stop me covering the war in any way.
And eventually with exercise my back did improve for a
while.

I had two of these bloody corsets made, because I had
to wash them. They were made of canvas with metal
ribs. Sometimes I'd take it off in the field, and the
soldiers would say, 'What the hell's that?' I'd say, 'That's
my flak jacket' and laugh and change the subject.

A severe emotional shock jolted Davis on his return to
Singapore. He had become extremely fond of a Vietnamese
girl, whom he hoped to marry.

Letter to Aunt Lillian, 16 February 1966
Orange Grove Rd,
Singapore

Rather a shock awaiting me on my return to Singapore
when I found my last letter to Mai returned unopened
with the words '*elle est mort*' written across the back.

Of course I immediately contacted friends in Laos and
Vietnam and received word back from one that she was
reported killed, but is OK — he spoke to her. Expect to
receive a letter shortly from her.

It is very difficult to explain, Auntie, so I won't try —
but there are many, many things regarding tradition,
custom, ties of country and history that make things very
involved for Mai. This I understand myself and she
realised that I do, but to explain to other people is very
nearly impossible. It is difficult enough even for people
who live in this area . . .

The war and distance intervened, so Mai and Neil Davis
were never able to marry.

She was one of the great loves of my life.

Letter to Aunt Lillian, 16 February 1966
Orange Grove Rd,
Singapore

. . . Visnews want me to go to South Korea sometime
soon, also Taiwan, Japan and possibly China. Visnews
are keen to keep me out of Vietnam more than before, by
tempting me with these other assignments, but whilst I'm
eager to go especially to Korea, I feel out of it if I'm not
in Vietnam.

Unfortunately things are very bad there at present. A
Singaporean Indian cameraman was shot and killed
there yesterday — making the total now about 16
cameramen lost since last May . . .

I'm still coaching my runners from here, and received

a cable from one to say he had been selected to
represent Tasmania in Perth late in March for the
Australian Championships . . .

Letter to Aunt Lillian, 6 May 1966
Hotel Majestic,
Saigon

There have been many riots here again, and the
government has been overthrown — possibly you saw
some of this on TV. I had the distinction of being
arrested by the Vietnamese police one day, then
managing to 'escape' to the rioters (who sheltered me).
Two days later, however, I was attacked by rioters! This
time, the timely arrival of the Vietnamese paratroops
saved rather an ugly scene.

There was quite a bit of Communist-inspired
anti-Americanism this time. All US personnel were
ordered off the street in the cities for some days.
Fortunately no Americans were killed . . .

Managed to get an exclusive interview with the
Buddhist leader Thich Tri Quang, which got very good
play overseas . . .

Letter to Aunt Lillian, 17 June 1965
Hotel Caravelle,
Saigon

The situation is about normal. The military have taken
control of the government again — this time for good.
Yesterday Saigon's civilian air terminal was blown up,
and at dawn tomorrow five naughty Chinese war
profiteers are to be publicly executed by firing squad in
the Central Market. That about sums it up . . .

Covering events in Saigon was often as lively as the battlefield. South Vietnam's involved political situation was further complicated by anti-government street riots involving
rival Buddhist factions. There was also an anti-foreign, anti-

American element to these protests, so being blond and tall was not an advantage for a Western cameraman, generally perceived by the mobs to be American.

The world was appalled in the early 1960s when Buddhist bonzes started pouring petrol over their saffron robes and publicly burning themselves in the streets as an ultimate protest. The burnings resumed early in 1966, and in the chaos of wartorn Saigon they almost ceased to be newsworthy. There was a story that two American oil company executives fell into a drunken argument in the seventh floor bar of the Caravelle Hotel about whether the bonzes were immolating themselves with Shell or Esso.

When the military government took over in South Vietnam in June 1965, they arrested Saigon businessmen accused of war profiteering and black market activities. Most of the merchants suffering martial displeasure were Chinese. Even the Saigonese, accustomed to bizarre happenings, were jolted when the new government began public executions in the central market.

Letter to Aunt Lillian, 3 April 1966
  Visnews Office,
  Singapore

  My first job back in Vietnam this time was to cover the execution of a Chinese businessman. His wife and eight children turned up, so it was memorable film. I have to treat something like that as just another job . . .
  otherwise one would be perpetually sad . . .

Whatever deterrent effect the government hoped these executions would have on the local population, the publication of still pictures and newsfilm in the wider world was a monstrous public relations disaster. Awful scenes with distraught wives and weeping children clawing coils of barbed wire as their men were shot invaded secure homes in other continents.

One of Neil's close friends, Donald Wise of the London

Daily Mirror, had been out of Vietnam for some months covering the Middle East and Africa. Donald, a tall man with a David Niven-style moustache, was both dashing and dapper in his well tailored tropical suits. He had been a paratroop captain in the British Army and a prisoner-of-war of the Japanese on the Burma-Thailand railway. Still in the army after World War II, he was involved in special operations against the Malayan Communist Party during the Emergency.

Because Wise had been away from Saigon for so long, he asked me to drive him around while I briefed him on what had been going on. I purposely didn't mention the public executions, and took him by a circuitous route which brought us back via the central market, where he got his first glimpse of five execution posts set up there surrounded by sandbags.

He knew there had been executions of Viet Cong terrorists and war profiteers, but not in groups.

He said, 'My God. Five executions!'

Donald Wise is a sensitive man, who abhors violence and discrimination, but covers his feelings with a rather black sense of humour. I said, 'Not only that, Donald, five in one go the other morning.'

'Did you see it?

'See it? I filmed it, old fellow!'

Wise was silent for a moment. 'Christ,' he said. 'You have all the luck!'

Over the next few days Wise had time to notice and reflect on the clasped hands on stars and stripes stencilled on so many commodities in Saigon — it was the symbol of US aid to the Republic of South Vietnam, and the urbane British correspondent used it to get back at his mate.

A few days later, Davis and Wise both covered another dawn execution in the central market. An open coffin lined with plastic waited on trestles barely three metres away from where the condemned man was being tied up.

He behaved splendidly, merely asking the Vietnamese firing squad why *they* were shooting him. Why not, he asked, let the Americans do it?

The executioners fired. The body was cut down and placed in the coffin. The bloody sand around the base of the execution post was hosed away and the central market resumed normal commerce.

As the shots rang out, Donald Wise saw a window flung open in a shop just behind the execution point. A man, obviously in ill humour because of the noise, looked down. Seeing that it was just another execution, he scratched his stomach above his pyjama trousers, yawned copiously, slammed the window shut and presumably went back to bed.

Donald Wise wrote that story for his paper, but he had not finished with Davis. He asked, 'Did you get a close-up of the clasped hands on the coffin, old fellow?'

Davis was aghast to have missed it. Wise let him agonise until lunchtime before he confessed that this image of Vietnamese and American friendship had *not* been emblazoned on the cheap pineboard coffin.

Davis and Wise typified the camaraderie and competition known to many foreign correspondents. Their jokes masked their mutual respect, and diverted them from the horrors that shattered other people and the horror that could affect them.

Davis used to joke with Wise that the British journalist would 'get his' before Davis did, and he would be standing by, laughing, to film it.

During the Buddhist anti-government disturbances in Saigon in 1966, there were morning and evening riots outside the Buddhist headquarters at the Vien Hua Dao Pagoda. The demonstration was always broken up by South Vietnamese troops using tear gas and this had happened so many times that the area seemed permanently impregnated with the acrid fumes.

The press got fairly used to it, and some reporters got themselves gas masks, but you could combat it with lots of lemon, hankerchiefs and water. One morning the demonstration was getting rowdy, and it was close on noon, the beginning of the three-hour siesta period. The soldiers were hot and sick of it, and the rioters were getting edgy and wanted to have a good old set-to so they could get home to their rice and noodles, and everyone knew the time for the tear gas was getting close.

At precisely one minute after twelve, the rioters stormed the soldiers, who broke a few heads with batons and fired some shots in the air. Then they fired tear gas canisters.

We didn't have time to get with the troops, and one canister fell right at Donald's feet, enveloping him in a cloud of gas. When it cleared some minutes later, I saw a hard-bitten South Vietnamese paratrooper, who had filled his doubtless sweaty helmet with gutter water. He was swabbing Donald's face and eyes with his pretty filthy scarf, and pouring some of this water into his mouth.

Remembering his standing joke with Wise, Davis rolled his camera. Wise fluttered his eyelids and came to, only to see his friend almost helpless with laughter as he fixed the moment for posterity. 'There you are, you silly bugger. You never thought I really would laugh when I saw you down on the ground and hit, did you?'

Wise said that was dead right; he hadn't thought Davis would laugh. But now he feared that if he were really hit, Davis would die in a paroxysm of mirth.

Australian troops had not long been in Vietnam at that stage, and Davis was always urging Donald Wise to go down and do a story on them. It was a bit of a sideshow for Wise's British readers but Davis wore him down. Things did not get off to a good start when Wise stepped from his transport chopper resplendent in a skintight camouflaged spotted parachutist's uniform he had had tailor-made. It was a startling contrast to the rather baggy fatigues that the Australians wore.

Two Aussie diggers, leaning against a pile of sandbags, took in this magnificent apparition stolidly. Then one said to the other, 'Thank Christ. We're saved — Tarzan's here!'

Unlike the Americans and other Allied groups fighting in South Vietnam, the Australians did not welcome foreign correspondents; they had a deep-seated distrust of the press. It was known in the trade as the 'feel free to fuck off' approach to public relations.

Wise reported to Davis that he was helicoptered out to a forward position and introduced to the company sergeant-major, who took him out to a bunker position. It was nearly dark, and the amiable CSM fussed about and found him a stretcher and even a mosquito net. The soldiers shared their food with him, and Wise felt that the anti-press attitudes of the Australians had been exaggerated.

He woke at dawn as the troops were getting ready to move off, and heard the CSM being questioned by a young officer.

'Did you make Mr Wise comfortable and welcome?'

'Oh, yes, sir. We put him right out with the point platoon, like we do all these bloody correspondents.'

The point platoon, naturally, is the first to be attacked.

Letter to Aunt Lillian, 22 July 1967
Continental Palace Hotel,
Saigon

Air Marshal Ky came to power so quickly at so young an age that he pushed his luck too far. In very plain language, when they took a count of guns on the table, Ky didn't have enough. General Thieu will undoubted now be President. He will be OK. The main thing is to maintain stability. Another thing is that Vietnamese people respect age, and are wary of youth. Ky is only 36. Thieu is only 44, but a deeper thinker and open to compromise . . .

Respect for age is one of the main reasons why Ellsworth Bunker was appointed American Ambassador. The Americans *at last* in some small way, are starting to understand the Vietnamese. Bunker is about 73 years old, a fine upstanding, grey-haired, distinguished, quietly spoken, humble gentleman. This counts a tremendous amount with the Vietnamese. The previous Ambassador, Cabot Lodge, was a schemer, almost assuredly a more astute politician, but he wasn't old enough or humble enough. General Maxwell Taylor, before Lodge, was a disaster, although in the situation he was the logical choice. A fine military man, decisive, straightforward — but too prone to try and force his ideas, and not enough 'Vietnamese-style' dignity . . .

Letter to Aunt Lillian, 27 July 1967
Continental Palace Hotel,
Saigon

The Australian Minister for the Army, Malcolm Fraser, is here at the moment — young and impressive-*looking*, but really a dreary bore with little intelligence to look further than he is *officially* shown. Which is in direct contrast to another young MP, Andrew Peacock — who recently visited here at his own expense. He holds old Bob Menzies' blue-ribbon seat of Kooyong, and was really inquisitive and intelligent. He's only about 28 years old . . .

Neil Davis did not spend a great deal of time with Australian troops, but covered major news events such as the visits of Prime Ministers Harold Holt and later John Gorton and the arrival of the Australian Task Force at Nui Dat on the aircraft carrier HMAS *Sydney*. He had a high opinion of the operational efficiency of the Australians, but had to assess their contribution to the war as a whole.

I didn't go out with the Australians much, because relatively speaking they didn't do much fighting. They did have two or three very stiff battles, but that was over a period of several years. As an Australian I was very proud of the Australian troops. They were very professional, very well trained, and they fought the people they were sent to fight — the Viet Cong.

They tried not to involve civilians and generally there were few civilian casualties inflicted by the Australians.

The Australians were highly trained in jungle warfare. They rarely made contact with each other by voice, but used hand signals. Unlike the Americans they didn't wear flak jackets or helmets, so did not get so tired on patrol. They also adopted a policy of not using jungle tracks, which Davis believed worked against them.

I believe that fifty per cent of Australian casualties were caused by land mines and booby traps. When the Communists found the Australians weren't using the tracks, they became very smart about this, and the Australian practice of not walking down the jungle tracks but fanning out through the jungle was turned against them. The VC would discover and sometimes reposition Australian mines that had been left in ambush positions, which were then triggered by the Australians themselves. Meanwhile the VC were using the jungle trails like highways, because they knew the tracks were free'.

Nevertheless, Davis conceded that the Australians did win military control of their designated area.

But when they pulled out, the area at Nui Dat in Phuoc Tuy province reverted to Viet Cong control. They had not, in the phrase of the time, 'won the hearts and minds of the people', but had some limited success in the same way the South Koreans did.

Over the years in Vietnam, Davis saw more of the members of the Australian Army Training Team, thirty to forty warrant officers and sergeants who acted as advisers to Vietnamese units all over the country.

They gave them training in the field on fire discipline, and how to outflank an enemy, and it was all done by demonstration. They were very effective, and well liked by the Vietnamese. They shared the same hardships as their men, and generally got on well with them and with Vietnamese villagers.

Neil spent more time with the 50 000-strong Korean ROK force in Qui Nhon province than with the 6000 Australian troops. He was one of the first foreign correspondents to visit the Koreans in their operational area, and he told the ABC's Don Simmons to go and take a look at them. 'Jesus, they're a tough mob of fuckers.'

Letter to Aunt Lillian, 27 July 1966
Hotel Indonesia,
Jakarta

I was notified yesterday that I had been named Cameraman of the Month for June, or perhaps May — it wasn't quite clear. The award was for, as they say, 'his splendid coverage of the Korean Tigers operating in South Vietnam in particular, and his coverage from this extremely dangerous theatre of war in general. His coverage was hard, yet sympathetic; brutal yet tender, and full of understanding for the almost overwhelming task facing them.'

Oh well, it doesn't mean all that much, so I donated
the prize money to a suitable fund for the relief of
Vietnamese war victims in London . . .

When Davis first arrived in Saigon in 1964, the city was still
French in style, with tree-lined streets and outdoor cafes.
But terrorist grenades drove the customers indoors behind
sandbagged walls, and the narrow streets reverberated to
the unceasing roar and clatter of heavy military vehicles,
countless thousands of farting two-stroke motorcycles,
three-wheeled motorised cyclos and a solid phalanx of
battered Renault taxis and assorted private vehicles.

The English-language newspaper, the *Saigon Post*, used
to run daily ironic cartoons under the heading 'Saigon —
Pearl of the Orient' and Davis was saddened over the fate
of this once lovely city, as he was over the wretched
situation of many of its inhabitants — particularly the
beggars and orphans who lived on the streets.

Letter to Aunt Lillian, 4 January 1971
Continental Palace Hotel,
Saigon

Saigon is more crowded than ever, and pollution is at a
fantastically high level. The pollution recording
machine — or whatever it's called — refused to work in
Saigon some months ago.

It's worse now, which is terribly unhealthy for
everybody and everything that lives here. Even the trees
are dying.

13

Tet

In January 1968, Neil Davis was covering anti-British pre-independence riots on the Indian Ocean island of Mauritius. He was therefore away when the North Vietnamese and Viet Cong unleashed their surprise attacks throughout South Vietnam to disrupt what the Allies had hoped would be a peaceful celebration of Tet, the Lunar New Year.

Recalled to Singapore on 31 January, he found himself cut off from the biggest story in the world. All flights to Vietnam were cancelled. He made it to Saigon on 8 February courtesy of the Royal Australian Air Force, flying from Butterworth in Malaya into Saigon, which was still besieged by the Communist forces. One week earlier, Saigon had been devastated by co-ordinated guerilla attacks, one of which almost captured the Allied citadel — the American embassy.

Tony Ferguson, Davis's colleague from the Australian Broadcasting Commission, recalls being peacefully asleep in the Continental Palace Hotel on the hot and humid night of Tuesday 30 January. He was woken by a phone call at 2 a.m. from fellow Australian correspondent Pat Burgess who was staying at the Majestic Hotel. Burgess said, 'There's something funny going on.'

Ferguson, a bit irritated, replied that it was a funny town and what did he expect? There was a crash from the phone as it fell on the marble floor of Burgess's room, and other unexplained noises. Ferguson looked out of his window down Tu Do Street towards the Majestic (which was closer to the Saigon River than his hotel) to see tracer bullets bouncing off its facade, coming from the direction of the South Vietnamese naval headquarters. He grabbed the phone again to hear Burgess (by now under his bed) shouting, 'They're shooting through my fucking window!'

Tony Ferguson's first thought was that there had been a military coup d'état of some kind, and it didn't seem wise to go out on the streets just then. At first light he began to walk up to the Reuters office, which happened to be near the presidential palace. He got as far as the Roman Catholic cathedral at the top of Tu Do Street.

The first person he saw was a big Australian military policeman, standing alone in the traffic roundabout near the cathedral, holding a .45 pistol over his head and firing it aimlessly into the air. He was obviously panic-stricken.

Ferguson walked up to ask what was going on, but the policeman ignored him and kept firing frantically. An American journalist came running down the road with the news that the Viet Cong were attempting to take over the American embassy.

The Viet Cong assault team had failed to blow the main security door of the embassy with a satchel charge and when Ferguson arrived they were trapped between the compound walls and the embassy building, while American troops lobbed grenades over the wall. An American colonel had been asleep in an upstairs room in the guardhouse, just inside the gate of the compound, when the attack started. He had no weapons, and there is some now-famous film footage of American soldiers trying to throw a pistol up to him. While this was happening, an armed and wounded Viet Cong guerilla was crawling up the stairs of his house towards him.

Ferguson says, 'It was almost B-grade movie stuff. The colonel finally caught the pistol as the injured guerilla dragged himself up the stairs and propped himself in the doorway, trying to raise his rifle. I understand the colonel fired and missed, then threw the pistol at the VC, and actually strangled him with his bare hands!'

More incredible scenes followed, according to Ferguson. General Westmoreland, the commander of all American forces in Vietnam, was waiting around the corner in his limousine until the last of about thirty of the Viet Cong assault force were killed in the embassy compound.

'As the last one died, a siren was heard, and around the corner came Westy with his outriders. He was wearing a World War II-style paratrooper's outfit, and he immediately held an impromptu press conference in the compound. It was an extraordinary occasion. There were bodies literally everywhere — fellows draped in fountains, some half blown apart.

'His opening remarks were something to the effect that the enemy had overreached himself, we are in pursuit and we will annihilate him! People couldn't believe it. And amongst the bodies, sad to say, were some very young American MPs who had been in the pillboxes at either end of the garden, so there were some very incongruous scenes.'

Ferguson went to the Reuters office to file his copy, and was surprised to see what appeared to be a soldier in steel helmet and flak jacket with a pistol lying beside him on the desk, pounding away at a typewriter.

'I thought "Good God, what's the army doing here?" when he gave me a wave and I realised it was a *New York Times* correspondent I knew who had started to play John Wayne. The next time I saw this character he was sitting in a military jeep cradling an Armalite rifle!'

Back at the Continental Palace Hotel, with a strict dusk-to-dawn curfew in place, Ferguson met an angry Roland Challis of the BBC. Tony asked him what was the matter.

'The bastards are in the Dalat market,' said Challis.

'So what?' commented Ferguson.

'The strawberries Tony, the strawberries! We'll never see them now!'

Neil Davis arrived the following evening after some difficulty getting in from Tan Son Nhut airport through the street fighting. When Tony Ferguson made contact, he had unpacked his camera gear, was showered, spruced-up and rearing to go. The curfew was already in force, but Davis announced he was going to visit his girlfriend. Ferguson told him he was bonkers.

'Where does she live?'

'Out near the airport.'

Earlier that day, Tony Ferguson had tried to get some film and tapes to the airport in a taxi, but had been turned back only about two hundred metres from the gates. As Ferguson drove back, he saw bodies lying in the gutters and signs of recent action everywhere.

Davis listened to all this patiently, and went off to spend the night with his girlfriend. There was no bravado, but Ferguson was convinced he would not see him again.

The next morning Davis was back in time for breakfast — without strawberries — and told Ferguson that the only moment of concern had been in the middle of the night, when his girlfriend woke him to say there were people running up and down laneways and that they sounded to her like Viet Cong.

Their first joint Tet assignment was to a village about twenty-five minutes' drive out of Saigon, where twenty-seven Viet Cong had been surrounded in a paddy field by tanks and mown down. They had no chance, and bodies were draped all over the rice stubble. As Davis filmed, Ferguson could not believe his eyes. One dead Viet Cong was lying on his back, hands clasped on his chest holding a card — the ace of spades!

Ferguson yelled out to Davis to have a look, and Neil held a straight face for as long as he could. He had put it there himself, not to film, but as a macabre joke for his colleague. Davis had heard of the practice from American helicopter units operating on the Laotian border.

Letter to Aunt Lillian, 29 February 1968
Continental Palace Hotel,
Saigon

Well, the Allies are really in trouble now, and frankly I can see no real hope for victory. Not that it will be a bad thing for the Vietnamese anyway.

The Communist attacks were astounding in the way that they sustained their various offensives, particularly in the old Imperial capital of Hue — it was my favourite city in Vietnam. Besides Hue, other cities and towns all over the country have been devastated — mostly by Allied bombing and shelling as the Americans and South Vietnamese recaptured the towns. Many were up to fifty per cent destroyed.

Hue was eighty per cent destroyed or damaged. About four thousand civilians were killed there, plus thousands of North and South Vietnamese soldiers besides Americans. Actually the South Vietnamese Army did most of the fighting throughout the country, which I suppose is contrary to the press reports from here, where one would think only the Americans were doing anything. In Hue, for instance, they retook only about one-fifth of the city, while the South Vietnamese recaptured four-fifths.

On 21 February Davis and the Australian newspaperman Pat Burgess flew from Saigon to Hue. The Viet Cong, the southern-based National Liberation Front, had predictably failed to hold Saigon and had been savagely mauled in the process — not an entirely unwelcome development for the North Vietnamese, who dominated the political and the military conduct of the war from then on. The North Vietnamese troops had set themselves the task of taking and holding the old imperial capital of Hue in the extreme north of South Vietnam. In late February the attention of the world was focused on the battle for Hue.

Davis and Burgess flew to Phu Bai airport but had problems going any further. The North Vietnamese controlled most of Hue, the South Vietnamese had quite a big military compound, and the Americans held a much smaller area. The Americans were trying to keep clear a sixteen-kilometre corridor from their compound to the airport but military traffic was often ambushed.

At Phu Bai we were adopted by a damned American marine, who had arms and ammunition festooned all over him, who was going to protect us goddamn Aussies no matter what. We had purposely worn civilian clothes, but we couldn't take local transport until we got rid of this mad marine.

They gave him the slip by paying a Vietnamese to drive them in a little three-wheeled Vespa truck. The driver refused to risk his life for $2, but an extra $3 did the trick. The little truck set off, full of cheerful Vietnamese and the two Australians, skirting around a convoy that had been ambushed just moments earlier.

The Americans were using a soccer field as an emergency landing zone for their helicopters to take out the dead and wounded. Davis and Burgess reasoned they could get from there to the northern part of Hue, which was being heavily bombed as both the Americans and the South Vietnamese tried to fight their way back into the city.

At about four p.m. we saw a small artillery spotter plane — a Cessna — shot down. It crashed very close to the soccer field, and just before dusk they brought in what was left of the pilot. There was little more than a charred skeleton wrapped in a plastic bag, which was placed inside one of the bigger regulation body bags.

By this time the Americans in Vietnam had the best of everything, and their body bags were heavy rubberised plastic with zips. They were about seven feet [just over two metres] long, and could stand on their own like a collapsible coffin.

The two Australians knew they would not be able to move away from the soccer field until morning, if then. They had a little two-man pup tent and tried to make the best of the situation. The climate in the north of Vietnam in February could be quite cold; Davis knew this and had brought his sleeping bag. From his quilted comfort, Davis said a cheery goodnight to Burgess.

Burgess was dressed in light cotton tropical gear, and by 8.30 p.m. he was getting very cold. (Burgess disputes the fine detail of this story, but Davis was adamant.)

> I heard Pat say, 'Well, father, at least that pilot's warm out there.' It was just a passing remark, and I didn't take much notice. Then at eleven I heard him flapping his arms and muttering about having to get warm somehow. I was half asleep by then, and heard a kind of dragging sound.
>
> I thought I knew what it was, and then I heard the unmistakable sound of a long zip being pulled open, followed by a crackle of plastic as an object was lifted and moved. Then there was some rustling and grunting of Pat settling down for the night, and the *ziiiip* sound again, and I knew he was in the body bag.
>
> Pat did have the grace to go through the whole thing in reverse just before first light . . . the *ziiiip* sound again, the rustle of plastic and a few thumps as the remains of the pilot went back, another zipping sound, and the scraping noise as the body bag went back to the stack.
>
> Pat was always reticent about that — but he had a good warm sleep, anyway.

Next morning they hitched a lift to the northern part of Hue on a helicopter that had delivered its latest load of dead and dying men. They took only seven hits on the short flight, which the pilot said was lucky. Davis and Burgess joined a platoon of twenty South Vietnamese soldiers, under the command of an Australian warrant officer, Terry Egan, one of the military advisers assigned to the ARVN in various parts of the country.

> We went out with this patrol into the streets, and it was really like being one bubble in a glass of soda water, the situation was so fluid. The bubble next to you could be a South Vietnamese or American soldier, or it could be a North Vietnamese. That was the situation in Hue, with these bubbles, these little units of men moving about.

There was no water in the pipes and food was scarce. They had some canteens of water and American tinned field rations, but after two days holed up in a partly bombed house, with their unit exchanging fire with a North Vietnamese patrol at the other end of the street, supplies were short.

Into no man's land at this time walked a large, strapping pig. Firing on both sides stopped instantly, and Communists and capitalists began willing this potential banquet to walk, not only their way, but close enough to be shot and retrieved. If it was killed too far away, neither side would get it. The atmosphere was taut with projected willpower.

> This fine baconer actually started to move towards our side, when it stopped and looked around. Pigs can be alert and almost human in some of their reactions. Then we noticed the dead and decomposing body of a North Vietnamese soldier lying on the side of the street.
>
> The pig hesitated, looked one way and then the other, turned as if it was going to come our way again — and then darted across the road and drove its snout into the putrid mess of the dead body. It was a ghastly thing to

see, and one of our soldiers aimed and shot the pig through the head. It dropped dead right over the body of the North Vietnamese.

Immediately there was an outcry. Even from the other end of the block we could hear the North Vietnamese obviously saying, 'Oh, my God, what have you done?' Our soldier defended his action by saying that if the pig had been eaten, we would have been cannibals because the pig had been feeding from a fellow Vietnamese. Reluctantly the soldiers agreed with his argument.

The desire for roast pork had disappeared, but food of some kind had to be found. A foraging party went off and met a group from the North Vietnamese-held area doing the same thing. Hungry enemies eyed each other off and got on with their scrounging and left the shooting until later.

Someone brought back a bottle of Japanese whisky called Gold King — I never saw it anywhere ever again, but it was just dreadful. As we had very little water or anything else we drank it. It was about one a.m., and it gave me an instant headache.

Despite that, the Gold King party went on. The group was joined by another correspondent, Beverley Diepe of the *Christian Science Monitor*, who didn't drink alcohol and who settled herself down in a corner to sleep.

Beverley was a very fine correspondent and we were delighted to have her with us. Meanwhile the Australian WO Terry Egan, Pat and I finished off the Gold King, and were wondering how to fill in the rest of the night when Pat Burgess had a bright idea.

'Hey, Beverley, Beverley, wake up!' he kept shouting,

and Beverley thought it best to ignore him. Perhaps she thought she was about to be propositioned by this Australian monster.

Pat kept going. 'Beverley, you work for the *Christian Science Monitor*, don't you?' Still not a sound from the corner.

'Well, come and turn this bloody water into wine then!'

Burgess was glad he had the water in the morning for his teeth-cleaning ritual. Davis thought it wasteful of the little water they had, and told Burgess it was dangerous to clean his teeth anyway. He was right. While the big Australian was out in the little courtyard of the house scrubbing and foaming away, Neil heard the unmistakable 'plop' of a mortar shell being launched.

Three things happened at once. I yelled out, the mortar exploded in the courtyard and Pat crashed in the door, frothing at the mouth with toothpaste. He was spreadeagled at my feet in a cloud of dust and debris, having missed death by a fraction of a second.

I said, 'Told you it was dangerous to clean your teeth in the morning!' He never did it again, on that trip, anyway.

Davis's work diaries for the next three days are masterpieces of understatement.

Hue, Saturday 24 February

Located ARVN 1st Div. 2/3 Battalion and accompanied them to captured section of wall. Major Dinh, Btn CO raised VN flag from main Citadel flagpole at 1100.

PM: Assault on Palace with ARVN. Stayed till dark. Only scattered opposition.

Unable return to ARVN HQ through city due heavy

sniper fire, so crossed to south side over footbridge now in place. Stayed south side.

INCOMPLETE: The battle for Hue (150 ft today)

Hue, Sunday, 25 February

Returned north side early AM. Filmed in devastated area in Citadel, also snipers (NVA) who made last-ditch stand last night. Then through entire palace grounds, and filmed comprehensively.

Returned ARVN HQ early PM and filmed NVA POWs just brought in. Then to south side, walked to outskirts of city to get private car to drive me to Phu Bai.

There by 1530. Get Marine CH46 to East Da Nang, taxi to Press Centre — arrive there 1730.

Stay overnight.

COMPLETE: The battle for Hue (600 ft 250 ft today)

Taxis
Hue-Phu Bai 800 P.
E. Danang — Press Centre 500 P.

Da Nang, Monday 26 February

0900. Leave Press Centre. Wait at airport till 1330 takeoff. Tan Son Nhut Airport by 1600. City by 1700.

Evening — wrote and recorded ABC taped voicepiece with actuality sound on 'Ethics of War'. Shot listed (very comprehensive) all Hue footage. Labelled all film.

Expenses: One night Da Nang Press Centre, 300 P.
Taxis, Military Airport — City, 1000 P.

On Wednesday 21 February, Davis noted in his diary: 'Shot and filmed Man With The White Flag.'

He was with the American marines on the southern bank of the Perfumed River. The North Vietnamese had complete control of the northern bank, which included the old stone citadel of the imperial palace. The opposite bank was under very heavy bombing and shelling by air and artillery. The marines were right down on the bank of the river, which was about a hundred metres wide at that point. In the midst of the action, a young man — a civilian wearing black pants and a white shirt — came down to the opposite bank. He was one of the Vietnamese civilians trapped by the fighting. He waved his arms, obviously wanting to swim over to the American side.

There was a brief pause, and the marines opened fire on him. He ran into a little shed like a boathouse and the Americans continued to pour a lot of fire into it. How the man wasn't killed then, I don't know.

When the firing died down two or three minutes later, he ran out waving his white shirt like a flag. His intentions were perfectly obvious. He was a civilian, a refugee. After waving his shirt for two or three seconds, he didn't know what to do, and started to run.

Davis had his camera and tape recorder rolling. Here is the transcript of the sound tape from that point onwards.

(The man runs out of the boathouse waving his white shirt.)

'Hey there, he's waving a white flag . . .'

(Sergeant's voice): 'Bullshit! Cut him down, cut him down . . .'

(Heavy gunfire)

'Cut him down!'

(Very heavy gunfire for about thirty seconds)

'Can't see him any more.'

(A pause)

'Cocksucker waved a white flag and then ran right for us.'

'Oh?'

'He waved a white flag and then ran right for it.'

Davis said, 'He disintegrated right in front of my eyes.' He believed the incident was essentially racist, that if the man had been a Caucasian — a Frenchman — the marines would have welcomed him across.

> But I can't in my heart blame the marines. It was their indoctrination, their commanders and ultimately their government who sent them into that situation without knowing why they were there and who they were fighting with and against.

Davis was not surprised some months later when the story of Lieutenant Calley and the My Lai massacre came to light.

> There were other instances of torture by the Americans, and I filmed two or three of these. That is not to say the South Vietnamese did not do it. They did, and for a purpose — to get information. So did the North Vietnamese. But I found it sad that the Americans mostly did it because they wanted to be cruel to the people concerned, their defeated enemy.
> The South Vietnamese never did that to their enemies. They might be brutal and torture a prisoner initially to get intelligence, but when that was over, they treated him with great compassion. There is a difference, I think.

The sound tape Davis had recorded was more damning evidence than the film which, for reasons never entirely explained, was not shown. He passed on transcripts to several American correspondents who wrote the story. The consequences were serious.

> The American military then hounded me for the next twelve months, first to get back the tape, then to have me expelled from the country, but the South Vietnamese weren't going to have any of that. Their view of the argument was quite the opposite.

The Americans did momentarily take away my military accreditation, which only meant I couldn't cover the Americans. I couldn't travel on their very comprehensive transport system, but it didn't worry me too much because I covered the Vietnamese side of the war mostly.

Eventually I was let off the hook, because Lieutenant Calley's My Lai massacre came to light and the fact of shooting down one man with a white flag was lost. It became relatively unimportant.

After the citadel fell and the devastated city of Hue was retaken, camera crews and journalists came in droves from Saigon. Pat Burgess was still in Hue with the Australian adviser, Warrant Officer Terry Egan. One of the cameramen, secure in the knowledge that the action was over, began filming the dead bodies of the North Vietnamese who had been lying in the cold, wet streets for several weeks.

He began taking closeup shots of the face of one dead Communist. The soldier had obviously died in agony, mouth open, teeth showing, and Egan as a soldier was outraged by this violation.

'Watch my flank,' he said to Burgess, meaning the rest of the television crew. It was a big outfit, and there about ten of them.

The Australian warrant officer walked up behind the cameraman as he crouched over the dead soldier and booted him in the arse so hard, that he fell over on top of his camera.

'Don't do that,' said Egan. 'Me or my mate' (indicating Burgess) 'could have looked like that three weeks ago. That's the point.'

It was during the 1968 Tet offensive that one of the Vietnam war's coldest and most horrific images was photographed and filmed — the shooting of a Viet Cong suspect in the head by General Loan, Saigon's chief of police. Even now, the watcher is fascinated and wants the action to stop, recoils, and is revolted. Eddie Adams of Associated

Press took the still picture, and Vo Huyn, a South Viet-namese cinecameraman working for NBC, shot the news footage.

Neil Davis did not excuse this killing of an unarmed man, even though it was common.

> There was a reason from General Loan's point of view. Only an hour before he learned that the Viet Cong had swept over the police compound in Saigon, and his best friend, a police colonel, and his wife and six children were murdered. The children had their throats cut. Loan was a godfather to some of them.
>
> When the Viet Cong suspect was brought before Loan in the street, he asked where he had been captured, and it was near the police compound. What went through Loan's mind one can only imagine, but he immediately took out his pistol and shot him.
>
> He never really recovered politically from that incident — but his attitude to the press didn't change much. He understood the press pretty well.

Some days after the celebrated street execution, Loan flew to Hue while the battle for the Citadel was on. One of the first people he saw as he stepped out of his helicopter was Davis.

> He lifted his arm to which he had strapped a machine pistol, pointed it at me and said, 'Some day I kill you.'
>
> Well, he didn't really mean that. I knew what he meant, it was another way of saying that there had been too much publicity, too many pictures. He certainly wasn't going to kill me. But it rather startled a British television crew who were standing right behind me filming. They thought they were going to have yet another execution on their hands!

Loan himself was badly shot up in an action in Saigon later that year. Pat Burgess helped to carry him from the scene.

He liked Loan and had been invited to his house. The general spoke fluent French and played the piano — there was a red rose beside him as he performed, Burgess recalls. It was just after the street execution, and his wife gave him the rounds of the kitchen when it was published in the papers.

Loan said in French, 'Well, what do you expect me to do? Go back to shooting them in the basement?' His wife pointed out that he had sergeants for that sort of work.

The Communists' 1968 Tet offensive was the biggest victory the South Vietnamese and the Americans ever had in South Vietnam. Neil Davis saw the irony of public misconception reversing battle reality.

The Viet Cong committed most of their troops to that offensive. They controlled most of Saigon for several days and captured some other cities, but at enormous cost.

The agents who had been there all the time had to surface and were identified. After the towns and villages were recaptured, they had to flee. The Allies were in the best position they'd ever been in, but paradoxically the antiwar movement in America gained great momentum because of what appeared to be an Allied defeat.

Most of the lost territory was regained by the South Vietnamese. That wasn't factually presented on most of the world's television sets. Most people believed that the Americans were doing most of the fighting. They did do a lot of fighting, but it was the South Vietnamese who physically recaptured most of the towns and cities in South Vietnam, much to the surprise of the North Vietnamese and Viet Cong.

Until the start of 1968 the Allies were allegedly winning the war and the media believed that. It was the Tet offensive that shocked them into the realisation that it wasn't so.

The media at that time did a complete turnaround. They presented the attack on the American Embassy as a moral defeat — I think they were right in that, but wrong in presenting the whole offensive as a military defeat.

One immediate result was that the southern-born guerillas, the Viet Cong, were effectively destroyed. After that it became war with the North Vietnamese versus South Vietnam and America.

In the final pages of his 1968 work diary, Davis noted the text of a letter recovered from a wounded North Vietnamese soldier during the battle for Hue on 25 February 1968. It was written in North Vietnam on 30 September 1967.

Dear Brother Thu,

Today the weather is cool. I take the pen to write some sentences to you. Brother, you are just 16 years only, but forced by the wild dog army to leave. Other people are staying home and enjoying life, whereas you have to be in another land.

Brother, as you live in the jungle you hear neither birds sing nor cocks crow, but you see only the breeze and water current in the streams, and see nobody at all.

We are born and raised by our parents. I never forget you.

The war is not over yet, but it seems that if you enjoy the war, you live.

Brother, the night is long and the moon is light. I think life is pearl and gold.

I wish you more successes in your career. I assume the chores at home. If you receive this letter, please answer me.

Your younger brother,

Dang Van.

14

The Safest Place
is the Front Line

Sound, sound the clarion, fill the fife,
Throughout the sensual world proclaim,
One crowded hour of glorious life
Is worth an age without a name.

Neil Davis wrote the last two lines of this verse by Thomas Osbert Mordaunt in the flyleaf of every work diary he kept in South-east Asia from 1964 to 1985. He said it was his motto and summed up his philosophy to life and combat.

Sometimes the dangerous thought would occur to me that I had an immunity, that I was safe from wounding or death or being caught in any unpleasant happenings, and that is a very dangerous assumption to make, because of course you are not immune. Whenever I got that feeling, I'd immediately stamp on it, and be extra careful for the next few times and make sure that I did everything in my power and experience to protect myself.

Sometimes when you are looking through your viewfinder you get the impression you're watching a television story. And you are not part of it. Maybe you can switch it off, or switch to another channel. It's an extremely dangerous feeling.

Yet despite conscious efforts to shake off the 'it can't happen to me' syndrome, Neil Davis did have enormous faith in his own luck. Later in the war his Cambodian friends called him 'Mean Samnang' (the lucky one).

Letter to Aunt Lillian, 6 May 1966
    Hotel Majestic,
    Saigon

    I managed to get to the Gulf of Tonkin (off North Vietnam). This was very lucky, and some kind of mix-up I think. Since some American warships were attacked there in 1964, no correspondents have been allowed. I got there by a roundabout method, and was less than 32 kilometres from Haiphong (the port for Hanoi) for over two days on an American frigate on station there to rescue American pilots downed over North Vietnam. That is, of course, if they are close enough to the coast to ditch in the water. The frigate carries a helicopter for this rescue work.

    It was very interesting, and fortunately (for me) the Americans have securely closed all the loopholes for those correspondents trying to do the same. So it made my film the only one to be shot in the Gulf since 1964 . . .

Donald Wise was with Davis on that chancy assignment. The two men were winched down to the rescue ship after a ninety-minute full alert flight on a Sea King helicopter. They spent two nights on board, then their reluctant hosts arranged a chopper to pick them up.

As Davis and Wise waited to be winched from the deck, the frigate's own helicopter started up its rotors for a short patrol. There was a sudden crash and shower of sparks as a chunk of its rotor blade detached itself and spun into the bulkhead just behind where the two correspondents were sitting.

'Jesus!' said Wise. 'It nearly got us.'

'No, old fellow,' said Davis, 'it nearly got you!'

The remark was only partly in jest. Davis later admitted to an addiction to combat and to his heightened perception in adrenalin-charged moments. He instinctively felt that the fragment of rotor was not going in his direction.

The BBC's Brian Barron said that Neil Davis had the best jungle instinct of any journalist he ever met. Davis believed that his survival in combat could be rated at 10 per cent luck and 90 per cent experience — allowing for the fact that combat was never the same twice running.

> I was always optimistic, and took the soldier's view that it always happened to someone else — and it always did, although I was wounded on a number of occasions. It's rather like learning to drive a car well. There's always the fool that might come out and do the wrong thing, but I felt the more experienced I became, the more chance I had of staying alive. Now many people hold the opposite view that the more times you go into dangerous situations, the odds are greater that your number will come up — that you will be killed. I didn't subscribe to that. Every time was new, and my chances of survival increased with my experience.

But Davis also put great emphasis on instinct or a sixth sense that he felt civilised man had largely lost.

> There's a famous clairvoyant in Holland called Le Croiset who doesn't claim to be able to predict the future, but he has a natural instinct for knowing what has happened. The police sometimes use him when they are trying to trace missing people. Sometimes the people are dead, and Le Croiset can visualise that — he has a feeling about it.
>
> He's a very simple man and he lived with his widowed father, who I think was a woodcutter or rural

worker, in a cottage in the forest. The most plausible explanation for his success is that he has never lost that sixth sense, that instinct caused by living close to nature.

Davis believed that playing the survival game for long periods reactivated an instinct for life. It was that reserve force that a desperate jungle animal may draw upon when hard pressed by predators. It knows instinctively the right moves to make.

There is a great feeling of accomplishment when you recapture that, and the addiction comes when you keep testing it. It's amazing how many times you are right.

Soldiers under extreme stress sometimes sensed that state of intense awareness in others, and immediately followed the man they thought was 'hot'.

They're happy for you to have that electric feeling, because your instincts might be working more powerfully than theirs on that particular day. Sometimes you will see Vietnamese soldiers going a little slower and looking apprehensive — much the same as a nervous dog when strangers are around — and there'll be a definite feeling that something is about to happen. It often does.

Sometimes Davis was with a Vietnamese unit searching villages in a Communist-controlled area. It might be the fifth or sixth village before the feeling was generated — for no apparent reason — that the Viet Cong soldiers were there. They almost invariably were.

Davis experienced this phenomenon powerfully one day in 1967. He was south of Saigon with an ARVN unit commanded by his old friend Captain Long — the man who had taken him on his first combat assignment. The battalion was advancing across open paddy fields towards a treeline ahead. Several hundred metres to the left was a small clump of trees, which seemed unlikely cover for the Viet Cong as it was isolated and easily surrounded.

> Normally I would have been concentrating on the treeline about half a mile ahead, but I had the very strong feeling that this clump of trees was dangerous, and I kept glancing back to it as we moved past. Captain Long noticed this, and laughed. 'Ah,' he said, 'I see that you know.'
>
> I didn't know anything, and said I had a strange feeling that there were Viet Cong in that group of trees.
>
> He said, 'Of course you are right, and they are in the woodland ahead, too.'

The Viet Cong had expected the ARVN troops to attack the treeline first, and then the troops in the small copse would have counter-attacked from the rear. But they had miscalculated the instinct of Captain Long and his soldiers, who skirted around the smaller group and wiped them out.

Davis actually felt safer with Asian troops, but sometimes his instinct would tell him not to cover a particular operation. On one occasion towards the end of 1964, before the big American build-up had begun, he went to cover a set piece battle in a rubber plantation not far from Saigon. The several thousand ARVN troops involved had been fighting for three days when Davis arrived.

> The South Vietnamese troops were preparing to move into the rubber late in the afternoon as the sun was going down. I knew the light would be bad, that I couldn't get any film out for thirty-six hours or so, and I had an uneasy feeling about the operation anyway. So I didn't go.

Next morning Davis was helicoptered to the same area to film the 28 survivors of the battalion of 430 men he had nearly accompanied. The Viet Cong had ambushed them in the rubber trees, and the South Vietnamese Air Force could do nothing to help them under the tree canopies.

Jim Bennett, an American television correspondent, says simply that the first time they met, Davis saved his life. It was at a hot landing zone in the central highlands of Vietnam. They were both trying to get a chopper out with film taken of one of the first major clashes between the South Vietnamese and North Vietnamese troops. A Chinook, one of the big double-rotored, troop-carrying helicopters, came in to disgorge fresh troops and ferry out the dead and wounded. Bennett and his crew were about to dash on board when Davis advised against it.

He was alone, carrying a small Bell and Howell cine-camera with a cassette tape recorder strapped to his belt, and he looked to Bennett like a soldier with a camera. After Davis had identified himself as a Visnews cameraman, Bennett asked what was wrong with the Chinook. Davis said, 'The bloody thing's a death trap. They're too damn slow, and the bad guys are shooting hell out of them.'

Bennett took the advice, despite the Australian accent, and the Chinook left without them. It was some hours before they were able to get on one of the smaller, faster Huey choppers. When they got to Pleiku they heard that two Chinooks (including the one they had let go) had crashed, killing all on board. Dinner and booze were on Bennett that night.

For Davis, the exhilaration of survival was a powerful aphrodisiac.

When you have been to the edge and played your life against the odds and you've won, it heightens the joy of living and loving. Not just at the time, but afterwards, back in Saigon, when I go out to meet people and eat in a nice restaurant — you have a far greater sense of what's good about life and how to enjoy and appreciate it.

I liked to work alone because I didn't want to be responsible for the life of any other person. I felt I had enough to do just to stay alive myself. If I was tied by the umbilical cord connecting me to a soundman who was relatively inexperienced, I couldn't concentrate on my work and on staying alive. If you have to make a decision for yourself, right or wrong, you stand by that decision.

I didn't wear a steel-lined flak jacket, because it was too heavy, and made me hot and tired. Besides, I had other things to carry like food and water and extra film.

Davis refined his field gear down to a load of twenty to twenty-two kilograms. In the pre-videotape days he used a hand-held Bell and Howell camera with a clockwork mechanism to power 100 foot (30.4 metre) reels of 16 millimetre film through the shutter. That gave a little over two minutes of film before the roll had to be changed. To capture sound, he had a small cassette tape recorder strapped to his belt. This was not synchronised sound, and meant that the film editor back in London had to work very precisely to marry the picture with the recorded sound. It could not be used for a news interview, but was adequate for combat coverage. In less desperate circumstances he used a bulky sound-on-film camera.

The Bell and Howell camera became part of me, an extension of my arm. Everything became automatic. By using this gear I was much more mobile, and able to get more worthwhile film.

I would always go to the extreme front line to film. The main reason is that's where the best spontaneous film is.

Contrary to popular belief it was not, Davis believed, the most dangerous place. That was the second or third line, several hundred metres behind, because the troops there were more likely to be shelled, mortared, rocketed or hit by propelled grenades. The enemy's aim would be to knock out the command post for the attacking unit, and the area would be peppered with thousands of pieces of shrapnel.

I don't like shrapnel, because you can be killed by any one of a thousand — ten thousand — pieces of metal from one shell slicing through you. I preferred bullets in the front line, because you take cover from your immediate front and you don't have to worry about things dropping on top of you or around you.

During one desperate action in 1965, Davis's unit was actually in hand-to-hand combat, while South Vietnamese Sky Raider aircraft bombed and strafed within fifty metres of his position.

Many of our unit were being killed and wounded by shrapnel from our own bombing. I lay down alongside one body and pulled another corpse half over me as a sort of wall of protection. That was one occasion where the front line and the shrapnel were too close for comfort.

A lot of people used to think I was foolish, because I always went forward with the advancing troops, and I even heard the expression 'death wish' used. That was absurd. If I was going to cover an action, I wanted to be in the best place to film and the safest place in my way of thinking was the immediate front line.

You can't get the spontaneity of the action if you are not there. There is no use trying to get it with a telephoto lens from the second or third line. You don't see the faces, and the expressions on those faces — the compassion that they may show for their wounded comrades — or their enemy, for that matter.

You are also testing the unknown and something that has to be experienced to assess your own capabilities

With hand-held Bell and Howell, Neil Davis is pictured in action by his Pulitzer prize-winning New Zealand friend Peter Arnett in the Mekong Delta region of South Vietnam in 1967.

VIỆT-NAM CỘNG-HÒA
PHỦ THỦ-TƯỚNG
TÒA TỔNG TRẤN SAIGON – GIA-ĐỊNH
Đ.T. : 51586 – 92510

THẺ
LƯU THÔNG ĐẶC BIỆT
TRONG GIỜ THIẾT QUÂN LUẬT
(TÌNH TRẠNG CHIẾN TRANH)

SPECIAL PASS
for movement during periods of Martial Law.
(War situation)

REPUBLIQUE KHMERE

ទីស្តីការរដ្ឋមន្ត្រីក្រសួងឃោសនាការ
MINISTERE DE L'INFORMATION

PRESSE

N° 55/INF/DAE

No. 040

Name
Nom   Neil Davis

Organization
Appartenance   Visnews

Date   September 23, 1970

This identification card is delivered to qualified journalists by the
COMMITTEE FOR THE SAFETY OF FOREIGN CORRESPONDENTS
IN CAMBODIA, Room 25, Hôtel Le Royal, Phnom-Penh, Cambodia.

Cette carte d'identité est livrée aux journalistes qualifiés par le
COMITE POUR LA PROTECTION DES CORRESPONDANTS ETRAN-
GERS AU CAMBODGE, Chambre 25, Hôtel Le Royal, Phnom-Penh
Cambodge.

Mementos of a foreign correspondent.

properly. Most people are not sure how they're going to react under great personal stress and tension — that's always an unknown. The ultimate, I suppose, is to be placed in a position when your life is threatened, and you have to make a decision which may save your life or may kill you.

Not to be in the front line meant what Davis called 'aftermath' film, in which the viewer sees wounded soldiers coming back, and guns and artillery can be heard in the distance.

Battle photographers could suffer a dangerous delusion. Because they watched the action through a camera lens they would begin to feel displaced from the violence around them.

You are looking through a viewfinder which looks very much like a television screen, blocking off everything else. You simply have to keep reminding yourself that this is not so!

As a professional athlete, Davis had learned a lot about reaction speeds. He calculated that it took at least a quarter of a second for the mind to assess a situation and give the order for the limbs to move — which could be a long time when bullets were flying.

You first hit the ground, that's the first cover. Don't run to the nearest tree or you are dead. You have to keep an eye on what the troops are doing, and maybe roll over and over towards a small indentation in the ground, and then perhaps make it to a tree or a paddy dyke.

There was also the all-important question of luck — and sometimes Davis needed every point of the 10 per cent he felt was involved.

On one occasion in the Mekong Delta area south of
Saigon in 1966 I was moving across open paddy fields
with an ARVN unit. There were a few tussocks and
bushes, but not much obvious cover. Suddenly a Viet
Cong jumped up only about 3 metres ahead of us and
shot the radio operator dead.

The Viet Cong sniper was shot and killed seconds later. But
he had selected the radio operator out of a group of five
which included the battalion commander, his adjutant, an
American adviser and Davis. It was, Davis conceded, just
blind chance and luck that he himself had not been the
target.

Selecting the right unit to accompany was also a key
factor in survival.

You had to have confidence in a unit — and if you
didn't, it was better not to go.

Davis preferred regular army units to part-time reservists,
as they were continually in combat and had time to develop
their sixth sense.

In a small unit you would get to know the soldiers
right down to the last man, as well as the commander.
The commander quite often was not good, and you had
to watch that. If he was a political appointee, or had
been given the job because of his wealth or influence, it
was best not to go with him — unless he happened also
to be a good soldier. A career soldier was the best
proposition.

Don Simmons, an Australian Broadcasting Commission
journalist who also covered the fighting war, remembers
the high quality of Neil's early work in Vietnam. His film
was never just a collection of shots; feeling was always
there. Maybe it was expressed in shots of tight, taut faces,

children, burnt hands and the humanity of war to underline its basic inhumanity. Davis was a film essayist who composed stories in his camera often using less than 100 feet of film to fix details in a sequence able to engage the viewer and expand comprehension.

He believed that frontline combat brought out the best in people.

> You see a person stripped of all pretensions, and if they do have annoying or irritating personal habits, that is completely unimportant. What is important is how they react in the most dramatic situation you can present them with — when your lives are on the line. A very close understanding and camaraderie develops from that.

That friendship could even cross over to the other side, which Davis found personally most rewarding. It was most often seen following the capture of prisoners.

> Initially there's a sort of anger, and it's very dangerous for the prisoners. After all, until a few moments before, both sides have been trying to kill each other. They can be killed in the first minute or two, but if they survive that, they are treated more or less as comrades.
>
> On their way back to the rear lines, villagers sometimes get angry and want to get at the prisoners, and the soldiers protect them because they identify with their situation.
>
> The Americans could feel that, too. In November 1967, the Americans took Hill 875 in the central highlands. It was called that because it was simply 875 metres high. There had been a three-day battle as the North Vietnamese defenders on the mountain were pounded with artillery and air strikes. No Communist soldiers on top of Hill 875 could survive. It was devastated. Every tree was knocked down and stripped of all its leaves. There were great craters everywhere and its deep

bunkers were breached and there were bodies in every position.

I was with an American infantryman as he looked down into a bunker with several North Vietnamese soldiers who had died at their weapons, and he said very quietly, 'Poor bastards'. He understood their situation.

15

Gooks,
Dinks and Slopes

The Americans called their South Vietnamese allies 'gooks',
'dinks' or 'slopes'. The Australian troops called them
'noggies'. The cultural gap between Westerners and Asians
in Vietnam was awesome. Understanding was not helped
by foreigners' bewilderment with the Vietnamese language.
Hearing its sung vowels and glottal stops was, Donald Wise
once said, 'like listening to ducks fucking'.

One tragic result of this cultural impasse was the inability of the average American soldier, on a year's tour of
duty, to see a Vietnamese as a fellow human being. It was a
situation that Neil Davis, with his compassion for all
human beings, found a source of constant anguish.

I found the Americans overall a terribly kind and
thoughtful people. By 1966 there were half a million
Americans in South Vietnam. Most of them were
soldiers, but they were drawn from all walks of life, and
there were many civilians too. They did have the milk of
human kindness, and they were unfailingly courteous
and helpful.

But this behaviour related mainly to Westerners. They
really didn't associate bombing or punitive action carried
out against the South Vietnamese people living in Viet
Cong-controlled areas as action against people — it was
action against gooks, dinks or slopes.

The American soldier didn't understand what the Vietnam war was about — but that wasn't his fault. After a few months in the country, the fighting soldier knew more about the Vietnamese than his commanding officers. The American command was completely divorced from the realities of the situation. They saw it in totally conventional terms. There was a war to be fought, and you had to pursue that war in conventional terms and destroy the enemy.

But they didn't understand who the enemy was.

They could talk about all sorts of ideas for furthering the cause of human dignity in the Western world at the same time as they were blowing a village of people away right in front of your eyes.

Moments of insight and concern did surface. One afternoon down in the Mekong Delta, Davis stood with a young GI from Kentucky, watching a village burning after an action. There were a few Viet Cong killed, but the entire village and the livelihood for hundreds of people were destroyed.

This young GI from Kentucky had had six years of primary school education, and like his brother soldiers had had no proper indoctrination from the army why he was fighting in Vietnam. As we watched the destruction of the village he said, 'I dunno, it seems to me that there's something wrong with this; we're killing these people in their own homes. What are we doing here?'

He understood very well, but it took a long time for most Americans. Then their one-year tour was up. Most American GIs understood there was a great deal wrong with the war. Their commanding officers in general terms never did understand.

The civilian pacification programme 'Winning the Hearts And Minds of the People' could make some wondrous miscalculations. The unfortunate acronym WHAMMO did not foreshadow gentleness and subtlety. Davis recalls that one programme was to distribute portable toilets to Vietnamese farmers who had been managing quite well with their own arrangements for several thousand years.

In almost any large town in Vietnam you could buy American Zippo cigarette lighters engraved with the WHAMMO slogan. I saw one with an extra comment engraved on the back: 'Let me win your heart and mind or I'll burn your bloody house down.' And that is what happened.

Few American soldiers ever met their hard-fighting counterparts in the South Vietnamese army, because each force operated independently, and even in combined operations they never actually integrated with each other's units. Effectively the American soldier never met a South Vietnamese soldier. He was more likely to meet the Vietnamese hanging around the fringes of his base camp peddling sex, dope or any commodity to grab a fast buck.

When the GI went on leave to Saigon he'd head for the bars, into the restaurants and brothels, so he'd meet more pimps and prostitutes or shoeshine boys and taxi drivers, whose main purpose at that time was to win quick dollars from the Americans.

He got a distorted view of the Vietnamese character. He never really knew the farmer and the peasant in the field — the person he was killing most of the time.

What little indoctrination the American soldiers received was that they were in South Vietnam to fight the Communists because the South Vietnamese forces were incapable of doing so.

That was totally wrong, of course, because the South Vietnamese proved themselves very good fighters except they lacked assets like air support, helicopters and artillery that the Americans took for granted.

The Viet Cong guerillas didn't share this view. They knew when the Americans were coming — all they had to do was watch the helicopters coming like a swarm of flies. Underneath the helicopters were the Americans so they could literally run circles around them.

There is no doubt that the American commander-in chief in South Vietnam, General Westmoreland, was one of the most brilliant generals of modern times. He was a superb logistics expert, but as a tactician, fighting in Vietnam, he seemed completely at sea. He was fighting a conventional war on a massive scale, whereas the Viet Cong and North Vietnamese were running in and out of his hundreds of thousands of troops. He never could seem to locate them.

Although there were five hundred and fifty thousand American soldiers in South Vietnam at the height of the war, there were never more than eighty thousand actually fighting. There were ten non-combatant troops backing up each fighting soldier in the field. So it was easy for the Communists to sever their lines of communication, to cut their logistics, force them to resupply by air and then bottle them up and decimate them piece by piece in the mountains or the paddy fields.

The usual rifle used by the Americans was the M16, known to the Australian troops as the Armalite.

It was a very sophisticated weapon, high-velocity and hard-hitting. So much so, that if you were hit anywhere on your body by a round from an M16 you were either dead or very severely wounded.

But being so sophisticated, it had faults. Often it would jam for a number of reasons. It had to be kept very clean, and that was very difficult in the jungle or paddy fields, where soldiers might be up to their waists in mud and slush a lot of the time.

The Viet Cong and North Vietnamese used the Communist assault weapon the AK47, Russian-designed and Chinese-made. It was very reliable, but not as hard-hitting as the M16. Nor was it as accurate, but you didn't need accuracy in the type of warfare in South Vietnam. But it was easily kept in working order, and would keep working in the mud and slush and general wear of a tropical country, where the M16 didn't.

The M16 caused the death of many Americans.

I remember seeing one platoon of thirty-two men that had been wiped out. Nineteen of those soldiers were lying there with their weapons half stripped down or jammed, which meant that nineteen out of thirty-two men died without being able to offer any resistance.

The Communists had another advantage. They could use captured American ammunition, but the reverse was not possible.

The Communists used sixty-one-millimetre mortar, the Americans sixty-millimetre. So if the Americans captured enemy mortar bombs they would not fit down the tubes. On the other hand, the Communists could make use of the American ordnance.

The Americans actually employed a device called a 'people sniffer'. It was carried by helicopters or low-flying aircraft over jungle areas, and it responded to the exact body temperature of a man — ninety-eight point four degrees Fahrenheit [36.8°C].

But it didn't always work out. Many a time the Americans went scorching in with a bombing raid after the people sniffer had scented men — only to find they had wiped out a herd of water buffalos or a few elephants.

The Communists had a few technical tricks, too. The

Americans were very dependant on their thousands of helicopters, not only to move troops and supplies about, but to get their wounded to hospitals.

During the spring offensive of 1972, American helicopters became terribly vulnerable to a small heat-seeking rocket only a metre long, which could be carried and fired by an infantryman. If it were fired in the direction of a helicopter or a low-flying aircraft, it homed in on the heat of the exhaust.

It took a great toll for a while. Apart from the loss of life, most of the helicopters being downed were worth one and two million dollars each. The Americans had to think of something quickly, and they came up with what we called the 'stove boat'.

It looked like a country shack gone wrong, with a chimney stove arrangement which extended from the actual exhaust and took it out in an L to an S shape at the back of the helicopter.

They still got a nasty jolt in the helicopter because the rocket would still explode just outside, but it did the job for the time being.

Most civilian casualties in the field occurred in what the Americans and the South Vietnamese designated 'free fire zones'. These areas were categorised as being under Communist control, so everybody inside the zone was by definition a Communist or a sympathiser. They were therefore likely to be killed in the open, even if they were just farmers ploughing their rice fields. The Americans and the South Vietnamese had a so-called legal right to attack anything in that area by air, artillery or by any other means.

Many farmers and their families were killed in those free fire zones. They had nothing else — it was their home, their means of livelihood. If they left for a refugee camp it meant leaving land they had occupied for hundreds of years, as well as abandoning the graves of their ancestors. They didn't see any real reason why they should leave. No one likes living in a refugee camp, and they didn't consider themselves Communists. So they were targets, and thousands of Vietnamese civilians died in this way.

Davis was not surprised when the My Lai massacre was exposed, and the world suddenly had endless details about Lieutenant Calley's gunning down of unarmed, unprotected women and children.

Letter to Aunt Lillian, 5 December 1969
    Orange Grove Rd,
    Singapore

I am afraid the massacre story has almost completely destroyed the credibility of the Americans. In the past all I could do was to suggest that it wasn't only the Communists who perpetrated atrocities. But if I ever spoke too strongly — especially in Australia — I always came under suspicion of being a Communist myself.

Well, war itself is an atrocity and it is rarely just one side that is totally to blame. However, I feel sorry for the Americans because this has done them more harm than any peace demonstration back home could possibly do. They will never recover from it.

It is interesting to observe that the Vietnamese people themselves understand all this, and have more or less ignored the incident. They are aware that these things happen in war, and know that they always have. They are rather amazed to think that other people throughout the world haven't understood about that before now.

Napalm was a horrible weapon of war. Dropped in canisters from aircraft or helicopters, it spewed out jellied petroleum in obscene explosions of orange fire and jet-black smoke.

It sticks to your skin and burns straight through to the bone. Excruciatingly painful, and almost always fatal.

At the same time napalm consumes all the available oxygen in the surrounding air. So if it is dropped on top of bunkers which may be very well protected from the initial blast of all the jellied petroleum, the people below ground suffocate.

One of the most devastating sights I saw was after a napalm bombing raid when American advisers went into the area with South Vietnamese troops. There were a number of survivors, and a little old peasant woman came out with what I thought was the remains of a baby in her arms.

She walked right up to one of the American officers without saying a word, but deep hatred in her eyes, and threw a bundle at his feet.

It wasn't a baby, but the grotesquely burned carcase of her little pet dog which was all she had left.

Davis had strict rules about his own personal conduct when filming the ugly face of war. Always the impartial observer, he determined to keep his cameras rolling.

There's almost no situation in which I'd stop filming to do something, because I think a film record of a given situation is ultimately more effective, and has greater impact. In the end it helps more people than if I put down my camera to lend a hand.

I did stop filming once in Cambodia to help drag wounded soldiers behind a tree for safety, and was quite badly wounded myself. Had I kept filming, I might not have been injured.

Some unscrupulous cameramen encouraged soldiers to mistreat or even shoot prisoners for their cameras in tense and difficult situations. Once, after a savage action in the Vietnamese highlands, Davis came upon some South Vietnamese who had custody of three North Vietnamese regular troops, just captured. Seeing his camera, they cheerfully offered to shoot their prisoners. The film would have led television news bulletins all over the world. Davis just smiled and slowly put his camera down on the ground.

> They were probably shot later — but not because of any action of mine.

But on some occasions, Davis used his camera to alter the course of events. In 1970 he was with South Vietnamese troops inside Cambodia.

> There was a wounded civilian — a man. One of the soldiers went down on his knee to shoot him, and I got behind him with my camera to film, thinking that the very act of filming would stop him, and it did. He hesitated. I thought he might shoot me, actually! But he stopped, and did not kill that man.

Neil Davis guarded his impartiality jealously. He always said his sympathies were with the Vietnamese people, whether they were northerners, southerners, Communists or non-Communists.

> Sometimes in discussions, I'd find myself arguing for the South Vietnamese side, and at other times for the Viet Cong's stated position. Nothing is black or white.

On leave in Australia in 1972, Davis threatened to take legal action against a television station and newspaper that had published a story saying that in action he would put down his camera and fight Communism with an M16. He not only regarded this as professionally damaging but potentially lethal if he were captured by the Communists in Vietnam or Cambodia.

Although Vietnam has been called the first television

war, its horror was not at first apparent on the world's television screens. There were a number of reasons for this. In the mid-1960s colour television was relatively new to the United States, and it was not introduced to Australia until a few months before the end of the war. Blood loses its impact in black and white, and there was also a policy (not absolutely enforced) that American dead and wounded should not be shown on the screen.

The restrictions were laid down by the American government, and the television networks imposed self-censorship by greatly restricting the footage of American casualties. They didn't restrict film showing Vietnamese casualties.

I agreed with this to a certain extent, because it wasn't a good thing to have the wives and parents of Americans seeing their men dead on the screen. It could be the first they knew about them being involved in an action.

However, I did object in overall terms that the American public was denied the right — and it is a right — to see the worst aspect of the war, that large numbers of Americans were being killed and wounded every day. If more of that had been shown, the full horror of the Vietnam war would have been brought home to the American public much sooner.

One way this censorship could have been overcome, Davis argued, was for the film to be held up for several days until the relatives of the dead and wounded Americans had been informed, and then the footage screened.

It was a sad thing for those relatives, but a sadder thing that more and more American soldiers were killed in a war in which they should never have been involved in the first place.

Americans are very conservative in many ways. Many things will not be shown on American television that will be screened in England, Japan, or France, but the

Americans are much like the Australians in this sense, very conservative, particularly where their own people are concerned.

There wasn't as much blood shown on American television as on Japanese, British or European.

Letter to Aunt Lillian, 27 December 1968
Continental Palace Hotel,
Saigon

The Americans have not been pleased with me for some years, mainly because my films are now shown in many countries throughout the world, and they have not always been flattering to the Americans. It's just as simple as that, Auntie.

The Americans are quite Fascist in some ways, and very frightening . . .

Despite frigid relations with American military authorities in Saigon, Davis continued to be offered lucrative jobs with American television networks. The disadvantages from his point of view were that he would be a cameraman working with a reporter, and subject not only to the editorial direction of the reporter, but to the prevailing editorial policy on the war at head office — invariably American-oriented.

He valued his independence with Visnews, selecting, shooting and scripting his own assignments. He was also aware his footage was distributed to more than one hundred countries — some in the Communist bloc.

His own attitude to his work was uncompromising. He believed it was the journalist's and cameraman's job to bring truth to people. It was the primary professional obligation. His scripting and shot lists were always meticulous and he was profoundly irritated when the editing and rescripting of his material were less than adequate.

I was confident that Visnews wouldn't butcher my films. But no cameraman or correspondent is ever completely satisfied with the way someone else handles his stories. In overall terms, I was happy I worked for Visnews, and not for an individual television organisation or network.

What Australian viewers saw of the Vietnam war on their television screens — and Davis estimated that about 50 per cent of the film coming in would have been his Visnews coverage — was governed by a rather arbitrary system of censorship. In order for newsfilm to be allowed to come in quickly without going through the usual formalities of Customs and a censorship board, the news editors of each of the television networks and the Australian Broadcasting Commission were designated as official censors.

It was Davis's view that censorship was applied more rigidly under this scheme than if the film had been reviewed by the Commonwealth's Censorship Board. Jack Gulley, the ABC's newly appointed Director of Television News in 1967, remembers his incredulity when called into the office of the controller of news and told, 'Forget about objectivity, we are at war!'

Davis believed his Vietnam footage was cut much more drastically in Australia than anywhere else in the world.

You'd think it was a war without violence, that it was all sweetness and light. Just our Australian boys patrolling and keeping the dreaded Communists in check.

The hierarchy of the ABC's news department believed that news programmes were a family affair, and they didn't want the wife and kids watching blood and guts over seven o'clock dinner — even in black and white. Therefore Australian viewers were deprived of the right to see exactly what was happening in Vietnam, and many other parts of the world, for that matter.

Some of the censorship was crude. In 1966 ABC correspondent Tony Ferguson and an ABC film crew managed to get to Cambodia, then closed to the Western media. Ferguson was being driven along a Phnom Penh street by an Australian embassy diplomat when he did a double take. Australian journalist Wilfred Burchett was walking down the street. At the time Burchett was *persona non grata* with the Australian government, as he had reported the Korean and Vietnam wars from the Communist side. Often travelling in Communist countries closed to other Western journalists and denied a passport to return to his native land, Burchett was hated, admired, and he had extraordinary information.

Ferguson knew that Burchett had been in South Vietnam with the Viet Cong, hiding in their tunnel complexes while being strafed and bombed by American and South Vietnamese firepower. An exclusive interview with this enigmatic man would be of great interest in Australia. He asked his diplomatic chauffeur to stop the car. Burchett agreed to an interview and they made an appointment for the next day.

The interview went well and a delighted Ferguson cabled the ABC in Sydney that his Burchett footage had been despatched, and gave the usual flight and waybill details.

Meanwhile in Sydney, all hell broke loose. Burchett was regarded by many in Australia as a traitor — a view shared by the ABC's controller of news. He ordered the Burchett film to be destroyed on arrival. It never even made the processing lab.

During some home leave in 1967, Neil Davis was interviewed on ABC television in Melbourne about the way Vietnam war footage was being censored in Australia.

Letter to Aunt Lillian, 1 May 1967

It seems my personal fortunes are going up and down. The ABC is very angry about the interview I did in Melbourne. Apparently the General Manager, Mr Duckmanton, was watching it and immediately rang a senior news executive to ask was it so about the censorship. The man was caught off balance, and made the foolish blunder of saying outright, 'No'. Then an article appeared in the *Australian* newspaper quoting me.

So at the moment Duckmanton has taken the word of his senior news executive (as of course he should), but when it is pursued further this will not stand up. Anyway, I am right and they are wrong, so I'm not worrying at all.

The political repercussions of the drastic 1968 Tet offensive were felt worldwide when President Lyndon Johnson announced he would not seek a second term in office. The US started to pull American troops out of Vietnam, and Davis's company Visnews wanted to do the same with him.

Visnews believed that because the Americans were coming out, the war was over. I don't know why they thought that, because the war continued at exactly the same rate for another seven years. The only difference was that there were more South Vietnamese soldiers being killed to replace the Americans who weren't getting killed any more.

In September 1968, John Tulloh of Visnews visited Hong Kong and wrote to John Hartley, the managing editor in London, that something urgent had to be done about Davis to stop him being poached by the Americans. Tulloh suggested that Davis be made 'a bloody good offer as soon as possible'. It would, said Tulloh, be a savage blow to Visnews if they lost him.

Visnews executives in London felt that Davis had done enough, and it was time to move him back to head office for a spell, and then perhaps go to another posting in a less hazardous part of the world. John Hartley had also heard that Davis was suffering from back trouble and recalled him to London for talks on the Vietnam situation and for medical consultations. For Davis, a London winter was a severe culture shock.

Letter to Aunt Lillian, 19 January 1969
   White's Hotel,
   London.

   Well, I'm still cold! I think the English people are equally as cold in some ways. I didn't realise how accustomed to Asia I had become — or Tasmania too, I suppose. You know, I like to walk down the street and talk to people, and in Saigon and other Asian cities everybody is so happy (with so little) and always anxious to talk.
   Everybody here is in such a hurry, and doesn't have time or the inclination to worry about others. However, my company has been very good, and wined and dined me.

Davis thought he might have damaged his back in South Vietnam jumping from a helicopter. When the pilot told them he couldn't land because of enemy fire, Davis, in full kit, plunged two metres to the ground. Many years later the affected disc in his back collapsed completely and he was operated on in Bangkok. But in London in 1969, Harley Street specialists could find nothing wrong with him. They came up with an ingenious explanation. It was all in the mind. He was suffering from battle fatigue, a stress syndrome in which the nervous system reproduced pains in areas of old injuries or wounds, even though they had totally healed.

Letter to Aunt Lillian, 7 February 1969
   White's Hotel,
   London

   I won't be returning to Saigon until May at least . . . three doctors say I am suffering from 'battle fatigue' — which is a bit of a laugh. My bosses seemed a little

surprised and even disappointed when I didn't throw
a fit when they told me.

I won't be able to go near any fighting for three
months.

Davis resisted Visnews' efforts to move him from Asia,
negotiated a new contract and returned in 1969 on the
understanding he would not go back to Vietnam for three
months. By June he was back in Saigon and fully operational again. When Cambodia came into the war in 1970,
Indo-China was clearly going to stay the world's top story.
Davis continued to turn away offers from American television networks and stayed loyal to Visnews. But strains
developed in their relationship.

The operational difficulties of providing a newsfilm service from Asia, let alone from a war zone there, prompted
some queries on the efficiency of Davis's operations towards the end of 1969. It became apparent that head office
had very little understanding of the way he operated.

In November the editor of Visnews, Tony Whyte, wrote a
memo querying — among other things — the number of
assignments shot by Davis in the six months from 1 April
to 30 September, the costs incurred in that period, why he
had not worked from Singapore or Malaysia, and why his
excess baggage costs were so great.

In a further memo of 26 December 1969, the editor of the
day at Visnews, Peter Marshall, wrote that Davis seemed to
have become too remote from 'our prime objectives and
requirements'. He added what must be one of the great
understatements from a chairborne head office man: 'Obviously there are problems of communications, contacts,
security, etc. which we do not experience elsewhere.'

Davis's sharply argued nine-page response to Whyte's
queries left London in little doubt as to their man's dedication, operational efficiency and fieldcraft. But he was
obviously hurt by the implication that he was doing less
than his best. He detailed forty-three assignments carried

out in the six months under review. Here is one 'routine' assignment from that report.

ARVN Search VC cradle: FILMED 4-6 JULY 1969

The 'cradle' is the birthplace of the Viet Cóng, an area in the Mekong Delta where few troops still venture. It is alive with booby traps. It is totally VC. It is difficult and dangerous to even reach there, and obviously dangerous when one is there. Our opposition have never covered this area. The filming was actually done 4−6 July, but I left Saigon city at a little after 0600 on 3 July. Could only get to Can Tho in the Delta that day, where I received an up-to-date briefing on the area I was interested in. Before dawn the next day I left again and finally arrived at My Tho, the ARVN 7th Division HQ. Finally there I was able to get a jeep to Ben Tre (by road and ferry) through VC-controlled territory. From Ben Tre I hitched a ride on a chopper to the field, where a reconnaissance company of the Vietnamese 7th Division was operating. Reconnaissance companies in the Vietnam war mean those that precede a larger sweep in order to seek out and engage the enemy, then hold them off whilst the larger units can reinforce. I spent the night of 4 July in the field in Kien Hoa province — sometimes walking, sometimes catching a 'rest' in a swampy paddy field. From before dawn on 5 July till at least one hour after dark we operated non-stop through paddy fields and jungle, across streams, through VC villages — all studded with booby traps. I spent the night of 5 July the same as 4 July. On 6 July we started again (of course) before dawn, and I managed to get a chopper out at 0800. This was the first resupply since I landed — I carried food for the time spent in the jungle as always. By great good luck I managed to get three quick chopper rides and arrived back at Tan Son Nhut airport by 1000 — the fastest I can remember from the Delta. I did complete

shot lists and scripting immediately and managed to
'buy' (bribe) the package aboard an aircraft before noon.
I managed to get a shower by 1400. On 1−2 July I made
at least six different calls (in person) to obtain full
permission for this coverage. So besides 3−6 July out of
Saigon (and two nights in the jungle), at least several
hours were spent on this job on 1−2 July. We obtained
exclusive footage. Is this again a statistic? Would AHW
care to give his opinion on what he thinks might be a fair
thing to take off after this little jaunt? This is classed as
one job — so surely a little more attention can be paid to
circumstances. Oh, I took no time off. Those days just
become 'normal' working days.

A London-based Visnews man, Tom Hudson, visited the
Asian area at this time, and on his return weighed in with a
memo to Tony Whyte. It read:

'January 10, 1970
'I approached the region with the "attack" of a Europeanised
HQ mind — just couldn't see what the reasons were for
delays, non-arrival of film, communications unanswered,
transportation breakdowns, official obstinacy, mishandling
of freight, etc., etc., etc. I soon learned.

'It's *mañana* land ... I likened working there to trying
to run in the sea with water up around your neck. Sometimes you are held to a frustrating speed despite the effort
involved.'

Hudson graciously admitted that Neil had not become
remote from Visnews' prime objectives and requirements:
'generally speaking there is no such thing in Southeast Asia
as a straightfoward assignment'.

He concluded: 'I admit that my first reaction to Neil was
that we should remove him from this area and replace him.
On second thoughts I don't think this would be such a
good idea.

'His replacement would have to be a white, single, good-story-minded cameraman, a good technician, administrator, with unbounded patience and good humour, with an excellent knowledge and understanding of this peculiar area. My experience among his contemporaries leaves me with the distinct impression that Neil is apparently the best of those available.'

16

The Man Who Liked Everybody

By 1965, the Davis legend was already growing. Australian Broadcasting Commission correspondent Tony Ferguson admitted some prejudice before he met him. The stories sounded like grand-standing stuff, racing around the paddy fields and getting shot at. Ferguson thought Davis might be a bit of a larrikin, a cowboy. He was relieved to be disarmed when he met him in Saigon. Davis's unassuming friendliness made an immediately favourable impression.

The celebrated Korean cameraman Yosep (Joe) Lee also met Davis in 1965. Lee later worked for Visnews (and Davis) as a stringer. He says, 'I remember Neil as a kind person at my first glance.'

After a year of working together, the two became close friends.

'I can recall those days so easily. We used to go out for shooting pictures, and came back to look for restaurants to eat and find pretty women at the same time.

'We used to compete who can get this girl's attention first. Frankly speaking, it is always Neil is the one to catch her heart!'

Many and varied girls were caught, and as quickly released. Davis's instinct for a wager — on women as well as everything else — could cross the bounds of good taste, but the bets were always serious. During a night's carousing in Singapore, he and a fellow expatriate Tasmanian journalist waged US$50 (a considerable sum in 1965) on who would be the first to have sex with a nun.

Davis returned to South Vietnam and immediately went down to the Mekong Delta on assignment. He chanced on a Catholic orphanage and became friendly with a young Vietnamese nun. Very friendly indeed, as it happened, and he couldn't wait to get back to Singapore to claim his bet.

'I did it, boy — you owe me $50!' he announced.

His colleague was deeply suspicious.

'Was she a proper nun, then?'

'Of course!'

Davis was scrupulous in matters of honour. His fellow Tasmanian was silent for a moment.

'Name the order, then.'

Davis did so. Another silence.

'Well, did she have all the gear on? The robes and stuff?'

'Come off it, old fellow — it's the tropics. She was in civvies.'

'Doesn't count then. Doesn't count!'

He wouldn't pay up. Davis was outraged.

There were always wagers. Back in Singapore between assignments in 1969, Davis loved to play the Filipino dice game, *balut*, and he had an enormous win against Bill Pinwill, an Australian ABC correspondent. Pinwill couldn't pay so Davis arranged a deal. Pinwill would have to make a bed available to him — if necessary his own — under any circumstances anywhere in the world.

He was remorseless about this, and delighted in asserting his rights in hotels and apartments whenever he and Pinwill coincided. Davis tried to insist that whatever lady happened to be sharing Bill's bed was also part of the deal, but that remained an area of dispute. Several years later the dice fell differently during a mammoth Singapore *balut* session, and Pinwill won. Davis traded him his stereo gear, but refused to cancel the bed bet.

It was no small tribute to Davis's charm and personality that he remained a welcome guest at Singapore dinner tables presided over by the wives of colleagues. These forbearing women could only guess at the riotous bar and bordello expeditions he shared with their husbands during his periods of leave from Vietnam.

With so much war-generated awfulness assaulting their sensibilities day after day, the Indo-China press corps developed the 'joke method' to stay sane. Davis played that game to the full. ABC cinecameraman Derek McKendry recalls walking back with him one night to their hotel after an excellent French dinner. On Tu Do Street they passed a beggar who had been shockingly burned and disfigured by napalm, sitting against a shopfront. Davis stopped, gave the man some money and exchanged a few words in Vietnamese with him before rejoining McKendry and another journalist, one of the many 'quick story' visitors to Saigon.

McKendry remarked to Davis very seriously that the beggar was really the leader of the local Viet Cong cadre in deep cover, the master puppeteer who was pulling the strings and controlling all the VC forces within eighty kilometres from his vantage point on a Saigon pavement. He concluded by saying that if the CIA knew that Davis was contributing to the VC coffers, he would be in a lot of trouble.

Davis agreed with the flicker of a smile, but said that it was worth taking the risk because the beggar was one of his best sources and always told him where the VC were going to start a firefight the next day and he would go there to get a good story. All this, he said, for a few piastres.

McKendry glanced at the face of the visiting journalist and saw that he believed every word. The Davis legend was at work.

Although the Indo-China war claimed most of his professional attention, Davis did an enormous amount of travelling to keep up with the major stories of the region. His diary for 1969 records the travels of a fairly typical year.

January: Singapore, Copenhagen, London
February: London, Paris, Geneva, Bonn, Vienna, Berlin,

Rome, Tel Aviv, Singapore
March: Singapore, Hong Kong, Tokyo, Saigon
April: Singapore, Jakarta, Bangkok
May: Singapore, Jakarta, Kuala Lumpur, Bangkok
June: Singapore, Manila, Saigon
July: Saigon, Hong Kong, Manila, Bangkok
August: Bangkok, Vientiane
September: Vientiane, Saigon, Singapore
October: Hong Kong, Karachi, Manila
November: Saigon, Phnom Penh, Singapore
December: Saigon

His visit to Kuala Lumpur in May was to cover the extremely nasty race riots that threatened the fragile communal relationships between the Malays and Chinese.

Letter to Aunt Lillian, 22 May 1969
Federal Hotel,
Kuala Lumpur

I managed to get in on the last flight before they closed the airport. It has been really terrible. There is nothing worse than Chinese-Malay riots. 'Officially' about 170 have been killed, but it is obviously up over 300. There have been some terrible things, with Malay soldiers shooting Chinese in their own homes, and helping Malay mobs kill and loot in Chinese areas.

The Malaysian army and police are almost entirely Malay. Forty per cent of the people in Malaya are Chinese, and the Malays are afraid of them — mainly because the Chinese are a more clever, hard-working people. So now it is a Malay dictatorship, with a 'National Operations Council' taking over from the Government. So much for democracy.

The press is being suppressed, harassed and misinformed in every direction ...

A strict curfew was in force and the BBC's Brian Barron recalls that it was Davis who discovered that opposite the

ABC and Reuters office was a Chinese nightclub packed with charming and terrified Chinese hostesses who had been unable to leave the building for at least five days.

According to Barron, Davis skilfully ran several quick missions of reassurance. He brought the hostesses food and confidence and he took away cases of cold beer and an endless series of assignations with them, including a truly stunning singer from Hong Kong.

Barron reports that while Davis's efforts were certainly rewarded, he did help a group of people who were in a jam.

Davis and Barron were together again in November 1970 covering the aftermath of the cyclone and tidal waves that engulfed low-lying areas of East Pakistan before it became Bangladesh. The Pakistani government handled the disaster so ineptly that its callous incompetence was a major cause of the Bangladesh war of independence.

Letter to Aunt Lillian, 20 November 1970
Hotel Inter-Continental,
Dacca

. . . There is little I can say about the devastation here. It is just beyond description, and leaves one numb. The reports are comparatively conservative. Tonight's local newspapers carry the death figures — estimates really, because on dozens of smaller islands in the Bay of Bengal there is nobody alive to give an accurate description of what happened there. Or even how many people previously lived there.

But as one leading newspaper said tonight: 'Not a million, but *millions* are dead.'

Davis, one of the first into Dacca for this story, managed to inveigle himself onto the helicopter of Pakistan's president, Yahya Khan. His exclusive footage was bounced from satellites to screens around the world. But there were some amazing unrecorded scenes in the President's helicopter.

As Davis crouched and filmed against the shaking interior of the helicopter, Yahya Khan was downing a mountain of cold beers and bellowing orders to his luckless staff as they circled the disaster zone. The president, Davis told Barron, hadn't looked out of the window often. He was too busy opening cans and didn't bother to conceal his colonial-style contempt for the devastated Bengalis below.

Correspondents who knew Davis in the early years of covering Indo-China attest to his willingness to share information and give useful tips to his brother and sister correspondents — even if they were in direct competition. This was most unusual in a cut-throat business, with egos and deadlines usually fostering taut, tense relationships between rival media groups and individuals. Jim Bennett of the American ABC News network thought that Davis had worked so long and hard in developing a keen sense of how to cover combat that he did not want to see such expertise go to waste. He was just as helpful to the adrenalin-fringe freelance freaks as to the heavyweight 'names' of the major agencies and networks.

Korean Yosep (Joe) Lee was trained by Davis in the bizarre art of combat reporting, and Davis recommended him to Bennett for assignments in Cambodia. The three men became close, except for one thing. Davis had a real aversion to letting others join him in the field. He did not want the responsiblity for anyone else's life when the chance came to venture just a bit further than others might have dared.

Documentary film producer Jim Gerrand believes Neil Davis helped him to survive. Gerrand says Davis took people as he found them and shared without asking anything in return. That information was priceless in Cambodia where press casualties were higher than in Vietnam. The ferocity of the fighting and the lack of helicopter transport — coupled with the lackadaisical approach of Cambodian villagers giving guidance to impatient pressmen — could be a lethal mixture. Gerrand was once directed to an enemy mortar position by Lon Nol troops who honestly believed it was theirs.

In the early years of the Cambodian war, before the Khmer Rouge took over the main combat, the Lon Nol forces were actually fighting the Viet Cong and North Vietnamese. Davis told Gerrand to beware of the VC habit of booby-trapping corpses, and the very next week he saw Cambodian troops killed by a grenade-primed body.

Davis, Gerrand believed, took great pleasure from this generosity, and being able to earn the admiration of his peers and protégés.

Davis confirmed this.

I value friends and friendship above everything else — I never forget or forsake a friend.

A good friend of mine, Jack Langguth, who worked for the *New York Times* but who also wrote books of great depth and compassion on many subjects, once asked me my opinion about a certain politician in South Vietnam.

Before I could answer, he laughed and said, 'But it's no good asking you, because you like everybody.'

I took that as a compliment actually, because I do like everybody, or at least try to see their better side. I'm also always optimistic, and even on the battlefield when the situation looks hopeless, I will find kindred spirits everywhere. That's why I liked being with Cambodian troops. They laughed and joked in the face of adversity and then came up with militarily ridiculous plans which, because they were so crazy, often took the other side unawares and led to a miraculous escape.

Langguth also had reason to be grateful for Davis's field-craft. He had planned to enter Cambodia from Vietnam with the troops of one Vietnamese general.

'Never!' said Davis. 'But go with General Di. He'll get you in and out alive.' He did.

Fellow-Australian Don Simmons, who was in Saigon for the ABC when Davis first arrived, believed Davis saw himself as an Errol Flynn figure.

Simmons, a loner himself, shared his apartment with Davis in Saigon for a month in 1965 while they went into the field covering combat. They passed like ships in the night, Simmons remembers. He did not feel he ever really understood or knew Davis. He believed Davis was afraid of people knowing him too well and did not encourage intimacy above a superficial level. There was a personal space around him which could not be breached.

Davis's dress sense could at best be described as execrable — he was partial to powder-blue shirts with white piping around the collars and pockets, alternating with repulsively garish tropical shirts of the sort worn only by American ten-pin bowling teams on tour or by Cuban hoods in Miami. A penchant for brown suede boots stayed with him all his life, and in later years he affected bright red socks to bridge the gap between suede boots and trousers in varying pastel shades. Gary Burns of Visnews swore Davis must have been colour blind. There might have been an element of inverse snobbery, too. Taken to an exclusive London club once by the managing director of Visnews, he turned up in a sports coat, skivvy — and brown desert boots.

But on the field of battle, Davis gave away the Hawaiian shirts and red socks to blend in with his surroundings.

In South Vietnam it was army fatigues, because the military was generally well outfitted. When I went with the Viet Cong a couple of times, I wore a black shirt as they did, like most of their cadre and guerilla soldiers. In Cambodia I wore a mix of military and civilian clothes, because few Cambodian soldiers had a complete uniform. I dressed for my surroundings — with a green floppy bush hat, favoured by the Australian troops, to cover my blond hair which made an inviting target.

My motto was: blend in with your surroundings and you'll live longer.

But his pathological inability to resist a wager often shortened those odds. On one occasion he went up to Da Nang in the north of South Vietnam to film a story on the Australian Army Training Team. These men were all warrant officers and most were also trained as paratroopers. They received extra pay for this, but had to do a certain number of jumps per year to maintain their rating.

During a solid night's drinking some of the WOs bemoaned the fact they would have to be up at five the next morning for a parachute jump. Davis unwisely said, 'Fancy getting money for that! Anyone can fall out of an aeroplane.'

One thing led to another and he accepted a bet to jump with them. At 5 a.m. he was hungover and scared witless, but he went through with it not only for his own honour, but the reputation of journalists generally.

All the country around Da Nang was crawling with
Communist troops, and I'd never parachuted in my life.
They strapped a parachute on me, and gave very
rudimentary instructions of what to pull when I got clear
of the plane, and pushed me out.

I thought I'd broken my leg when I hit the ground.

Getting on an aircraft at Saigon's Tan Son Nhut airport on 1 November 1968 proved equally hazardous. Davis was to fly to Phnom Penh to meet Tony Ferguson for an assignment. Taken in for questioning by the Vietnamese police at the airport, he was interrogated about currency violations and black market operations.

Davis was carrying a wad of undeclared US dollars at the time and operated on the black market, as most did in those days. (In fact he had an Indian money changer called Dema conveniently operating from a broom-cupboard-sized room in the Visnews Saigon office.)

He was taken to a room, where two civilian Americans appeared and began questioning him at length about the origins of his currency deals. The plane left without him and the questioning became not only insistent, but accompanied by violence. Unwisely, he got a bit cheeky with them and said, 'All right, all right — I'll tell you where I'm buying it.'

The two Americans huddled closer to him and said, 'Yes, yes,' expectantly.

Davis lowered his voice and muttered, 'From Robert W. Komer.'

Komer was the senior American official enthusiastically in charge of the pacification program WHAMMO — Winning the Hearts and Minds of the People.

At this, the Americans really whaled into him with fists and boots, and things were not looking at all good. They left him alone for a while, and Davis later told Tony Ferguson in Phnom Penh that he had not been at all sure how he would get out of it.

He was left in the care of Vietnamese security officers, one of whom, it turned out, had a brother in an ARVN unit Davis had just filmed in the Mekong Delta region south of Saigon. Davis was able to tell the security guard that his brother was happy and well and doing a magnificent job for his country!

The guard conferred outside the room with the two Americans and shortly afterward Davis was allowed to return to his hotel — with instructions not to try to leave the country.

He told an influential American journalist what had happened, and the journalist demanded a meeting with the American ambassador, Ellsworth Bunker. The American's simple message was that if such crude assaults on journalists did not stop immediately, he and other pressmen would publish a list of all the American officials whom they knew were dealing on the black market.

Bunker ordered an investigation, and it was discovered the two Americans who had beaten Davis were not US officials but standover men in league with some corrupt Vietnamese police, running an extortion racket over currency dealers.

Economic necessity made dealing on the black market normal practice. ABC correspondent Jim Revitt cannot recall why Davis let Dema the Indian money changer operate in the Visnews office. It was certainly convenient for visiting correspondents who needed his services, but in a city that lived on its nerves, Dema lived on the edge of a nervous collapse.

Dema certainly faced the confiscation of his funds and a prison term if he were caught in his currency deals — a fate that Davis often predicted with devilish glee. He would sometimes make a huge commotion, coming back to the office, shouting in Vietnamese and kicking the door before bursting in on the petrified Indian.

Revitt said Dema never had the personality for money changing. Every deal with visiting journalists used to send him white with fear. One day, Jim Revitt recalls, Davis came back from a field assignment with an excellent captured Viet Cong flag — a highly marketable item among American officers. The sight of the flag sent Dema into a frenzy of fear.

His state of mind was not improved when Davis announced his intention not of selling the flag but of displaying it on the office wall.

'Oh no, that is not a very good idea, Mr Neil,' stuttered Dema, visibly paling. 'More better you sell it to some American colonel.'

Davis thought for a minute and said, 'Well, if we've got to sell it, we've got to advertise. I'm going to hang it out the window.'

Revitt was relatively unconcerned, knowing Davis's habit of teasing Dema. Outside in the street were dozens of armed troops and police and dozens of notoriously trigger-happy guards in front of a building directly across the street. There was no way, he thought, that Davis would actually do it.

Davis attached the Viet Cong flag to the windowsill with sticky tape and flung it out. Revitt was stunned, but only momentarily. He collided with the terrified money changer as they dived forward to pull the flag in, while Davis collapsed on the floor helpless with laughter.

'Got you, Revitt,' he said. 'I figured you'd be just as scared as Dema when the crunch came.'

A visit to the 'Bank of India' (as Dema's modest operation became known to the cognoscenti) was more than a simple exchange of greenbacks into piastres. In the first place, the actual black market rate was usually a good indication of how the Allied war effort was going — the piastre would plunge in direct relationship to the state of health of the South Vietnamese government. The Tet offensive in 1968 caused a giant leap in the value of the US dollar.

Bill Pinwill remembers Dema gravely discussing the latest government reverses as his fingers sped expertly over his calculator. If the client queried the rate, alleging a better deal from a rival money changer down the street, Dema would often hold a muttered phone conversation with some mysterious overlord.

It was widely believed among the press corps that the ultimate destination of the dollar bills so changing hands was Peking, via Saigon's Chinese quarter in Cholon and Hong Kong. This posed an ethical problem for some in that they might be helping to provide hard currency for Red China, the Viet Cong's principal backer and supplier of arms.

Another theory was that the CIA actually manipulated the currency black market. But such moral dilemmas did not greatly concern most foreign correspondents patronising the 'Bank of India'. They considered they were entitled to a little profiteering as a return for the risks and discomfort they encountered in Vietnam.

Although Davis had a live-in black market currency dealer,

he did not make a habit of boosting his expenses for personal gain. In a war situation, most correspondents loaded things up a bit, but Davis's diaries record his expenses accurately and fairly. That he was always a straight shooter on expenses is confirmed by Bruce MacDonell, NBC's Asian manager, for whom Davis worked in the post-Vietnam years. 'If he paid a dollar fifty to a bellboy to move his equipment, he could easily have put down — as everybody else did — twenty dollars. He always put down the dollar fifty. He just had no time for that kind of petty dishonesty.'

What Davis did with money he saved he revealed only to Aunt Lillian.

Letter to Aunt Lillian, 11 November 1968
  Hotel Monorom,
  Phnom Penh

I gave $4000 to help war victims and orphans in Vietnam. I found somewhere I could be sure that it really would help. I suppose many would say it was silly — but there you are. I felt like doing it, and I did it. Strange twist was that when I arrived in Cambodia and got my mail, there was a letter from a friend in Tasmania to say that the legal firm which handles my investments is really down the financial drain, and my money is as good as lost. So now I'm back to square one, I suppose.

It is a bit of a blow, but I reasoned fairly quickly that I had the choice of jumping from the nearest high building or accepting fate with a laugh. I wasn't about to jump, but the funny side took a lot of seeing!

It did indeed. Until 1968 Davis had invested his savings in property in Tasmania, through the legal firm that collapsed in that year. But as he later told Aunt Lillian:

I'm afraid I don't keep my money very long, anyway. I have lots of Vietnamese friends here, and just a few dollars can make a tremendous difference to them.

One thing about the Vietnamese is that they accept gifts graciously and with genuine affection and don't mess things up with false pride. So ... I don't have much money, but lots of friends, and I am glad to say they were friends before I was able to help them out financially.

Most journalists and cameramen in Saigon forced themselves to ignore the beggars and street children hustling a living on the pavements of downtown Saigon. Davis could not.

Letter to Aunt Lillian, 28 January 1969
  White's Hotel,
  London

I've had a letter from the Vietnamese girl who runs the Visnews office for me in Saigon. She said all the children of the streets keep coming up to the office and asking when I was coming back. They are the waifs who have been living on the streets as beggars, thieves, salesmen — anything at all — since they were very young. Nearly all are orphaned by the war.

They are great kids, although when we all go riding in my jeep it becomes a handful. We seem to arrive back with all sorts of bounty! Rather unnerving with all the police around ... however, even they understand rather well. Traffic is so congested there that the kids take advantage of the traffic jams to relieve unwary commuters of anything loose ...

One of the street children was a little girl with a hauntingly beautiful face who used to hawk a tray of cigarettes around the streets balancing expertly on one crutch — her other hand supporting her meagre wares. Her right leg was withered and bent back and around, a pathetic flap of useless flesh.

On 19 November 1969, Neil sent Aunt Lillian the newspaper clipping reproduced on page 209.

Only Aunt Lillian knew that Neil had brought Tran Thai Sa to the attention of the Terre des Hommes and helped to finance her journey to Germany for a series of operations.

Letter to Aunt Lillian, 12 December 1969
  Orange Grove Rd,
  Singapore

  Well, the little girl with the leg was injured in an explosion (I think) when she was very tiny — maybe about three I think. It withered and never grew from then on. I was amazed that they said they could rejuvenate it, because it's exactly similar to the useless limbs you have probably seen many times as a result of polio many years ago, before Sister Kenny's methods changed things . . .

One year later, little Tran Thai Sa was mentioned again.

Letter to Aunt Lillian, 7 December 1970
  The Oriental Hotel,
  Bangkok

  A great surprise awaited me in Saigon, as the little crippled girl had returned. She has an extra high boot, but the leg is no longer withered. It's still smaller than the other and always will be, but it is much stronger.

  She now walks without crutches, and when she learns to handle the boot better, it will be difficult to know the leg is not normal — particularly with the Vietnamese national dress, which has long silk pantaloons underneath and a light flowing sort of cheong-sam over the top. It completely covers the legs.

Aunt Lillian must have asked for more details.

Operation Saves Tot From Saigon . . .

FRANKFURT/SAIGON — Eleven-year-old Tran Thai Sa is just one of Saigon's numberless cigaret vendors.

But, unlike most of the other preteen tots who make their livings hawking "smokes" to GIs, Sa gets around on one good leg and a crutch. Her right leg is withered and practically useless.

After years of limping through war-torn streets, Sa came to the attention of Terre des Hommes, a Swiss charitable organization. The group agreed to send her halfway around the world — to Frankfurt, Germany — to have her crippled leg mended.

The tiny, black-eyed, black-haired girl arrived in the orthopedic clinic at the City hospital in Hoechst, a Frankfurt suburb, on July 4. On July 22 doctors operated, then put her shriveled leg in a cast. Doctors hope a series of operations plus the cast will straighten out the leg.

Apparently Sa became confused while in the hospital. She wrote home and told her parents that in the second operation, scheduled in three or four months, her "bad" leg would be amputated.

"She has it all wrong," the clinic's chief, Dr. Wolfgang Bechtold, said, "we certainly aren't going to cut her leg off. After the second operation she will be able to walk and run on her own with both of her own legs."

Sa limped way through Saigon.

Now leg is being straightened.

Letter to Aunt Lillian, 9 January 1971
Visnews Office,
Singapore

The little girl in Saigon is well. It's remarkable when one sees her leg. It's still in a brace — and probably will be for most of her life — but it's practically the same size as the other. Before it was just a withered, tiny little flapping piece of — almost nothing.

No, she doesn't know that I helped her much. She only knows I helped arrange for doctors to look at her. I don't think it really matters that she doesn't know. Probably better otherwise. We are just friends, as I am with the rest of her family. So if they are genuinely pleased to see me, then I don't have to wonder if it might be partly because I gave them money, or helped in some other way.

17

With the Viet Cong

Letter to Aunt Lillian, 1 March 1973

Goodwood Park Hotel,
Singapore

I wasn't able to tell you by letter from Saigon that I spent some time in South Vietnam with the Viet Cong. And that was really strange! Especially when a South Vietnamese helicopter sighted us and attacked.

So I was in the very peculiar position of crouching in a bunker with five VC soldiers, whilst my friends above did their darndest to wipe us out. However it was intensely interesting, to say the least.

Filming the Viet Cong had been a long-term goal, but it was not practical in the early years of the war. But following the Paris peace talks and the involvement of the International Control Commission, it was politically desirable for the Viet Cong to show the world that they had areas of South Vietnam under their flag and control. Fighting was still going on, of course, and Davis knew that the South Vietnamese government would do all they could to stop foreign correspondents giving a propaganda advantage to the enemy.

I wanted to film the other side in action, to hear what they had to say, to see how they lived, and to see the response they got from the people they were living with and fighting for. I did the same thing continually with the South Vietnamese, and I had sympathy with both groups. Each was fighting for their people, yet were ideologically diametrically opposed. That is the sad thing about any civil war.

To make contact with the Viet Cong, Davis had to find a reliable double agent. He knew that the Communists had such agents all through the South Vietnamese army and civil bureaucracy — and the Viet Cong later admitted that their districts and institutions were well penetrated by government agents.

I finally made contact with a double agent who happened to be a sergeant interpreter for an American major in the Mekong Delta. Paradoxically he was a trustworthy double agent.

To complete this *Alice Through The Looking Glass* world of spy and counter-spy, the American major was well aware that his sergeant was a double agent — a fact Davis discovered after some delicate verbal fencing with the major over his wish to film with the Viet Cong.

Finally the major said, 'Perhaps you should talk to my sergeant.' I admitted I already had, and the American said, 'OK, stick with him, he'll get you there.'

I said, 'Don't you worry about this?'

'Oh, no,' said the major. 'He's a complete double agent and he's useful to both of us.'

I found out that the sergeant knew the major was aware of his role, but they never mentioned it. The major wasn't afraid for his life because he saw that the link was necessary. The sergeant respected the American as a good man, and used his influence with the VC to stop him being killed. Of course the Viet Cong didn't really want him there, but they didn't kill him either.

The sergeant told Davis to drive his jeep along a certain stretch of Highway Four and look out for an old man, who would hail him for a lift.

I had to meet him at eleven a.m. near a bridge. He was a nice old man of about seventy who looked a bit like Ho Chi Minh — with a little wispy beard. We drove up and down the road for about half an hour discussing the situation and my credentials. They knew who I was, and he said they had checked me out.

I said, 'How could you check me out?' The old man said, 'Through the Ministry of Information in Saigon. We have our people working there, too.' And of course they did.

Davis met the old man on three occasions, and was asked all kinds of leading questions. One was: What would you do if you were bombed?

It was a pertinent question. The Americans were using massive pattern bombing by B52 aircraft which flew from Guam. The Vietnamese called the giant bombers the 'Whispering Death', because they were so high they could not even be seen from the ground. Each B52 carried 30 tonnes of bombs and they flew in an arrow formation. Thirty or forty aircraft could drop their loads simultaneously.

The first thing the Viet Cong would know was that they were being obliterated. The carpet bombing was incredibly accurate, and a mixture of bombs were dropped. High-explosive bombs were meant to shatter deep bunkers as shock waves surged through the ground. Cluster bombs were detonated at treetop level, spewing out tens of thousands of tiny needle-sharp fragments of shrapnel that could riddle your body and tear you to pieces.

Also included in the mix were phosphorus bombs which not only set fire to everything on top of the ground, but burned up all the oxygen in the air. People on or below the ground who might have survived the high explosive and cluster bombs were suffocated.

But the blast killed most people. It ruptured everything inside, and blood poured from every orifice. You can imagine the tremendous blast created by fifty to one hundred bombs dropping within the space of a few seconds over a limited area. It was just devastating, and sounded like rolling thunder from a distance. The Americans called it 'arclighting'. 'We'll arclight them,' they would say.

Afterwards the ground was intersected by overlapping craters two metres deep and five metres across, and it was like walking over a giant pockmarked face.

It is very difficult to imagine that anyone lived after being pounded by the B52s, but in fact they did. The Viet Cong told me that they would come out of their bunkers and lie on top of the ground, because the shock waves would kill them inside. On top, it flowed over them 'like the sea', and it was possible to survive.

Davis was more apprehensive about the B52 strikes than about his reception by the Viet Cong. He discussed this with the American major, who said he could guarantee to hold off the B52s for three days, because he was the senior adviser in that area of the Mekong Delta and the raids were mounted on his advice. However, there was also the possibility of being attacked by South Vietnamese helicopter gunships. That could not be ruled out, but Davis decided to take the risk.

From an arranged entry point on Highway Four, about eighty kilometres southwest of Saigon, Davis began the walk that would briefly convert enemy to ally. Practising the Vietnamese phrase for 'liberated area', he crossed the paddy fields and entered light jungle.

I field tested this phrase on the first Vietnamese farmer I saw and he pointed to a line of trees. I walked straight in and came to a crossroads on the jungle path. A young man there just nodded in the direction I had to go.

The rendezvous was in a small jungle clearing over which flew a Viet Cong flag, and where several serious young soldiers were waiting. It was a tense moment, not helped when some small boys raced up to me, pointed dramatically at the soldiers shouting, 'Vee Cee! Vee Cee!'

I was stunned. 'VC' is a derogatory expression coined by the Americans, meaning roughly 'Vietnamese Commie'. The soldiers' reaction was to laugh delightedly. It broke the tension, and they embraced me in welcome. An old man came forward with an outstretched hand and said, 'Welcome to the liberated area.'

The old man led me to a rickety sampan, and a boy took the paddle to pull us further into the 'liberated area'. All along the river bank, the Viet Cong flag — a yellow star on a blue and red background — fluttered from the houses and huts. 'Nothing to liberate here,' said the old man, and smiled.

We were still only a few kilometres from the busy highway running to Saigon.

Stepping from the sampan, Davis was met by an older French-speaking Vietnamese who was the leader of the village, and assigned to stay with him the whole time he was with the Viet Cong, or National Liberation Front as they called themselves.

None of the soldiers I saw wore the legendary black pyjamas. Most wore tattered black trousers and blue shirts and looked the hard-working sons of farmers. Some had captured American M16 rifles, but most carried Russian or Chinese made AK47 rifles which stood up better in the rough conditions of guerilla warfare.

The soldiers crowded round Davis with all kinds of questions. Why was he not married if he was over thirty? Many of the Liberation Front soldiers much younger than Neil boasted families of seven or eight children. But some of these were the adopted children of captured or killed comrades.

The soldiers posed with fierce expressions as I shot film, but invariably broke into laughter as the children shouted at them.

Everyone wanted to offer tea to the foreign newsman, and Davis drank at least thirty scalding cups of green tea in the next five hours.

During the twenty-four hours he spent with the Viet Cong, he was taken deeper into the jungle, where he visited a number of villages. But Davis was very sensitive to anything in the air because he had had no experience in handling such an attack. About 5 p.m. that afternoon, his fears were realised.

There was a village meeting going on, and I saw a helicopter pass over, flying high. I could see it was a gunship, which had banks of machine guns mounted four by four, which could spew out six thousand rounds a minute in a pattern. It was death to anybody on the ground if you were caught in it.

The soldiers didn't take any notice of the helicopter when it went over, but I did . . . I didn't like it at all. It went on and almost disappeared. Then it turned and I realised it was coming back again.

This time everybody went quiet, and sort of slunk back into the shadows, and they said, 'Careful — we have to watch,' and they told me they thought he was going to attack. This was their instinct. They didn't take any notice the first time, but as it was on its way back they had a clear premonition that the pilot in the helicopter had seen something on the way over and was coming back to check them out. And their instinct was absolutely right, because as he appeared to be going

216

past, the pilot suddenly banked and went into a dive, and I could see he was going to strafe.

Even as the helicopter started to tip, the Viet Cong shouted '*Di, di mau!*' ['Go, go quickly!'] and we all fanned out, running out in a 360-degree radius. By the time the helicopter started to strafe — he could only pick one area — we were in bunkers in the jungle.

The pilot had picked a building in a clearing to attack and some were killed and wounded in that area before they could get to the bunkers. The gunship strafed up and down for half an hour, while I crouched in a bunker with saplings on top of it, with five Viet Cong soldiers. I thought, my God, this is the way I'm going to die, at the hands of the South Vietnamese people. I have spent nine years with them and now they are doing their best to blow me away right now.

When Davis emerged, the jungle was stripped. Leaves were hanging in shreds, and trees had been almost cut in half by swathe after swathe of gunfire.

I wanted to get the hell out of there very fast. But they said, 'Never mind, we've got a few minutes, and then we'll trot off.'

Fortunately I was very fit. They jogged off like long-distance runners. We went through a very complicated minefield. The soldier with me said to follow him exactly, but I had that habit anyway, after moving through the countryside with government soldiers, knowing that there were mines and booby traps everywhere.

Davis was impressed that the Viet Cong soldiers regarded the South Vietnamese soldiers as easily their hardest opponents on the other side. They did not regard the American troops as being terribly difficult to defeat or elude.

In fact, during our run they said we must be careful of the South Vietnamese commandos, because they sometimes came in to a situation like this, and they were difficult opponents.

Each time the soldiers came to a hut they whistled a bird call and waited for an answer before going on, to guard against a possible ambush from the commandos. From a vantage point two kilometres away they watched an air strike on the area they had just left. Davis asked why they were not in much of a hurry to leave the spot when they could have been caught in the air strike. The Viet Cong soldiers laughed. 'No no,' they said, 'surely you know the system. To get an air strike, that helicopter pilot has to report to his commanding officer, and the commanding officer then has to go through the area commander, and he has to get the province chief's approval for a strike. That gives us plenty of time.'

They did admit to Davis that it came five minutes earlier than anticipated. As they watched, the fighter bombers devastated the bunkers they had just left. It was highly probable that the South Vietnamese authorities knew he was in the area.

The Viet Cong themselves conceded that, and warned that within twenty-four hours the South Vietnamese would not only know that Davis was with them, but exactly where. They weren't surprised when the group was attacked. The South Vietnamese government was not keen for correspondents to get to the Viet Cong. If correspondents were killed while doing so, the South Vietnamese could not be held responsible because it was an ongoing war, and it might discourage other journalists from doing the same thing.

I don't think they wanted to kill me. I got on very well with the South Vietnamese, and even after they found I had been out with the VC, they didn't hold it against me personally. The knew it was my job, what I had to do. But they didn't want to encourage journalists either, and

the easiest way to discourage them was to attack the
areas where they were known to be.

In the early stages Davis kept asking if he could film this or
that and the Viet Cong told him he could film anything he
liked.

But after the attack by the helicopter gunship I could
see some dead and wounded, and they were adamant I
could not film that. There was no debate about it, it was
simply not to be done. I don't know whether it was
because they didn't want to be seen taking casualties, or
whether it offended their sensibilities.

Crossing back to the South Vietnamese side was far more
difficult than getting to the Viet Cong. Davis also knew that
his chances of getting his film back to Saigon were fairly
slim — and without the film, the whole operation would
have been a waste of time. The Viet Cong told him that
government agents in the villages would have already
reported his presence, and that the authorities would be on
the lookout for him.

I asked if they could take me by another route, and
they said only if I had another week to walk a further
hundred kilometres. There was nothing for it, I had to
take my chance.
The Viet Cong soldiers said they would take me to
within a kilometre of Highway Four, and then a group of
children would take me the rest of the way. There were
a group of ten- and twelve-year-olds from the VC area,
who skipped and played around me as a kind of cover as
we entered a South Vietnamese government-controlled
village.

No more than fifteen minutes after Davis reached Highway
Four, he was arrested by South Vietnamese troops and
taken to a nearby town. He had no way of knowing whether

the events that followed were just lucky or whether they were planned.

I was taken to an army captain who happened to be a friend of mine. I certainly didn't know where his political sympathies lay. He asked me where I had come from, and I said Saigon.

He said, 'Well, you are very dirty and unshaven, I think you have come from somewhere else.' I kept insisting that I had come from Saigon that morning. Then he said, 'I've got to go out and do some business in my other office, and I will be away from this room for at least five minutes. You will be alone during that time. While I'm away I'd like you to get your film together ready to give to me, because higher command has ordered it to be handed over.'

Of course, that was deliberate. He went out and closed the door, and I got my exposed film and strapped it to the insides of my legs. If I had been searched, it would have been found immediately.

The captain came back and said, 'Now have you got all your film?' I said yes, and gave him all the unexposed film and cassette tapes that had not been used. He gave me a receipt, and said, 'You won't be searched again, because of this receipt. If they ask you about your film, just show it to them. You are now about to be taken for interrogation.'

Davis could not have known whether the captain was protecting him out of friendliness or whether he was also a double agent. After the war, it was revealed that many middle-ranking ARVN officers were Viet Cong.

The interrogation was much tougher, and went on for eight hours.

Eventually I saw that I was going to be kept overnight, and that's what I didn't want at all — some nasty things can happen to you. So I said I had to get back to Saigon to report to my embassy, who knew that I had come into the countryside and would be expecting me. The ruse worked, and the commander didn't really know what to do because he was not anxious to make trouble with the embassy of an ally of South Vietnam. He let me go, and I was able to get my story out, including the helicopter gunship attack on the Viet Cong.

Back in Saigon, Davis quickly shipped his film out of the country to London and took stock of the situation.

I came away with the feeling that the Viet Cong did represent the people — but no more than most of the South Vietnamese did. Both sides wanted the same things — independence, freedom and peace. But the big powers were pushing both sides for an ideological victory: Communism versus so-called democracy. If they'd been allowed to settle their own differences way back, after World War II, the war in South Vietnam would almost certainly not have come to pass. They would have evolved and created an independent national government. Perhaps it would have been left-wing, Communist if you like. But nobody criticises a country like Yugoslavia much.

The foray with the Viet Cong was an enormous personal triumph. The film was circulated to more than one hundred countries and Visnews allowed Davis to write and publish the story widely.

By his actions, he had demonstrated the complexity and confusion of the war. To see the conflict as one people attacked by rapacious and ideologically misguided foreigners was one of the most absurd simplifications imposed on a situation of sporadic and terrible violence. Good or frightened Vietnamese all had to keep their options open; they had responsibilities to families and they could not foresee the future.

Letter to Aunt Lillian, 14 February 1973
Continental Palace Hotel,
Saigon

I have had some interesting times lately — a bit different from everything else I've ever done here. Will tell you about it when I write from elsewhere . . .

I had a byline story in the *New York Times* last week, which is all a bit strange, as American journalists strive for that. It seems their ultimate aim.

18

Death
is a Lady

If Neil Davis is reincarnated, there is little doubt he will be a Cambodian. As one American journalist said, 'Every correspondent should fall in love with a country.' Davis fell in love with Cambodia and Cambodians, and from 1970 until Cambodia fell to the Khmer Rouge forces in April 1975, he spent his happiest and most eventful days there. He always hoped that one day he could return to Cambodia to live.

The Cambodians were what remained of one of the greatest empires in the world, the Khmer empire, and reigned supreme in Asia for about six hundred years. It was like the rise and fall of the Roman empire in some ways, great periods of architecture and culture, but also periods of war. They took on Buddhism, and came to a compromise with life that I think was admirable. They weren't aggressive, their society was rural-based, and the balance between the rulers — the monarchy of Cambodia — and the people was also admirable. They had a good relationship with the French, who had been more or less the colonial masters.

I had an enormous admiration for the Cambodians, their outlook and their courage. They were also a fun people, who always made the best of things, always saw the humorous side, and were very hospitable and kind, to me — and all foreigners.

Davis was captivated by Cambodia on his first visit to cover the country's independence celebrations in November 1964. He took some superb footage of the Angkor ruins, and Visnews (on his advice) sent a copy of the footage to the Cambodian head of state, Prince Sihanouk. The prince, a man of many talents, was also a film buff. As he tried to keep Cambodia apart from the Indo-Chinese conflict, Sihanouk took an anti-Western stance, but from this time, Davis usually managed to get Cambodian visas by appealing directly to the prince.

During his 1964 visit, he also made contact with the Australian journalist Wilfred Burchett. Davis got on well with Burchett, and regarded him as a superb source of information through his close contacts with the North Vietnamese and Viet Cong. In return, Davis taught Burchett how to use a cinecamera and encouraged him to get the first television coverage of the Viet Cong in action. Through Davis, Burchett sold his footage to Visnews and later to CBS.

This friendship with the idiosyncratic Burchett once saved Davis's life under extraordinary circumstances. Burchett, although not a young man, made several forays into South Vietnam with the Viet Cong, sometimes hiding in tunnels from bombing raids and artillery strikes. During one of their Phnom Penh meetings, he told Davis he had seen him on an ARVN patrol in the Mekong Delta region on such-and-such a date. Burchett said his NLF unit was hiding in the village that Davis's patrol was passing through. The Communists had planned an ambush, but Burchett, recognising Davis, convinced them not to shoot.

Davis thought it was too good a story to be true. The odds of the two Australians attached to enemy armies meeting in the thousands of kilometres of South Vietnam were greater than a million to one. But Burchett told Davis to check his diary, and named the village and the time. It all checked. Davis later told this as a funny story, but it had obviously shaken him.

In August 1966 France's President de Gaulle visited Cambodia and Davis was granted a visa. It was a visit that de Gaulle, Sihanouk and Davis would remember for a long time. Things did not start well with a water pageant laid on for the French president, during which a flotilla of royal barges were to row past a saluting point. Davis was having some difficulty in fitting the almost-two-metres-tall de Gaulle in the same frame as the short, rather tubby Prince.

Prince Sihanouk told de Gaulle that he would now see an exhibition of rowing a royal barge.

The boat crew were trying a bit too hard, and taking quite a lot of water on board. As they got right up to the official dais, they were all supposed to raise their paddles in salute . . . but the boat just sank. Suddenly there were all these guys in gold helmets, Cambodian silk stockings and traditional dress floundering around in the water.

All I could see through the viewfinder was de Gaulle's huge nose, which had been inclined up to take the salute, come slowly down to take in what had happened, point across to look at Sihanouk, and then go back up into an elevated position. De Gaulle seemed unimpressed with Cambodia and Cambodian organisation.

Fresh embarrassments lay ahead. Prince Sihanouk had organised a sound and light show at Angkor Wat to re-enact a great historical battle. Elaborate lighting and sound effects were prepared, and forty elephants were standing by for the battle scene. Two thrones were set up near the stage for the two heads of state.

Davis said it looked fantastic, enclosed by the jungle,

225

Angkor Wat behind, with lights, elephants and hundreds of soldiers with bows and arrows, spears and swords, re-enacting the battle.

In the middle of it all the lights failed. All I could hear was the trumpeting of frightened elephants cantering about on the stage, and Prince Sihanouk's high-pitched nervous giggle saying, 'He, he, he, mon President, are you still there?'

Davis kept his camera running through the entire blackout in case he had an international incident on his hands when the lights came back on.

Letter to Aunt Lillian, 6 September 1966
Manohra Hotel,
Bangkok

Things finally turned out well in Cambodia, and I had a cable waiting for me here from London to say that 'de Gaulle coverage scooped everything' — which meant it beat all the other companies. This didn't actually surprise me in the least, as I'm a little ashamed to say that I 'suggested' to a friend in the Cambodian Customs that the American companies didn't have the necessary clearance for their films. The official found it worth his while, with the result that their films of de Gaulle's arrival in Phnom Penh and his first day in Cambodia left the country 24 hours after mine!

I had the honour to be invited to lunch with Prince Sihanouk last Sunday in the Royal Palace in Phnom Penh. Only French correspondents were invited, and I wondered how I came to be there at all until he mentioned how much he liked my colour film of Angkor which Visnews sent him.

In March 1967 Davis was granted another Cambodian visa to cover the visit of Australian Prime Minister Harold Holt.

By then Australian troops were fighting in South Vietnam and Prince Sihanouk had been forced by circumstances to allow the Vietnamese Communists to use the Cambodian border areas as a sanctuary. The Australian Prime Minister's visit was diplomatically dangerous for the embattled Prince Sihanouk. Davis attended the Palace to film the two leaders greeting each other before their talks. As he did so, he saw out of the corner of his eye the Australian journalist Wilfred Burchett walk in the door at the end of the room.

Burchett was obviously unaware that Holt was in the room, but a diplomatic incident of some note was in the making.

I knew that Harold Holt would not know what Burchett looked like, and, being a friendly bloke, he would probably shake his hand and ask to be introduced.

I saw Sihanouk's eyes glaze over with horror as he caught sight of Burchett over Harold Holt's shoulder — and fortunately Wilf got the message, turned around and walked out.

It would have made wonderful film had they met!

In his mercurial way, Sihanouk steered a course of independence and managed to keep Cambodia out of the Indo-China conflict. But in 1970 he was deposed by a clique led by his Prime Minister, General Lon Nol, who quickly made himself Marshal Lon Nol.

He organised himself a nonsense election to become president of the first Khmer Republic in 1972.

The Cambodian people did not want to be involved in the war at all; the Americans dragged them in. President Nixon and his national security adviser Henry Kissinger were mainly responsible for Cambodia entering the war. Of course the Viet Cong and the North Vietnamese had sanctuaries in eastern Cambodia, and the Americans had wanted to wipe those out for a long while. They thought that by dragging Cambodia into the war on their side, they would eventually win the war in Indo-China. The only thing they were successful in doing was almost totally destroying twelve hundred years of Cambodian culture and civilisation, and the Cambodian people.

Of course President Nixon and Henry Kissinger were deeply involved in the secret bombing of Cambodia in 1969, a totally illegal act in which many Cambodian civilians, and very few Communist troops, were killed.

I believe that the actions of President Nixon and Henry Kissinger in dragging Cambodia into the war were criminal.

Letter to Aunt Lillian, 21 May 1970
Continental Palace Hotel,
Saigon

Although I am back in Vietnam, I have been spending nearly all my time in Cambodia — but advancing from this side with Vietnamese troops and a couple of times with the Americans. Or should I say West Vietnam and not Cambodia? I actually went to Phnom Penh without a visa! With the Vietnamese Navy.

It is all so terribly mixed up, with all the centuries-old Vietnamese-Cambodian animosities being stirred up. Last week an editorial in a local Saigon newspaper vilified the Cambodians for massacring Vietnamese living in Cambodia and confiscating their property. They ended the editorial on an ominous 'Hitler-style' note when they said: 'If the weakling Cambodian government is unable to ensure the security of Vietnamese residing there, whom they should consider as Allies now — then we shall take care of it ourselves.'

And they have been doing just that. All of Cambodia east of the Mekong River is in fact now South Vietnam.

Neil Davis saw the Cambodians go to war with great enthusiasm and tragic consequences.

228

It was very moving — a spontaneous feeling of patriotism and nationalism. The Cambodians were fighting their traditional enemies the Vietnamese. There was no need for conscription; in fact, there were too many volunteers, including boys and girls barely in their teens. Some were university students.

When the war started, the Cambodian army numbered only 35 000. They were ill-equipped and inexperienced. They were a people's army, and had been building roads most of the time. They had not fought a war for twenty or thirty years, and they were thrown straight in against some 50 000 North Vietnamese and Viet Cong — one of the best armies and some of the most experienced fighters in the world.

They marched off to war behind their flag, which had on it the towers of Angkor Wat, the twelfth-century palace of the great kings of Cambodia. It was rather like it must have been in the eighteenth century, with soldiers walking to meet their enemy in blocks of four by four or three by three, disdaining to take cover. The flag was generally carried in front of the advancing troops by a young boy.

When he was killed — and he was usually among the first killed — it was a race to see who had the honour of carrying the flag in front of the troops again.

It was all very courageous — and magnificent in its own way — but, oh, how they got slaughtered by those little men in black pyjamas flitting around like will-o'-the-wisps.

The war in Vietnam was fought mainly for the countryside, off the main highways. The reverse was true in Cambodia, where the fighting was for control of the main highways. When Davis first arrived in Phnom Penh to cover the war in 1970, he was told 'just go down any road'. There were seven main highways radiating out of Phnom Penh, and they all led to the war.

Generally I went by car, and when it got too close to the front I would pick up a motorcycle — a motorcycle taxi service to take you to the war! Some boys from Phnom Penh or the country towns were running this service to get you right to within two or three hundred metres of the fighting.

It was a remarkable scene. The noodle sellers were there, too. They would be less than two kilometres from the fighting, selling noodles to the soldiers and their families and to the correspondents, and sometimes sightseers as well.

The Cambodians never had the sophisticated equipment that the Americans gave the South Vietnamese. In Davis's view, they fought better without it. They were on equal terms, fighting in the mud and slush of the paddy fields with the Communists.

In the first two years of the war, however, they mounted frontal assaults on the enemy because they believed these unnerved them.

The Viet Cong had never faced an enemy like the Cambodians. The great spirit of the Cambodians carried them to some early victories, but soon the heavy casualties began to take their toll. The people had to evacuate the villages and move into the cities, creating a refugee problem.

The Cambodian army never recovered from the first six months of devastation and heavy attacks by the Vietnamese Communists, during which they lost two-thirds of the Cambodian countryside. But they never lost their fighting spirit, despite defeats and setbacks.

Neil Davis's camera recorded the cheerful calvalcades of young Cambodians setting off for the front on buses, open trucks, motorcycles and three-wheeled cyclos. All too often they returned dead on the same transport on the same day. The naive enthusiasm of the boy and girl soldiers was heartbreaking. Worse, the war was often a family affair, with wives and small children accompanying husbands or fighting sons to the front. At the end of the day, Davis filmed poignant scenes: a Cambodian soldier, weeping after the death of his wife, holding his surviving five-year-old son, or a dazed and suddenly orphaned six-year-old girl left absolutely alone in a strange and violent world.

The boy soldiers used to fish and climb coconut trees between actions. They may have carried lethal weapons, but they were just kids. A Cambodian major told me once, 'If we don't let them join, they cry.' There was a nice rapport between the adults and the boy soldiers. The men would rather have been home farming or fishing, too.

They had no sophisticated means of gathering intelligence in the field, so a soldier would put on civilian clothes, hide a couple of hand grenades under his shirt and cycle off down the road to find out where the Communists were. If he was lucky he got back with the intelligence. Or he died.

This well-meaning amateurism was potentially lethal for war correspondents, and a whole new set of survival rules had to be learned. Davis knew he could depend on the bravery of the soldiers he was with and that they would not break and run, leaving him stranded. But they often died to the last man and that was little comfort. There was sparse cover in the open paddy country and a tiny depression in the ground or a low paddy dyke could determine life or death.

The only way to advance over open fields was to run and I had to run with them. It was far more dangerous to stay back. They would move to close quarters and throw grenades. They had the unnerving habit of standing up to fire at the enemy so they could see better. It made them better targets, too. Girls would often be among the frontline troops, and they fought well, too.

The Cambodian troops always tried valiantly to recover the bodies of their dead and wounded. In the absence of any organised army medical service, only the families could tend the wounded, and the Cambodians believed it important for the dead to be farewelled with the proper Buddhist ceremony. This was one of the main reasons their families came out so close to the action — as well as to provide food and moral support.

Later in the conflict, the Khmer Rouge, who had thrown away all their religious beliefs, would deliberately mutilate the bodies — and that was bad from a Cambodian point of view, because that mutilation, they believed, stayed with them in the afterlife. In the case of reincarnation, it prevented their bodies going whole into the second life.

It made the Cambodian government soldiers fight very hard and not give ground. They fought and fought long after a Western army would have retreated in similar circumstances.

Letter to Aunt Lillian, 22 November 1971
Apartment 403,
Phnom Penh

Had a good coverage yesterday of Khmers atop a hill fighting, and unfortunately losing their position to the Communists. But they were really magnificent in defeat — today's papers are full of it — in much the same way that Australia's biggest military day commemorates their Gallipoli defeat.

Well, you know, Auntie, it wasn't a big battle, but that

(Left) 'If we don't let them join in — they cry!' Cambodian boy soldiers ready for action against the battled-hardened North Vietnamese Communist regulars, in 1970. *William Pinwill.* (Right) Neil Davis and a Khmer army nurse help to carry a wounded Cambodian soldier from a disastrous action at Phnom Kieu (25 kilometres west of Phnom Penh) in 1971. *Tea Kim Heang ('Moonface')*

Shortly after the ailing Lon Nol had declared himself President of Cambodia in 1972, Neil Davis obtained this exclusive interview with him. *Joe Lee*

(Left) Recording a sound commentary in Cambodia, 1970 with his driver and soundman Srun. (Right) Davis with Cambodia's famous soldier-monk, Lieutenant May Um — known as the Friar Tuck of Cambodia. In 1973 the 51-year-old May Um commanded a territorial unit about 60 kilometres southwest of Phnom Penh.

In moments of extreme danger and tension, often before charging an enemy position, Khmer soldiers put the image of the Buddha worn around their necks into their mouths. In this frame from Neil Davis's action footage, tension and fear are clearly evident on the face of this soldier.

matters very little, really. We had about 100 soldiers, along with some of their wives and children (very common here and in Vietnam). Twenty were killed plus four or five of their dependents, and fifty per cent of the remainder were wounded. But they held on, and eventually drove back the Communists, but were so depleted that they had to make a sorrowful withdrawal carrying the wounded (and leaving the dead) on an eight kilometre trek. So I don't blame them for casting their soldiers as being heroic in defeat. I didn't hear a harsh or bitter word. Not one of them — or their families — became hysterical or tried to break and run.

The Cambodians carried a protective image of the Buddha slung around their necks. In moments of extreme stress, in close combat or when about to make a final charge on an ememy position, they held the Buddha in their mouths. Davis was sometimes seen to bite on a Buddha, too.

During this time, he achieved the most graphic combat footage of his career. The unit he accompanied was surrounded, with waves of Communist troops coming in on all sides.

I couldn't film everything I saw because I was trying to save my own life. The film reveals a look of uncertainty on the faces of the troops because they weren't sure where the enemy was. The Buddhas were in their mouths, though, so they were close.

Sometimes the Communist positions were overrun so quickly that the Communist soldiers were coming up behind the advancing troops. On this occasion I found myself right on top of a bunker with a Communist soldier inside. He showed himself once, and went back inside. One of our soldiers threw a grenade in the bunker and at the same instant the Communist soldier shot him dead.

It was exhausting fighting, with temperatures

approaching one hundred degrees Fahrenheit [about 37 degrees Celsius]. In this particular action there were fifty government soldiers killed, but they won the battle.

Hand-to-hand fighting did take place in these skirmishes. It came at the climax of the battle when the Cambodians or the Communist troops rushed in from fifteen or twenty metres to overrun the other's position.

There was a lot of grenade throwing, and quite often some actual grappling with the opposing soldiers. They didn't use the bayonet very much, but sometimes swung their rifles like a club. I was never actually able to film that, because by that stage I was too busy trying to stay alive. Had I tried to film it, I am sure I would have been killed on the first or second occasion I tried it.

Although the Cambodians were mainly Buddhists, their religion had some overtones of Hinduism. Davis believed that, because they lived close to the soil, they had the 'sixth sense' he believed he shared in highly charged moments. To the Cambodians death did not come as the Grim Reaper.

The Cambodians had a saying, 'Death is a lady'. She might appear as a laughing girl, or an older woman — but she was a very gentle, warm lady who was there to protect them even in death.

During one very dangerous and close contact within about twenty metres of the Communist forces outside Phnom Penh, I was lying behind a paddy dyke watching the young Cambodian soldier nearest to me. He had his necklace Buddha image in his mouth, ready to move forward in the attack, and I saw his eyes go out of focus, as though he was thinking about something.

He caught my eye and laughed, saying, 'She's here, she's here!' and he laughed again. His glimpse of the Death Lady was a happy one for him — she had come to protect him.

Another combat cinecameraman who worked for Visnews, Tom Aspell, believed that Davis never took what he regarded as an unacceptable risk. Aspell was with him during a number of actions in Vietnam and Cambodia. He says, 'I don't think I ever once saw Neil run a road or a wall or a paddy field without first spending a lot of time watching and waiting, checking where the fire was coming from and waiting for the safest moment to move. He sometimes sat for hours in one place without rolling a frame of film, while others moved around.

'It didn't stop him getting hit a few times, but that was the way he worked. When he did move, he always looked for dead ground or shelter to take cover behind if something happened. He did this even in safe areas.

'I remember this very clearly because on one occasion we were in a fight in a clearing a few kilometres east of Phnom Penh. There were mortars landing and a lot of small arms fire directed at the company of soldiers we were with. It was reasonably safe to crawl around. The company commander was moving from position to position, trying to get his men to return the fire. At one stage his wristwatch was shot off, but he kept moving. I crawled around a bit too.

'It went on for a good three hours, but during that time Neil did not move. When we eventually did get out I asked him why he hadn't moved to film, and he replied that in his judgment it had not been safe to move at any time. Besides, he added, there were fights going on every day and there would always be safer and more spectacular ones to cover.'

Aspell said that Davis had been absolutely right. His own film looked the same that day as on most other days, and he had never been more scared in his life.

He says, 'Another battle on a different highway produced what I think was one of Neil's best one-liners. We were working in the same area as government forces prepared to launch an all-out attack on a Khmer Rouge position in the middle of a large, flat plain. It was one of those days when you seemed to be able to get every single weapon in the world's arsenal performing for the cameras. First aerial attacks by T28 aircraft, dropping great big bombs which set the village on fire, with black smoke everywhere. Then helicopters using rockets and miniguns poured tracer through the air. Then came the armour, APCs rumbling through the paddies firing machine guns, followed by the infantry running and firing.

'The whole plain looked like a scene out of a David Lean movie. I mentioned this to Neil, who replied, "Yeah, but we could do with a few wounded to round it out".'

Documentary film maker Jim Gerrand said that Davis always warned his colleagues against becoming involved in assisting either side. Once a Cambodian radio operator was having enormous difficulty in directing an American radio operator where there should be an air strike. Because of confusion over the French word *ami* for 'friendly', and 'enemy', the operator succeeded in directing the air strike on his own position! Jim Gerrand said: 'With the poor Cambodian scared out of his wits, I spoke on the radio to the American to call off the strike, explaining that he was using the "friendly" not the "enemy" co-ordinates. Neil later ticked me off for this, as he had every right to do. The press had to keep their noses absolutely clean — trying like the Red Cross to be absolutely apolitical in the field — because of the risk that the Communist forces would show no sympathy or respect for captured reporters.'

In fact, few captured reporters survived capture by the Khmer Rouge, and Neil Davis himself was once forced to pick up a weapon and help defend a Cambodian government position that was about to be overrun. He knew prisoners were seldom taken.

Our position was being overrun and at least one-third of the defending troops had been killed. Many more were seriously wounded and four or five Cambodian soldiers and myself were cut off. There was no way but to pick up a weapon and help defend the position, which we fortunately did successfully to enable us to escape. That action was over in a few minutes, but it took us three days to get out.

I always thought such a situation would pose a moral question. In actual fact, there was no moral question in my mind. It was either be killed or defend myself, and I chose to defend myself. I only did that on two occasions in the battlefield. I could have done it dozens of times if I had wanted to. I was shot at many times in close combat situations, and all I did was duck.

Australian Broadcasting Commission cameraman Derek McKendry remembers one Cambodian assignment where impartiality became academic. He went with Davis and some Cambodian troops to check the situation at a town called Kompong Speu. To their dismay they realised the troops they were with were wearing reconnaissance patches on their uniforms, and both men agreed that only idiots would go along with a recon section, as they were usually the ones to spring an ambush.

But as McKendry said, they hadn't shot a decent bang-bang for a few days, and so decided to risk it. Kompong Speu was very quiet — too quiet, as it happened. Just as the recon troops were radioing back to give the all clear, the North Vietnamese troops opened fire from the ambush they had planned. The two cameramen scrambled for cover as rockets and automatic weapons fire engulfed the street. McKendry says, 'We raced through the front door of a house, out the back and dived into a monsoon drain running parallel with the road. A sniper on a rooftop started to shoot at us with an AK47. Every time we moved, he fired.'

The two men crawled very slowly along the drain, the sniper's bullets thudding into the bank millimetres from their backsides, until they came to an unpleasant obstacle — the body of a very dead and stinking soldier. McKendry says, 'He'd been there about a week, and his body had swollen in the heat and split his uniform, and his face was just starting to become a skull. Naturally, this impeded our progress somewhat.'

Davis, who couldn't see the obstacle, urged McKendry forward. The choices available were all unpalatable — to crawl over the rotting body, to go back, or lose cover and go around. Meanwhile the sniper was still shooting. Stalemate.

McKendry noticed that the dead Khmer soldier still had a couple of hand grenades attached to his webbing. 'I reached forward and took one, handing it back to Davis, and kept the other for myself. The pins were out — still attached to the webbing — but the clips were clutched firmly in our hands, I said to Davis, "Count three and throw" which I did in the direction of the sniper, and took off like a cut cat down the monsoon drain and back onto the road, which had some tree cover. I stopped to rest and wait for Davis.'

But Davis had disappeared. McKendry came under fire again, and withdrew from the too hot town of Kompong Speu back to a schoolhouse some distance away, where he met ABC correspondent Bill Pinwill. McKendry told him they had been under close fire, and had been too busy staying alive to shoot any film. 'We were quite worried about Davis, but he turned up safe and sound shortly afterwards. I asked him where the fuck he had got to.

'"No problem," said Davis. "After all that bullshit I decided to stay a while and get some film".'

McKendry believed that made the difference between 'a fair-to-average cameraman like me', and a great cameraman like Neil Davis. He never asked whether Davis threw the grenade he had given him.

Sometimes Visnews editors would cable to ask Davis why he had not taken film of troops firing their weapons when he had obviously been in a big battle, because the firing could be heard in the wild sound tape he recorded.

The answer was simple. I'd been in a firefight so heavy that the soldiers I was with had to keep their heads down. Their colleagues in another part of the battlefield were returning the fire.

Some cameramen used to get troops to re-enact firing their weapons after the battle was over. I've always categorically refused to take film of them firing for firing's sake. It may seem a silly thing to say, but they might kill somebody on the other side simply because I have asked them to fire their weapons. I was determined my coverage would be historically correct.

Once Davis saw a foreign cameraman ask a South Vietnamese soldier to stand up and loose off a burst from his M16 as though he was in a firefight. The soldier obliged — and died, falling victim to an answering volley from an enemy no one had known was out there. Davis also believed that correspondents had to be completely self-sufficient in the field. With some anger and bitterness he told the story of a foreign correspondent who did not have a steel helmet, so borrowed one from a South Vietnamese captain — and then saw the captain take a bullet in the head.

Davis's acute awareness of the military situation would often lead to exclusive stories. Jim Gerrand remembers an incident during action on the east bank of the Mekong River, across from Phnom Penh in 1971. All the press's interest was focused on this battle. They had a ringside seat, there was access and a genuine firefight to cover.

But Neil Davis absented himself quietly for a couple of days and reappeared with a better story. The east bank action had distracted attention from an unknown but disastrous series of government defeats at a place called Srang. Davis had noticed that helicopters had been arriving at Pochentong airport from an unexpected direction.

Only the Cambodian war could produced an official army spokesman called Colonel Am Rong. Davis asked about the Srang action, and the urbane Am Rong lied to him. Davis did not argue with the colonel, but quietly went to the airport, established where the wounded were coming from, and made his way to Srang the next day to film the appalling carnage there. The press corps became terribly edgy if Davis were not around. He was generous with information, but only if he had covered a story first.

Colonel Am Rong remained steadfastly true to his name throughout his undistinguished career. Early in the Cambodian war, newsmen died as a result of false information given out by him. He was a charming, gifted man whose chief qualification to be military spokesman was that he had been a film director for the deposed Prince Sihanouk.

Bill Pinwill noted that he was a delightful but dangerous anachronism, his mind still in the fantasyland of his films that magnified the past glories of the Khmer nation. The unpleasant reality of the guerilla war consuming his country distressed him deeply. Once when he was obliged to announce a government defeat because newsmen on the spot had witnessed it, he declared with nostalgic defiance, 'We prefer classical battles to all these ambushes.'

Am Rong spoke beautiful French, but no English — which made him an ideal spokesman for a foreign press corps composed largely of American, British, Australians and Japanese. He acquired an official interpreter named Chang Song, a sensitive intellectual and poet of some note. Pinwill recalls that after one particularly bombastic briefing, during which Song had translated Am Rong's ringing declarations of non-existent victories, the distraught intellectual sought out a group of Americans and Australians he knew. 'For God's sake,' he muttered, 'can anyone get me out of this country?'

Armed with the latest intelligence from the filmmaker Am Rong and the poet Song, the international press corps fanned out across the countryside to cover the war. This meant hiring a car and driver at exorbitant rates. A knowledgeable driver was the key to success and survival.

Davis's first driver Srun said he had been a tourist guide. He spoke near-perfect English and had been to university in Peking. Bill Pinwill said he combined inordinate courage and coolness with a wry sense of humour. During one of several battles for control of Kompong Speu, a provincial capital forty kilometres from Phnom Penh, Davis, Pinwill and a number of other correspondents found themselves on the losing side. They made a dash for Srun's car, which was waiting with its engine running.

'Let's go,' someone shouted as the journalists piled into the car.

'Everyone lie on the floor,' yelled another voice.

'I assume that does not include me,' said Srun quietly but audibly as he drove the prone press to safety.

The drivers earned their money, and several were killed or captured.

Davis's friends often found his highly individual approach to covering combat alarming. One particular stretch of road north of Phnom Penh was known as Ambush Alley. Bill Pinwill, not long in Cambodia, went with Davis and the unflappable Srun in the hired white Mercedes to cover a story on a military convoy pushing through this notorious area. As they approached the danger zone, Davis told Srun to drive to the head of the convoy.

An apprehensive Pinwill asked if that was abolutely necessary.

'Of course, dear boy,' said Davis, laughing, 'if we're stuck in the middle of the convoy during an ambush, we'll just get shot at and not get any film.'

Mindful of the excellent example of *The Gondoliers'* Duke of Plaza-Toro, Pinwill suggested dropping back to the rear of the convoy.

'What!' said Davis. 'Miss all the good pictures? No, if we're out in front we have a good chance of getting through before the ambush starts, and getting good pictures as well.'

Jim Gerrand admired the way Davis handled the Cambodians. He never shouted at them or became angry (as many frustrated Westerners often did) but was always smiling and polite. This did not mean he drew back from covering unpopular stories.

Gerrand said that Davis's friendship with officials often compromised them and they were furious when he got on to stories they were hoping to hide. Their superiors gave them a hard time for not keeping the press out, but Davis would joke and jolly his way back into favour.

'In short,' Gerrand says, 'he had a measure of the Cambodian way of seeing things — smile and imply by your casualness that, in the greater scheme of things, nothing matters all that much. So he always reported a story, even if it meant the risk of being kicked out of Cambodia. He assumed that his official friends would have to learn to respect his professional duty, just as he was prepared to accept their lying or bullshit.'

Davis's unrivalled Cambodian contacts gave him entrée to the top. General, Marshal and finally President Lon Nol consolidated his power, despite a crippling stroke that paralysed him down one side in 1971. Shortly before Lon Nol proclaimed himself president in March 1972, he granted Davis an exclusive television interview.

On 30 December 1974, only hours before the final Khmer Rouge offensive against the failing Cambodian Republic began, Davis filmed the last interview Lon Nol ever gave.

The apple of Lon Nol's eye was his baby daughter, three-year-old Srey Sras, nicknamed 'Charming Girl'. Srey Sras and I hit it off immediately, and whenever we met I always found her a tiny gift — a fresh flower, a ribbon for her hair or a coloured pencil — things dear to the heart of a little girl. It did me no harm to have a supporter at the president's table.

I took a seaside holiday, where Lon Nol was also vacationing. I'd requested a TV interview with him, and contrived to bump into Srey Sras taking a walk with her nanny along the beach. She waited expectantly for the usual gift, and the presentation of a pretty seashell

ensured that 'Charming Girl' would tell daddy I was
close by.

Lon Nol agreed to see him, and after the interview Davis
sprang a surprise. Could he film the president taking his
daily swim? Horrified aides tried to intervene, but Lon Nol
waved them aside, and the whole party went swimming —
the crippled president, Srey Sras, aides and Davis with his
sound camera. It was as colourful as Mao Tse-Tung's
famous Yangtse River plunge.

Other notable stories evolved through Davis's long association with Cambodia. In November 1969, only four months
before Prince Sihanouk was overthrown, Davis was the
only Western pressman invited to cover Cambodia's independence celebrations. During that visit, Davis stayed at a
Buddhist pagoda in the countryside, later overrun by the
Communists who executed twelve monks. Just one escaped,
May Um, aged fifty.

The Venerable May Um decided not to turn the other
cheek, and formed a company of irregular troops from
boys who had been his former students, and led them
into battle. He never carried a weapon, and the only
concession he made to danger was to occasionally wear
a steel-lined flak jacket. It was quite a sight to see him
leading his troops into battle with his saffron robes
flowing under his flak jacket. His young troops believed
he was protected by the Buddha.

May Um shunned the press, but Neil prevailed on their
previous association in the Pagoda and filmed a story titled
'Cambodia's Friar Tuck'. It delighted the soldier-monk, a
longtime Robin Hood fan.

Always drawn to inspired eccentrics who tackled problems laterally — even guerilla warfare — Davis was
captivated by an old man called Danh Kroch, nicknamed
'Grandfather Tiger'. Davis estimated his age at about sixty-

five, and he used to disguise himself as an old peasant dressed in tattered shorts, and walk ahead of his troops to test the situation.

Then he would lead them into battle, after putting on a helmet. So you had this old man in shorts, helmet — no shirt — and carrying a staff, walking ahead of his troops. Sometimes he wore boots, although I don't know why, as his feet were as tough as leather.

He would walk down the road, while his men fanned out on either side, because the bullets bounced off him. That is what his men believed, and I'm sure old Danh Kroch believed it. To my knowledge he was never wounded, and there were plenty of stories to back up this superstition.

Danh Kroch was a stern disciplinarian, and earned his nickname 'Grandfather Tiger' from his habit of giving his young troops a good lathering with his bamboo staff if they stepped out of line.

The first time I met him I thought he was a peasant, but he was introduced as a colonel. He was about to lead an attack, and was burning some brush sticks and praying over a pig's head. I took some film of this, and he took a bowl of rice and set it on a tree stump, and explained that he was praying in front of the pig's head for the spirits of soldiers killed in battle to come and help them. The rice was for the spirit soldiers. He and his men then went into battle, and fought very bravely and won. They knew Danh Kroch couldn't be killed.

But in another battle, Davis wondered if his faith in Danh Kroch was misplaced. He and his men were surrounded by Vietnamese Communist soldiers. They had no food and only three rounds of ammunition left per man. The old man made sure that the besieging troops knew that he, Danh Kroch, was in command, and ordered his own men to lie low, not to speak, smoke, light fires, or move at all. They were not to open fire unless ordered to.

The Vietnamese had heard of 'Grandfather Tiger', and regarded him as a bit of a joke, and after sundown launched their first attack — which was something of a feint to gauge the strength of the Cambodians. However there wasn't a murmur from inside the village, no sound, no lights, no nothing. This nonplussed them, and they gathered strength and launched another attack about an hour later.

This fell a bit short when they discovered that all the shooting and yelling was coming from their side. And it was dark, and they started to think about this old man in there with his reputation, and began to get a bit spooked.

They rather nervously called out insulting things to try and get a response from the soldiers inside, to reassure themselves, I think, that human beings were there, with no mystic stuff going on. But there was no response.

They launched another half-hearted attack about midnight, but it faded fairly quickly and mutterings could be heard from about fifty and sixty metres away, and some swearing — all Vietnamese soldiers, Communist or not, used to swear a lot. But they were definitely spooked, and never did launch another attack.

Resupply helicopters came in at first light with fresh ammunition and supplies, and the situation was saved. Old Danh Kroch had won out again.

Davis firmly believed that Grandfather Tiger in his peasant disguise would have survived the Pol Pot atrocities after the fall of Phnom Penh.

Always on the lookout for a new angle, Davis took an opportunity in January 1973 to drop in by helicopter to the particularly vicious siege of the little railway town of

Romeas, northwest of Phnom Penh. The siege had been going on for three weeks. Neil flew in with two companions, a Cambodian photographer Costaud (nicknamed 'Muscles') and Associated Press photographer Lee Rudakewych. They took a lot of small arms fire as they came in, and the chopper took off immediately for Phnom Penh. Obviously the three had to overnight at Romeas.

They were warmly welcomly by the defenders, about a hundred soldiers and two hundred part-timers. And what an assortment! It was tailor-made for Davis, who attracted cheerful eccentrics with uncanny magnetism. One old man presented himself proudly, ramrod-straight, wearing a frayed but recognisable World War I French infantryman's coat. The old soldier was wearing his French and Cambodian campaign ribbons, and carrying the oldest working blunder-buss Davis had seen outside a museum. He was over seventy-five and assured Davis that he was delighted to serve again, although there had been a bit of a gap since he fought with the young de Gaulle in France from 1914 to 1918.

The three visitors hunkered down with a family group manning a forward mortar pit, with the Communist soldiers just across the railway line.

They were marvellous people. The old man's son was about sixty — a leather worker by trade. His rather jolly, robust and saucy wife was about twenty-five years younger. She took rather a fancy to me, and there were lots of explicit suggestions made, not helped by Costaud who suggested Ma take me forcibly and start a harem!

Outside their little lean-to shelter were their two 'babies', the sixty-millimetre mortar in its pit, and a livewire monkey tied to the bare pole of a tree which went up about ten metres, but had been stripped of all foliage by constant strikes of shrapnel and bullets. They swore the monkey was their lookout. The little chattering creature would shin up the scratched and battered pole and warn of any attacks from across the railway line.

A bare three hundred metres away, several hundred Khmer Rouge troops supported by North Vietnamese and Viet Cong regulars poured in mortars, automatic rifle fire and B40 rockets that screamed past the monkey lookout like an express train.

Davis was intrigued to find that the twenty-five-year-old Romeas commander Lieutenant Chan Lim spoke English and French fluently and had spent some months at the Australian jungle training centre at Canungra, Queensland. The previous commander had been killed in a night assault a few days before.

The Communist troops knew that there were Westerners in Romeas and it promised to be a rough night — with the strong possibility of the camp being overrun. Through the night, from less than eighty metres away, came mocking voices speaking in Khmer, Vietnamese and pidgin French: 'We know you are in there, Americans. We're coming in to cut your throats,' and other similar pleasantries.

Lee Rudakewych thought we might as well arm ourselves, and Lieutenant Chan said that was not a problem, because so many had been killed and wounded there were plenty of weapons.

While Costaud and Rudakewych went off looking for weapons, Davis settled down in a dip in the ground on a low stretcher bed he'd scrounged. It had been a long day, and there was a pleasant evening breeze to help lull him to sleep.

Gunfire never stopped me from sleeping. But about twenty minutes later Rudy arrived back. 'I've got us some weapons, Digger. Hey, Digger? Christ, the son of a bitch is asleep!'

Costaud said, 'He's resting, *mon cher ami* — it's a good idea, right?'

Davis slept the sleep of the just until 5.30 a.m., when between intermittent bursts of fire from the besiegers, the defenders heard President Nixon broadcasting on short-wave radio his 'peace with honour in Indo-China' message, saying that the war was over.

The Cambodians were delighted with this twist, and called out the news to the Communists outside the fence — then ducked.

Shortly afterwards the three newsmen were whisked away by an American helicopter which was not officially taking part in any combat-related flying. Lieutenant Chan Lim politely invited them to 'visit again any time'.

Early in March 1974, Neil Davis filmed an incident that again demonstrated the confused and fearful impact of the Cambodian war on its people. It was also an occasion with a bizarre personal twist for Davis himself.

I managed to get to a Khmer Rumdos camp, about thirty kilometres southwest of Phnom Penh. The Khmer Rumdos were allied with the Khmer Rouge, but they were not Communists. Unlike the Communists, they were devout Buddhists, and considered themselves nationalists.

The Khmer Rumdos were considering changing sides, provided the Phnom Penh government assured them of political integration. When Davis visited them, they were camped in a Buddhist pagoda in a kind of 'grey' zone between the Khmer Rouge and the government forces.

I took a chance and joined them. While I was there they were attacked from the jungle side of the pagoda by the Khmer Rouge, but they fought them off. Less than two kilometres on the other side were the government troops, but they didn't take any part one way or the other.

Davis filmed the tough Khmer Rumdos guerillas praying in the pagoda.

Another group sat in a circle around a teenage soldier playing a haunting Cambodian melody on a bamboo flute — like I'd never heard the flute played before or since. It brought tears to my eyes, and some of those wiry guerillas were sitting there silently, tears rolling down their cheeks.

Many of the Khmer Rumdos and their families were suffering from malaria. Anticipating that, Davis had brought in hundreds of malaria tablets. After a couple of hours they relaxed and began talking freely. Davis asked them where they had been fighting during the past few months. 'Oh, up and down Highway Four,' they said, 'mostly past Kompong Speu.'

Davis had been lightly wounded in the back by shrapnel from a mortar bomb the previous December near a bridge at a town called Mohasaing, and told them so.

There was hardly a pause. Their twenty-two-year-old battalion commander pointed at a well-built young man sitting on the ground. 'He did it!' The young soldier blushed self-consciously. 'He's the mortar layer,' the commander continued, 'and we think he's the best. He might not have put the actual round in the tube that wounded you, but he did set the positions of all the mortars. We only had three sixty-millimetre tubes down there, you know.'

I didn't know — it seemed like the buggers had twenty. Anyway, the commander pointed dramatically again at the youth, who was by now on his feet and scuffing the ground with one foot in his embarrassment. 'He did it!'

'Congratulations,' Davis said. 'All it'll cost you is a cigarette.'

The young man laughed, and handed him a Fortune Cambodian cigarette in his fingers, which is the way a guy hands his mate a smoke in Cambodia.

The changeover eventually fell through, and the Khmer Rumdos returned to the Communist side, to be killed almost to a man by the Pol Pot madness after 17 April 1975.

19

Dean of the Phnom Penh Press Corps

Letter to Aunt Lillian, 17 March 1971
  Visnews Office,
  Singapore

  I expect to send my furniture to Phnom Penh by ship
  early in April. Only one ship goes up the Mekong River to
  Phnom Penh now, and it's no good sending anything to
  Kompong Som (formerly Sihanoukville) the port,
  because almost nothing can reach Phnom Penh by road
  from that direction. So I hope the old ship makes it this
  time.
    I have a flat in Phnom Penh, which although not as big
  as the one in Singapore, is quite good. And I like the city
  of Phnom Penh . . .

Neil Davis's deep affection for Cambodia and Cambodians
undoubtedly influenced his decision to move his Visnews
operation from Saigon to Phnom Penh in 1971. He had
been spending more time there since Sihanouk's overthrow
in 1970 and the Lon Nol government's subsequent commitment to the allied cause. Jim Bennett mentions another
pressing personal reason; a Vietnamese girl who had surrendered her virtue to Davis amid vague references on his
part to nuptials, home and hearth, was pressing her claim
too insistently for comfort.

Davis set himself up in some style in Apartment 403 off Monivong Boulevarde in the heart of Phnom Penh. Tastefully decorated with artifacts from his various trips to Angkor, wood carvings and paintings from India, Indonesia and the Philippines, his Cambodian home reflected how far he had travelled in cultures as well as space. Through his apartment passed a parade of Cambodian beauties, although as Bennett recalled, none stayed for very long.

Neil Davis was a compulsive and successful womaniser — one of the few things he did boast about. Jim Bennett said he thought Davis was 'long on lust and short on love', although Davis did have a number of deeper involvements with the key women in his life.

Phnom Penh was under enormous pressure as the Communists tightened their grip on the city and the country. Refugees crammed in to expand its normal population of six hundred thousand to nearly three million people.

Davis bought a white Mercedes-Benz, driving to the war in air-conditioned style. He was now the acknowledged dean of the foreign press corps, and the ABC's Richard Palfreyman recalls that he was unfailingly courteous and helpful to newly arrived journalists. After a good meal at the Café de la Poste, he would gallantly offer to drive the newcomer back to his hotel. His old white Mercedes would cruise through the blacked-out streets well after midnight, way beyond the 10 p.m. curfew. Every Khmer soldier on duty in Phnom Penh knew Davis, the white Mercedes and his late-night drives home. But Palfreyman says it was unnerving for the newcomer sitting in the back.

'Somewhere along Monivong, the main boulevarde, Neil would tell the unsuspecting passenger in the back to wind his window down — and when Davis said to do something, it was done without question. He'd then swing the car into a dark alley where the headlights picked up what seemed to be hundreds of white bats bearing down on the vehicle.

'Suddenly all you could hear were shrill cries of "Neil, Neil", as dozens of girls tried to climb into the car. They were street girls who used the alley as a not-too-secret rendezvous for anyone who dared brave the blackout.'

Davis would roar with laughter as the visitor fought to actually stay in the car. Then he'd accelerate away, sometimes with one or two girls riding the bonnet or fenders, to drop the shaken newcomer back at his hotel.

Al Dawson, a former GI and correspondent, remembers seeing Davis shaking his head with disbelief one night in Phnom Penh. 'You know, Al,' he said, 'I don't honestly think I've got a sexual fantasy left.' Closer questioning revealed he had enjoyed the favours of a comely Cambodian girl soldier. This sustained encouter had taken place in the back seat of Davis's air-conditioned Mercedes returning to Phnom Penh from a day's filming at the front. The Cambodian had begun her assault on pleasure in full army gear.

Davis's celebrated coolness under fire often translated to Phnom Penh night life. Each evening the foreign correspondents would attend the press briefing on the war situation given by the information officer Colonel Am Rong. The briefing was a casual affair, conducted, if it was raining, under a bamboo-roofed lean-to next to the main press building. Afterward, the journalists would go to the Grand Lac Bar on the banks of the Mekong, just below the bridge that the Khmer Rouge blew up so many times throughout the war.

In the later years of the Cambodian war the biggest danger in Phnom Penh after dark was from disaffected bands of army veterans — men who had been either demobbed because of injury or had deserted. They had a habit of standing over and shooting up bars and restaurants that refused to hand over money.

Richard Palfreyman has reason to remember one particular night. 'We had just got into our second beer when the door of the Grand Lac opened, and three guys in ragged army uniforms came in. I looked around to see that one had only one leg and an M16 rifle crooked under an arm between his body and the crutch. Another carried a bag that looked heavy with other weapons or grenades.'

The girls sitting with the correspondents and behind the bar fled screaming to the back of the room. Neil Davis, in his usually calm manner, muttered, 'Stay where you are, don't look around.'

The group sat there trying to be nonchalant, ignoring the three ragged figures coming up behind them. Suddenly there was a commotion at the door where stairs led up to the next level. The owner, a colonel in the army, was trying to pull on his trousers while he covered the three with an M16 swaying in his one free hand. As he barked orders at the intruders, they backed off slowly towards the front door. The colonel followed, and having got his trousers on, bullied them out into the street.

Davis resumed drinking, the girls came back and the colonel went upstairs to continue his interrupted moment of passion. One of the journalists remarked that Neil was the only drinker not suffering badly from the shakes.

'Oh,' said Neil, 'I happen to know the colonel always takes his M16 with him when he pops upstairs for a quick one!'

Letter to Aunt Lillian, 8 February 1972
>   Apartment 403,
>   Phnom Penh

There is fighting going on around the Angkor temples. I do hope they don't fight among the temples themselves — it would be just too dreadful if anything happened to them. At present they are occupied by the North Vietnamese, and you can imagine the frustration of the Khmers.

They were able to work off a few frustrations the other night in Phnom Penh when they fired many bullets to frighten off the dragon trying to eat the moon! It was the eclipse of the moon, and the dragon is the younger brother of the sun and the moon, who hasn't got any work to do, and gets angry about it. So periodically he tries to eat the sun or the moon. All the soldiers everywhere fired off their rifles and people beat drums, plates or trees — anything. Of course several people were killed and more than sixty wounded.

Nixon's peace proposal caused a stir, but naturally the Communists rejected it, even though it accepted virtually everything they had asked for. However, the poor old Cambodians are the ones to be sold down the drain.

Davis's aversion to working with anyone else in the field in case he might be responsible for their safety was sometimes relaxed to help a friend or a Visnews client visiting Cambodia. In that case, he would uncomplainingly go to a reasonably safe spot to help record a story. He did such a favour for Richard Palfreyman and drove him in the air-conditioned Mercedes some twenty kilometres out of Phnom Penh where a key Lon Nol division was pinned down on three sides by the Khmer Rouge.

The only way in was along a road raised above the paddies exposed to enemy fire, and Palfreyman says it was the scariest ride he has ever had. Desperately wishing he had not come, Palfreyman was left crouched in a bunker with one of the Khmer commanders while Davis and the American freelance photographer Al Rockoff went off to investigate.

Three-quarters of an hour later, Davis came back. 'I've found a place for you to do a stand-up piece to camera. It's quite safe behind the perimeter wall,' he said. Ignoring Palfreyman's suggestion that they do the sound piece when they got well away, they crouched and ran to the suggested spot. Palfreyman did a shaky TV piece beside a Khmer soldier sheltering in a hollow in the earthworks. Relieved to be finished, the nervous Australian asked how close the Khmer Rouge were.

An interpreter interrupted to say that a B40 rocket was about to be fired at the position from fifty metres away.

They left as it hit and drove away still under fire. While on his own, Davis had filmed what he described as 'a few bits and pieces to go with your story'. The film was later described by the ABC's foreign sub Ivan Chapman in Sydney as the best item ever received from Cambodia. It had all the ingredients of the war — mortars, tanks, and air strikes — all shot while Palfreyman was sheltering in the bunker. Davis had done it as a 'soft' story to oblige a friend.

Perhaps Davis's ultimate example of professional selflessness is in this story told by David Brill, also a Tasmanianborn cinecameraman who had been sent in to Cambodia by Visnews in 1973 to do freelance work — in direct competition with Davis, who by then no longer worked for Visnews.

The first thing Brill saw at the airport was Davis's driver An Veng holding up a sign with his name on it. Davis apologised in a note for not meeting him personally, as he was covering a battle that day, but he would meet him later at his hotel to brief him on the general situation.

It was the classic Davis treatment, extended even to the man who had been sent in by his former company as his opposition. Two days later Davis asked Brill if he would like to come with him to film a major action on the Cambodian-Vietnamese border. Davis had his Bell and Howell spring-loaded camera and cassette recorder strapped to his waist. Brill had a soundman with a Nagra and he carried a relatively bulky Eclair camera on his shoulder.

'It was ridiculous,' Brill said. 'We had clapboards — the lot. It was as though we were going to make a feature film. "Stop the war — slate 20. Clap".'

As the action hotted up, Davis asked Brill if he wanted to come in further, and Brill prudently declined. He watched Davis walk off nonchalantly behind an APC. Two hours later he was back.

'Are you all right, mate? Got a cigarette?'

Brill recalls his almost uncanny calm. He lay in a hammock for a time, smoking, almost as though he was coming down from a 'high'. In the background, some American crews were paying Cambodian soldiers to re-enact the battle scenes they had been unable to film.

Jim Gerrand remembers that if Davis were caught with other journalists under fire, he would always crack jokes to jolly along those who might otherwise panic. He had a very genuine compassion, Gerrand said, for others who were frightened, and never thought less of them, then or later. Sometimes his tension-relieving jokes would not be appreciated; he was fond of whistling to imitate an incoming shell.

Correspondent Jim Laurie tells of one occasion when Davis's generosity to a colleague was misplaced. A certain American radio reporter nicknamed 'Snitch' accosted him one day outside the Phnom Penh PTT as he was about to file a Reuters despatch.

'Snitch' rarely ran the roads, and Davis's firsthand account was just what New York would want. So after a few minutes' debriefing, 'Snitch' turned on his heel and raced back into the PTT, where he filed his story for CBS radio. But Davis got his revenge; from then on, 'Snitch' only got stories from him that were complete inventions.

Letter to Aunt Lillian, 5 September 1972
> Apartment 403,
> Phnom Penh

> I'm afraid things are not too good here, but everybody keeps their spirits up — it is quite amazing.

> I passed by the Royal Palace today and saw the two elephants inside, where they stay most of the day. They are kept in stalls for most of the daylight hours, and anybody could walk in. There is no front to the stalls. They have a heavy chain on one leg which allows them to walk a few feet.

> A sign says in five languages: 'ATTENTION THE NAUGHTY ELEPHANT', really meaning 'Beware the naughty elephant', because they will trample people underfoot if they get

the chance. I saw a dozen children playing their games a few feet from them, taking no notice whatsoever. They treat the elephants as kids in Australia might regard a 'naughty' dog next door who might nip them on the ankle.

Only Neil Davis, with his penchant for disaster in investment, would put money into a floating nightclub on the Mekong River in the middle of a war. He went into the venture with another journalist, Denis Cameron, known as the Gardener because of his great ability to cultivate tender cannabis plants on his patio.

Jim Bennett was also invited to put his money in. The pitch, as outlined by Cameron, was for Bennett, Davis and Cameron to go into partnership with some wealthy Chinese merchants in Phnom Penh to open a dance palace on one of the abandoned floating barges along the Mekong River front. It would be renovated, stocked with fine foods and booze and an appropriate number of comely bar girls.

As Cameron put it to Bennett and Davis, not only would they get rich but they could audition all the dance partners before they were hired. Bennett declined and Davis took up his share.

Sure enough, Bennett says, they got that barge open for business. 'The Khmers flocked aboard. Denis and Neil personally selected a bevy of about thirty-five absolute beauties as "hostesses" — and I am sure they both took every one of those lovelies to the casting couch before making their final selections. Business was apparently booming. They were shitting in high clover and rubbing it in to me for having dropped out.

'The first week went by and the Chinese merchants said there wouldn't be any profits to split because of the high cost of opening this emporium of fun and revelry — naturally it was the Chinese who presided over the cash register and kept the books. The second week went by and that old barge nearly sank from the weight of all the dancers crowding aboard that ancient and honoured vessel. It had been Prince Sihanouk's private royal barge before he was overthrown. But there was still no money forthcoming from the Chinese partners.

'By the third week, Neil was getting a bit antsy, but he said he was getting a lot of good stuff on the side, and free meals in the restaurant. But business was booming, and there was even talk of opening another dance hall on a barge further down the river. Both Neil and Denis figured they were destined for greatness as the Dance Kings of the Mekong, while the tills clinked merrily away.'

The dreams of gold and glory shattered with a reverberating roar halfway through the third ill-fated week. The music had stopped and the weary dancers were straggling home when an enormous explosion ripped through the deserted barge, sending the inflated hopes of Davis and Cameron with it to the bottom of the Mekong.

It seems that all the late-night carousing had disturbed the peace and rest of the Khmer Rouge across the river, and they sent a team of frogmen over with a plastic charge. Bennett says he thinks Davis and Cameron harboured unworthy thoughts that he had somehow had a hand in this dastardly deed.

Undeterred by this disaster, Davis cheerfully entered into a joint investment in a vineyard in South Australia with Visnews man John Tulloh. The vineyard grew only red wine grapes at a time when the whole of Australia had taken to drinking bulk white. Drought, disease and a wine glut did the rest and, like the barge, the vineyard slid beneath the murky waters of failed enterprise.

Some of Davis's money, however, was being invested in rather different activities.

Letter to Aunt Lillian, 21 January 1972
　　Apartment 403,
　　Phnom Penh

　　So now a few friends and I support an orphanage!
　　Actually, despite the war, there are almost no

orphanages in the Khmer Republic. Khmers are very warm-hearted, and gladly take in kids who have lost their parents — they don't have to be relatives.

But all our orphans are cripples, or amputees, or bedridden with disease or for some other cause . . . We look after about 40 kids, aged from a few weeks up to about eight years old. My friends are all correspondents resident in Cambodia. Kate Webb is one — you may remember she was the Australian girl who was captured for about a month by the Communists here. Then there is a Britisher working for an American news agency, an American freelance photographer, an American radio correspondent, the Tass news agency correspondent (Russian), and a Frenchman.

We supply everything from mosquito nets (very important as malaria is a killer) to rice, clothes, dried milk and medicines. Some we buy, some we beg (from the Americans mostly) and some we steal, when begging has no effect!

Anyway, the kids at least have a chance, and I managed to persuade a British pediatrician who has been working in Vietnam to come across for several days . . .

Many of Davis's friends who knew him as a hell-raiser were unaware of his support for Asian children in Saigon as well as in Phnom Penh. Then there was the saga of Towser the Wonder Dog, a paralysed mongrel that had been partly run over by a tank in the town of Kompong Chhnang. Davis brought Towser back to Phnom Penh and importuned the chief French surgeon in Phnom Penh, Paul Grauin, for medical attention. Grauin, not amused by being woken at 2 a.m., protested he was not a vet, but Davis was adamant.

Grauin put Towser in a plaster cast and Davis fed him and encouraged the dog to walk again. He became something of a mascot and minor legend. It was typical of Neil Davis's concern, literally, for the underdog.

That was Phnom Penh. The madness of war and work in the daytime; fine food, women and wine at night. On Sundays, the press corps gathered at Le Royale Hotel, later the Phnom. In the early 1970s its pool was jealously presided over by the French, who gradually retreated to one end, while the non-French (mainly Americans) gathered at the other. The two groups rarely spoke, preferring to glare across the water with proprietary disdain.

Jim Bennett and Davis would go there for a few drinks and a swim. Bennett said that one of the Sunday highlights for Davis was the sight of a voluptuous Frenchwoman they dubbed 'Bobbie Boobs'. She would float majestically past Davis, her magnificent chest thrust towards the sky. 'My God, mate,' Davis would say, 'those bloody tits would float a tank. You could leap on her in the water and she wouldn't even sink.'

In Indo-China, Davis moderated his drinking from the excesses of his Tasmanian footballing days, but he had a great capacity for booze and could drink his way through the night if necessary. He developed a penchant for grass in Indo-China and smoked the occasional pipe of opium. Brian Barron remembers that he could spend a night drinking beer, topped with a dozen pipes at Madame Choum's opium den, and still make it to the front line by first light the next day. Denis Cameron goes further, saying that Davis had the strongest and most robust constitution he ever encountered. Malaria was the only force that could beat him to his knees. Says Cameron, 'He could smoke more grass than Rockoff, and on one evening in Phnom Penh Davis and a senior Western diplomat drank more than half a bottle of Scotch apiece and had more than a dozen joints!'

Grass and dope of almost any kind were easily obtained in Phnom Penh, and a group of correspondents used to wind up at the Golden Pagoda restaurant on occasions for soup and couscous stew, a fragrant dish generously laced with Khmer Rouge, the local dope.

Derek McKendry recalls that an American Senate Foreign Relations Committee on Drugs sent two officials through Asia to get firsthand information about the narcotics trade. They spent three days in Cambodia and were given Denis Cameron's name as a contact. He invited the delegation to join the regular group at the Golden Pagoda.

The two delegates turned up and really enjoyed the soup and couscous casserole and asked for second helpings. McKendry said they all got terribly stoned and lurched off into the night. They were not sighted for the remainder of their stay. Even the American ambassador lost track of them for a while.

Davis reckoned that they were extremely lucky to get such firsthand information on how drugs worked.

20

If You Weep Once,
You Weep Forever

Letter to Aunt Lillian, 19 October 1965
 Gleneagles Hospital,
 Singapore

 I am a little depressed (other than through hepatitis) as a
 cameraman I knew was shot down and killed in a
 Vietnamese fighter aircraft the other day, and an
 extremely good Vietnamese photographer friend was
 shot and killed in a battle just two days ago. So that's
 three friends in about as many weeks . . .

There were to be many more. Neil Davis calculated that
between eighty and ninety Western and Asian cameramen,
photographers and journalists were killed in Indo-China
from 1965 until the fall of Saigon in April 1975.

 I knew most personally, and at least twenty of those
 killed I considered good friends.

Even experienced correspondents such as Larry Burrows,
Dickey Chapelle, Francois Sully and the distinguished war
historian Bernard Fall died in combat, helicopter crashes,
by stepping on land mines or directly at the hands of the
Viet Cong. Less experienced photographers and reporters
died in greater numbers. Some died very hard.

Davis had become good friends with Sean Flynn who, like his famous father, made a living out of B-grade movies. Bored with making potboilers for Run Run Shaw in Hong Kong, he would fly into Vietnam and join Tim Page and other notorious characters who alternated pot and parties with risky combat coverage.

The ABC's Don Simmons remembers Sean Flynn as a shy, rather soft young man, perhaps lured to adventure by his father's reputation. But in Cambodia in 1970, Flynn and another photographer Dana Stone rode their motorbikes through a government checkpoint and disappeared in Communist-controlled territory.

Letter to Aunt Lillian, 26 April 1970
Visnews Office,
Singapore

. . . Have heard nothing of Sean Flynn and my other friends missing in Cambodia. An unconfirmed report said that Sean had been killed — crucified, in fact. Unfortunately the report is outlandish enough to be true. Things like that are not usually reported without foundation, and a few years ago another American met the same fate in Vietnam . . .

Flynn was never seen again.

In October 1974, Neil Davis wrote a despatch for the *Far Eastern Economic Review*, noting that nine pressmen had been killed up to that time in the Cambodian war and that twenty-two foreign newsmen were missing with little hope of finding more than four or five of them.

Nine of the missing are Japanese, five French, four Americans and one each from Switzerland, Germany, Austria and Australia. Additionally, several Khmers working as interpreters and drivers are not accounted for.

Most newsmen covering the action in Cambodia were wounded more than once. Some were very cool about the danger. Kyoichi Sawada, who won a Pulitzer Prize for photography in South Vietnam, was one of them. He came to Cambodia early in the war.

Sawada was a man of charm and subtle wit. Early in 1970 he was captured by the Communist troops, and after waiting several hours for his promised release, he decided it was time to go. 'You may shoot me here or here,' he said, pointing first to his forehead and then to his back, 'but I am leaving now.'

The Japanese then bowed politely and walked off down the road towards Phnom Penh, followed by an American correspondent who was with him on the assignment. They did not shoot him then — Kyoichi Sawada died later that year in an ambush south of Phnom Penh.

Al Rockoff, a former American GI, arrived in Cambodia in mid-1973 and, Davis said, promptly made up for his late appearance by getting good photographs in the front line. He was one of the small group of Western correspondents to stay for the fall of Phnom Penh, and he is portrayed in the film *The Killing Fields*. Rockoff took enormous risks to get his combat photographs, and justified this by saying he had already died once. Rockoff and Joe Lee were wounded when a mortar shell landed between them. Rockoff, who had been wounded twice before in Cambodia, took shrapnel in the chest, and Lee was hit in the leg.

They were rushed to the overcrowded hospital in Kompong Chhnang but Rockoff's heart stopped beating shortly after arrival. A Swiss medical team working there for the International Red Cross immediately performed open-heart surgery. Rockoff's breathing also ceased, and for the next nine hours he was kept alive by the use of a hand pump on an oxygen balloon. His life was saved.

Newsmen adopted a fatalistic approach to their chances in the Cambodian conflict. Before he left for Kompong Chhnang in October 1974 on the assignment that nearly killed him, Rockoff bade farewell to his colleagues in Phnom Penh with the words, 'Well, so long. Been nice to know you.'

One of the few foreign correspondents to be captured by the Communists in Cambodia and return to tell her tale was the UPI correspondent Kate Webb, an Australian. She was taken prisoner by the North Vietnamese in April 1970, after a heavy action not far from Phnom Penh.

Later, a body believed to be hers was found. However, three weeks later, on the day memorial services were to be held for her in Australia, Kate reappeared from captivity.

A journalist charged with the melancholy duty of trying to have the teeth recovered from Webb's supposed body verified from dental records, was driving across the Sydney Harbour Bridge when he heard on his car radio that she had been released unharmed in Cambodia. He threw the teeth out of the car window.

Kate Webb had that rare privilege of reading her own obituary, and nearly made it to her own memorial service.

By 1970, approximately two thousand Allied soldiers were being killed every week in Vietnam. As Neil Davis noted in a letter to his Aunt Lillian in September of that year, 1800 were Vietnamese and 200 Americans. The phased US withdrawal meant fewer American dead but more Vietnamese. It was inevitable that some of these deaths would occur in front of Davis's Bell and Howell camera.

Davis made many friends in his sorties with the ARVN and when he saw that Nguyen van Phuc was with a five-man unit about to go into action only fifty kilometres north of Saigon in November 1972, he decided to centre his coverage on him. Phuc was known simply as 'the grenade thrower'. Davis was fascinated by Phuc's combat tactics, which were to take off his heavy flak jacket and military gear, put a cluster of hand grenades in a plastic shopping bag and crawl forward in his pants and shirt to within a few metres of the Communist position to throw his grenades. Phuc represented the antithesis of complex engines and electronics of war: he was flamboyantly mundane. Phuc was backing his own skill and bravado to take him to the edge of death and back.

Davis had known Phuc for about four years and they enjoyed meeting again. His unit, from the 15th Regiment of the ARVN 25th Division, was preparing to move against some North Vietnamese troops dug in to a cemetery.

Most Westerners tended to forget that the Vietnamese soldiers on both sides were nice, simple people with ordinary human thoughts and desires. I tried to bring out the human element whenever possible.

He gained some superb film of Phuc who, as expected, stripped down to his pants and T-shirt and while the rest of his unit covered him with their fire, wriggled forward to lob his grenades over the tombstones to knock out the North Vietnamese position.

He used one of the tombstones as cover, standing up to throw his grenades and then crawling back under fire. Late in the day, Phuc made his third and last sortie. He actually stood and scampered the last three metres very cockily. He thought he had killed all the defenders, and he made his one fatal mistake. He stood up to put his heavy flak jacket back on.

I was half-lying behind a tree and Phuc stood in a shallow trench laughing and excited about it all. A burst of automatic weapons fire came in, and I ducked my head down. When I looked up again at Phuc I could see that he had been hit — stitched right across his body with bullets. He said just one word, '*Chêt*' which means, 'Dead'. And then he fell forward.

Letter to Aunt Lillian, 14 November 1972
Visnews Office,
Saigon

I suppose it was a reflex action, but I started my camera running on him. And it was a difficult decision to make, because the inevitable question I will be asked later will be, 'How could you just lie there and film your friend in that situation?'

All I can say is that many things raced through my mind. I knew that Phuc was well aware of battlefield chances — a whole world unknown to those that haven't been there exists under those circumstances. Contrary to many thoughts about this is the lack of hatred for the man trying to kill you from a few yards away. He is very much like you, and he might die at any time, just as you might.

I knew that I had film of this laughing young man displaying the joy of life as he knew it just an hour before — and I knew if I showed the shock of him suddenly dying it would impress on people at home very graphically what it was like to be a common soldier out there, no matter what side he was on.

So I ran my camera.

Phuc lifted his head, his eyes went out of focus and it was obvious he was dying quickly. He died with dignity, and quietly slumped forward about ten seconds later without another word.

The film has received enormous praise but they really miss the point, I think. They see it rather as a piece of film taken in unusual circumstances, and not as I see it — intended to bring home the awful reality of war — particularly on a personal basis.

However, it's done, and there's little doubt I won't ever do it again.

Davis said later that he was aware some people might say his actions showed a lack of feeling and compassion.

If Phuc had been able to speak to me, I think the last thing he would have said was, 'Keep the camera rolling.'

Because I don't show outward emotion doesn't mean I don't feel emotion. It's just that in a war situation one has to control those emotions. The Vietnamese have a saying: 'If you weep once, you weep forever.'

Letter to Aunt Lillian, 16 February 1971
Lane-Xang Hotel,
Vientiane

I have been covering the Vietnamese offensive into southern Laos. It was very difficult, with absolutely no co-operation from the Americans — on orders from Washington. They refused to carry us on American helicopters, which were doing most of the troop carrying into Laos. We had to fly with the Vietnamese, many of whom were inexperienced.

This duly resulted in the death of three of my longest and dearest friends. The pilot got lost in the mountains, and flew into a barrage of anti-aircraft fire from the Communists. Two of the cameramen killed I have known since my first days in Vietnam, an Englishman and a French-Vietnamese. Another, an American, I had known for three years. So my heart is heavy at the moment. They were such wonderful people in every sense of the word. There were other pressmen killed also — one Japanese, and two Vietnamese . . .

ABC correspondent Bill Pinwill had flown to Vientiane with Davis to try to cover the combined South Vietnamese and American incursion into Laos in February 1971. In the bar of the Lane-Xang Hotel, he heard that Larry Burrows, Kent Potter and the Frenchman Henri Huet were missing, presumed dead, in a helicopter crash. Only a few weeks before,

Pinwill and Davis had been working with Potter, a young UPI photographer, in Cambodia. Huet was an old and close friend of Davis's, and Burrows, one of the great lensmen for *Life* magazine, had seen almost as much Indo-China combat as had Neil Davis himself.

Pinwill went to Davis's hotel room to break the news. Davis was shattered, and sat on the bed with his head in his hands.

'Suddenly I feel mortal,' he said to Pinwill. That night the two men got very drunk indeed.

Letter to Aunt Lillian, 17 March 1971
Visnews Office,
Singapore

Unfortunately my old friend General Tri was killed in Vietnam when his helicopter was shot down. Another old friend was with him — Francois Sully — a Frenchman who had been the correspondent for *Newsweek* for many years in Indo-China. So many old friends killed lately . . .

It was traumatic enough coping with the news of the death of close friends. But Neil Davis regarded the saddest day of his life as 7 January 1973, when a Cambodian photographer and close friend Iang Chamroeng was badly wounded in action and had to be left dying on the battlefield.

We were caught in an open paddy field. The rice had just been harvested, so there was superficial cover. If we lay down, we could not be seen. The platoon of thirty Cambodian soldiers could not go forward, and we had to retreat.

Chamroeng stood up to take a photograph and he was shot through the throat and that's usually fatal. He was unconscious and having great difficulty, and another Cambodian photographer friend Costaud and I got to him, and for the next hour managed to drag him with us, and keep him under cover, or at least out of sight.

There was no cover from the bullets, rockets and grenades, and the Khmer Rouge were trying to complete the encirclement of the stricken platoon. The soldiers managed to reach a little bit of dry ground with a few trees and some cover, and tend their wounded.

The commander, a major, said to me, 'We are almost surrounded. We have to get across fifty metres of open ground right here in front of us. No wounded man is going to make it. I'm sorry, but no wounded men. If you want to bring your friend, you do so, but it's up to you.'

Just as he was saying that, two soldiers tried to carry a wounded friend across and they got cut down and killed before they were ten metres across that clearing. It was obvious that the Khmer Rouge had the area covered with machine-gun fire, and the only way was to run, go down and roll, pick yourself up and run again — and you could not do that with a wounded man.

Davis told the major he wanted a minute to think. The major said that was about all the time they had before moving.

I looked across to where Chamroeng was lying, and he looked very, very bad. There was no hospital, not even basic medical attention for another hour at least, even if we got out. He looked as though he was just about gone. Costaud was already leaning over him, taking all his identification cards, because the Khmer Rouge hated journalists and killed them in a very nasty manner if they caught them — particularly Cambodian journalists. I knew Costaud realised we had to leave him. And we did leave him. We left about five or six other wounded soldiers, too.

Eleven of us survived out of the original thirty. Two or three were killed crossing that open space, and six of the eleven survivors were wounded.

By the time we fought our way back to the area several hours later, Chamroeng was dead.

Only three months before, Neil and a Korean cameraman Joe Lee had been covering an action in Vietnam in a wooded area near Quang Tri City. Both Davis and Lee had an uneasy feeling that they should get out of the area. There were no outward signs that disaster was about to strike. But some North Vietnamese troops had actually infiltrated old foxholes and suddenly opened up at point-blank range.

We were about a hundred and forty metres away from Terry Khoo, a Singaporean Chinese working for the American Broadcasting Company and his crew. As we looked up, we saw Terry's soundman, Lee Tae Hung, a Korean, running zigzag style towards us as bullets whistled overhead. He told us what had happened, and Joe and I doubled back in a semicircle and tried to get close. We got to within about five metres of Terry, who was motionless in long dry grass. Two other newsmen were also dead nearby. We couldn't get any closer.

Letter to Aunt Lillian, 13 July 1972
Visnews Office,
Saigon

Just returned from a long stay in Quang Tri Province — where fighting has been very fierce, and heavy losses on both sides. Came upon the remains of a convoy of trucks, cars and buses that was destroyed south of Quang Tri City during the retreat of the South Vietnamese early in May. The North Vietnamese had destroyed more than 400 vehicles in all — each loaded with refugees, mainly women and children.

It was unbelievable and horrifying — quite the worst thing I've ever seen — and will surely rank as the blackest day in Vietnamese Communist history. The soldiers I was with were stunned for a while. Then many of them just wept . . .

Friendship was all important to Davis. He was prepared to put his life on the line for a friend.

In November 1970, he was in East Pakistan covering the aftermath of the cyclone and tidal waves that killed more than 300 000 Bengalis. On hearing that his colleague Yosep (Joe) Lee had been reported missing, presumed killed or captured by the Communist troops in Cambodia in November, he flew back to Phnom Penh. Lee had been on assignment for Visnews, working with Davis. The Australian and Korean had become extremely close friends.

One of Davis's first calls was to the East German embassy. He always cultivated good relations with journalists and diplomats from the eastern bloc, not only for useful information, but always mindful of being granted his long sought-after visa for Hanoi. In any case, he liked the East Germans, and they enjoyed drinking with him from time to time.

But there was a delicate diplomatic problem. The Lon Nol government was profoundly anti-Communist and while Davis presumed that the East Germans maintained some kind of contact with the opposing Communist forces (Vietnamese troops at that stage of the war) the East Germans certainly could not say so.

On 30 November Davis spoke with two East Germans known to him to see if it were possible to get a message to the Vietnamese Communist troops to release Joe Lee. The fact that Lee was Korean was not helpful, as South Korean soldiers were fighting in South Vietnam. Davis knew that Lee would say he was Japanese.

One of the East Germans told Davis he had tried to drive down Highway Three south of Phnom Penh on the previous day, but had been turned back by government troops at the thirty-kilometre mark. Davis presumed he had been trying to make contact with the Vietnamese Communists.

A wonderfully oblique conversation took place.

'Of course if you were to drive down there,' the East German said, 'you would probably get through.'

This was true. The East Germans had been refused passage by Lon Nol government troops. Davis would undoubtedly be allowed to drive his white Mercedes through the last government checkpoint, but what then? If word were not passed to the Communists, Davis would be ambushed, shot or captured himself.

'I was thinking of driving down towards Takeo tomorrow,' Davis ventured.

The following day was Tuesday. The East German looked thoughtful, and said casually, 'That seems a bit soon, don't you think? Why not wait till Wednesday?'

Davis assumed he was being given a message, but he could not be sure. On Wednesday he gave his driver the morning off and drove his car out of Phnom Penh at 6.30 a.m., heading south. His work diary for that day is asterisked at that point with the comment, 'Shall not enlarge here'.

As expected, he was not stopped at the last government roadblock, and he drove on through a deceptively peaceful countryside. His options were strictly limited. If word had been passed through by the East Germans, he would probably be OK. If not, a burst of gunfire or an unheard sniper's bullet would end his mission.

By now deep in Communist-controlled territory, he slowed his Mercedes when he saw some crossed palm branches on the road. That was a signal that travellers should proceed at their own risk. Davis could only assume that the sign was for him, and he drove cautiously into the next village. A young Communist soldier flagged him down. His nonchalant manner suggested to Davis that he was expected, but he still could not be sure.

Speaking in a patois of French and Vietnamese, Davis asked to be taken to the area commander. He got out of the car and the young soldier led him across the rice paddies for about a kilometre to a small hut at the base of a lightly timbered hill.

Inside, a small group of uniformed men asked him why he had come. Viet Cong and North Vietnamese Communist soldiers did not wear badges of rank, but Davis knew by their manner and bearing that he was in the presence of high ranking officers.

They listened politely and in silence while he explained that his friend, an international journalist from Japan, had been captured by their troops and that he had come to request his release. He hoped they would be able to contact his friend's captors to deliver that message. The only concern of international journalists was to report fairly on both sides of the conflict, and Mr Lee could be relied on to do that if he were allowed to return safely to Phnom Penh.

The Communist officers said they did not know anything about Lee and that it would take time to relay a message to the area concerned because there was no radio contact. But they would make inquiries, even though they could promise nothing. There was little small talk.

Davis asked if he could drive back to Phnom Penh without being stopped again and permission was granted. One of the men told him bleakly that it would be unwise to attempt a similar mission again — for any reason.

He drove back to Phnom Penh without incident.

Five days later, in Bangkok to cover the 1970 Asian Games, Davis heard that Joe Lee had been released unharmed after seventeen days with North Vietnamese troops in the jungle on the Cambodian-Vietnamese border.

21

'Someone is Trying to Kill Me!'

In Cambodia Davis's diaries record twenty-eight combat coverages for the month of April 1973. During the spring offensive in the northern regions of South Vietnam in 1972, he spent three months in the field with the South Vietnamese marines and he calculated he was in combat three days out of four.

By 1985 he genuinely could not remember how many times he had been wounded.

> I usually tell people I was hospitalised six times. The Americans award a decoration to their troops called a Purple Heart — all you have to do to earn one is to have blood drawn by enemy action. Had I been a GI, I would have been eligible for about twenty Purple Hearts, from little bits of shrapnel dug out of my back in the field and similar injuries. Only six were serious enough to put me temporarily out of action.

The odds of being injured jumped dramatically if soldiers on the other side deliberately set out to kill you. In April 1974, one day before Davis received his most serious combat wounds, he was filming an action fifty kilometres southwest of Phnom Penh when he had to join a scrambling retreat.

It was the usual set-up. Only one small paddy field separated us from the Khmer Rouge. We were just hanging on, the government troops having advanced well, but the Khmer Rouge were in bunkers and had the advantage.

Two other cameramen, Joe Lee and a Cambodian, Sou Vichith, were further away to the right, and saw that Davis's group was about to be encircled by the Khmer Rouge. They called to Davis to pull back, but he had a problem.

A Communist soldier on the other side had decided I was his target. This often happens in the front line; a soldier fixes on one individual and concentrates on him. It might be because he is taller than other troops, or wearing a distinctive scarf or hat.

You can easily tell when you have become a target, even if there is a lot of gunfire coming over. It is partly a sixth sense, but whenever you move, a bullet whacks in close, and you know it is for you.

There are two checks to confirm this situation if the target lives long enough. The sound of a rifle being fired away from you sounds different from the sharp 'crack' of a weapon pointing in your direction.

You get to know the sounds made by different weapons, and when an AK47 is fired absolutely directly at you, that is a different sound again.

The other indication of a bullet coming so close is that it sucks the air away from your ears as it whistles past only a few centimetres away from your head. It is as though someone put both hands on either side of your head and smacked you over the ears at the same time. It scares the hell out of you.

The soldiers with me realised what was happening after this happened to me about three times. 'Oh, Davy, they're after you,' one said.

Meanwhile, Joe Lee and Vichith were yelling out to Davis to pull back because he was being cut off by the Khmer Rouge. Feeling rather foolish, and conscious of the *Catch-22* echo in his words, Davis called back; 'I can't — someone's trying to kill me!'

I knew Joe would understand, and of course he did. We laughed about it later. But I still had to get out.

The Cambodian soldiers with Davis suggested he show himself one more time while they tried to get a fix on the soldier who had targeted him with such enthusiasm.

As I did so, this dedicated bloody madman drew another bead on me. My troops said, 'Right! We can see him.' And while they laid down very heavy fire on his position, I ran. I only had about thirty or forty metres to go to get cover behind a couple of big trees and an armoured personnel carrier.

I swear that a couple of bullets chipped the ground near my feet in the last ten metres, and I knew that guy was still trying to get me, despite the fire being laid down on him.

Booby traps unleashing thousands of razor-sharp fragments of steel, or shrapnel from exploding mortar rounds, were the most likely source of injury rather than a direct hit by a well-aimed bullet. Davis, who said he was never afraid of being killed in combat, did fear being badly wounded by shrapnel and dying a slow and painful death on the battlefield.

His first wounds were from shrapnel in the Mekong Delta region of Vietnam. It was on Ho Chi Minh's birthday, 19 May 1967. He was with South Vietnamese troops, and they were deep in 'Charlie' country, having a midday rest on a patch of dry ground under some small trees.

I was very tired, because we had been marching since before dawn. Fortunately I had my head down on my knees, with my Bell and Howell camera still in my hand, when there was a hell of an explosion. Someone coming along the paddy dyke we had just walked over tripped a mine which my group had not set off for some reason.

Shrapnel went everywhere, cutting my hands, and gave me a gash on my head. It wasn't serious. I managed to walk out, and was later hospitalised for about twenty-six hours.

The next time shrapnel sliced into his hands and head, Davis almost filmed his own death. This action took place five years later in the north of South Vietnam, in an area made famous by the late war historian Bernard Fall, who called it 'The Street Without Joy'. Neil Davis was with a detachment of the South Vietnamese marines, who were making a frontal assault against North Vietnamese regular troops across scrubby sandhills.

A Communist hand grenade was thrown and I put my hands up to my face to try and shield my head. When it exploded, it cut my hands about and took a great jagged piece out of the left side of my jaw, but didn't break the bone. It also severed a minor artery somewhere near my temple, which immediately bled a lot. I fell back stunned, with my camera still in my hand, and I must have looked an absolute bloody mess.

At this moment the North Vietnamese decided to try to overrun our position. As I lay there half-reclining, with blood streaming down from my head and hands, a North Vietnamese soldier appeared literally a metre away over a slight rise.

My first reaction was, 'What a fantastic shot!' I looked down to adjust the focus and swing the turret of the camera on to a wide-angle lens. I mean, there was this man coming to kill me, and my first reaction was to get on to the right lens to get this dramatic shot.

As I tried to do so, I saw he was carrying his weapon, and I thought I was almost certainly dead. I'm a left-hander with a rifle, and if he had been too, he would have swung the AK47 just a little and shot me in a second. But he was a right-hander and his rifle was on the side closest to me, and it was pointing away.

All this of course happened in a second. I was going to adjust my camera, and he appeared to sum it up and decided that the quickest thing for him to do — he could see that I appeared to be badly wounded with blood everywhere — was not to shoot me. He would have had to swing around to do that. So he just swung forward and back with the butt of his rifle and smashed it into my forehead, while I was still trying to swing my lens turret around!

Davis lost consciousness for between one and five minutes, recovered in time to film the figure of a South Vietnamese marine dragging a wounded comrade back and correctly assumed that there had been a successful counter-attack. He managed to crawl back to safety and the shot of the marine rescuing his wounded comrade appears in the documentary film *Frontline*.

I was pissed off that I hadn't got a shot of the man coming to kill me. It would have been a great shot if anybody had recovered the film.

That night at the marines headquarters area, those coping with the dead and seriously wounded took little notice of Davis and his relatively minor wounds. The next morning he did not feel too bad — despite a bit of a headache — and hitched a chopper ride to Hue and an Air Vietnam commercial flight to Saigon.

Some of the passengers did look a bit oddly at me, but there were lots of soldiers and they were used to war scenes. I knew I was dirty, with some dried blood on me.

I got a taxi from Tan Son Nhut airport and the driver made no comment on my appearance. But when I walked into the Visnews office in Saigon, Juliette, the girl who worked there, looked at me and let out a scream and said, 'God, what have you done to yourself?'

I went to the washbasin in the corner and looked in a mirror, and on my left cheek I could see my white jawbone where the red-hot grenade fragment had torn out a chunk of flesh. But I needed to get the film away, and as I'd survived till then, I didn't think a few more minutes would matter. I packed the film up, wrote out the dope sheets and gave it to Juliette to take to the airport, while I ambled off to the American embassy doctor.

I did have to go into hospital for a couple of days while they watched it for any infection and things like that, but otherwise it was all right.

One enduring legacy of this encounter was the mottled imprint of the AK47's baseplate, which showed up on Davis's lower forehead whenever he was flushed or sweaty. The temptation to watch action through the viewfinder as though it were a television screen divorced from the reality of events had to be countered, but such intense professionalism could also be used to shield the mind from personal horror. Neil's friend and colleague Joe Lee was badly wounded three times in Cambodia, but survived to continue working as a newscameraman based in Thailand after the Indo-China war ended. In 1976 the intrepid Korean was on assignment in southern Thailand, covering skirmishes with Communists active on the border with Malaya.

Joe got caught in an ambush and trod on a land mine as he and his Thai soundman were taking cover. He was holding his sound camera, and when he came to he saw that his soundman was dying alongside him, and his own left leg had been blown off below the knee and was hanging by a thread.

Joe leaned back against a tree to get some cover, and filmed his dying soundman. He then refocused his camera, deliberately adjusted the aperture for the change in light and slowly panned down his body to film the stump of his leg and the severed foot.

It was as though he was pretending it was television, and that would be the most dramatic thing you could do, if you were watching it on television. It would certainly take your mind off this dreadful situation and the awful certainty that you'd just had your leg blown off — for a second or two, anyway.

Joe Lee survived that experience, and is still working as a newscameraman. Neil Davis saw a lot of him in hospital, gave him the book *Reach For the Sky* by Douglas Bader, the legless air ace in World War II, and encouraged him to play golf as soon as he had been fitted with his artificial leg.

Davis was lucky still to have two legs of his own. As he strode out on the Bangkok greens with the still-limping Lee, a close observer would have noticed a slight hesitation in his stride. In fact, Davis was kicking his own right leg forward to compensate for shattered muscles and tendons. His right leg had no feeling below the knee, a legacy of events on 11 April 1974 in Cambodia. The day after he had escaped from the unknown Khmer Rouge soldier who had tried to target him, Davis had returned to combat in the same area.

Once again it was very close fighting, less than a hundred metres. There were quite a lot of wounded on our side, and I had stopped filming to help my Cambodian photographer friend Vichith drag some wounded behind a large tree which was the only shelter. The Communists reasoned that there must be a command post behind the tree and homed in on it with rockets.

A young Cambodian officer in an armoured personnel carrier about forty metres away saw what was happening and called for the two men to take cover behind the APC.

He shouted that we would be killed if we stayed behind the tree. Although it seemed an obvious move to make, I had a strong feeling that I'd be OK if I stayed behind the tree. But my friend Vichith, who was only a young guy and not very experienced, said, 'I think we'd better go.' And so we went.

I looked up and actually saw the mortar bomb just before it hit. It blew up less than two metres from me, but the blast was directed slightly away from me, which saved my life. A soldier on my left was killed instantly. But the interesting thing is that everything went into super-slow motion, just like the technique of the film director Sam Peckinpah, who made *Bonnie and Clyde* and *Straw Dogs*. He showed ghastly scenes of people being blasted with shotguns in super-slow motion — where three seconds of action becomes fifteen.

So when I first saw the shell it was about three metres from the ground and coming down vertically. There wasn't time to do anything. I think I cried out, but it had hit the ground at that time anyway. On may left I saw a soldier disintegrate in front of my eyes, as though in slow motion. He had been hit full blast with shrapnel, and I thought, 'He's dead', as he was. At the same time, I felt a sharp pain and a thump on my lower right leg, and I knew there was serious injury there. Shrapnel hit my back, and I felt a thump near my stomach, and I knew instantly that it had hit a small tape recorder strapped to my waist and saved my life. I later found that to be correct. On my right a soldier was slammed against the

283

back of the armoured personnel carrier — again in slow motion. He put his hand to his shoulder and blood started to come through his fingers, so I knew he was wounded but not seriously.

Meanwhile, I was falling back through the air as though I was a skydiver. While I was in the air I saw my Cambodian photographer friend pitched forward and twisting at the same time. I noticed blood spurting from his left wrist, a vein was probably severed, and then as he twisted over further I could see a grave injury near his kidneys, and I knew he was in a bad way.

Then I hit the ground.

Although all those perceptions were gathered in split seconds, Davis was able to give a completely accurate description of the wounds suffered by everyone in the group.

The return of normal perception found the group in desperate shape, but little could be done. The Communist troops were in the ascendancy; they were trying to overrun the position with human wave attacks. Davis lay where he had fallen behind the armoured personnel carrier, the dead soldier was left where he was and the other two wounded were put in the APC. Someone managed to put a pressure bandage on Neil's shattered lower right leg.

I had to get medical attention as quickly as possible, certainly within an hour or two, because I knew the main artery on my leg was severed. I had seen similar wounds on others many times.

The young Cambodian lieutenant who was lying on top of the APC leant over and dropped me his pistol, with two or three rounds in it. I knew what that was for — it was not to defend myself, because if it got to that stage we were all dead, anyway. It was to take my own life if we were overrun, because the Khmer Rouge Communists were very brutal. There was no way they would take us prisoner, they wouldn't even shoot us quickly. There would be torture, and very slow death.

In one strong Communist push to overrun the position, an attacking Communist soldier was shot and killed at point-blank range right in front of the APC. But the assault was repulsed, and after an hour the APC, acting as an ambulance, set off to cover the three kilometres to the main road. There was an extremely primitive aid station there, with one medical attendant. He did his best, and Davis was given a transfusion of coconut milk straight from a nut taken from a nearby palm.

This was a recognised emergency field procedure in Indo-China. The Viet Cong did it as well. It provided a sterile fluid to boost the volume of blood.

I was fairly groggy, under a sort of tent, but I saw them puncture the green coconut with a primitive little gun, which fired a needle into the heart of the nut, and they gave me the drip. It was a pretty fast drip, because they had no vehicle at that time to take me to the hospital in Phnom Penh fifty kilometres away.

Davis had instructed his driver An Veng to drive back to Phnom Penh to ship film already completed at 1 p.m. if he had not returned to the car by then. Fortunately, the worried and concerned An Veng had not carried out these instructions. Just over two hours after he had been wounded, Neil was on his way to Phnom Penh's Calmette Hospital.

I knew, because I had seen similar wounds, that I was in grave danger of losing my leg because my main artery was severed just below the knee. Most of my calf appeared to have been blown away, and the artery was spurting blood everywhere. I knew it had to be rejoined, otherwise my leg was off.

The hospital was a scene of appalling chaos, with battle casualties being operated on in corridors. Davis was barely conscious through shock and loss of blood, but he managed to give instructions to his Cambodian photographer friend Costaud that he was not to permit the hard-pressed French doctors to amputate his leg.

Costaud did not actually pull his pistol on the surgeon, but he made it clear, in quite a threatening manner, that he was *not* to cut my leg off. The surgeon knew that it would take several hours to locate the severed ends of my artery and link them with an artificial plastic section. They also knew that I'd lost circulation for more than two hours, and you are on borrowed time by then. In their eyes it was a fairly hopeless case.

Costaud's real name was So Sokhan, but everyone knew him as Costaud, which is French for 'muscles'. He used to wrestle, and he was a big fit man, and he just stood in the doorway fingering his pistol while the surgeon began to try and save my leg.

It was quite a job. The leg was broken in four places, shockingly ripped and torn by shrapnel. The first and most urgent job was to restore the blood supply. After a four-hour operation under the watchful eye of the guardian Costaud, the artery was rejoined and the bleeding stopped.

The next day the Americans, God bless 'em, sent a special medical evacuation plane to fly me to Bangkok for further treatment.

The French doctor had told Neil that he was not sure whether he had saved his leg. The principal doctor of the Bangkok Nursing Home was Austrian and the consultant surgeon was Thai, but he had trained in Switzerland. French was their common language, and they assumed that Davis, being Australian, did not speak it. He learned that the two medicos had grave doubts whether his leg could be saved.

More operations were done. Dr Gerta Ettinger would come into my room in the morning and casually put her hand on my foot and ask me how I was feeling. She did this for two mornings and didn't comment further. I knew she was feeling my foot to see if the circulation was there, and my leg would be cold if it was not.

On the third day she casually put her hand on my foot and then said 'Oh!' and smiled. I said, 'Have you saved the limb, then?' She laughed and said, 'I gather you speak French.' But the leg was warm, and full circulation had resumed.

Davis, however, was out of action while the best and biggest news story in the world was moving to its climax. He was also deprived of his ability to earn money, as he was no longer under contract to Visnews. He had been undertaking freelance assignments for Visnews and other news organisations, but was worried about paying his medical bills, not knowing whether his Australian medical insurance was valid.

He set about regaining his fitness with the same fanatical determination that had had him out of an iron lung and playing football within four months of contracting polio in Tasmania.

I had my right leg in plaster for over two months and there were other shrapnel injuries to be coped with. The main task, when the plaster came off, was not only to regenerate my leg muscles, but to learn to walk again, because I had no feeling below my right knee.

It was almost as though I actually had an artificial leg. I had to learn to walk again by sort of swinging from the hips and by kicking my lower leg forward. It came naturally later, but it was extremely difficult for the first six months.

For instance, I kept falling *up* stairs by not being able to calculate the step, and I would often take my pants off at night and find blood running down the shin of my right leg where I had bumped into something and hadn't felt it.

Meanwhile, debate about how his considerable medical expenses were to be met was taking place in the Visnews head office in London.

Davis had been covering for Visnews in the absence of their new correspondent Tom Aspell, who was away from Cambodia on leave. There was doubt about the formality of this arrangement, which came to a head when John Tulloh wrote from Hong Kong to head office in November 1974 asking that Visnews pay half Davis's medical costs of US$4500 until the complexities of claiming on medical insurance from Australia had been ironed out.

The following telexes were exchanged between Visnews Executive Editor Roy Mack in London and the Asian Manager Russell Spurr in Hong Kong.

PRO SPURR/EXMACK. WE UNAWARE THAT DAVIS ON GENERAL ASSIGNMENT FOR VISNEWS. LAST MESSAGE FROM SPURR ON THIS SUBJECT (IN RESPONSE TO OUR OFFERING RETAINER FOR TWO WEEKS) WAS THAT NONE WAS NECESSARY SINCE DAVIS WOULD BE THERE ANYWAY.

WHILE I NOT SAYING WE WOULD CONSIDER CONTRIBUTION UNSYMPATHETICALLY I FEEL IT ESSENTIAL THAT WE DISPEL AT ONCE ANY SUGGESTIONS OF AUTOMATIC LIABILITY IF IN FACT SITUATION DOES NOT GENUINELY WARRANT IT.

LIKE EVERYONE ELSE I VERY CONCERNED DAVIS'S CONDITION, BUT FEEL WE MUST STICK TO THE LEGAL NICETIES SITUATION SUCH AS THIS.

PROMACK/EXSPURR. FEEL IT WOULD BE PREFERABLE FOR REPUTATION OF VISNEWS IF YOU STUCK TO MORAL NICETIES.
1. DAVIS WAS OFFERED RETAINER FOR TWO WEEKS BUT THEN ASKED TO STANDBY FOR GORST ROAD SPECIAL WHICH NEVER MATERIALISED.
2. WHILE STANDING BY (BUT STILL WITHOUT RETAINER) HE AGREED TO COVER DURING ASPELL'S ABSENCE.

3. IN THAT CASE BOTH LEGALLY AND MORALLY YOU BOUND TO
BE MORE THAN SYMPATHETIC. AND IF YOU TRY TO WEAZEL OUT
YOUR OBLIGATIONS TO DAVIS SO EYE SHALL MAKE QUITE CLEAR
THE ENTIRE PROFESSION KNOWS ABOUT IT.
4. CHEERS.

Davis's parting with Visnews had been a difficult decision.
He set great store by the freedom they gave him to film and
co-ordinate his coverage of the Indo-China war and other
Asian assignments. He had refused a number of lucrative
offers from American television news networks because he
liked to shoot and script his own film, and with the
Americans he would be restricted to camerawork only. But
there was another, deeper reason. Visnews was the Reuters
of the newsfilm business, it had no national barrows to
push, and it distributed film to more than one hundred
countries, many in the Communist bloc. Davis took his
work very seriously and the international impartiality of
the Visnews service meant more to him than a hike in
salary.

No cameraman is ever completely happy with the way
his film is handled back at head office. Despite Davis's
deep and hardwon insights into the Indo-China war, his
contribution to the rest of the world's understanding and
interpretation of the turmoil had to be expressed through
short news clips that ranged from one to three minutes.
Occasionally a feature treatment might expand to four
minutes.

He knew that Visnews would not deliberately distort or
falsify his film, although the pressure of work in handling
stories flowing in from all parts of the globe sometimes led
to omissions or inaccuracies. Davis followed up whenever
he could, patiently advising the harried editors and writers
why it was incorrect to shorten Vietnamese names as detailed in his original script or to call the propeller-driven
Skyraider aircraft used by the South Vietnamese 'American
jets'.

The narration and pictures are history. History must not be tampered with in any way whatsoever, not even if it's harmless — that is, if the editors want to run the film longer. If they think there is not enough footage of helicopter gunships attacking in the air and want to put in say twenty-five more seconds, it is possible to splice in similar footage from a coverage the day before. Nobody will know the difference.

But it is not the same. It's not the same helicopter, and if you could not get that footage on the same day, it's unacceptable. There should be no exceptions whatsoever. It must be one hundred per cent historically correct.

I want to be able to say at the end of my working life that I recorded history faithfully. But you have to keep at it, and this means battling head office. I think I battled fairly successfully under the circumstances. But it did get me into many arguments with London.

Visnews executives were very pleased with Davis's extra-ordinary achievements in the Asian region. But they were genuinely concerned about his continued exposure to the dangers of combat, and felt that he should consider a change of scene. It was company policy to move corre-spondents around after three years in a particular posting, and by 1973 Davis was beginning his tenth consecutive year in Asia for Visnews. In 1968 they had tried to pull him out of Saigon for three months after Harley Street specia-lists had diagnosed battle fatigue.

In 1973 they called him to London again to negotiate a new contract and perhaps a new posting in Washington or Cairo. There had been some niggling irritations. For in-stance, it infuriated some of the cost-conscious London-based Visnews executives to note that Davis was flying around Asia first class. There was a simple explanation, later accepted by London, that the concessions on excess baggage for the camera equipment more than compensated for the higher fare. For a number of reasons, it was time to talk.

Letter to Aunt Lillian, 26 June 1973
Hertford Hotel,
London

I don't know yet what my future holds. Visnews want me
to come to London to work in the office as an 'adviser'
on Asia. I would go mad in a week!
So maybe I will work alone as a freelance. I like
Britain to visit, but I just must work at something
interesting.

Visnews management failed to perceive that Neil Davis's
commitment to Asia was absolute, or if they did realise
that, they were unsympathetic to it. Of course, in their
terms he was just one of many correspondents operating in
quite difficult areas of the world. Davis won out on staying
in Asia, but a new contract had to be negotiated.

Postcard to Aunt Lillian, 18 June 1973
London

Still staying on a week or two as Visnews are now
'revising' their offer. I've already told them it's no use, as
I've lost confidence in them somewhat. I want freedom
to work as I wish. No doubt I'll make less money, but I'll
feel better about it.
I saw the Queen the other day, also Marlene Dietrich,
who was appearing for maybe the last time in
London . . .

Agreement on a contract could not be reached, and Davis
set off on a quick swing through Europe, signing up as a
stringer for a number of European news organisations.

Letter to Aunt Lillian, 27 June 1973
Frederikhotel,
Copenhagen

The only thing certain is that I am no longer working for
Visnews. The Managing Director and the four men

immediately below him took me to lunch the other day in an effort to persuade me to change my mind. As I told them — I can't agree that I'm now worth 50 per cent more than I was two weeks ago, and 'negotiation' of a contract to me means just that. Not threat and counter-threat . . .

Davis sank most of his ready cash into buying his own sound camera, a Commag CP 16, and headed back to Phnom Penh to take his chance with freelancing and survival as the Communist pincers tightened on that once-gracious city.

His coverage was eagerly accepted by European television outlets and by NBC in the United States. He was able to satisfy a long-suppressed desire to write more about the Indo-China situation and began regular contributions to the weekly news magazine *Far Eastern Economic Review* and occasional pieces for Australian newspapers and the Australian Broadcasting Commission.

He was able to keep writing while convalescing in Bangkok after his April 1974 wounding.

I did all sorts of amazing exercises even with the plaster on. Some of these were so violent that the sections around my ankle and knee broke.

By early August he was back in Phnom Penh hobbling about doing city-based assignments. He continued merci-lessly exercising his damaged and nerveless leg, he regained his fitness, and by December was once again covering com-bat. It was only a little more than four months since the mortar round had ripped its shrapnel into his lower body.

I wanted to get back and see how the old reflexes and instincts were working, and I found they were OK. They might even have accelerated a bit. I was pleased to note within myself that my wounding hadn't affected me adversely. I was just a little more careful — that's all.

22

Man Soup

Not long after Neil Davis began filming the Cambodian war in 1970, he became aware the Khmer soldiers practised ritual cannibalism.

It would generally occur after a very torrid, close battle with either hand-to-hand combat or within grenade-throwing distance of the Communists. In the heat of victory some soldiers would take out their knives and very expertly cut out the liver of one of their dead enemy. Sometimes they would eat a slice of it raw then and there, or they would take it back a few hundred metres behind the lines and cook it.

Davis did not regard this practice as barbaric, but rather akin to the Holy Communion rituals of the Christian church.

The Cambodians believed if you ate a part of the heart or liver of an enemy who had died bravely, you gained the strength and courage of the vanquished soldier. They respected and liked a brave man and so they ate his liver. It was more often the liver than the heart.

It wasn't a slaughterhouse with soldiers slicing up their dead enemy everywhere. If they were very tired after a long and protracted battle and they had many wounded, they looked after their wounded and did first things first. Eating the livers of their dead enemy was not a high priority.

Nevertheless, it was done consistently through the five years of the Cambodian war from 1970 to 1975, and Davis estimated that one in five Cambodian soldiers performed that ritual act.

If they had overrun a Communist position and killed their enemy at close quarters, they would eat the liver immediately. In those moments of high excitement they would hold it up to their mouths in the same way we might eat a hamburger.

Although Davis saw this on many occasions, he did not film it.

They did not consider it unusual, and in their trusting way they did not think I would either. I felt sensitive about filming them with the liver actually in their mouths. I certainly did film them after they had taken it from a body, carrying it away.

The South Vietnamese did it sometimes, too, but not as much as the Cambodians. The Vietnamese liked to think they were more sophisticated. But they did it.

I suppose it would have horrified me had I seen it during my first introduction to battle, but I had covered many interesting and unusual events in war so by the time I first saw the liver of a man being eaten by his enemy it wasn't all that much of a shock.

Davis deliberately held back on that story because he did not want the Cambodians portrayed as savages, and ritual cannibalism was the kind of story that would be sensation-alised around the world. In his view, the Cambodians were a gentle and cultured people. Their history and civilisation would have been unjustly distorted by reports of frenzied troops eating raw meat sliced from dead enemies. The short television film and the tabloid headlines of the Western media would give no space to the compassion and cultural interest that Davis himself brought to exotic events.

I know Westerners in general find it hard to accept. However, Cambodians for their part find it difficult to accept a lot of our customs. For example, there are no old age homes in Cambodia, Vietnam or in most of Asia. Family life is so close, and they feel so strongly about their aged relatives, that they look after them. The Cambodians find it inhuman of us to put old people in homes until they die, even when their children or close relatives live close by.

That's what they find inhuman — not eating the liver of a brave enemy.

During the Cambodian war, cannibalism for survival was also practised. Neil Davis first became aware of this in September 1974, when he wrote a story for the *Far Eastern Economic Review* detailing the plight of a town called Kompong Seila, which had been besieged by the Khmer Rouge for four months.

The siege in fact continued for nine months, and was lifted only when the Khmer Rouge withdrew to concentrate their final assault on Phnom Penh in May 1975. The defenders of Kompong Seila came to assist in the defence of the Cambodian capital and Davis gleaned details of the extraordinary and bizarre story only days before the Khmer Rouge took over the country.

Kompong Seila was situated on Highway Four, approximately 115 kilometres southwest of Phnom Penh and 70 kilometres northeast of the port of Kompong Som (formerly Sihanoukville). It was twelve kilometres from the southern side of the Pich Nil Pass, which winds through the Elephant Mountains. The area was heavily wooded and precipitous. To the south of Kompong Seila was another smaller mountain range.

From early May 1974 no one could enter or leave the town, and all supplies had to be dropped by air as an anti-aircraft barrage by the Khmer Rouge in the surrounding hills prevented helicopters from landing.

There were nine thousand men, women and children and a force of one thousand soldiers at Kompong Seila. These ten thousand people were besieged in an area about one kilometre long and half a kilometre wide in a valley.

After four months of isolation, the defenders were in bad shape. They were under daily attack by mortar, rocket and cannon fire. On some days, they might be the targets of only ten or twenty shells, but Davis reported in the *Far Eastern Economic Review* of 13 September 1974 that in one thirty-six-hour period 700 rounds had been fired into the town. There were also frequent ground attacks against the perimeter.

On average, they were receiving about three hundred rounds of mortar shells, artillery or rockets each day. During the total nine-month siege, approximately two thousand people were killed and five thousand injured.

The Kompong Seila defenders dug in and lived underground in home-made bunkers. They had no doctor, but a medic who had only received fifteen days' medical training carried out major operations. They dropped him books on how to do them; he was a very astute and intelligent man.

Every one of those five thousand wounded had been operated on or treated by that marvellous medic. They called him 'doctor', as well they might.

The Lon Nol government could not adequately supply the garrison with essential equipment, ammunition and food.

Air drops of food and medical supplies were made, but 50 per cent fell into enemy hands due to the small area of the town and the necessity of flying high to avoid anti-aircraft fire.

As can be imagined, a population of ten thousand needed a lot of food and other goods to keep them going, tons and tons every day. They obviously ran short.

They ate all the dogs and cats — and the rats of course — birds, lizards, anything that was edible.

After four months, the situation was becoming desperate, but surrender was unthinkable.

The Cambodians were very good defenders, it seemed to be part of their character. The people of Kompong Seila took part in the longest siege since World War II, and they stood up to it remarkably well. I think they were better defenders than the Vietnamese, and certainly better than Australians or Americans would have been. I don't think Westerners would have had the patience or the grit to hang in there under those exceptional circumstances.

They were called on to surrender a number of times, and they refused that alternative over and over again.

The defenders of Kompong Seila desperately needed more protein. Although the soldiers were familiar with the concept of eating parts of the liver of a dead enemy, that was not considered cannibalism. Eating a dead body for food was cannibalism, and it was abhorrent to them. But eventually hunger and determination to stay alive were stronger than revulsion and learned taboos.

It was four months before they actually ate their first man — and he was a Khmer Rouge soldier who had been killed on the perimeter attacking the garrison. Someone dragged him in, and after some debate, they ate him.

The leaders of Kompong Seila decided that for the garrison to survive, cannibalism would have to continue. They did not, however, want to eat each other, so a policy evolved that only the enemy would go into the pot.

I followed this story quite closely, and just before Phnom Penh fell, I talked at length to many people who trusted me and told me in great detail what had happened.

They established special hunting parties to exfiltrate their own positions — through their own minefields and barbed-wire defences — in order to hunt and kill the Communist soldiers.

This was the ultimate hunt, because your prey was also armed and ready to kill you. It was also possible that your quarry would kill and eat you in turn, because the Communist soldiers were short of food as well. This was revealed later when the siege was lifted and the skeletons of government soldiers were found where they had been killed on these hunting parties.

After a while they evolved certain procedures. The hunting parties went out almost every night. They didn't take it in turns — the men who went were selected from those who were best at it.

They not only had to be skilled hunters, but sensitive to their surroundings and with a good knowledge of the area.

The hunting parties were formalised in teams of four to twenty men.

One hunter told me, 'We got thirty in one night!' And the cook raised his eyebrows and said, 'And that wasn't enough.'

I'm sure it wasn't. They had a lot of people to feed.

The Kompong Seila garrison had some rice, which was airdropped to them, and grew some vegetables despite the hazards of the daily bombardment. They had some spices, dried chillies and a few basic ingredients, all of which were in short supply. To this they added the meat — their enemy.

They learned how to butcher the bodies, and told me which were the best cuts. Of course there wasn't enough to give everyone steaks, although occasionally the hunters had prime cuts. They told me that the rump, the buttocks, was the most wholesome part as far as they were concerned.

The liver and heart were naturals, they had eaten them before anyway. One particular man kept on butting in to tell me he liked the lungs — the lights, I suppose. The calves of the legs and arm biceps were quite good. They didn't like the chest — one might say the spare ribs.

The head was hardly touched at all, and they did not eat the cheeks or tongue. But they did eat the brains.

Fingers were quite a delicacy, apparently. Not that many could be spared, but they were given out for some special reason or on a special occasion. One of the hunters might get a finger, or it might be given to a pregnant woman or a child.

Generally they made what they simply called 'man soup', which was literally chopped-up man. The flesh and offal were all cut up and cooked with a few vegetables and chillies if they had them.

I asked some of the Kompong Seila soldiers what man soup tasted like, and they said, 'Quite nice'.

I said, 'Well, what's nice then, like pork?'

'Oh,' they said, 'better than pork!'

The people of Kompong Seila supplemented their diet with man soup for five months of their nine-month siege. Understandably, their behaviour became a little odd.

They were living underground, in fear of violent death at any moment by incoming shells, and they were fighting for their lives. The soldiers dressed in a bizarre way, and had no fear of battle any more — in fact, they quite looked forward to it.

I think that was something to do with the ultimate hunt, the challenge of stalking and killing another armed man. They admitted to getting a great kick out of that. And it must not be forgotten that the people they were killing and eating were the ones besieging them. They didn't have any doubts about it, nor any remorse. Somehow I agreed with them.

The story of the long siege of Kompong Seila, the hunting parties and man soup was submerged in the chaos surrounding the final assault on Phnom Penh. The siege was lifted only a few weeks before the Khmer Rouge won the war, as there was no strategic reason to sustain it. Neil Davis managed to speak to the surviving Kompong Seila soldiers at this time, when they came in to do what they could to defend Phnom Penh.

> They went back into the front line. Of course for them it was like a holiday by comparison. They could go into Phnom Penh, and they had plenty of open country to defend about twenty-five kilometres from the heart of the capital.

Davis became fascinated by the Kompong Seila soldiers and dropped in on them whenever he could. Only two weeks before the end of the war, there was heavy fighting all around Phnom Penh.

> I asked them how much fighting they had had, and they said that they had good fighting — they enjoyed it — for about five or six hours when they took up their position on the perimeter, but for the last twenty-four absolutely none, and they could not understand it.

I understood, all right! Under those situations the

This expression clearly indicates that Davis has spotted a girl he wished to get to know better. *Nancy Nash.*

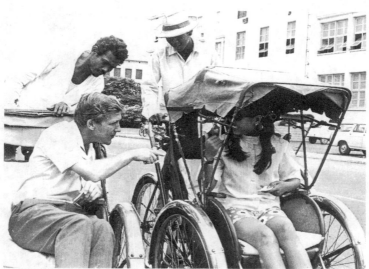

Bill Pinwill gleefully captured Davis in action, picking up a Cambodian girl from adjacent cyclos in Phnom Penh in 1970. The smiling maiden is holding Davis's card with details of his address for their assignation.

Davis steadies himself on the body of a dead Khmer soldier during hectic action around the Oudong Pagoda on Highway Five in Cambodia in June 1970.

Close action in Cambodia, in open country north of Phnom Penh in 1973. During the fighting, a Khmer soldier used the palm of his hand to catch and return a Communist hand grenade 'volley-ball style'!

opposing sides are only about a hundred metres apart and often shout insults or trade information over that distance, as well as listening to each other's radio. Within a few hours they know which units they are opposing.

As soon as the Khmer Rouge learned that they were fighting the soldiers from Kompong Seila — which they knew all about — they weren't all that keen to attack, knowing they would probably finish up in the pot! Although the Communists were supposed to have renounced their Buddhist religion, they did not like the idea of their bodies being cut up after death.

During one of his visits, Davis found a company of the Kompong Seila boys, about forty men, lounging about, not doing any fighting, about a kilometre from the front line. As it turned out they were on strike, refusing to fight until they had been paid. Their salaries had not been paid for four months, not an uncommon state of affairs in the Lon Nol army.

They were quite happy to fight, and indeed were looking forward to it, but said they were waiting for their pay. They believed the paymaster was coming out from Phnom Penh the next day to give them their money.

At 2 p.m. the next day, Davis caught up with them again, and they seemed rather surly and withdrawn. He chatted with them for a while until they seemed more relaxed, and asked if they had been paid.

'No, we haven't,' they said.

Davis asked if the paymaster had come on schedule. Yes, they said, he had come.

'What happened then — didn't he have any money?'

There was a pause.

'We ate him!' they said.

Gradually Davis extracted the story. The paymaster, a captain who lived in Phnom Penh and who had not seen

301

any hard fighting, had come down and rather imperiously ordered them back into the front line. Their lieutenant refused to do so until they had been paid. The paymaster pulled his pistol and repeated the order. Again the lieutenant refused, and the paymaster shot him.

> The paymaster was dead seconds later, because the lieutenant was much loved and respected by his men, and because he had been through the siege of Kompong Seila with them.
> Then they then ate part of the paymaster, but it was more a ritual than necessity. They ate the liver, heart and lungs. The man who kept telling me he liked the lights ate the paymaster's lungs.
> They got into the swing of things while they were telling me, and said they had cut the paymaster about a bit because they did not have any respect for him. That is why they ate more than just the liver.
> Then they said, 'Do you want to see him?'

Davis felt it was unwise to say 'no' to anything the Kompong Seila men suggested, and reluctantly agreed.

> The paymaster's body was lying under a tree, and even as a layman I could see how expertly they had cut out the heart, liver and lungs. They had also taken the biceps and had made man soup, actually.

On his way back to Phnom Penh, Neil met the general commanding the area and told him he had a problem with the soldiers from Kompong Seila.

> I said, 'They've just eaten the paymaster.'
> He didn't show any great surprise, and just said, 'Heavens, I suppose we had better pay them then.'

Davis said he thought that might be a good idea.
Thinking back on those events, Neil was inclined to agree

with the general's attitude that non-payment of salary was more important than cannibalism.

When I read books on Africa and somebody wrote they had known a cannibal, I thought it was something exceptional. But I suppose I've known many cannibals, and I don't think any less of the Cambodians for doing that. They never tried to hide the fact that they had eaten human flesh either through necessity at Kompong Seila, or for ritual reasons.

It was highly likely Davis had, too.

There always seemed to be some liver in the pot after a battle, and there weren't many animals about by then. Cambodian soldiers are always very hospitable and offer you part of their meal, and are disappointed and even hurt if you don't accept.

I never asked questions about this. But I would often see Cambodian soldiers walking back from the front line with some liver, and you could only assume it came from a body.

When I had eaten under those circumstances, there was one chance in five that I was having a bit of man soup or stew.

23

'The Situation is Desperate But Not Serious'

Letter to Aunt Lillian, 25 March 1973
Apartment 403,
Phnom Penh

Dear Auntie,
Not so much doing here — the situation is desperate but
not serious! That's an old Indo-China saying and
strangely true. A crazy ex-pilot stole a light fighter
bomber and tried to bomb President Lon Nol out of
existence in his Palace last Saturday, and then
disappeared into the unknown with the plane — so the
Khmer Communists now have the nucleus of an air
force!

Things are bad here — the worst they've ever been. I
don't really know what will happen. The Government
forces control almost nothing of the countryside, so the
Communists roam at will, and thereby control what they
like, when they like.

Of course it's always easy to be the attacker, with little
or no responsibility to the population regarding security,
communications, health services, local trade,
administration and law and order. That's why a
Government must have a superiority of at least eight or
ten troops to one so that they can protect all the
services, installations and people. The British had about

304

that ratio — ten to one — in the Malayan Emergency and it took them twelve years. The Khmers have nothing like that, in fact at times they are battling one-to-one ...

I'm now listening to the American Forces Radio Saigon — AFRS — which is what it was called when I first went to Vietnam. They had stations all over Vietnam as well as TV and they changed its name several times, the last being AFVN (Armed Forces Vietnam Network). But now there's just the Saigon station again, and in three days' time that will finish.

It's just gone 9 p.m., and that's now the curfew time. So the traffic has suddenly stopped, and the soldiers' whistles are blowing as they stop those late out. But at least it's nice to sit out on my patio above the normally crowded and terribly noisy street. It's the hottest time of the year here now.

Must go,
Cheers to all,
Neil

Aunt Lillian Davis, who had been living in a home for the elderly in Warrane, a suburb of Hobart on the eastern shore of the Derwent River, died on 9 September 1973. Davis was deeply saddened by her death. She had been a strong and rather stern figure to him after his mother died, but they had grown very close in his adult years. It was through Aunt Lillian that Neil Davis communicated with his family, learned of the generally disastrous efforts of his beloved Clarence football team and revealed details of his own life and personality carefully hidden from his hell-raising friends in Asia.

It is only through correspondence with Davis's Aunt Lillian that we know of his generous support for Vietnamese and Cambodian orphaned and handicapped children. This care and concern extended to old friends back in Tasmania. Davis had been shaken to learn when he arrived in Saigon for the first time in 1965 that his best footballing mate Ron Batchelor had died of liver failure, a legacy of the heavy drinking bouts they had enjoyed together. But Batchelor had become an alcoholic. So had another boyhood friend, Johnny Wright.

Johnny Wright had lent Neil the Box Brownie camera with which he captured his clandestine photograph of the old eccentric Adam Featherstone, who later collapsed and died while digging his own grave in the churchyard at Sorell. Wright had engineered Neil's first job at the Tasmanian Government Film Unit. Davis returned the favour by clandestinely sitting the public service examination for his friend, who was weak in English and maths. He overdid things a bit, and topped the state! When Davis left Tasmania for Asia in 1963, Johnny Wright succeeded him as an ABC news cinecameraman.

But Wright's drink problem was dragging him down. In the late 1960s Davis made several trips to Tasmania to counsel his friend and dry him out. He was successful in motivating Wright to voluntarily enter a hospital specialising in the treatment of alcoholism in 1970. Wright began work as a cameraman again with the Tasmanian Government Film Unit. Unfortunately he had irreparably damaged his health, and he died in 1974.

Letters to Aunt Lillian reveal Davis's patient counselling of Wright, encouraging him to write letters and send tapes to him with Tasmanian news and whenever possible returning home to motivate him further.

Davis also told Aunt Lillian of the progress of the young runners he continued to coach in Tasmania, writing painstaking training schedules for them between his combat assignments and his film scripts.

On hearing of Aunt Lillian's death, Davis wrote to his sister Barbara.

> She was always such an anchor . . . it is difficult to imagine she is not there any more. The last time I saw

her, I couldn't help thinking it was very much as the last time I saw Dad. Both of them insisted on walking to the car with me, and seemed more demonstrative when they said goodbye. I didn't think of it much when I said goodbye to Dad, but I did when I saw Aunt Lil the last time. They looked so alike . . .

Davis's father had been killed fighting the Tasmanian bushfires of 1967. He was caught in a firestorm near Sorell, and died, his son always said, a hero's death.

The close call with the mortar bomb in Cambodia in 1974 had pushed the legendary luck of Neil Davis to the limit. A large chunk of shrapnel had smashed into the tape recorder he carried strapped to his waist, saving him from being disembowelled. He had kept his right leg against the odds. Despite making light of his injuries, he felt more vulnerable than he had ever been, and perhaps an acceptance of his own destructibility turned his thoughts towards a permanent relationship and marriage.

In January 1972, Neil Davis was sunning himself beside the swimming pool of the Lane-Xang Hotel in Vientiane when his eye was caught by a classically beautiful Chinese girl with long, black hair, wearing a swimming costume. Chou Ping Yen was a singer with a Taiwanese cultural group touring Southeast Asia. Because the Taiwanese government had no diplomatic relations with Laos, the troupe had been unable to perform, and was waiting to leave on the next leg of their trip.

Chou Ping (Julie) remembers that Davis was reading a book when they first noticed each other: 'I think he was very attracted to long-haired Asian girls.'

He asked Julie to have dinner with him that night, but the troupe was living as a group, and were due to move on the next day. Davis and Julie swapped addresses and later managed to meet briefly in Bangkok. Julie remembers liking him instantly because he seemed so gentle and shy: 'He spoke so softly, and seemed very kind.'

They continued to correspond, and Davis proposed at the end of 1972. Julie says, 'I wasn't surprised because I knew he really wanted to marry with me at that time. I was quite young, only twenty-two, and I said you must come to Taiwan to meet my parents and have their approval for the marriage.'

In March 1973 Davis went to Taiwan, but Julie's parents had misgivings. They were particularly concerned about Julie going to live in Cambodia during the war, and wedding plans had to be postponed.

Visa restrictions prevented Julie from visiting Davis in Bangkok after he was badly wounded, but they continued to correspond.

After the break with Visnews, Davis worked for American and European television news organisations, and did occasional assignments for Visnews. He began writing regular reports for the *Far Eastern Economic Review*, the English-language weekly published in Hong Kong and carrying its authority to the rest of the world.

He welcomed the chance to break from the frustrating brevity of his film scripts. As always, his keen eye for personal situations brought the war into sharp focus for his readers.

Far Eastern Economic Review — 4 October 1974

AN EXPLOSIVE LIST OF INCREASES
By Neil Davis

Phnom Penh: The soldier in the Phnom Penh market was dumbfounded, then angry. He knew the 45 kilogram sack of rice would have cost him over Riels 7000, but now the asking price was an even Riels 10 000 — only a little less than his monthly salary. Of course, that pay packet would be doubled next month, but, even so, the price was beyond him.

It was just one day after the devaluation of the Riel and the announcement that, to offset this move, salaries

of Government employees and the military would be
raised up to 100 per cent. Other economic measures
were also introduced.

The soldier delivered a tirade against rising prices in
general, and hawkers and bystanders scurried clear. A
wise precaution . . . the soldier concluded his outburst
by pulling the pin on a hand grenade and hurling it in an
explosive demonstration of his feelings. Fortunately,
there were no injuries.

The soldier's frustration was well understood by the
people in the market. For most were desperately
bargaining in order that they could return home with at
least something for their families to eat . . .

In the 29 November issue Davis relayed an even more
pertinent comment on the state of affairs in Cambodia five
months before its fall.

CAMBODIA'S 'CRAZY' DRAFT-DODGERS

In their desperation to avoid the dreaded draft and the
possibility of becoming one of the daily casualty figures,
many young Cambodians are willing to declare
themselves insane. Forged *lop-lop* (crazy) certificates,
declaring that the bearer is unbalanced or mentally
disturbed, can be bought in Phnom Penh for about Riels
50 000 (US$30.67) — quite good value in this sellers'
market.

To simplify the wordy description of the opposing forces,
Davis and other correspondents resorted to acronyms. The
Communist Khmer Rouge, because they had collected the
deposed Prince Sihanouk, were called the Royal Government of National Union of Cambodia (GRUNK). The Lon
Nol army fought under the simpler Khmer Armed Forces
(FANK). Somehow the juxtaposition of GRUNK and FANK
did not lend dignity to the most serious prose analysis of
a situation which, although superficially analogous to a

comic opera, was soon to degenerate catastrophically into one of the worst examples of national genocide ever known.

FANK was often criticised tactically for not following up some of its better performances against the invading Communist GRUNK. The American Broadcasting Company's correspondent Jim Laurie (who later joined Neil Davis to cover the fall of Saigon) recalls that Davis had a deep understanding of the problems facing the Khmer Republic's military leaders. Many Western correspondents dismissed them as good-for-nothing, hopelessly corrupted commanders. But Davis knew them, and understood their problems.

Says Laurie, 'Neil used to talk of the general charged with the defence of Phnom Penh who had literally to barter with thousands of riels to obtain artillery support from other commanders, and the occasional air strike. It was not simple corruption, it was a barter system simply to keep the army going, to achieve survival.'

Neil could not resist colourful individuals, and the *Far Eastern Economic Review* of 17 January 1975 carried his profile of the distinguished Cambodian surgeon, Colonel Dr Khun Son Soeung, whose normal workload of 1000 major operations a year had increased dramatically, helping to cope with the 600 or so military casualties each week, as well as civilian wounded.

Removing live grenades from human flesh was one of Khun's specialties. Once Davis watched him operating on a Cambodian soldier's wife who had an M79 grenade embedded in the flesh of her arm.

On the odd occasion, due to some freak maladjustment, the M79 fails to explode when it hits flesh from short range. However, it can still explode when the pressure is eased during this rather tricky surgery.

For this type of operation Col. Khun places the patient in a rough steel tank, and works with only his hands inside

— but he still runs the risk of being killed if the grenade goes off.

At the end of the operation Davis witnessed, Colonel Khun picked up the grenade, walked to a shallow, sandbagged hole in the ground and dropped it inside. A small crowd who had gathered to watch at a safe distance broke into spontaneous applause.

By February 1975, American and Cambodian officials admitted that Phnom Penh, with ammunition running low, had only enough rice and fuel supplies for one month. That estimate was thought to be optimistic, so there was considerable interest in the efforts of two tankers and four ammunition barges that managed to run the gauntlet of the Mekong River blockade from the Vietnamese border.

One tanker was crippled and had to pull into the government-held town of Neak Luong only halfway to Phnom Penh. The second tanker, the Vira One, made it to the besieged city. Davis went on board to interview the captain for the *Far Eastern Economic Review*.

Skipper of the Vira One is Captain Nguyen Van Chieu, a delightfully relaxed Vietnamese in his 50s. He has a twenty-man crew of mixed Vietnamese, Cambodians and Chinese and he speaks all their languages as well as French and some English. Captain Chieu has made 'oh, so many runs' to Phnom Penh since 1971, and says he will continue to do his job. Morale on the tanker, which carries nearly two million litres of fuel, is surprisingly high. This seems to stem from the captain himself, who shows no outward sign of tension.

Captain Chieu agreed that the latest voyage was his toughest ever. 'Before, the Khmer Rouge only hit us at two or three spots along the way, usually from one side only,' he said. 'But this time it was for the entire journey, and from both sides.' He smiled broadly as he handed round coffee to his guests and crewmen in the tiny cabin. There was one cup short, so the skipper himself went without.

'It's a question of luck,' Chieu went on. Then he added, almost as an afterthought: 'When they strike at you from both sides, you can't run away — there's no way to go.' When he hurried off to complete the formalities of signing his ship into port, the Chinese mate completed the picture. 'We are all Buddhists on this ship — and we have confidence in our captain.'

By early 1975 the Communists had Phnom Penh completely surrounded and were within rocket range of five to seven kilometres. The Khmer Rouge proceeded to rocket Phnom Penh district by district.

It was specifically aimed at the ordinary people to demoralise them. That did not succeed, actually, because the will and the resolve of the Cambodian people to resist strengthened with each renewed rocket attack. But it did take heavy toll of civilians.

On Thursday 6 February 1975, Neil Davis was keeping a watching brief on the central district of Phnom Penh, which was being targeted by the Khmer Rouge. The area had many markets and schools, and up to one hundred rockets were coming in per day. He was one block away from a 107 millimetre rocket which scored a direct hit on a primary school, showering a classroom with deadly shrapnel.

I got there less than a minute later. The rocket had gone straight into a classroom with children aged six to nine years. There were fourteen or fifteen dead, thirty or forty seriously wounded and it was like a scene from Dante's *Inferno*. Bloodied children wounded and screaming in terror were trying to get out of the school. There were several hundred more children in other parts of the school who were also desperately trying to get out of the place, and calling for their parents. Some of the wounded children were being carried out by policemen and soldiers and some of their teachers and civilians.

It was the most horrifying sight I remember from the Cambodian war.

Davis had an agonising decision to make: to film or try to help. He filmed.

My instinct told me to stop and help those children. I did help later, but professionally I felt I could help them and other children and the people of Cambodia by presenting to the world what was really happening, on film.

I felt very strongly about these rocket attacks on civilian areas. There were many military targets that the Communists could have concentrated on, but they chose to kill civilians and children in schools. I felt revulsion and anger against the Communists. At the same time I knew I must cover this story to get the best possible stark and bloody film, to show exactly what the people of Cambodia had to put up with.

After the war ended, of course, it became apparent that the Khmer Rouge were the most repressive and bloody regime of recent times, so it wasn't surprising in retrospect that they did what they did before the end of the war.

Despite the barbarity of Khmer Rouge attacks on civilians, Davis maintained his even-handed compassion for fellow human beings. Early in 1975 he was filming action on the perimeters of Phnom Penh when he came upon two teenage Khmer Rouge soldiers who had just been captured.

The government soldiers had many of their dependents killed in rocket and mortar attacks on

313

Phnom Penh in January 1975, and were mad with grief and anger. They were about to kill these two Khmer Rouge boys, and an officer who had lost control of the situation appealed to me for help. The troops knew me, and hesitated. I convinced them it was best to keep them alive for questioning. I remember the officer saying, his voice trembling with emotion, 'There will be no torture.' My reply was, 'I don't think there is going to be any torture, Colonel, just a killing.'

It was a close thing. I put them in my car and took them to the nearest HQ, near Phnom Penh.

The Cambodian government soldiers were tenacious fighters, despite lack of pay and, towards the end, food and ammunition. By early 1975, Neil Davis knew that Phnom Penh must fall. He faced some difficult personal decisions. He had made his home in Phnom Penh. In his apartment were all his prized artifacts, paintings, carvings and antiques. All his papers were there, his notebooks, diaries, scripts and other writings.

The situation had been desperate enough when he moved his possessions to Phnom Penh in 1972. Even at that stage only one small freighter was making regular voyages up the Mekong to the isolated city from the main port of Kompong Som.

His closest friends were Cambodians, although many had already died in combat and through random rocket attacks on Phnom Penh. His commitment to the country was strong and passionate, yet he knew he would have to go and that, by so doing, he would miss the last part of the Cambodian war he had covered so intimately. His love for the country, its people and the story was swayed by a calculated weighing of the odds of his being able to survive a Khmer Rouge takeover.

I had no doubts there would be a bloodbath one way or the other. I didn't, however, envisage the total evacuation of Phnom Penh's three million people.

I did know that the Cambodian Communists were not at all like their fellow-countrymen on the other side. They were a xenophobic clique of disenchanted radical so-called intellectuals, some of whom had graduated in France and other countries. But they had always been on the outside as far as the urban Cambodian people were concerned.

They had a vitriolic hatred of the Cambodian people because of their earlier rejections, and they disliked the Vietnamese — including the Communists — because they had earlier rejected them also. It was only the American involvement which moved the Chinese and Vietnamese Communists to support them. That is how they found themselves in a position to take over the government.

Davis knew that the Khmer Rouge soldiers, many of them only teenagers, had a kind of crazed indoctrination in lieu of education. He filmed the aftermath of massacres in captured villages, some only days before the end of the war.

It was very clear what they were going to do.

Meanwhile, the Khmer defenders fought with epic tenacity. Pushed back into the streets of Phnom Penh, they stopped only because they took so many casualties and ran out of supplies and ammunition because the Americans who had air-dropped supplies pulled out. In the end there was no alternative to surrender.

President Nixon had committed Cambodia to the war, against the will and knowledge of most Cambodians. At the same time he had promised them faithfully that the Americans would support them right throughout the war, that they could count on America.

315

As the situation in Indo-China in general deteriorated, the American policy changed. Americans are not always good allies, as they have proved in recent years. Eventually they deserted the Cambodians and the Cambodians fought their cause with greater strength and courage than any other army in recent times.

Weighing up whether to stay in Phnom Penh to film the Khmer Rouge takeover or evacuate was perhaps the most difficult decision Davis ever made.

On 1 April, the Australian Liberal Shadow Foreign Minister Andrew Peacock, and the Deputy Leader of the National Party Ian Sinclair, flew into Phnom Penh against the advice of the Australian Embassy in Bangkok, on a fact-finding mission. Peacock admitted later that the First of April arrival date was a suitable reflection on the lunacy of this foray into the stricken city.

They had with them the keys of the already evacuated Australian Residency, where Neil Davis sought them out. The next evening, while occasional shell and mortar fragments spattered into the Residency walls and garden, Davis told Peacock of his belief that the incoming Khmer Rouge would behave like the mad killers he knew them to be, and that he thought it best to get out of Phnom Penh to Saigon to cover the final chapter of the Indo China war there. He told Peacock that the Americans were only making plans to move their own nationals out, and asked him to intercede on his behalf. Peacock, who had met Davis on earlier visits to Vietnam, regarded him as one of the most outstanding journalists he ever encountered. He made representations to the Americans and the CIA and secured him a seat on an evacuation chopper.

There are conflicting accounts of Davis's reasons for leaving Phnom Penh in the final United States evacuation on 12 April. Jim Laurie was with him when the Operation Eagle Pull helicopters clattered into the sky from a school playground near the American embassy. Laurie later wrote,

'It was probably the only story from which Neil ever walked away, or in this case flew away. Emotionally he was exhausted.

'I remember him sitting in the Marine Corps CH53 cradling his CP16 camera that morning as the orange and gold pagodas of Phnom Penh disappeared beneath us and the cheering of schoolchildren still rang in our ears. Leaving Cambodia, I think, was the hardest decision of Neil's life.'

Later Davis became reticent about his decision to leave Phnom Penh while some Western correspondents had stayed. 'Truly humiliating, mate', he told a brother correspondent, Al Dawson. But, according to John Tulloh of Visnews, there was another infuriatingly pragmatic reason why he had to go. His camera had broken down.

Tulloh remembers Davis saying how depressed he was for some months after the Communists had marched into Phnom Penh while he had rushed off to Bangkok to try and get his camera repaired. By the time it was fixed it was too late to get back to Phnom Penh. 'He was concerned about the fate of his Cambodian friends, and not being there at that critical hour bothered him greatly for their sake, including the enormous responsibility he felt for any Asian who had worked for or with him.'

Davis's work diaries (carried out on the helicopter with him) confirm that. The last entry on the day of the evacuation was a note that he had paid his driver and soundman An Veng $US400 (including a bonus). There are one-line entries for the next three days.

April 13: Make arrangements to return Phnom Penh.

April 14: Try all avenues to get to Phnom Penh.

April 15: Repeat efforts to return to Phnom Penh.

Davis cabled his last Cambodian despatches from the US aircraft carrier *Okinawa* in the Gulf of Thailand. The evacuating Americans, guarded by grim-faced marines, were nervous that their former allies would turn on them as they abandoned them. That was not the Cambodian style. School-children waved and smiled and called out their few words of English, 'Hello, hello', and 'Bye bye', as the helicopters whisked the remaining 260 Americans, other Westerners and a few Cambodians to safety.

Phnom Penh fell on 17 April and two days later Davis took an enormous risk by re-entering Cambodia at the border town of Poipet.

I got the first film, and one of only two films taken, of the Khmer Rouge in Cambodia on that day when they occupied Poipet. I didn't like it at all, I was very nervous, and in some ways I guess I was more afraid than I'd been in most situations in Indo-China — combat situations or not.

He was immediately arrested by the Khmer Rouge and hustled back across the border, but he managed to get significant film of their occupation of the town.

Two days later Davis went into Cambodia again, to visit the last scrap of the Khmer Republic in the northern part of the country close to the Thai border. About 150 Lon Nol soldiers and their families were still occupying a twelfth-century temple.

The reason why it wasn't occupied by the Khmer Rouge was geographic. The temple was on a cliff and the cliff face was actually inside Cambodia, and to reach it easily you had to go into Thailand and walk up a hill.

The Khmer Rouge hadn't got around to that so I was able to take the last film inside Cambodia with the deposed government's flag flying over the one remaining square kilometre of the Khmer Republic.

He had already made up his mind to return to Vietnam and be in Saigon for the final part of the Indo-China war. In a letter to a friend in Tasmania written four weeks later in Saigon (by then Ho Chi Minh City), Davis allowed himself to pour out his bitterness about the Cambodian Pol Pot regime's unspeakable inhumanity at the moment of victory.

> The atrocity of that takeover is indescribable, and I can never bring myself to forgive those who perpetrated it. I think it has nothing to do with Communism, it was sheer, terrifying barbarism. Hundreds of thousands are dead, including innumerable friends of mine, in acts of wanton cruelty and destruction that cannot be imagined. Just for openers, everybody — but everybody — in Phnom Penh was driven out into the countryside forcibly, including people in hospitals ... all those in hospital. Nobody escaped — maybe that's the only democratic thing they will ever do!

In Bangkok, in the days following the fall of Phnom Penh, Davis was angry, shocked and homeless. He had only the clothes he wore, his cameras and his work diaries. All his possessions, souvenirs, furniture, all his notebooks and personal diaries, copies of all his scripts and writings in Southeast Asia for the past eleven years were lost.

On 27 April he boarded one of the last commercial flights to leave Hong Kong for Saigon. His ticket said HKG — SGN — HKG, but he was not planning to be on a return flight. His decision to stay in Saigon for the fall was absolute. There would be no last-minute evacuation this time. It was a deliberate gamble for the biggest story of his professional life.

24

'The Other Side
Will Be Here Shortly'

Just before lunch on the morning of 28 April 1975, Neil Davis strolled down Saigon's Tu Do Street with Rick Merron, a longtime AP photographer in Vietnam. As they passed Minh the tailor's shop on the left side halfway to the Saigon River from the Continental Hotel, Davis said to Merrin, 'You know, I need another correspondent's suit. I've only one left.'

Minh had been the first tailor to design and make the 'foreign correspondent's suit' with buttoned jacket pockets and slots in the sleeves to take pens and a notebook. Since Minh's originals had appeared in 1962, imitations had mushroomed not only in Saigon but all over Asia. Davis knew that no tailor's shop made bush jackets of the quality, style and fit better than Mr Minh the tailor.

Merrin thought the whole thing hilarious. 'I can't believe it,' he told Davis. 'You'll never pick up your suit.'

Mr Minh took at least forty-eight hours to make a correspondent's suit and it was doubtful that Saigon had as much time left. But apart from the quixotic nature of the exercise, Davis really needed clothes after losing all his possessions in Phnom Penh two weeks before.

It took quite a time to select the material and haggle over a price with the head tailor. Minh himself had rarely made the suits in recent years, leaving that to his deputy. Mr Minh had left for the United States several days earlier, to start a tailoring business there. As the head tailor ran the tape measure over Davis, General 'Big' Minh was being sworn in as the last president of South Vietnam — a position he would hold for less than forty-eight hours.

Davis decided on a cream-coloured cloth and the price for the finished suit was the equivalent of five American dollars. 'You'll never collect it,' gurgled Rick Merron. The delighted American regaled every pressman he met with the story. When the American evacuation began next morning, Merron was still chuckling: 'Davis can't come with us,' he told anybody within hearing. 'He's got to stay and pick up his TV suit from Mr Minh's.'

Late on the afternoon of 28 April only half an hour after 'Big' Minh had been sworn in, the Saigonese were made aware of how fast events were moving by experiencing the city's only Communist air raid of the war. The Americans and South Vietnamese air forces had previously dominated the skies.

But using North Vietnamese pilots, or perhaps defecting South Vietnamese air crew, some American A37 aircraft captured in Da Nang swept in low over the city and bombed Tan Son Nhut airport. It was pretty dramatic, because they came over at treetop level straight over the palace.

I thought the buggers were going to bomb Independence Palace as a symbol of the old regime, but they didn't. However, everybody in the city who had a weapon of any description fired up in the air. This was extremely dangerous in such a tightly packed and over-crowded city — soldiers in the street, policemen with their handguns all blazing away.

The signal for the evacuation came through at around 11 a.m. Saigon time the next morning, Tuesday 29 April. It was said the code was to be 'White Christmas' played over the American Armed Forces Radio.

I don't know whether they did or not, but the word came through anyway about twenty-four hours before the surrender and the whole city was in a turmoil.

Tens of thousands of Vietnamese, feeling betrayed and abandoned, were trying to get out. Vietnamese employees who had been promised evacuation and sanctuary in the United States were left stranded. Many Vietnamese wives or de factos of Americans had to stay, while some Vietnamese men seized the chance to get out with their girlfriends or de facto wives.

The whole evacuation plan got out of control because it really hinged on evacuation by fixed-wing aircraft from Tan Son Nhut airport, and that was by then under Communist bombardment.

Emergency pickup points were nominated for Vietnamese who had been given permission to go with the Americans, and other assembly points were designated for Americans. It all got out of hand because there were not enough buses to get to the airport.

Thousands of people on bicycles, motorbikes, motor scooters, motor cyclos, cars, small lorries and even on foot were following every American bus, literally screaming to get out of the city and escape with the Americans.

Davis had made a verbal agreement to cover the fall of Saigon for NBC and he met up with Jim Laurie, an American freelance radio reporter also working for the big American news network. Davis wanted a spare camera and found out he could get one from a French cameraman who was joining the evacuation.

At noon I went to the New Palace Hotel in the Street of Flowers, central Saigon. The Frenchman's room was on the sixth floor, and he sort of threw the camera at me and bade a hasty goodbye as his car was downstairs.

A Vietnamese girl in her early twenties, wearing slacks and well dressed, came out of another room and asked me in excellent English if I could help her and her family to get on a helicopter.

Davis could only suggest they went to one of the nominated assembly points, but the girl said the family had no authority. Through the door he could see the family of about six with her father looking hopefully at him.

The girl said they would pay anything to get out, and opened her satchel to reveal about fifty thousand dollars in American currency. 'We will pay ten thousand dollars to the helicopter pilot and pay you also if you can get us out.'

Davis could not help and was never able to find out what happened to them.

During that frenzied afternoon, he teamed up with Peter Arnett, a Pulitzer Prizewinning New Zealand-born journalist and photographer who worked for American Associated Press. The two men knew each other well, and they drove around Saigon everywhere seeking drama and melodrama, Arnett taking still pictures and Davis filming.

We went to the airport, and there was pandemonium as buses were being turned back from the bombardment. There were tens of thousands of hysterical people in the streets, everyone following American vehicles.

The American embassy was besieged by an enormous crowd of Vietnamese but behind it, about a block away, was a pickup point for Americans. Curiously enough when Davis and Arnett arrived, hardly anyone was there, except a very small — even for a Vietnamese — man of about forty in civilian clothes, with a boy of about eight.

It took a minute or two for Peter and me to recognise him. He was a lieutenant-colonel and had been press officer for the general commanding the Third Military Region, which included Saigon, and we knew him quite well.

When we spoke to him, he was most embarrassed and said that his wife and daughter were staying in Saigon, and he hoped they would follow later, but he and his son were trying to leave because he did not know what would happen to him when the Communists came in.

As we spoke, a jeep pulled up with about five or six Vietnamese paratroopers from the Airborne Division — one of the best-trained and elite units in the country. They were bristling with arms and ammunition and looking rather menacing.

A captain got out and swaggered over to us rather belligerently, looked us up and down with some contempt and said, 'Well, you are deserting us.'

Peter said, 'What do you mean?'

He said, 'The Americans are all running away, leaving us to our fate. You got us into this, and now you are deserting us.' He was quite threatening and his men were watching him very closely. I think they only needed his order and they would have done whatever his command was.

Peter said, 'No, we are journalists and we are not leaving.'

The captain was unimpressed and insisted that we were going on the evacuation. We said, 'Well you can see our cameras, and we have no luggage. We are waiting to see who gets on the bus.'

At that, the captain changed his tack and congratulated us, shaking us by the hand. But then he turned his attention to the lieutenant-colonel in civilian clothes beside us and it was immediately apparent that even if he did not know him personally, he knew that he was a high-ranking military officer waiting to get out.

He walked up to him with a look of absolute contempt

— I wasn't sure whether he was going to kill him or not — looked him up and down, then spat at his feet, sort of swaggered to his jeep and went off.

Davis believed that the presence of the little boy probably saved his father's life.

The Americans always seemed to blame the Vietnamese for anything that went wrong, but the Airborne were very well trained and not mad dog killers.

As the paratroopers drove off in their jeep, the evacuation bus arrived at the pickup point. It was jammed full, the American driver was shouting, 'Goddamn, no, no Vietnamese!'

Peter and I physically picked up the colonel and his son — it was easy, he was a light little fellow — and pushed them in over the heads of some people in the doorway. Peter kept shouting, 'He is the AP photo chief, he is the AP photo chief.'

I don't know what difference that would have made, but it was enough to hold the driver's attention and stop him closing the door while we bundled them in. The driver just gave up — it had been happening at every stop, probably — and off he went.

A few hours later Neil Davis and fellow NBC reporter Jim Laurie drove back to the same area.

The people were still running around hysterically like fowls with their heads chopped off. They didn't know quite what to do and were actually running around in circles some of the time.

A girl of about nineteen, well dressed, obviously well educated and speaking very good English, rushed up to us carrying her little suitcase, saying that she and her sister had to get to Canada to join their parents, but they had no papers.

Her teenage sister joined her and, bearing in mind

how Peter and I had helped the colonel and his son, Jim and I said we would do what we could. Just then a bus came along and we followed it with our vehicle. It had to stop at the next corner for traffic, and the people on board were pretty helpful. They opened one of the back sliding windows of the bus, and we actually pushed them through head first, and their little bags went after them.

It was a pretty sexy sort of operation in a way, and I was hoping under different circumstances that we could have got to know them better!

Ten years later, in April 1985, someone told Davis and Laurie that a girl had told him of how two foreigners — one an Australian — had pushed them through the back window of a bus and helped them to escape.

The situation at the American embassy was now utter pandemonium, with a crowd estimated by Davis and Laurie at about fifteen thousand trying to scramble over the gates and being pushed back by marine guards.

The American ambassador, Graham Martin, was courageously but unwisely insisting on returning to his house by car to pick up some personal effects, not fully realising that the city was in chaos and while the crowd was not necessarily anti-American, anything could have happened if he had gone out. In any case, these thousands and thousands of people were right outside the gate, and it would have been too big a problem simply to open it. We could see his car waiting behind a side gate.

Eventually he agreed not to leave. Helicopters were landing on the Embassy roof helipad, while people were actually managing to get over the high wrought-iron spiked fence all around, despite extra barbed wire. Some were managing to buy their way in. We did see money changing hands. A lot of people were waving money.

At dusk, Davis had to stop filming, and he and Laurie considered their situation. Davis was confident that a Communist takeover would not be accompanied by the kind of bloody bestiality that had been the trademark of the Khmer Rouge in Cambodia. But a breakdown of law and order seemed imminent, and anarchy would have its own dangers.

There was some danger that the South Vietnamese forces, in their frustration, would turn on any remaining Americans or other Westerners. There were already many deserters roaming the streets, and things were threatening to get out of hand.

You couldn't really blame the soldiers. Unlike Cambodia, where all but a handful of military leaders had stayed, the Vietnamese high commanders had left in droves. Now the troops were leaderless and penniless, and feeling understandably hardly done by. It seemed likely they would represent our greatest danger — not the incoming Communist troops.

There was a curfew of sorts that night, and Laurie and Davis returned to the Continental Palace Hotel for the night. They could hear the bombardment of the airport, and the fighting on the outskirts of the city as the Communists tightened their grip and prepared for the final push.

Davis, with his enviable ability to sleep under almost any circumstances, reported a good night's rest when he and Jim Laurie breakfasted at 7 a.m. on the morning of Wednesday 30 April.

When I went out into the street things were different, and for a minute or two I couldn't work out why. Of course there were no police, the White Mice we called them, as the Vietnamese police wore white uniforms and white hats and were rather small in stature. We were a bit contemptuous of the White Mice over the years as they were corrupt and not very efficient, but not to have them there was a big loss.

Suddenly we realised that there was no law and order

327

in a city of four million people which was out of control. It was a bit frightening.

Many people had cars stolen in the night. Davis and Laurie had two cars between them, one of which had disappeared.

> We immediately stole someone else's car so it didn't make any difference, and we drove straight to the American embassy by 7.30 a.m.

A crowd at least ten thousand strong was outside trying to get in as the last helicopters clattered away from the roof-top helipad. At vantage points in other areas of central Saigon, forlorn groups of people queued to stand on roof-tops for transport which would never come. The 'stairways to the sky' remained an enduring image of that undignified American exodus.

Neil Davis and Jim Laurie arrived at the American embassy to witness the end of that particular drama. As Davis filmed, American marines were lobbing tear gas canisters down into the crowd.

> Curiously enough, the mood of the crowd was not all that belligerent. They were shouting good old Vietnamese obscenities to the American Marines on the roof. So was I — in Vietnamese of course. The ARVN soldiers had taught me very well how to swear, and shouts of '*Do-ma*' — 'Motherfucker', or more literally 'Mummyfucker' — could be heard.

At a few minutes before 8 a.m. the last United States marine helicopter landed on the roof of the embassy. The crowd seemed to sense that and with a last violent effort they forced the front gates open.

> Very soon they had the doors open as well, and I couldn't help thinking that they had done what the Viet

Cong suicide sapper squadron had failed to do in the Tet offensive attack of 1968.

People were actually into the embassy as the last helicopter took off, leaving some Vietnamese still on the roof. I stayed outside filming the helicopter going and the people running into the embassy. There was a spirit of great camaraderie on the ground. After all, as far as we all knew, we were abandoned to our fate and a feeling of 'togetherness' pervaded.

It was very civilised looting, I might say. I didn't see one argument about who flogged what, and I was good-humouredly offered a nice shirt from an American's abandoned suitcase. It fitted me, too, and I was very glad to have it. There was bloody tear gas everywhere, as the marines had thrown several canisters down inside the building as well, but it barely hindered the looting.

The strangest things were taken. Air conditioners went. Some had to be turned off before being wrenched from their mountings. People took the telephones — some of which were still ringing! Light fittings, desks, papers, files, chairs and even carpets were carried away.

I saw one ARVN soldier take the end of an inbuilt fire hose from an upper floor and just walk solemnly off down the passage with it. Nobody took any notice and I didn't wait to see what happened when he finally unwound the hose to its full length.

I well remember James Fenton, the British correspondant for the *New Statesman*, walking out of the embassy with tears streaming down his face — not from emotion but tear gas — with his arms full of books he had looted. He triumphantly displayed some by Robert Shaplen, a reporter for the *New Yorker* and one of the old Vietnam hands.

Davis went outside again, near the main gate, and saw the BBC team of cameraman Eric Theiler and correspondent Brian Barron. As they spoke briefly, their attention was caught by a small man, obviously a Westerner, running down the street towards the embassy shouting and waving his arms.

> I heard Brian Barron say, 'I think we might have some good film here, Eric, better start rolling.' As the man came closer we saw he had a fur coat on, which was most incongruous. There are only two seasons in Saigon, hot and hotter, and this bugger was obviously all set to take a trip to a cold country, presumably the United States.
>
> He turned out to be an American aid worker who was absolutely terrified of what the Communists might do to him. He grabbed hold of Brian, babbling about being left behind, not realising or caring that he was making prime time on BBC television news. I didn't know whether to laugh or cry. He certainly illustrated the general mood that day of those who had been left behind. We eventually steered him towards the Red Cross hostel, where about thirty abandoned Americans were being looked after.

The only items not valued as loot from the Embassy were firearms. Davis saw discarded M16s and pistols everywhere. Some were thrown away by looting ARVN soldiers, others had been left by fleeing Americans. Davis and his Vietnamese driver went into the Embassy again and up to the roof. There were about half a dozen Vietnamese there, including a man of about thirty with glasses, wearing a steel-ribbed flak jacket and an American Services helmet.

> He looked very angry and was wearing a pistol, so I was a bit wary of him. He said, 'The Americans are coming back, aren't they? They promised they would come back and pick us up!'

I assured him they were, because I wasn't going to argue with him. He looked like he might take retribution on anybody who said they weren't coming back.

Then I looked down over the other side into the back of the American Embassy grounds where there was a swimming pool, and under the water I could see up to a hundred handguns which had been thrown there by those leaving on the helicopters. There were .45 Colt revolvers, .38 Smith and Wessons, automatics, down to Saturday night specials.

Fluttering about the roof I could see bits of notes of American dollars of all sorts of denominations. I was told later that several million dollars of valid notes had been destroyed in that area, which the CIA had used to pay agents.

Looking back down into the street, Neil's driver noticed a South Vietnamese soldier trying to make off with their latest vehicle, a minivan. The soldier had managed to get into the engine, and was trying either to steal the battery or to short-circuit the ignition so he could drive it away.

We didn't want to lose the vehicle because working cars were getting difficult to come by, so we left the irate civilian in his flak jacket waiting hopelessly for the Americans to return for him, and raced down three flights of stairs to convince the armed South Vietnamese soldier to turn his attention to someone else's transport.

The soldier was quite amiable about that and wandered off to try someone else's car, and Davis was able to drive back to the Reuters office further down Thong Nhut Avenue. There Neil heard Big Minh's historic radio broadcast. It was a statement of abject surrender turned into a plea for peace. The first broadcast was made shortly after 10 a.m., and repeated, not only on the radio network, but over the loudspeakers in the streets of Saigon.

'I believe firmly in reconciliation among all Vietnamese.

To avoid needless bloodshed, I ask the soldiers of the Republic to put an end to all hostilities. Be calm and remain where you are now. To save the lives of the people, do not open fire.

'I also call on our brothers, the soldiers of the Provisional Revolutionary Government, not to open fire, because we are waiting here to meet with their representatives to discuss the orderly turnover of the reins of government, both civilian and military, without causing senseless bloodshed to the people.'

It was time for Davis to take stock. The Reuters office was a small narrow building from which a battery of ancient overworked teleprinters had chattered out millions of words on the conduct of the war. Davis had been one of their correspondents in Cambodia, and was still on the Reuters payroll as a freelance contributor from Saigon. For the first time that he could remember, the machines were silent.

From a desk by the door, he could see the wrought-iron fence, the lawns and beyond to the presidential palace — Independence Palace as it was generally known.

I sat there quietly and considered where I would go. I could go to the airport where there was fighting — that would possibly be the last fighting of the war. But this would have been, in a sense, more of the same sort of fighting I had been covering for the last eleven years.

The Bien Hoa bridge was a possibility, where the last big resistance to stop the North Vietnamese and Viet Cong forces from entering the city was being mounted. Then I thought of the American embassy, which could be a focus for the Communists. They might want to destroy it, or raise their flag over it.

Davis rejected these possibilities because they did not seem significant enough. He knew that other Western journalists and photographers had also stayed in Saigon. He had to pick the place where the Communists would raise their flag to signify the end of the war. And he had to get it right, or his decision to stay would be largely wasted.

> I even considered the city hall, a fine old building in the centre of Saigon, or the post office, or the cathedral. But finally I was convinced that they would go to the presidential palace, because that symbolised the seat of power for what they termed the puppet government of South Vietnam, and that it would be there they would symbolise their great victory.

There was the question of timing. Davis believed that the Communists would enter the city quickly, and he hoped they would, because another night without any authority in the streets would have been extremely dangerous. The most likely course of events, he believed, was that the Communist forces would move in quickly, within the next few hours.

His driver (still loyally carrying on) drove him down to Independence Palace, but the front gates were locked, as they usually were. The palace was set back approximately one hundred metres from the gate, and a circular drive-way led to a flight of imposing marble steps at the front entrance. They drove down a side street to the service entrance, where tradesmen or journalists usually gained entry.

> The gate was wide open, and there were no guards which was quite surprising. So we drove from behind the palace, right around to the front, without being challenged by anybody. I thought the whole building had been abandoned.

Standing at the base of the huge flight of marble steps, Davis saw a young Vietnamese civilian running down with his coat over his arm, and recognised him as one of the palace bureaucrats.

333

He said to me, 'Are you looking for the president?'
I hadn't thought about it, but I said, 'Yes, I guess I am.'
'Well, he's up on the first floor.'

With a mounting sense of unreality, Neil Davis walked up
the steps and found himself alone with the then President
of South Vietnam, General 'Big' Minh. Big Minh had had a
chequered political and military career, but in Davis's view
he had vindicated himself at the end by staying and looking
after his people as best he could. The president was wearing a short-sleeved safari jacket, he had not shaved, and his
eyes were red with weeping. He had broadcast the official
surrender over the radio about an hour earlier.

'Oh, Mr President,' said Davis. The two men knew each
other quite well, but Davis was at loss what to say to him
at this moment of Vietnamese history.

I asked him if he was going to stay, and he said, 'Yes.
The other side will be here shortly.'

There seemed little else to say, and Davis filmed him walking down the long presidential hall with his head bowed,
going away from the camera.

Downstairs again, Davis met the elderly Mr Huyen, who
held the vice-presidency for those few hours. He knew and
liked the old man, a constitutional opponent of former
President Thieu. They embraced warmly, and Huyen said
he was going to drive home to be with his family.

I was stunned. It was all like a dream — as if I was
actually watching a movie plot unfold.

25

'Welcome
to Saigon, Comrade!'

At 11.30 on the morning of 30 April 1975, Neil Davis waited in the grounds of Independence Palace in Saigon to film a moment of history. The sun was high and hot. The relentless roar of Saigon's chaotic traffic — an unholy mélange of battered and ancient Peugeot taxis, buzzing Hondas and motorised cyclos making kamikaze dashes under the wheels of heavy military traffic — was stilled. An unfamiliar calm hung over the central district. All looting had stopped.

About forty or fifty South Vietnamese soldiers, their weapons piled, were sitting and lounging in the shade of some trees, waiting to surrender. Behind them, the circular lawns and ceremonial driveway led the eye to the impressive tier of marble steps in front of the main entrance to Independence Palace. Davis joined them, conscious of the curious dreamlike atmosphere enveloping the events he now saw unfolding. He felt euphoric but apprehensive, knowing that if he survived the hectic moments of the Communist takeover he could have a world exclusive on the end of the war. Most of the actors in that day's drama were victims of war, still under orders. But Davis was there by choice: he had planned to be there.

It was almost noon. As Neil waited a young captain came over and spoke to him in French, talking casually about the weather.

I thought it was significant that he spoke to me in
French. He'd already changed over in his mind. Rather
than speak in English, he wanted to speak French, as
France was considered a kind of neutral country at that
time.

After chatting about the weather, the two men discussed
the likely course of events.

Then Davis noticed a tank driving down the street beside
the palace, and as he watched a tongue of red flame shot
out of the barrel of its cannon. Milliseconds later, he heard
the crack of the shot.

The idea of a Communist tank in Saigon was still unthinkable to Davis. 'Jesus! What's that?' he exclaimed.

Almost nonchalantly the Vietnamese captain replied, 'It's
a Communist tank.'

Davis still couldn't believe it. 'Don't be silly, is there a
coup d'état or something?' He knew it was possible that
elements of the South Vietnamese Army would disregard
the surrender and keep on fighting.

'No,' said the captain calmly, 'it's a Communist tank.
Look.'

As the tank rumbled around the corner of the side street,
Davis saw the biggest Viet Cong flag he had ever seen
flying in front of the turret, and he recognised that the tank
was Russian.

I shook hands with the captain and we wished each
other good luck. And that was the last time I spoke to a
South Vietnamese soldier as part of the South
Vietnamese army.

He walked over the lawn to a point about forty metres
from the front gates and halfway between the high wrought-
iron fence and the Palace itself.

Neil Davis was not the only Western cameraman in the
grounds of the Palace at that time. Tom Aspell, covering

for Neil's old alma mater Visnews, had also positioned himself well. As the first tank nudged through the big wrought-iron gates of the Palace, Aspell left his camera on the ground, thinking that the tank commander might not have seen a camera before and might mistake it for a missile launcher of some sort. Davis put his camera to his shoulder and ran forward to the tank.

I started to film as that tank, No 843, smashed through the front gates of Independence Palace.

It didn't quite make it the first time, and one gate fell off its hinges. It backed off and smashed through again, and this time both gates broke wide open. The soldier on the front holding the huge Viet Cong flag jumped off and ran towards the palace, and I followed him with my sound camera rolling.

But out of my left eye — the one not to the camera — I could see a very determined Communist soldier racing straight towards me and calling out something. Because of the sound of the tank, I couldn't hear what he was saying, but I could imagine what he was telling me to do.

That was the last big decision I made in Indo-China: whether to keep filming or not at that specific moment, when that soldier was running towards me in a very threatening way with his rifle pointing at me and shouting out what I later found out was, 'Stop! Stop! Hands up!'

I thought, well, after eleven years of covering this war I'm here alone, and I have what the Americans like to call just about the greatest scoop one could imagine . . . and I'm going to keep filming. Maybe it's wrong, and maybe I'm going to die, but that's my decision.

And I did keep filming until he got right up to me and poked me in my guts with his rifle, screaming, 'Stop . . . hands up!'

Then I did stop, and put my hands up, still holding my fifteen-pound [6.8 kilogram] sound camera in my right hand, so I couldn't keep my hands up for very long. As quickly as I could, I got off my Vietnamese welcoming speech, which was, 'Welcome to Saigon, comrade. I've been waiting for you!'

He said aggressively, 'You are American?' I said, 'No, no, no, I'm an Australian.' I hoped that would fool him, and make him hesitate long enough to give me the breathing space I needed. I added quickly, 'I'm an Australian, and I've been waiting for the liberation of Saigon.' I wasn't too worried about political bias at that stage; I wanted to tell him what he wanted to hear.

So he hesitated. At that moment I knew I was going to stay alive because he was a disciplined soldier, and if he was going to shoot me, he really should have shot me by then.

Then his eyes went out of focus as he looked at something behind me. I knew what was happening then — the South Vietnamese soldiers were surrendering, coming out with their hands up. He dismissed me with a wave of his rifle, and I was able to keep filming the surrender and the Viet Cong flag being waved from the first floor of the palace.

They had forgotten to take down the South Vietnamese government flag actually, and it was flying only three metres above it. That was rather a good shot, and the last time I filmed the South Vietnamese flag.

By then, Aspell had picked up his camera and started filming, but only Davis had those vital first few seconds. The farm boy from Tasmania who left school at fifteen had reason to savour his triumph. He had captured on film not only a significant moment of history, but he had exclusive coverage of the biggest story in the world.

The full realisation of that would have to wait as events continued to move swiftly. Tank No 843 had outstripped its rivals to be first at the palace to ensure its place in Vietnamese history. A column of about twenty tanks followed

After a mortar blast nearly blew off his right leg in Cambodia in 1974, Davis reaches a field aid station where a transfusion directly from a green coconut helped to keep him alive. His concerned driver An Veng is pictured at the extreme left.

Five out of the six men pictured here in Cambodia on 28 September 1972 were later killed in action. From left: Cambodian photographer, name unknown (killed); Neil Davis, (killed); Major Chao Mei, (killed); Tea Kim Heang 'Moonface', (killed); Cambodian photographer, name unknown (survived); Ieng Chamroeung, (killed).

Only Neil Davis's camera was rolling when North Vietnamese tank No. 843 smashed through the gates of Saigon's Independence Palace on 30 April 1975. That moment symbolised for the North Vietnamese their moment of victory, ending the long and bitter Indo China war, and re-unifying the two Vietnams.

In 1984 Neil Davis posed on the historic tank No. 843 now in Hanoi's war museum.

through the broken palace gates and formed a semicircle, facing the palace. A detachment of infantry ran in with them.

> I saw James Fenton, the *New Statesman* correspondent, again. He had hitched a ride in on the back of a tank and was shaking hands with the beaming Communist soldiers.

Besides Davis and Visnews cameraman Tom Aspell, there were two other Western press representatives in the palace when Tank No 843 burst in, both from the French news-agency, Agence France Presse. One was Françoise Demulder, a photographer, and the other, Jean-Louis Arnaud, was in General Minh's office and was among those who escorted him to a jeep to drive to the radio station to announce the surrender.

Davis mingled with the curious North Vietnamese soldiers (Bo Doi) as they wandered around the palace staring in awe at the crystal chandeliers and opulent furnishings. Some of them found former President Nguyen Van Thieu's office and one sat down in his chair and put his feet up on the desk.

> Many of the soldiers were shaking hands with me and embracing me, and each other, and I talked with some of them. A shy young trooper was standing in the main hall. He looked a bit out of it and even homesick, which was probably true. Lots of handshakes were still being exchanged, so I went up and offered my hand to him, which he took shyly. He was probably about eighteen, but looked younger.
>
> 'Where are you from?' I asked. It was the standard question.
>
> 'Hanoi,' the youngster replied. That could mean anywhere in North Vietnam.
>
> I asked his name, which was not the usual question,

but I had a sixth sense about that kid. He hesitated many moments, obviously debating whether he'd tell, not because he didn't want to, but he was shy about it.

'Nguyen Van Thieu,' he said at last, and added, 'it's quite a common name you know.'

The war was over, but the fighting was not. Some South Vietnamese units had refused to surrender, and within three hours of the Communists entering the Palace, Neil Davis covered his last firefight in Vietnam — from the Communist side.

> They were puzzled to see me with them, but they accepted me. I was able to see why they had won the war. They were adept at street tactics, conserving their fire and cleverly seeking out their enemy. On this occasion they didn't launch a large attack, but played a waiting game. They called on the South Vietnamese rebels to surrender, and eventually after dark they did.

Many of the liberation army soldiers were South Vietnamese, and quite a number had brothers or cousins who had fought with the ARVN. Divided families were at last united.

> The former ARVN soldiers had to register, then they were allowed to go home. I met a South Vietnamese marine I'd known for several years during the war walking down a Saigon street between two Bo Doi — former Viet Cong soldiers — hand in hand. They were his brothers. I hadn't known he had brothers fighting with the Viet Cong until then.

The family had been divided many years before, and the young marine had gone with his mother as a boy, later joining the ARVN. His father had stayed in the countryside with his two elder brothers to help on the farm, but they were pressed into military service with the Viet Cong.

He was sad and he was happy, and the only comment he made to me was, 'Well, at least some of us were on the winning side.'

When Davis made formal contact with the new Communist regime, he asked to be allowed to stay in Saigon to cover events in Vietnam. That time was extended to three and a half months. He filed for Reuters and filmed for NBC. He was allowed to keep his room at the Caravelle Hotel, which also housed some of the Bo Doi (Communist soldiers). Although he had captured exclusive footage of the actual moment of Communist victory, his exposed film was still vulnerable. It was unprocessed and still with him in the newly named Ho Chi Minh City.

There was a CBS office on the same floor as my room at the Caravelle. A day or so after the liberation, a party of North Vietnamese soldiers — who turned out to be an army film crew — raided the CBS office and took every can of film they could see, most of it unexposed.

I was a bit apprehensive and went to make inquiries, but the authorities didn't know anything about it. I managed to find out that the North Vietnamese film crew were under great pressure from their superiors to come up with footage of the liberation of Saigon. As the tank column had raced in far ahead of the troops and the film crew, there was no way they could oblige.

They heard about this film office on the second floor of the Caravelle, and raided it in the hope that some film would be there. So I said to the authorities that I would be happy to make a copy of my film available, as long as they let me keep it. The officials agreed, and said my film would be safe.

Eventually NBC made a documentary film of the fall of Saigon, and the Vietnamese government was given a copy. Of course, that moment when Tank No 843 crashed through the gates of the Presidential Palace is the moment in history that Vietnamese Communists regard as the liberation of Vietnam.

Despite American-induced fears, the Communist takeover was surprisingly gentle. Policies tightened later, but Neil Davis believed that only one person was killed in the centre of Saigon on the day of liberation. The Communists themselves seemed bewildered by the speed of their own success and there was little alternative to letting Saigon, renamed or not, temporarily resume some of its old wicked capitalist ways while reforms could be organised. The bars and brothels were early casualties, but the black market continued to sell everything from television sets to petrol.

Five days after the end of the war, Davis had been keeping a watchful eye on Mr Minh's tailor's shop, hoping it would reopen so he could claim the foreign correspondents' suit ordered on 28 April.

Mr Minh's shop had stayed closed a few days, along with many other business establishments, while they waited to see what the new regime would do. But one afternoon at five p.m. I found it open. I went in and immediately took the head tailor to task for not opening sooner. A few minutes later I felt sorry I'd done that.

The head tailor told Davis the shop was about to be closed, because Mr Minh had fled and no one else could operate the business.

'Yours is the only thing I have to finish,' said the disconsolate tailor. 'There are two or three other orders, but I'm sure the people have gone, and yours is the only TV suit. Come back tomorrow, but not after five, because they are going to close the shop at that time.'

Davis returned at 4.45 p.m. the following day to witness a sad scene. The shop was still full of materials and some made-up shirts that were always ready for instant 'off-the-hook' sales. Mr Minh's head tailor wrapped up Davis's TV suit and gave it to him. At 5 p.m. precisely, the K4 Squad (the appropriation officials) of five soldiers marched up in a single line.

> The tailor turned out the lights, closed the door and I helped him pull the steel-mesh grille across. The leader of the K4 Squad put a lock on and snapped it shut, and Mr Minh's chief tailor walked off without a word down the street with his head down.

Before he left, the tailor gave Neil five extra buttons for his new suit, saying, 'I don't need them, so take them as a gift to an old customer.' Another light had gone out in Tu Do Street, which had been named Rue Catinat in the days of the French. There was no doubt that Neil Davis had scored the very last foreign correspondent's suit from Mr Minh the tailor.

With petrol almost unobtainable, the streets of Saigon were mercifully free of the hordes of motorcycles that were not only unbearably noisy but whose two-stroke exhausts added to Saigon's gross atmospheric pollution. A fascinated Neil Davis watched the city return to a place more suggestive of the 'Paris of the East', with bicycles taking over from heavy motor traffic. Vietnamese girls dressed in their graceful *ao zais* made a welcome change from the ugly war-related chaos of weeks before.

In the weekends, the Bo Doi strolled around Ho Chi Minh City, sightseeing and drinking tea or soup at wayside stalls. 'Surely,' Davis commented, 'one of the best-behaved conquering armies of all time.'

But their total control of life and death could surface at unexpected moments. One of Davis's friends told him of two motorcycle 'cowboys' of the old Saigon, who had somehow obtained petrol for their machines, and who had swooped down on an old woman in the central city area and snatched her bag.

> A Bo Doi calmly stepped out into the path of the oncoming motorcycle, raised his rifle and killed the two

cowboys — one riding pillion — with two shots. The old
woman whose bag had been snatched cried out in
anguish, 'I didn't want them killed! It was only two
hundred piastres!'

Davis also filed stories on the situation of the fifty or so
Americans who, for one reason or another, were still in Ho
Chi Minh City. Some had stayed on purpose, hoping to
continue their aid or welfare work with the new regime.
Others had simply missed the last flights out.

One contractor had come up from the Mekong Delta
region, got drunk and woke up to find the view from his
window full of Communist flags and victorious North
Vietnamese troops. Disbelieving and hung over, he went
back to bed and slept, presumably hoping they would be
gone the next time he looked.

Another case that fascinated Davis was the existence in
the city of a Western cyclo driver, a tall, rangy man who
might well have been a deserter from the American army.
He heard of this man from Vietnamese friends, and saw
him once pedalling his three-wheeled conveyance past the
Roman Catholic cathedral.

I jumped out of the car I was in and tried to hail him,
but he shook his head and pedalled away.

Eventually a Vietnamese friend of Neil's managed to hire
him and asked questions in English, to which the driver
steadfastly replied in Vietnamese. He said he earned enough
money to get by, and worked only every second day because
he had a partner. It was hard work at first, but he wanted
to continue doing it and stay in Vietnam.

On 15 May 1975, Neil Davis covered the victory parade to
officially celebrate the Communist takeover, during which
the South Vietnamese saw the North Vietnamese and Viet
Cong leaders in public for the first time. A great deal of
military hardware from Russia and China was on display,

but no marching soldiers. All the troops went past the saluting base in trucks.

There was a very good reason for this — the troops couldn't march, they had never learned! So much for Western preconceived notions that soldiers have to learn discipline and fighting ability first of all on the parade ground. These soldiers didn't have time to be on the parade ground, they were too busy fighting.

One morning Davis was having breakfast in a soup shop and a North Vietnamese cameraman recognised him and introduced himself. The two men realised that they had covered some of the same battles from different sides. They talked for a long time with the camaraderie of like-minded professionals.

Davis knew that his time in Indo-China was inevitably coming to a close and that he would have to rebuild his life elsewhere after eleven years of close association and ident-ification with Laos, Cambodia and Vietnam. As the two combat cameraman reminisced, the North Vietnamese leaned across the table and asked Neil an important per-sonal question.

'Did you enjoy covering combat?' he asked the tall Australian.

The question took Davis by surprise, but he admitted he did.

The North Vietnamese agreed he did also, and asked Neil whether he also missed it.

I was not able to give him a good enough answer, and again turned the question back, and asked him if he missed covering battle action.

'Yes,' said the North Vietnamese, 'because under those conditions everybody loves everybody else.'

I think he said it best. I built up many close friendships in Indo-China during the war, because they were formed

under extraordinary circumstances. When you are with
someone in times of stress, the small irritations of
people's behaviour don't matter, because when it comes
to the big things, they behave very well. I found the great
majority of people behaved superbly in very difficult
situations.

When you are under fire or under attack and
everything seems lost and you are facing death, I have
found people are naturally courageous.

That is what my North Vietnamese friend also realised,
and expressed so well when he said that under those
conditions, everybody loves everybody else.

The Indo-China war in general was easily the most
important news story I covered. I didn't expect to cover
a continuing story as important ever again. I think it was
also the most important story of my generation. The
repercussions, the social and political effects worldwide
were easily the most crucial events of our times.

I formed the strongest personal relationships of my
life in Indo-China and unfortunately I lost many of those
friends killed in Cambodia and Vietnam. It's very difficult
to recapture that feeling of comradeship I had with so
many people there.

In a sense, when I had to leave Indo-China a good part
of me died.

26

A
One-Man Band

When Saigon fell, there were about sixty journalists who had chanced their luck with the incoming Communist troops. Most were Europeans, a few were Americans; Davis was the only Australian. The Hanoi regime asked most to leave as soon as commercial flights resumed. After a month, only eight members of the foreign press remained and when Neil Davis finally left there were six.

> It got boring. Most of the stories I was permitted to cover were repetitive, and it was difficult to get film out because there was only one plane every two or three weeks.

It was time to go. And there was another compelling reason: Davis did not have a job.

> I was working for the American television network NBC News on contract, but I thought I'd better move on and get my life together again. I'd lost everything in Cambodia. I only had what I stood up in and my camera. It was time to get out into the world and see what was happening, and get a steady job.

It was a foregone conclusion that he would base himself in Asia. The obvious choice was Bangkok. It was as close as he could get to his cherished Indo-China, and where he could keep an eye on the continuing Cambodian story. To the day he died, Davis never gave up hope of one day being permitted to make his home in Phnom Penh.

Bangkok might have been the obvious base for him, but it was not a preferred choice. While recovering from his wounds in Bangkok in May 1974, he had written to an Australian journalist friend, Jim Revitt: 'Bangkok is now the most dangerous city by far in Asia. Robberies with violence never stop, and there are murders by the dozen — really ugly. Manila is mild by comparison, and Saigon and Phnom Penh positively gentle.'

Davis had covered the fall of Saigon for NBC, and the big news network was keen to have him working for them. The main reason he had not signed with an American network earlier was the almost certain loss of his independence as a journalist and cameraman. He would be one of a team of three, reporter, cameraman and soundman. But a deal was worked out. Davis would become a one-man band, working out of Bangkok and flying instantly to major news stories wherever they broke in Asia, Africa or the Middle East. He would shoot film, step in front of his own camera for on-camera pieces, file copy if need be and do radio pieces.

After thirty-six hours or so in a place where an international news story was breaking, he was to assess whether he could continue to handle the story on his own or whether NBC should fly in a second news team. Davis could continue to work by himself in hazardous circumstances without 'having to make decisions for other people'.

In a press release in January 1976 NBC called this one-man-band arrangement 'a new concept in television journalism'. The release highlighted another important advantage of employing Davis. 'Davis holds an Australian passport with no travel restrictions, and has less of a problem getting into Angola than American correspondents. So far he is the only reporter for any of the American networks who has consistently been able to get his reports and film out of Angola.'

Neil Davis had little time to brood on the ending of his active role in the Indo-China war — by November 1975 he was covering another war in Africa.

My first assignment was to cover the anti-Communist factions fighting in Angola, the FNLA and UNITA. They were the guerillas this time, as the capital, Luanda, was controlled by the Marxist MPLA — which eventually became the government of Angola.

In that vast turbulent ex-Portuguese colony of over five million people in southwest Africa, Davis had to learn new survival skills quickly.

On my first full day in Angola, I found myself twenty kilometres from the capital, Luanda, then occupied by the Communist forces. I hoped I was going to be with the liberating forces for once in my life, not on the losing side. But late on that first afternoon the Cubans attacked with great salvoes of rockets and we retreated very quickly.

I had never experienced such a retreat. By midnight we were sixty kilometres from Luanda and that ground was never recovered.

His Indo-China battle reflexes were little help in this type of guerilla warfare. He was completely disoriented. In Asia, an empty road was a warning of danger. Here, every road was empty.

There was no sustained, close confrontation as there had been in Cambodia or Vietnam, with troops required and willing to display courage in the face of innumerable difficulties. The Africans fought as they had done in their great tribal wars of yesteryear.

They would advance and confront each other, launch a salvo of spears from each side and retreat to take stock of casualties.

Maybe the Africans have got it right. If they see danger pressing they get the hell out of there, think about it, and plan their counterattack in another way.

Davis never saw any real battle action in Angola, only many withdrawals. He was once again covering the losing side and divided his time between the northern guerilla faction headed by the FNLA leader Holden Roberto and the rival southern guerilla group UNITA, led by Jonas Savimbi. Typically, he built up good personal relations with both men, particularly admiring Savimbi's swashbuckling style.

The FNLA 'government' was based in Kinshasa, the capital of neighbouring Zaire, the old Belgian Congo. 'Go-anywhere' pilots flew for both guerilla factions, and Davis became friendly with a number of them. For the next two months he was able to slip in and out of Angola.

Unfortunately, he had been sent to Africa before he had time to streamline the techniques of being a one-man band, which included talking to his own camera.

I taught some Angolan soldiers to hold my camera steady, frame me in centre picture, and push the button. Other soldiers took on the job of directing.

Davis was always sorry those performances had not been filmed by a second camera team!

The war was not going well for the guerillas, and Holden Roberto's FNLA recruited some British mercenaries.

Many were decent men — out-of-work British soldiers — but at least fifty per cent of them were ne'er-do-wells, and this group was commanded by the self-styled Colonel Callan. He was a dishonourably discharged British soldier whose real name was Costas Georgiou, described by his former commander as 'a mad dog on a leash'. The leash was off in Angola.

Callan was the name of the tough-guy hero in a British television series popular at the time. Costas Georgiou was undoubtedly mentally unbalanced, probably schizophrenic. Unfortunately the Callan-led faction of the British mercenaries gained control, and Georgiou was made the commander of the FNLA.

There were about a hundred and fifty British mercenaries in all, leading and fighting with several thousand black soldiers of the FNLA. Most of the British soldiers — even the decent ones — were not well trained. They were just British private soldiers with no particular leadership ability.

When things didn't go right for Callan, he reacted violently. One day, when he couldn't get some vehicles he wanted and a few other things had gone wrong, he got in the cabin of an old armoured personnel carrier, locked the door behind him and started screaming and crying and beating his head against the steel walls.

I realised then Callan wasn't the man to lead troops in battle.

Shortly after witnessing this crazed behaviour, Davis crossed north into Zaire only about fifty kilometres away from where Callan and his men were camped.

Some days later a group of twenty of the better of the mercenaries — the men who had been full-time soldiers — sought me out deliberately in Kinshasa to tell me that fourteen of their number had been executed by Callan and his crazy gang!

They wanted the story told because they were being hunted by Callan and his men, and thought they could get some sort of protection if the story was made public.

Davis was concerned about his own safety because Callan had already threatened to kill him if he broke certain 'confidences'. But he decided to file the story to NBC on 8 February 1976, which caused an enormous furore, including headlines in the London *Times*, *New York Times* and other leading papers throughout the world.

The story was not believed for several days. Eventually I got a cable from NBC in New York which said: YOU WILL BE DELIGHTED TO LEARN THAT THE BRITISH PRIME MINISTER HAROLD WILSON HAS CONFIRMED YOUR STORY. They had not told me about their doubts for the previous two days.

The story Davis gleaned from the frightened British mercenaries who had fled from Callan's homicidal wrath was chilling and bizarre. Things started to go wrong when a nervous seventeen-year-old British mercenary had mistakenly fired a rocket at Callan, who was returning to camp by car in the evening.

Nothing happened that night, but next morning Callan ordered the fourteen men out on parade who had been on duty when the incident happened, and asked who had fired the rocket. The seventeen-year-old stepped forward and said, rather sheepishly, 'I did, sir.' He expected to be docked a week's pay, or slapped in the brig for a few days or something.

According to the accounts given to Davis by the surviving mercenaries, Callan stepped forward and said to the boy, 'Do you think it's funny?'

The boy laughed nervously.

'No I don't, sir. I'm sorry.'

Callan then took out his pistol and shot him in the kneecap. As he fell screaming to the ground, he shot him again in the shoulder, and finally in the back of the head.

He then turned to his deputy, a man named Sammy Copeland — who apparently couldn't wait to help with the rest of the killing — to take the others out and 'waste' them.

Copeland forced some other mercenaries to accompany him and they later confirmed what happened. The thirteen men were taken to an open area covered with a kind of prairie pampas grass. They were ordered to strip naked and then told to run.

It conjures up an awful scene with these thirteen naked white men being told to run to nowhere on the high veldt of Africa. One of Copeland's henchmen was a man I knew only as Charlie, and they opened fire on the running men. Of course they were cut down, some were killed and others wounded.

Copeland and Charlie then went around executing the wounded. One man of about fifty had been recruited because he could speak and understand Russian. He was standing, grasping the limb of a tree, partly disembowelled and begging to be killed.

Copeland, who was a dreadful sadist, did not give him the coup de grace, and allowed him to die slowly.

One wounded man was lying face down, pretending to be dead. This gave Copeland the chance to play a ghastly game. He apparently nudged Charlie and said in a loud voice, 'Well, that's about all, Charlie, I guess they're all dead now. Let's go.'

The wounded man heard their truck start up and drive away. After the sound of the engine had faded into the distance, he waited a few more minutes and then slowly turned over.

You can imagine his terror when he saw Copeland and Charlie standing over him. They had crept silently back.

Copeland reportedly gave a maniacal laugh and shot him.

As soon as the FNLA leadership heard of the massacre, Holden Roberto, who had lost control of the situation, appointed another British soldier, a former sergeant named Peter McIleesh [phonetic spelling from Davis's transcript], as commander-in-chief. His first orders were to select one man to go with him and arrest Callan, Copeland and Charlie.

McIleesh was a good, well-trained soldier. The man he chose to go with him I had dubbed the Cyanide Kid because he carried cyanide pellets to take if he were ever captured.

It was all rather like the script of a B-grade movie, but it was true. McIleesh and the Cyanide Kid flew to the area where Copeland and Charlie were. Callan was still out on operations at that time.

Copeland and Charlie were not aware that events had moved so swiftly, and had no reason to suspect that McIleesh was their new commander or what he had been sent to do.

So McIleesh had the advantage. But he knew he was dealing with a very dangerous man — he'd known Sammy Copeland for about twelve years, apparently. Everybody was heavily armed.

The four men talked about the military situation for a time, and McIleesh asked Copeland if he had a map to give him a better idea of what was happening.

Sammy shouldered his rifle — which was what McIleesh wanted — knelt down on the ground and spread out the map with both hands.

McIleesh winked at the Cyanide Kid, and thumped Copeland across the temple with the butt of his rifle, while the Cyanide Kid held his rifle to Charlie's throat. After securing both men, they flew them back in the light plane to FNLA headquarters for immediate court martial.

Copeland was sentenced to death, but Charlie was not executed because none of the witnesses had actually seen him kill any of the men.

The execution was to be carried out immediately. McIleesh, who told Davis what happened, asked for volunteers for a firing squad. There was no shortage of willing recruits. McIleesh picked seven and discussion began whether to use one round each or full automatic.

The execution was to take place in the courtyard of a broken-down old colonial house where the court martial had been held. Copeland was standing nearby as the soldiers discussed the execution arrangements. Suddenly he began to run towards the crumbling two-metre wall surrounding the courtyard.

He ran — and McIleesh described it to me very well — as though he was possessed by the devil. The group of eight men stood frozen to the spot as Copeland ran with manic jerky strides towards the wall. McIleesh said there was something terrifying and evil about the way he ran.

As he reached the high wall and tried to climb over it, McIleesh came to life and gave the order to fire. And the firing squad did execute Sammy Copeland as he was climbing the wall. He fell back and they buried him where he was.

Costas Georgiou (Callan) was captured by the MPLA, the Communist forces in Angola, and put on trial. He and three of his colleagues were executed by firing squad.

But on 8 February 1976 Davis knew that breaking the Callan massacre story would put him at risk. Some of Callan's men were in Kinshasa. He told UNITA of his plans to break the story and was promised protection, not only for himself, but for the British mercenaries who had fled from Callan's homicidal rage.

Davis needed to alert NBC News in New York to his

story without drawing too much attention to its sensational revelations, before he filed it. He sent a cryptically worded telex: SOME TOURISTS HAVE BEEN CANCELLED OUT BY THE TOUR OPERATORS.

They left it up to my judgement whether to file or not.

Before he was captured, Callan had given orders for Davis to be killed.

I took this fairly lightly, because while I was in Indo-China a lot of people had been trying to kill me!
Callan briefed an American mercenary to do the job and I was told later he was initially fairly serious about it. But Callan's mob weren't so tough. They crumbled astoundingly under pressure, both in the battlefield and when this story became known, and they became once again the rather frightened, unsure little men they always were.

As stories went, Neil Davis did not look back on the Callan affair with any particular regard.

It wasn't a difficult story because the sources came to me. It wasn't something I had developed and sought out. Although it was rewarding in a news sense, I've done stories of which I am more proud because they involved more work, more deduction, contacts and a lot more time.

In early August 1976, Davis was again at the centre of remarkable events in Africa.

Libya's Colonel Qaddafi had just launched an abortive invasion right into the heart of the Sudan's capital, Khartoum, and called it a coup d'état attempt. But he'd been outsmarted by President (General) Nimeiri, who turned out to be quite a man.

In true Arab Muslim style, Nimeiri ordered the execution of eighty-one of the ringleaders in one day, seventeen the next, and that was that!

As Davis flew into Khartoum, he reflected that all he knew was based on schoolboy stories of General Charles Gordon's siege there in 1885.

I didn't have a visa, and the immigration people really turned on the heat. There is no gentle Asian approach with Arab Muslim Africans.

Just as the customs officials were about to tear Davis's gear apart looking for hidden weapons and subversive literature (he did have a copy of *Playboy* in his luggage), an information ministry man appeared with the all-important news that President Nimeiri had okayed his visit. Suspicion and distrust turned instantly to smiles and the courtesies of traditional Arab hospitality.

Before he had time even to check in to his hotel, Davis was caught up in an anti-British street riot. Apparently the BBC had been broadcasting excerpts from material put out by the Libyan news service.

I got separated from my Ministry guardian long enough to be positively identified as a Brit and set on by the mob. Fortunately the Ministry man appeared with seconds to spare. I was then hailed as a hero when I explained that I was a Tasmanian, a victim of Pommy exploitation, and we'd only recently managed to get our leg irons off.

Khartoum was extraordinary. At any second I expected to see Gordon on horseback sweep out of the cantonment at the head of a motley crew of mad-dog Englishmen and dervishes.

This fantasy was enhanced by seeing paintings of Gordon, who looked astonishingly like Charlton Heston in the movie *Khartoum*.

357

Davis's priority was to get an interview with the new president.

Nimeiri's minister of information at that time was a big black man from the Christian south of the Sudan called Bona. He was a charming fellow, but he made Idi Amin of Uganda look like an undernourished midget.

Bona casually picked up the phone — just after I'd escaped the anti-Pom mob — and called the president to arrange the interview. I was told to come to the government TV station the next day.

The station was a broken down collection of Quonset huts and as Davis set up his camera in a 'studio', the president was broadcasting live to the people from another of the huts.

He was opening letters from people on camera and replying to their questions immediately. There was a mixture of 'Dear Abbie' style letters to rather more racy queries like, 'When are we going to see some more mass executions on TV?'

As Davis prepared his equipment, a posse of armed guards swept in. As he reached for the ceiling, they checked him and his equipment against any assassination attempt on the president. That set him back about thirty minutes in his preparations and he was untypically testy when a rather unassuming man in fatigues but no badges of rank asked him if he was ready.

I told him pretty roughly that I couldn't be ready for another ten minutes because of the guards' interruption, and he left.

Twenty minutes later, with lights and everything at last in place, the station manager came in with the same man

who sat down at the table and looked at me expectantly.
He said, 'Ready when you are.'
It was, of course, President Nimeiri.

The interview went well, and Nimeiri asked him what
else he wanted. Davis asked to see some prisoners from
Qaddafi's invasion — and to see them alone. Nimeiri agreed,
and Davis did.

I also wanted to see the south of the country, where
there had been a devastating civil war. Nimeiri had
stopped that war, and had actually made the guerilla
leader his commander in the south.

The president scrawled a note on the back of one of
Davis's cards, and said, 'Show them this.' Pushing his luck
further, Davis asked if he could travel with the president
when he went into the countryside, but not on a public
relations tour.

Nimeiri said, 'You want to go where they don't like me,
right? Next week I'm going to the western border. They
don't like me at all there, and Qaddafi thinks he has a
chance with those people.'

He was as good as his word and Davis travelled with him
and filmed his courageous forays into hostile territory.
Otherwise he could not move without a minder from the
Ministry of Information or the president's little notes.

Davis was less successful in establishing rapport with
Uganda's President Idi Amin in July 1976. It was not long
after the Israeli raid on Entebbe airport, and Amin was
furious that the Israelis had refuelled at Nairobi en route.

Idi worked himself into such a rage — and he was not
at all a figure of fun at such times — and was killing
people right, left and centre in Uganda. Visitors arriving

at Entebbe airport were being given a rough reception, and foreign correspondents were absolutely barred.

Davis thought there might be an outside chance that he could get in to report on the situation — and a possible imminent war with Kenya — if he could get the president's personal permission. He was also aware that Kampala could be phoned direct from Nairobi.

Idi Amin had delivered one of his crazy outbursts a few weeks before and invited any journalist or foreign correspondent to ring him, and had given his telephone numbers. There was one for his palace, another for his office, and one for a place he called the command post, which was in the middle of Kampala — his own personal military headquarters.

Davis called the command post. Idi Amin answered the phone himself.

He actually said, 'Who dat?' in the Rastus-style voice and dialogue used by *Punch* magazine in London, who were satirising him in a weekly column.

Davis introduced himself as an Australian and asked if he could come to Uganda.

Big Daddy was in an expansive mood, and said that as a Commonwealth citizen I could come anytime without a visa.

I replied that he might not be so happy about that, because I worked for an American company.

'Oh, dat's OK,' said the president, and went on to explain that it was not the American people he disliked, but the government of the day.

Idi had eyes that fascinated me — as lethal as a bloody snake's when he was really mad. They were normally friendly enough, but a bit hooded. They quickly changed to mean little piggy orbs when he was starting to go crazy.

Davis took the plunge and revealed that he was a newsman.

There were five seconds of absolute silence, and I could imagine his eyes changing! He was really close to the phone, and I could hear his heavy breathing, and the memory of his threatening whisper haunted me afterwards for quite a while.

'You bastard journalists!'

He handed the phone to a maniacal aide who abused me roundly. I felt safe enough sitting in the Intercontinental Hotel in Nairobi. But I didn't go to Uganda.

Another African story that claimed Neil's continuing attention was Rhodesia's unilateral declaration of independence (UDI). The white-dominated government led by Ian Smith could play it rough with journalists when the occasion arose.

In June 1977, Davis (reporting for NBC) and Gary Burns (Visnews) were in Salisbury on assignment. Gary Burns, at twenty-six, was new to the game, and Davis took a friendly interest in the progress of his fellow-Australian as they covered the bloody and bitter war between the Ian Smith-led forces and black guerillas.

Davis alerted Burns to a film story following information that the Coca-Cola company intended to withdraw permission for its trade name to be used in Rhodesia. The company was going to support the United Nations-directed economic sanctions against Smith's rebel regime. The two men took some fairly innocuous film of the Coca-Cola plant, with trucks of bottles coming and going and the familiar international logo.

The following morning Burns was showering in his hotel room when two Rhodesian Special Branch men kicked in the door, forced the still-dripping Australian to throw on his clothes and said he was being arrested under the country's Counter-Espionage Act. He was frogmarched out of the hotel, taken to Special Branch headquarters and locked in a soundproofed cell with padded walls. With mounting concern, Burns noticed manacles and chains set into the wall and bloodstains and claw marks on the acoustic padding.

While Gary Burns mournfully contemplated an uncertain future, he heard a commotion in the corridor outside. As the sounds of loud argument came closer, he heard a familiar voice. The door burst open to reveal Davis struggling with his burly Special Branch escorts and yelling abuse: 'You're just like the fucking Gestapo, the bloody SS. Take your hands off me, you fascist bastards . . .' and more in similar vein. The guards hustled Davis in with Burns.

Seeing Gary Burns' obvious disquiet, Davis muttered quietly, 'Don't worry, keep calm, it'll be OK.' Then to his escorts: 'You bastards, you sons of bitches, they've got a name for you where I come from . . .' until the soundproofed door slammed shut.

Apart from his anger at being locked up, Davis was furious that the Special Branch men had searched his room and read all his private correspondence, some of which was extremely personal.

Burns said, 'Jesus, I don't like the look of this room much. It's soundproofed, and I think those marks are bloodstains.'

Davis took a look: 'You're right.'

At that moment the Special Branch men came back into the cell, and Davis said, 'You bastards — I suppose the torture starts now, does it?'

They said, 'Look, no one is going to be tortured. We've brought you a cup of tea. Calm down.'

Davis took a sip and spat it out. 'You *are* torturing us!' he howled. 'No bloody sugar in it!'

Gary Burns began to feel that everything would be all right. Two hours later, both men were released.

Although Davis spent a great deal of time in Africa and the Middle East in the post-Vietnam years, he never identified with either region as he had with Indo-China.

I just slogged along and covered what came up.

In May 1981, NBC assembled a team in Beirut from its foreign bureaux in case the SAM missiles that President Assad of Syria had placed in the Bekaa Valley would provoke Prime Minister Begin of Israel into invading Lebanon or attacking the missile site.

David Phillips, an Englishman, knew of Davis's reputation as a top-notch cameraman correspondent and a hell-raiser — 'a legend in his own lifetime'. Phillips was pleasantly surprised when he met the tall, softly-spoken Australian for the first time. Davis did not join the carousing press corps that night, but went to bed early. Phillips was grateful for the low-key approach and quiet demeanour of his colleague because the work for the foreseeable future was to be the crushing boredom of stakeouts.

NBC booked into a small family hotel where the rooms overlooked the missiles at Chatura in the Bekaa Valley. Neil Davis, soundman Bill Latch and Phillips moved in and set up their camera with a special 'doubler' lens trained on the missiles. The three men arranged a roster to babysit the camera and filled in the time as best they could.

Davis read, jogged — sometimes in company with Syrian soldiers — read books and sipped an occasional cold beer. The stakeout had been a good idea, but the only excitement during two weeks was a sonic boom from a fighter aircraft that had the NBC men scurrying to their fixed camera.

NBC gave them their orders. They were to drive to Damascus to do their turn babysitting the story at that end. Phillips recalled that NBC was only interested in the big one — if President Assad let rip at Israel or Begin let go at Syria.

But the news on Monday 8 June was dramatic — Israeli jets had attacked the nuclear reactor being built by the French for Iraq just outside Baghdad. Phillips, Davis and Latch joined the international press brigade in a scramble to get there. Because everyone arrived without visas, all camera and sound gear was impounded by Iraqi customs.

The foreign press were corralled in the same hotel and told not to leave for the reactor site until permission had been granted. Phillips recalled that it looked like another stakeout — the third of that summer.

This boring prospect prompted the NBC team to try to break this stalemate. Why not make a reconnaissance of the reactor site without taking the camera? They reasoned that if they got close enough to assess the success of the raid and talked to eyewitnesses among the French contractors, they would at least have the first story on what had happened.

They were also concerned that some of the other hotshot foreign correspondents fretting around the bars and lounges of the Mansour Melia Hotel would break out and beat them to it. They decided to sleep on it and if there was no hint of an official visit by midday on Wednesday 10 June, they would slip away at lunchtime.

Bill Latch remained behind as the contact with NBC New York in case anything went wrong. Phillips said that he and Davis strolled out of the hotel without alerting any of the security men. The French Embassy was closed for the afternoon.

The duty officer told us that the French community were in their compound at the nuclear reactor, about nineteen kilometres southwest from Baghdad's city centre.

David Phillips said he and Davis felt happily adventurous, delighted to be out after a summer of waiting for something to happen, and their spirits were buoyed up by the hot cloudless day: 'We expected to see some spectacular wreckage caused by the Israeli jets. Instead, a structure like a modern monument to the Pharaohs loomed ahead: a massive concrete wall running parallel to the road for about two kilometres, and seemingly as high as a ten-storey building. All of it intact.'

At the French camp, the two journalists walked up to the guardroom. There was no guard, so they simply signed the visitors' book and strolled down a path towards a group of French people who were about to be evacuated in case the Israeli jets returned.

Davis spoke in French to some of the French technicians sunbathing beside the camp's outdoor pool, explaining that he and Phillips were from NBC. He learned that the Israeli jets had badly damaged the reactor and that one of the French technicians had been killed in the raid. They did not know if they would stay on to rebuild it, but many of them had decided to send their families back to France.

'Unfortunately,' David Phillips says, 'there was a plain-clothes security man among the evacuees, and he heard us talking to a Frenchwoman who spoke English. He was livid we were in the camp, and could not believe we had walked in unchallenged.

'We were escorted back to the guardhouse. Embarrassingly for him, there was still no guard there. His security had been made to look foolish, and we were to pay the price.'

Davis and Phillips were driven the length of the protective wall to a security HQ at the back of the site. They managed to get a good glimpse of the reactor itself on the way, and were surprised to see that it looked more intact than they had been led to believe.

They were taken into an office block and confronted by a bruiser in plainclothes.

'The two of us felt dwarfed — he bulged with muscles.

He was told where we had been detained, and was not amused. We both anticipated physical violence. He bundled Neil into a back room and I braced myself for the thumps. None came.'

After their details had been taken, the Iraqi commanding officer of the reactor site arrived. Phillips said he was 'very Sandhurst' in looks and bearing and it did not seem likely that there would be any beatings-up while he was around.

The commandant took a statement from them and seemed happy with the explanation that they were journalists. He drove them back to Baghdad and their spirits rose as they quietly discussed how they would capitalise on their scoop story.

Their destination was not the hotel, but a top Iraqi military security jail run by tough red-bereted paratroopers. They began eight days of solitary confinement and interrogation.

From Neil Davis's Diary

10 June 1981

At 1800 taken to Bagdad Security HQ. Then later to security prison at 1945. Changed into prison clothes (blue and white striped pyjamas), everything confiscated, and led blindfold to solitary confinement — entered there about 2025. Brick room, 10 feet by 8 feet [3 metres by 2.4 metres] one blanket and nothing else.

11 June 1981

Taken out of cell (Cell 12, prisoner number 254) at about 0800, led with David and five other prisoners (all appeared to be Iraqis) downstairs to have prison record photos taken. Blindfolded at all times, except for photography session of one minute.

(Funny incident in elevator on way back when all prisoners and one guard locked briefly inside — guard panicked!)

Decided on return to cell to not eat for one week, then take stock of my position. Reasons being obvious lack of medical attention if one should fall ill plus the fact that water not running in my cell, except for very slow drip into sludge of water in blocked 'pan' of shower. (Toilet flushing, but unable to open cistern and bowl unspeakably filthy.) Have just one small plastic cup and one small plastic bowl. Central air conditioning. Small slatted window, but can only see slit of sky. One cup of tea given at about 0600, again about 1800 — this the only liquid I have. Took first drink in 28 hours when I had 1800 tea.

12 June 1981

Nothing. Did not eat. Two cups of tea only — about 0600 and 1800. No real hunger.

13 June 1981

Ditto yesterday.

Feeling OK as far as going without food concerned.

Just occasionally — twice so far — have received a little extra tea into my bowl . . . about half a cup extra.

No word, no talking, nobody entered cell — nothing. Guards offer food three times a day, twice with tea at 0600 and 1800 and at about 1200 (without tea). It is usually one meal with rice and 'slop' — one simply watery soup, and maybe one other — or nothing!

14 June 1981

Same all day as previous two days.

At about 2230 taken from cell, blindfolded, downstairs, then upstairs in adjoining block to carpeted office, seemingly well furnished. Interrogated for about one and a half hours, blindfolded at all times. Questions continually stressing possible links with Israel, one interrogator claiming to have seen me on the streets of Tel Aviv several times last year! Also straight offer of a 'deal': . . . 'If you help us we can help you'! Finally taken back to cell around midnight — light turned out shortly after return.

Interrogators metioned my 'second passport' (actually a cancelled passport) so I knew they had been to my hotel room. Passport was in my bag.

Interrogators gave me a glass of water which was a life-saver, and seemed to help me overcome the shortage of water, not only immediately, but in the long term.

15 June 1981

Same routine as all other days.

Now five days without food, and feeling absolutely no hunger. Even appear to be holding weight! (Although it is apparent may have lost 1 kg.)

16 June 1981

Same routine as always.

Decided to end my 'fast' tomorrow afternoon and take food. Have now found that by standing in the slop up over my ankles, hold the plastic cup for two hours (in 30-minute stretches) I can get two-thirds of a cup of water. Drip does not always appear, plus fact that water is cut off intermittently.

Getting more drowsy, and fitfully sleeping more — maybe due to lack of food.

Interrogated again at about 2200 for about 45 minutes. Just the senior interrogator this time. Same theme — 'Do you know Mossad?' [the Israeli security organisation].

'No, I don't know him!'

17 June 1981

Guard came at about 1000. Blindfolded, then joined by David. Downstairs, waited standing and blindfolded — about 20 minutes — then given clothes back and told to dress.

I received back only $221 — $100 short. (David noticed this also.) I didn't complain! Driven back to hotel by 1040 and released in foyer!

> Not hungry — didn't eat till 1600 (then small plate of
> spaghetti). Checked bags. Obvious somebody had
> checked shoulder bag and $570 missing from 'blind'
> wallet (missed $2000 in lining of toilet bag in suitcase).

The two men had different experiences. David Phillips's
cell had a working shower, and no shortage of water. His
interrogation had been equally alarming, with the thrust of
the questioning seeking to identify him as an Israeli spy. At
the end of one torrid session, Phillips's interpreter whispered to him, 'Don't worry. It won't be long now.' This was
a tremendous psychological boost.

Davis said his worst moment was to be taken for an
interrogation session into a room that smelled like a den-
tist's surgery.

> I could smell the anaesthetic and heard what sounded
> like the buzzing of a drill. I broke out in a cold sweat,
> visualising torture in a dental chair as in the movie
> *Marathon Man*.

Fortunately, Davis was returned to his cell with his molars
intact.

Both Neil Davis and David Phillips firmly believed that if
the Iraqis had wished to believe they were Israeli spies,
they could have been held there for years.

High-level negotiations by NBC News (involving the US
State Department and the United Nations Secretary-General
Kurt Waldheim) had taken place. Journalists in Baghdad,
including Mike Lee, the American Broadcasting Company's
senior London correspondent, kept nagging the Foreign
Ministry, insisting the two men were only erring journalists.

NBC sent an executive jet to fly Davis and Phillips to
Amman for television interviews.

When Davis returned to base in Bangkok, the press corps
marked his return with an enormous banner hoisted above
the Grand Prix bar in Patpong Road: WELCOME HOME DAVIS

— JUST ANOTHER TASMANIAN CONVICT.

During the solitary confinement, Davis said, he had whiled away the time by mentally calculating his accumulated salary if he were imprisoned for three years.

I wasn't too impressed with the result, either!

27

'Patrons Will Please Check In Their Weapons Before Entering the Club'

Five days before Neil Davis died violently in Bangkok, he recorded what became the last cassette tape of reminiscences for his proposed autobiography.

The tape arrived in Sydney a week after his death, and detailed his experiences in the Philippines — a country he visited often and knew well. He had been at Manila airport when opposition leader Benigno Aquino was assassinated on 21 August 1983. He returned in later months to report on the Marcos regime's desperate attempts to hang onto power. But when he recorded his comments on the Philippines, he could not know that elections would soon be called early in 1986 — or that Cory Aquino would stand as a candidate for the presidency. Most observers at the time thought Mrs Aquino had about the same chance of becoming president as did Imelda Marcos of wearing out her wardrobe of imported shoes. But Neil Davis said this about the realities of opposition to the Marcos machine.

Only Ninoy Aquino was a serious alternative to Ferdinand Marcos.

There may be another, because I believe the one person who could carry that mantle on her own is his widow, Corazon Aquino.

Cory Aquino, I believe, has her own personal charisma.

371

Of course there would be great sympathy for her because of Ninoy. But she is also a charismatic lady in her own right.

She would deny that — she is a rather beautiful lady and denies political ambitions. However, she does have the love and support of the people.

Cory Aquino is capable of toppling Ferdinand Marcos.

Neil Davis knew the Aquinos personally. He first met Ninoy (his preferred nickname) in 1964 when he was vice-governor of Tarlac province. Then thirty-one, Aquino was only two years older than Davis.

He was a rising star right from the time he could talk, I suppose. He came from the old established and well-respected Aquino family in Tarlac. His grandfather had been a general, and his family had always been mixed up in politics. They were landowners, not so rich — although they were comfortably off.

Ninoy was a journalist at seventeen and eighteen and covered the Korean war in the early 1950s.

Aquino continued his career in journalism, working for a Manila newspaper until he became vice-governor of Tarlac province, but he lost the post because he was found to be under age after he was elected.

He was duly re-elected, and at the time I met him he had been vice-governor of Tarlac for two years. It was clear he was destined for big things, and even at that stage he was spoken of as a future president.

Davis's first visit to Manila was to cover a meeting of the South East Asia Treaty Organisation (SEATO) in April 1964. The Philippines was the first major assignment for the young Tasmanian cameraman outside Singapore and Malaysia. He struck up a friendship with Ian Ward, a fellow Australian who worked for the London *Daily Telegraph*.

Wardy is very positive and assertive in his views —
and doesn't care for people he calls 'pinkos' and 'lefties'.
Over the years I have had many outspoken arguments
with Ian, but never in bad blood. I well remember he was
enormously helpful on my first visit to the Philippines.
He gave me a good backgrounding in Filipino history, the
current political situation, and introduced me to the two
men who were going to play such dramatic roles in the
future of the Philippines, Benigno Aquino and Ferdinand
Marcos. Marcos was then a handsome young senator in
the Nationalist Party.

Neil never forgot the value of Ward's informed assessment
of the Philippines situation, and was himself unfailingly
generous to visiting journalists in later years, giving them
not only background briefings on countries and particular
situations, but immensely valuable practical advice on the
best way to ship film, tape or copy out of difficult situations. Needless to say, Davis's film was always first out.

Manila in the mid-1960s was a wonderfully volatile and
exceedingly dangerous city.

The press was astonishingly free, with stories of murder
and scandal splashed across newspaper pages, accompanied by allegations of political and personal improprieties
of the leaders of the land, which paid scant regard to libel
and defamation laws.

The Manila columnists of the day wielded enormous
power and influence. Ward introduced Neil Davis to one of
the most influential — Ernesto Grenada, later to be imprisoned by President Marcos after heavy press censorship
was introduced in the Philippines under martial law.

Of course there's always a lot of gunplay in the
Philippines and Ernie had bodyguards who didn't
hesitate to use their weapons whenever necessary. There
were some pretty wild killings, particularly in nightclubs
along Roxas Boulevarde — the famous nightclub area in
Manila.

Neil Davis met Ernie Grenada in Taboys, a small piano bar with a few hostesses.

It was a pleasant place. The owner, Taboy, used to insist on singing during the evening and playing the guitar. He did both badly, which is rare for a Filipino, but he was rather funny. His favourite tune was a bawdy version of 'Bye Bye Blackbird', which he sang at least three times a night.

Taboy was an amiable host, and one of his bar girls, an extremely attractive girl named Ligaya (the name means 'happiness'), was Ernesto Grenada's girlfriend.

I didn't know at that stage that Ligaya was Ernie Grenada's girl, otherwise I'd have steered well clear. Filipinos are a volatile race, prone to flaring up on the spur of the moment. After they have done some damage they are awfully sorry about it, but it is sometimes too late then.

On his second visit to the Philippines in 1965, Davis, who knew by then that the lissome Ligaya was Ernie Grenada's girlfriend, continued to pay attention to her. He was sailing in dangerous waters, and one night just before midnight when he was sitting with Ligaya, Ernie came into Taboys.

There was a pretty dramatic silence, of course, and Ernie casually sidled up and sat down next to me. I knew Ligaya very well by this time. She was a sweet girl but she didn't have a lot of conversation. Ernie said, 'You like her, do you?'

Davis, heart thumping, said, 'Oh yes, she's a nice girl,' trying to make it sound casual as he glanced over Ligaya's shoulder, expecting to see Ernie's thugs moving in to deal out rough justice.

Ernie said casually, 'But she's boring though, isn't she? She's really boring.'

'I'm not certain what you mean, Ernie.'

'I mean she's got no conversation, she's just a bore.'

Ligaya, who was listening to this conversation, stalked off in a huff. Davis, who did not know Ernie well at that stage, hastily bought him a drink.

To his dismay, Ernie said, 'Let's go along the Boulevarde.'

Davis knew that people could be 'accidentally' shot in a fracas along the Boulevarde.

'Where along the Boulevarde, Ernie?'

Ernie said, 'Oh just the nightclubs; I know the nightclubs well.'

'I don't think so, Ernie. I'm a little bit tired, and it's a bit too expensive for me,' said Davis.

Ernie was in like a flash. 'I'm inviting you as my guest.'

There was no way out. Davis was sure he was being set up.

> The only solution seemed to get blind drunk and enjoy what would either be my last hours or before I got the shit beaten out of me.

The two men went out on the town. Ernie was as good as his word, bought all the drinks and introduced Neil to some stunning girls in each nightclub.

> It wasn't a put-up job at all, it was just Ernie. And so we became quite friendly over the years.

When President Marcos declared martial law in 1972, Ernesto Grenada was one of the first pressmen to go to jail. Most were jailed on suspicion of having Communist contacts.

> Some might have had Communist contacts in the sense that journalists have all sorts of contacts. Ernie

---

375

spent several years in jail. He died of cancer in the early 1980s. Only then did it emerge that Ernie had actually been a member of what is now called the New People's Army — the Communist insurgents.

So whether Marcos and his intelligence people knew it or not — and I suspect not — they did in fact have a Communist in jail when they had Ernie. He was a most unlikely Communist, which I suppose is the best cover of all.

Because Taboys was a journalists' bar, it tended to get going even later at night than the general bars and nightclubs in the Ermita district of downtown Manila. Serious drinking began around midnight, and carried on from there.

One night Neil was at Taboys with an Australian journalist Arthur Cooke (not the British *Daily Mail* correspondent Arthur 'Shoulders' Cook, who was also working in Asia at that time).

It was around midnight, and Arthur and I had sunk quite a few noggins. I was sitting at the bar with a Filipino reporter who worked for UPI, Vic Maliwanag. Arthur was dozing on a benchlike settee against the wall. As he woke up, he stretched out his arms, one of which fell nicely around the shoulders of a young lady sitting next to him.

Cooke took advantage of this happy accident to strike up a conversation. But he was unaware that her boyfriend, a dapper little man in a suit, was sitting on her other side.

Vic suddenly said, 'Oh, my God — Arthur's in trouble!'

Davis peered through the gloom to make out the silhouette of Arthur Cooke — who was not a big man — tapping the smaller Filipino on his chest and saying, 'Now, put away that gun and I'll fight you outside.'

I could see the Filipino had a pistol in his right hand pointed at Arthur's middle.

The other people in the bar took the incident seriously enough. The pianist went to ground behind the piano and the drinkers at the bar scattered.

Arthur was most indignant at having a gun pulled on him, which he regarded as distinctly un-Australian behaviour, and Vic went over to try and straighten things out. Eventually Arthur produced a rather grudging apology and the angry Filipino and his girlfriend left the bar.

Vic came back and sat down, saying, 'Phew! That Arthur — he gets himself in a gunfight and he ain't got no bloody gun!' Davis said he always thought they were the worst sorts of gunfights to get into.

. . .

In 1965 Davis covered the presidential election won by Ferdinand Marcos.

There was enormous goodwill and high hope resting on Ferdinand and Imelda Marcos. Like the Kennedys in America, they were a very handsome couple, and Marcos was a marvellous orator and seemed to have the right credentials.

No one believed that Marcos was sweetness and light itself, but the Filipino people thought he would do better than his predecessor President Macapagal. But people couldn't take Macapagal seriously either. One of the greatest advantages Marcos has had over the years has been the weakness of his opposition.

In 1968 Neil returned to the Philippines again and as usual, contacted Benigno (Ninoy) Aquino.

> To claim to know Ninoy Aquino well is no great accomplishment. It was the duty of every foreign correspondent who visited the Philippines from the early 1960s to know him — if you didn't meet him, you were not doing your job.

Davis found Aquino an engaging character and admired his agile brain and personal magnetism.

> You really got the feeling that he had the capacity to finally lift his people and unite them. Although there was a Communist problem, he was able to talk to the Communists.
> He was finally charged with being pro-Communist, which was ridiculous. He was non-Communist, but whether he was anti-Communist is another thing. He basically believed in free politics.
> Although he believed in the capitalist system, he did not believe in absentee landlords owning tens of thousands of hectares of land and bleeding the tenants dry.

Davis had come to the Philippines to cover an unusual story — a rat plague. Millions of rats were eating rice crops and invading whole districts.

> There were extraordinary stories, like the three fishermen who were drowned after rats overturned their boat. The rats were evidently swimming en masse to or from an island.

One of the worst-affected provinces was Ninoy Aquino's Tarlac. The story of the rat plague had political implications.

One of the things that can be done to combat a rat plague is to cultivate the ground, which deprives the rats of a haven for their nests. But the absentee landlords in certain areas of Tarlac province were deliberately leaving tracts of land uncultivated so that the rats could breed.

Adjacent to their land the poor farmers would be working strenuously to grow rice or maize to eke out a living. The rats would come from their haven on the rich men's land, and eat all the poor farmers' crops.

The subsistence farmer would be forced to take out a mortgage on his little patch of ground, then a second mortgage. Eventually the landlord would take over the poor farmer's land. One of the worst affected areas was a little town called La Paz.

The town was more or less under Communist control. At that time they called the Communists the Huks — shortened from the Tagalog term Hukbalahap, which had been the People's Army Against Japan during the war. Government officials from outside did not care to go there. There was a small police station with a couple of policemen who one assumed had made an accommodation with the Huks because they were still alive.

Davis spoke to Aquino about visiting La Paz to cover the rat plague story and was given a note to take to the mayor of the town. It all worked out, and he made contact with the mayor and the judge of La Paz, both men in their early forties.

I was there for three days and I drank with them every night. They asked me what I wanted to drink on the first night, and I said 'scotch'. They produced a bottle of scotch. The judge drank brandy, and the mayor gin.

The unwritten rule on these occasions was that the bottle had to be finished. Every night, Davis drank a bottle of whisky. The job took three days instead of one.

That's where I first saw rats on sale in the market. The people were so poor they were eating the rats.

Some years later, Davis (whose ability to eat or drink absolutely anything rivalled his reputation as a cameraman) ate a rat on camera during his coverage of a lesser rat plague in Thailand.

The La Paz story had been covered with Ninoy Aquino's help. Davis kept contact with the mayor, who also owned shares in a small Manila nightclub called the International Executive Clubhouse.

It was very swishy. To get in you had to know the signal — so many knocks on the door and a password. You passed through a tiny room, and on into the club where there was nude dancing, which was illegal in Manila at the time.

You could have a meal there, too. They gave marvellous receipts — I think they spent more money on their stationery than the food. The mayor gave me a note to say I was a close friend of his.

The mayor confided to Davis that he was actually a Communist, and so was the judge. Perhaps the La Paz police were too. Davis was not able to confirm that. They all did their jobs.

I had become accustomed to this sort of thing in Vietnam, so I was not all that surprised.

During his 1968 assignment to cover the rat plague story, Davis was in Manila when a major earthquake rocked the city. He was asleep in the Tower Hotel in Ermita, one of

Manila's few high-rise buildings at that time. The Tower survived with a few cracks, but some 250 people died when a big apartment block collapsed.

His coverage of the earthquake aftermath won him an award for the British Commonwealth newsfilm of the year, but he was rather dismissive of such accolades, which he believed merely signalled that someone was lucky enough to be in the right place at the right time.

In 1969 Davis covered the last 'legitimate' presidential election in the Philippines. Marcos was running for a second term against Senator Osmena. If successful, it would be the first time a Filipino president had been twice elected. It would be his final term. Neil received a useful briefing on the state of democracy in the Philippines when he asked a Western ambassador for a rundown on Senator Osmena.

The ambassador said, 'He's even more corrupt than Marcos.' In the Philippines that was saying something!

Neil remarked in a letter to his Aunt Lillian at the time that the high level corruption in the Philippines generated fantastic rewards for those in power. He never knew that Marcos measured his loot in billions rather than millions of dollars, thus raising the art of political nest-feathering to an undreamed-of level.

When Cambodia was dragged into the Indo-China war in March 1970, Neil Davis was not able to visit the Philippines so often. President Marcos declared martial law in 1972, jailed Benigno Aquino and many other political opponents and effectively ruled under martial law for the next ten years.

In 1981 he had an election of sorts and was elected for a six-year term.

Aquino was allowed to go to the United States for a heart bypass operation. He decided to return to the Philippines when it was possible that elections were going to be scheduled for late 1983 or maybe 1984.

In theory Ninoy was still under sentence and would be arrested when he came back. He wasn't worried about that, but he was obviously worried about the possibility of assassination. He spoke of it in Taiwan only hours before he boarded the China Airlines flight which took him to the Philippines.

Davis had flown to the Philippines on 20 August 1983 and talked with Aquino's sister Lupita Kashiwara, whose husband Ken was a correspondent for the American television news network ABC and who was travelling with Ninoy Aquino.

I knew Lupita well. She was waiting at Manila airport with Ninoy's mother and other members of the family and close friends.

Also at the airport was a crowd of about twenty thousand people who had tied yellow ribbons around the electricity poles and the trees everywhere on the route from the airport to the Aquino suburban home. 'Tie A Yellow Ribbon Round The Old Oak Tree' was one of Ninoy Aquino's favourite songs.

There were 'Welcome Home Ninoy' banners everywhere in English and in Tagalog. And so there was great excitement at the airport. There was some tension too. We all believed that Ninoy would be arrested and we probably wouldn't see him.

Of course it's a big, busy airport with noises of planes landing and public address system announcements and crowds of people, so that some things could happen and we were unaware of them. We did not hear any shots fired.

The press were allowed into the terminal building, and inside the immigration section, but they were kept away from the big open windows overlooking the tarmac. Aquino's China Airlines flight came in at Chute No 8.

We were waiting approximately fifty metres away on the same floor, expecting him to emerge from the covered walkway leading from the plane.

The China Airlines plane drew in to Chute No 8 and some minutes passed. The waiting reporters saw many security guards running about and guessed that something was up. They correctly surmised that Aquino was being taken down the emergency steps directly from the plane to the tarmac, into some kind of military vehicle to be driven away.

It was five or ten minutes more before the first passengers from China Airlines started coming towards us. There were Chinese from Taipei, Filipinos returning from vacation or business and a few Westerners.
We were looking for a phalanx of security which would surround Ninoy Aquino as he came and we hoped to get a word from him on the spot.

A press statement from Aquino had already been released as he landed because his advisers and family believed he would probably be whisked away without being able to make his statement in person.

We tried to talk to one young Chinese man before he reached immigration, but he just shook his head and did not appear to be disturbed in any way, although he must have been aware that something fairly dramatic had happened.

Several more people went past, ignoring the group of press. Then a European couple, either Scandinavian or German — Davis estimated they were probably in their sixties or seventies — came past and were stopped by the press. The first query was whether Aquino was actually on the plane, because that was by no means certain.

The man spoke English and said, 'Yes, yes . . . he was on the plane but he was taken off.'

We asked him if the military had taken him away.

'Well, I don't know,' he said. 'You see, he was taken out of the plane first and down the steps. I don't know what happened after the shots.'

There was a complete silence for what seemed like two seconds.

Then all of us shouted in a chorus, 'Shots . . . shots . . . *what* fucking shots?'

The guy backed off, astounded at our reaction. He didn't realise we hadn't heard the shots. While everybody was screaming, 'What shots? What shots?' his wife plucked his sleeve to lead him away. As he walked away he said, 'I don't know . . . there were these shots and I don't know what's happened to him.'

Then there was just turmoil. I saw Ken Kashiwara, Ninoy's brother-in-law, looking very, very upset hurrying along obviously to get to his wife — Ninoy's sister — to tell her and the family the news.

I said, 'Ken, Ken, what's happened?'

'They've killed Ninoy, they've shot Ninoy.'

No one knew what to do. The press group of about fifteen people went back down to the VIP lounge, which was close to the immigration area. Designed to hold about twenty people, it was crammed with about one hundred and fifty, including Ninoy Aquino's mother, who was well into her seventies.

Cory Aquino and their children — four girls and one boy — had all remained in the United States to see whether Ninoy was going to be arrested or not before deciding what to do. But his mother, sister, brother and

384

friends were all waiting in the VIP room.

There was little information. There had been shots, a lot of blood, and Aquino appeared to be at the very least seriously wounded and probably dead.

The prominent opposition politician Salvador 'Doy' Laurel was also there and he went out with Aquino's brother to make some statement to the thousands of people waiting outside. Although this was now half an hour after Aquino had been shot, no announcement had been made.

The enormous crowd outside was still happy, waiting to give a joyous welcome to Ninoy Aquino, not only at the airport, but right along the road to his home, with yellow ribbons all along the route.

So when Doy Laurel and Ninoy's brother came out of the arrival hall, this whole host of people believed that Ninoy was among them. Ninoy was not a tall man, and they assumed there'd be bodyguards grouped around him, but eventually he would appear and talk to them.

This enormous crowd was pressing around the small group shouting, 'Ninoy! Ninoy!' and waving clusters of yellow ribbons. The welcome home banners were there, and it was really a happy occasion for them. Their beloved Ninoy was home, and there were great expectations of what could happen.

Wherever Ninoy went, there was always excitement and expectations — and love, he generated tremendous love. Indeed, Ninoy could generate a great deal of love. He was very much a ladies' man, although he loved his wife and family very dearly. In the past he had been rather conceited, but his period of imprisonment had made him, in my view, a much greater man. He became more philosophical, more able to accept his fate, whatever it might be, and to see his destiny more clearly.

The large crowd was waiting for him, screaming his name, calling out and laughing.

It took Doy Laurel almost ten minutes to clamber up on top of a vehicle and call for quiet. But no one could hear him. Eventually someone found a loud hailer, and he called on the crowd to quieten down.

> The crowd began to sense from his serious demeanour and his look of anguish and despair that something had happened. I think they assumed at that moment that Ninoy had been arrested.
>
> He told them simply that Ninoy Aquino had been shot, and we did not know his fate. As he said that, the whole crowd, thousands of people collectively, groaned almost the same words: 'Oh, no!'
>
> I didn't know what the crowd would do. I thought they might do anything — even tear the place to pieces. And I give Doy Laurel his credit. He asked them to remain calm, and concluded by saying: 'Pray for Senator Aquino if it is not already too late.'
>
> And they did, they went off to the churches. I followed them to a nearby church, people wearing their Ninoy Aquino T-shirts, carrying their Ninoy Aquino banners, waving the yellow ribbons and trudging off disconsolately, many of them weeping. It was a very, very sad scene.
>
> Aquino's body finally arrived at his home late that night, and was put on view there the next morning.

Hundreds of thousands of Filipinos viewed his body that day and for another ten days. Aquino's body was then taken from his home to a church and then to his home province of Tarlac, and then brought back to Manila.

> Each of these moves was like a ticker-tape parade, as if a candidate was on show. The banners said 'to Ninoy'. The predominant one was 'We love you, Ninoy'.
>
> T-shirts and little caps started to spring up with all sorts of sayings of Ninoy on them. One I remember said

'The Filipino is worth dying for'. Others asked questions: 'Who killed Ninoy Aquino?' 'Who killed our hero?'

This amazing outpouring of grief was sustained through the ten days before his funeral.

The cortege began from a church in downtown Manila to a big cemetery on the outskirts of the city, and took a circuitous route of about twenty-five kilometres. It's estimated three million people lined that route and it took approximately twelve hours to negotiate the distance.

It was an extraordinary sight — I'll never forget that. People were weeping, some were applauding as the cortege passed with Ninoy's coffin visible and they called out many things. The most often heard cry was simply, 'Goodbye, Ninoy, goodbye', or, 'We love you Ninoy!' said thousands of times that day.

I don't think Ferdinand Marcos ever heard that except from his wife and family and a few of his more ardent supporters. He's never heard it en masse. If he didn't know of Ninoy Aquino's great popularity and charisma before, he knew it that day. And he's known every day since that they haven't forgotten Ninoy Aquino.

His place in Philippine history is assured. The whole history of the Philippines changed course when Ninoy Aquino was shot on 21 August 1983.

28

Children
of the Dust

On 2 January 1977, Neil Davis received a desperate telephone call from Jim Bennett, asking for his help. Bennett's cameraman Yosep (Joe) Lee had been blown up by a land mine in southern Thailand while filming Thai military action against the Communist forces on the Thai-Malaysian border.

Joe Lee's Thai soundman Annant Chamchun died in the explosion and Joe himself had lost a leg and was close to death from loss of blood and shock.

Davis recruited a German doctor and a medical team in Bangkok and helped arrange a charter aircraft to fly them to Songkla province to pick up Lee.

Always the professional, Joe Lee had actually filmed the death of his soundman and then coolly altered focus to film his own severed leg.

Eyewitnesses described how Joe Lee was still filming as they lifted him into the rescue helicopter. But the slow deliberate pan down his leg to reveal his severed foot was considered too alarming for prime time US television, and was not shown.

Neil Davis met the aircraft bringing Joe Lee back to Bangkok. Lee recalls, 'I saw Neil walking to me. He didn't even say a single word but just held my hand and walked to the ambulance. He was with me in the ambulance to the Bangkok Nursing Home, which was coincidentally the same hospital Neil was taken to after he was wounded in Cambodia.'

Before Joe left the Bangkok Nursing Home, Davis came to him one day with a surprising announcement. 'Joe, I'm going to get married.'

Lee was astounded. He had known Davis for seven years and each time he or his wife had asked him about marriage, he said he would remain a bachelor for life. Joe asked Davis if he was sure.

'Yes, I'm very sure, and it'll be soon. I have a girlfriend in Taiwan.'

Only days later Davis flew to Taiwan to marry Chou Ping (Julie), promising to ring his dumbfounded friend immediately after the ceremony.

Since their first meeting beside the swimming pool at the Lane-Xang Hotel in Vientiane in 1972, Davis and Julie had kept in close touch. They met in Hong Kong and Bangkok, and with the Indo-China war over, parental opposition to the marriage had been overcome.

Even so, Davis's decision to marry astonished his correspondent friends, who found marriage difficult to equate with his freewheeling lifestyle. As Joe Lee said about the early post-Indo-China-war years, 'At night Neil and I used to go to Patpong Road, a popular night zone in Bangkok, to ease fatigue and enjoy young girls' nude dancing. I later heard that Neil's nickname was "The Old Fox".'

The adjective 'old' did not seem appropriate for the ever-youthful Davis, so he became simply 'The Fox'. Somewhere, his friends said, a portrait hung in a dark cupboard, like that in Oscar Wilde's classic tale *The Picture of Dorian Gray*, on which the ravages of Davis's lifestyle were clearly etched. But the nickname of 'The Fox' was appropriate for other reasons. Davis guarded his private life with obsessive secrecy. He was coy about his age. When they first met in 1972, he told Julie he was thirty. He was in fact thirty-eight.

Julie, a citizen of Taiwan, had not been able to get a visa

to visit Davis in Bangkok when he was recovering from the mortar blast that nearly severed his right leg. His decision to marry Julie might have been confirmed at that time. Later he confessed to Joe Lee in a rare expression of personal feeling that he had felt very vulnerable at that time. He told Joe that he was shocked at his friend's injury, and it confirmed his already formed view that if he were badly wounded or incapacitated, it was better not to be alone.

His diary of 29 January 1977 has a one-word entry — 'Married'. At the bottom of the page is a reminder to call Joe Lee at the Bangkok Nursing Home as he had promised.

After a short honeymoon in Taiwan and Hong Kong, the couple returned to Bangkok. Julie's life had changed, but Davis's had not. In April that year he flew to Africa for a three-month assignment. Julie made what life she could in the apartment, in an unfamiliar city where she knew few people, while the one-man band jetted off to assignments in Africa, the Middle East and Asia.

With Davis's sympathetic understanding, Julie visited her parents in Taiwan during his longer absences from Bangkok. She could not travel with him on local assignments, because they often involved complex political situations or danger-ous stories on the volatile Thai-Cambodian border. She tried to get him to pull back from risky assignments, but knew that was a hopeless task.

The man who valued friendship above everything else found it difficult to share his intimate thoughts with his wife. Their conversations stayed on a curiously superficial level. Indeed, Julie says that she never really knew him: 'We would talk about his work, or the people he knew in Cambodia. But he would never talk about himself — from inside his mind.'

Julie believed that Davis was not able to share his inti-mate thoughts with anyone. The mainspring of his deepest feelings stayed tightly wound up inside. Julie thought he made an effort to change his lifestyle after they married, but 'it was impossible'. They did try to have a child, but without success.

By January 1980 they had separated, although they corresponded and met from time to time. Divorce was never discussed.

The pattern of Davis's life never changed. Returning from assignments, he relaxed in the bars and nightclubs of Bangkok's notorious Patpong Road, cadged other people's cigarettes and made preposterous sporting bets with other journalists.

He was probably the heaviest smoker of other people's cigarettes ever known. The origins of this quirk are unclear. It was once said that he was caught in a tight combat situation in Vietnam and vowed that if he got out of it, he would never buy another packet of cigarettes. In any case, he never did.

'G'day, mate. Got a cigarette?' was his invariable greeting as he removed a packet from the friend's top pocket and helped himself. His best one-liner in response to a disgruntled 'I've only got one left' was 'Well, I only need one.' Those with a full packet usually heard him say, 'One for now and one for later.' He was the most generous of men in all other ways, but quite remorseless in his quest for smokes from others.

ABC correspondent Richard Palfreyman forgot the rules when he brought a carton of American cigarettes into Ho Chi Minh City in April 1985 while Davis was helping to organise NBC's live satellite coverage of the tenth anniversary of the end of the Indo-China war. He tried to hand them to Davis.

'No, no,' Davis said. 'Give them to Gary Burns. I'll enjoy them more that way.'

On assignment, Gary Burns used to keep his suitcase locked with a combination lock. Once in Ho Chi Minh City he found his suitcase burgled. Considerable sums of money were untouched, but his cigarettes were gone. In their place was the drawing of a skull with the words, 'The

Tassie Phantom strikes!' Burns realised that Davis had been so desperate for a cigarette that he had sat in his room for hours to crack the combination lock. But he never bought any of his own.

Fellow Visnews man John Tulloh remembers a birthday party for Davis in Singapore in 1969. Of course, no one knew his actual age. The diners caroused in an Indonesian restaurant for some hours, then Davis was presented with a gift-wrapped package the size of a tea chest. His eyes glowed with anticipation because he thought it might be an ancient Asian artifact to enhance his collection. His expectancy mounted as he burrowed through the piles of rice paper filling the crate. Finally he got to the bottom to discover an exquisitely wrapped box the size of a fountain pen case. A hush fell on the drunken company as he slowly removed the paper and opened the box.

Inside was a single cigarette.

'Happy birthday, Neil,' bawled the guffawing journos. Tulloh remembers that as one of the few occasions when he saw Davis embarrassed.

Always intensely proud of his Tasmanian origins, Davis was a founding member of Tasmanians in Thailand, or TIT. Crates of Cascade beer were freighted to Bangkok for TIT's meetings, and their activities were gleefully reported in Thailand's English language newspaper the *Bangkok Post*, resulting in headings like 'TIT EXPOSED'. On 17 January 1982 the *Post* reported that TIT was anxious to liaise with the Tourist Authority of Thailand (TAT) to promote tourism between the two countries. It was a case of TIT for TAT.

An apogee of awfulness was attained in the *Bangkok Post* of 1 October 1984, under the heading TITS BOUNCE BACK: 'After a break of two years, TITs bounced back into prominence in Thailand last week. Tasmanians In Thailand (TIT) and Tasmanian University Graduates (TUG) got together for a TUG-A-TIT luncheon at the Sheraton Hotel in Bangkok ...'

Davis was a keen tennis player. The game brought out

the best — and the worst — in him. He revelled in the physical competitiveness but would resort to scoundrel gamesmanship if things were going against him. He would carry on a non-stop patter of insulting comments about his opponent's game, morals, politics and general appearance. The fact that there was usually money on the game added an extra edge.

Creighton Burns, later the editor of the *Age* newspaper in Melbourne, once reportedly stormed off the court in Singapore in the late 1960s after enduring a sustained burst of Davis's invective.

But Davis was quietly confident when he agreed to play Bobby for a barrel of beer in Bangkok in 1982. Bobby ran a bar on Patpong Road. He was some said, part Portuguese, part Chinese. It was an exaggeration to say that his circumference was running a close race with his height, but Bobby did not look like an athlete. Appearances were deceptive. Bobby had been a junior tennis champion in Hong Kong, and it was said that he had even been paired with Australia's Ken Rosewall at one stage.

Despite his war-smashed leg and his age of almost fifty, Davis could still wield a forceful and subtle racquet. But Bobby wiped him off the court and Davis's first response was to drink most of the barrel of beer he lost. His second was to turn Bobby's unlikely skills to his own advantage.

Davis engineered the set-up. A newly arrived American helicopter pilot was well built, brash and given to hinting at a record of great deeds on track, field and court. After a night's drinking in the Grand Prix Bar, the helicopter jock was on for $US1000 to beat Bobby and Davis in consecutive singles matches.

One of Davis's major worries was to keep Bobby off the booze for a few days beforehand and make him do some practice. But it all worked out. Bobby toyed with the helicopter jock over three sets in Bangkok's dry-season heat, and Davis delivered the coup de grace.

Although his track record in investment in collapsed

property deals, sunken floating nightclubs and hail-stricken drought-prone vineyards was magnificently disastrous, Davis's instincts for a bet won him a lot of money. The bets were posted on a notice board behind the bar at the Grand Prix in Patpong Road. It was an early port of call for Davis after he returned from eight days' solitary confinement in the Iraqi security jail. He wanted to know if two or three people who owed him money on boxing bets had paid up, or whether they were holding off to see how things went in Baghdad.

Gary Burns and Neil Davis had $US10 000 between them on the Hagler-Hearns middleweight title fight in Las Vegas in April 1985. The two cameramen were in Ho Chi Minh City at that time, where Davis was helping to organise the ground station facilities for NBC's live satellite coverage of the tenth anniversary of the end of the Indo-China war, but they hoped the fight would be broadcast by Voice of America or Armed Forces Radio.

Davis had engineers from NBC rigging antennae out the window of their room at the Majestic Hotel, but Armed Forces Radio was broadcasting a baseball game with only occasional progress reports on the fight. Gary Burns recalls that the first report they got said: 'Round Two's over, another torrid round, and it's Hearns in front in the fight, Hagler is bleeding badly.'

Their $10 000 was on Hagler. Davis turned grey and railed against the sporting broadcast policies of Armed Forces Radio while the baseball coverage went on for the next forty-five minutes. They had no way of knowing that Hagler had reversed the tables, and knocked Hearns out at the start of the third round. When the news came through, Davis leaped into the air.

'I wasn't worried for a moment! I knew he'd win it!'

The Vietnamese government allowed Davis to return to Vietnam on a number of occasions after he covered the fall of Saigon. He got back in April 1980 for the fifth anniversary of the end of the war, first to Hanoi and then to Ho Chi Minh City in the south.

In the former Saigon, he had always been popular with the street orphans of Tu Do Street. Apart from friendly badinage, he used to pass on little presents. After he had been booked into his hotel, the Doc Lap (the old Caravelle, where he had stayed when he first came to Saigon in 1964), he went for a stroll and was shocked to see children still eking out a wretched existence on the streets. Most were Amerasians — the results of liaisons between American GIs and Vietnamese women. They were known colloquially and accurately as 'Children Of The Dust', a continuing reminder to the Vietnamese of the American invasion of their culture, and were effectively regarded as non-people by the Vietnamese. The Vietnamese government did, however, have some orphanages for these children and Neil Davis was allowed to take some film at one of them.

Outside the orphanage, he saw a Vietnamese woman whom he recognised as Mai Chi, wife of a UPI correspondent Paul Vogle. He talked with her briefly, and arranged to meet her again.

> A few minutes later, an unseen hand thrust a note into my hand which said, 'Somebody follow you'. Not more than three minutes later I was handed another note which said, 'Somebody follow you Neil!'

This was not melodramatic. Davis knew that he was being kept under surveillance during his time in Vietnam.

> The loss of many civil liberties was the biggest change I noticed then. It is, for example, against the law for any Vietnamese to have contact with a foreigner — even to talk to one.
>
> They can have contact in a shop, selling something, but no other comunication is allowed. A foreigner may go into a Vietnamese home — but within minutes the security police will be along. It is a very doctrinaire Communist state. There must be no talking against the government — only the actual members of the

Communist Party are free to criticise from within.
Anybody else among sixty million Vietnamese who
speaks out critically can be put in prison.

Davis was able to take up Mai Chi Vogle's case with the
authorities and acted as intermediary. Eventually she and
the children were reunited with her husband and the Vogle
family now lives in the United States.

A number of foreign correspondents took up the story of
the desperate plight of the Amerasian children and their
mothers at this time. Australian film maker Jim Gerrand
heard his name whispered several times during some street
filming and was nervously enticed up back alleys to be presented with a petition with five hundred names and photographs of Vietnamese women and their half-caste children
wanting to leave Vietnam.

He passed on this document to the United Nations.
Eventually the Vietnamese government issued exit visas to
some of the women concerned, but this often added to
their desperation. There was still nowhere to go, and they
had forfeited their rights to rations, housing, health services
and schooling for their children. They lived in limbo as
non-persons.

Davis did what he could by featuring the story on NBC
News and by personal involvement. Gary Burns believes
that the impact of his stories on American television was
largely responsible for the US government reluctantly taking
some responsibility for the Amerasian children and their
mothers.

Among Davis's papers are pathetic letters and messages,
some thrust into his hand on the street, others posted to
him in Bangkok. One mother who had a child by an
Australian soldier wrote: 'In addition I have one more Vietnamese son, named Nguyen Goc Tuan, born 23 December
1965 in Saigon, whose father was died in an auto accident
before I met the Australian. This Australian knew well
about my son, while my mother brought him to my house.

'Children Of The Dust' — some of the Amerasian children in Ho Chi Minh City (formerly Saigon) whose mothers organised petitions to be carried out of Vietnam by sympathetic journalists. They hoped not only to contact the fathers of their children, but to emigrate to the United States.

Khmer Rouge followers fleeing from the Vietnamese invasion of Kampuchea in 1979 across the Thailand border. *Bangkok Post.*

Neil Davis interviewing a Khmer Rouge cadre, Mit Veth, on the Thai/Kampuchea border in November 1979. *Jim Gerrand*

'Actually I have been living in the unmarried situation, and trying to foster my children in agony and sweat.

'Therefore, I call upon your generosity and humanity to assist me and my children in emigrating whether to USA as refugees in order to seek a better way of our living there, for the sake of my children's future, or to Australia under your help, so we can be saved from the difficult and miserable situation that we have been suffering.'

One scrap of paper obviously torn from a school exercise book and written in a childish hand says simply: 'My father's name is Richard John —— of [an Oklahoma address].'

'My name is Stephanie May Jeanne, of [Ho Chi Minh City address].

'Please, Sir, try to help me to find my father and try to help me and my mother get out from here. Thank you, Sir.'

Yet another letter from a refugee camp on the Thai-Cambodian border has a photograph attached of two young ARVN soldiers, carbines slung nonchalantly over their shoulders, posing for a happy snap. The writer hoped Davis would help find the young man on the left-hand side of the photo. 'Mr Hung was also a soldier of Republic Vietnam, attended Division 18 at Long Thanh Province, and Phuoc Tuy later on. He was on his way to Vung Tau carrying serious wounds on many parts of the body when Phuoc Tuy was taken over in 25 April 1975. After that he stayed at a shelter while his friends were on boats going out to the sea to other countries. He is still wearing many stigmas as a mark of the war . . .

'Mr Hung's aspiration is always to be sent to the United States because only this place, he will be able to meet his relatives facedly.

'I send you his photograph in the Army that he keeps as his precious souvenir, and desire you will help him sufficiently.'

Davis found time to follow up on behalf of Miss Tuyet, the former news secretary for NBC in Saigon who, in company with many Vietnamese who worked for the Americans, was not able to be evacuated when Saigon fell. He wrote to head office in New York about payments owing to her. She had courageously worked on after the Communists took over the city.

> She now has no job and an ailing father. There is little money coming into the household. She never complains, and never asks for money, but I know she feels things deeply . . .
> I suggest we offer her $1000 to tide her over. It's sad . . . Miss Tuyet is now in her mid-thirties and the prime years of her young life have passed her by as she waited patiently to obtain her freedom . . .

Davis was so well known in the streets of Ho Chi Minh City that he could take only a few steps outside his hotel before the street urchins descended on him. 'Oh, no,' he would say as they came running up. Australian Broadcasting Corporation correspondent Geoff Leach has an enduring memory of Davis being trailed down Tu Do Street like an Antipodean Pied Piper, distributing little gifts for the children — sweets, soap or shampoo. The children would usually pass letters to him for posting outside Vietnam.

In May 1983 he returned to Phnom Penh for his second visit since it fell to the Communists.

> It was a traumatic experience, because I was returning to a city I had lived in for five years and although it physically resembled the rather beautiful city I had known, everything had changed. It was a city of impermanence, like a giant refugee camp.

He had the keys of his apartment, letter box and Mercedes car with him, and went to his old apartment.

> It was being renovated to allow Russians to live there. So I walked into the downstairs foyer, to the bank of

letter boxes. Mine still had my name on it. As I put my
key in, I had a funny feeling something would be in it.

Among the cobwebs and dead spiders were two letters.
One was a small cheque from the *Far Eastern Economic
Review* for some articles he had contributed and the other
was from a South African group of newspapers.

They had been delivered four days before the fall of
the city, so the postmen can be proud of their dedication.
They had made their rounds as the city was being
constantly hit by rockets and artillery fire.

He was also curious about the fate of his beloved Mercedes.
He found it in a car graveyard. The Khmer Rouge had
actually shot it 'between the eyes' through the radiator
grille as a symbol of Western capitalist decadence. All the
'executed' cars had been stacked on top of each other in
what could only be called vehicle burial grounds.

But for Davis, the biggest shock was the lack of people
he knew. Phnom Penh was occupied by country folk who
had never lived in a city before.

I knew hundreds, or maybe even thousands of people
in that city before and they weren't there.

Davis was quartered in one of Prince Sihanouk's old villas
just outside Phnom Penh with a group of American correspondents, while his fellow Australian newsmen Gary
Burns and Barry Wain scored the Russians and Eastern
Bloc journalists in another crumbling mansion nearby. The
two Australians found the company of the Russians and
Bulgarians rather stolid.

They decided to go into the city for dinner but the guard
on the high wire gates would not open up. Burns and Wain
began to climb over the perimeter fence and the armed
guard came running up to stop them. 'You'll have to shoot

us in the back then, mate,' said Burns cheerfully as they strolled off down the street.

Davis had also flown his coup and the three Australians joined forces to walk into town.

Gary Burns was astounded when a cyclo pedalled by an aged Khmer trundled up with the driver calling out, 'Mr Neil, Mr Neil!' It turned out to be a man known as the King of the Cyclo Drivers, who used to operate in a low-life area called Ambush Alley full of pimps and prostitutes. As Burns and Davis were pedalled into the drab and sterile heart of Communist Phnom Penh, the driver made his pitch to Davis for help in emigrating to the United States. Neil asked the King if he thought he could find his former driver, An Veng, who had worked for Davis devotedly and bravely through the Cambodian war years from 1970 to 1975. He gave the cyclo man his business card and some money to pass on to An Veng if he could find him.

An Veng had actually seen Davis in the street when he made his first postwar visit to Phnom Penh with a group of journalists invited by the Vietnamese to witness the withdrawal of troops from Kampuchea in June 1980, but at that time An Veng would have been compromised had he made the slightest gesture towards contact.

After Davis left Phnom Penh, the King of the Cyclo Drivers found An Veng and gave him some money and Neil's business card. The old man took great heart from the realisation that Davis had been looking for him. Three of An Veng's children had been executed by the Khmer Rouge because they were deemed too intelligent for the forced labour squads into which they had been drafted, but eventually he and his remaining eighteen-year-old son managed to escape over the border to Thailand in September 1985. An Veng's wife Chea Kruy made it over the border into Thailand independently in 1986.

The chain of events begun when the King of the Cyclo Drivers passed on Davis's message and money in Phnom Penh in 1983 could not be completed. Neil Davis planned to go to the border to meet An Veng and begin the complex processes to enable him to emigrate to Australia, when an attempted coup d'état in Bangkok on 9 September 1985 diverted him to his last assignment.

29

'Tomorrow
Will Be Too Late'

Neil Davis's return to Phnom Penh in 1983 shocked him
into the realisation that it would be many many years
before he could hope to live in Cambodia again.

> It brought home to me that it was going to be a long
> time before Phnom Penh recaptured the spirit that the
> city had had before 1975.
> I didn't want to go back to the city again unless there
> was a re-establishment of the Khmer culture, and Khmer
> independence.

With other foreign correspondents, he had tried to follow
events in Pol Pot's Kampuchea from the Thai border. The
border town of Aranyaprathet became the headquarters for
the press, where they gleaned what scraps of information
they could. Refugee movement on the Thai-Cambodian
border increased dramatically in April 1979, as an estimated
55000 to 80000 Cambodians fled over the border into
Thailand south of Aranyaprathet and then crossed back
into Cambodia about thirty kilometres south from where
they had entered Thailand. They were fleeing from the
Vietnamese invasion of Kampuchea and the dreadful bestiality of the Khmer Rouge administration.

The Thai government was anxious to secure its territory
against international embroilment and against a mass of

escapees. There were anguished scenes at the border as Cambodians tried to enter Thailand. Many of the desperate Cambodians crossed the small stream at the border and pleaded to be accepted as refugees. Those forced back faced death from three sources — the Khmer Rouge, the Vietnamese invaders, or the border minefields they had to traverse.

On Friday 13 April, Davis witnessed a group of about two hundred trying to cross the border.

> There were men, women and children of all ages, all suffering from malnutrition and various diseases.

They were led by an old man of about seventy. He was gaunt, but had what Davis described as a kind face, and his tattered clothes only enhanced his distinguished bearing and air of quiet dignity.

> He had a small monkey in his arms, and they were obviously devoted to each other. Despite the lack of food, some refugees went to tremendous trouble to keep a companion — particularly if they had lost their families.
>
> All were pleading with the Thai soldiers to allow them to stay. It was very tense, because behind them in the shadows of the forest were the dreaded Khmer Rouge dressed in black, silent, waiting and very forbidding.

The old man was particularly eloquent in his pleas for himself and his people. He spoke French beautifully, probably having been a schoolteacher from one of the provincial capitals and a graduate of the French education system. He also spoke Thai, which was rare for a Cambodian.

> The Thais were nice, but insistent that the refugees would have to return.
>
> The old man said he was a dead man if he went back,

403

because the Khmer Rouge now knew he was educated
— enough to bring death — as they had heard him
speaking French. Sensing the tension, the monkey
snuggled close to its master and jumped on his shoulder,
stroking the old man's head with his tiny hands.

The people were rejected, and started to move back across
the stream into Kampuchea, clearly terrified.

I was standing on the lip of the bank close to the old
man. He started slowly down the bank, and a Thai
soldier stopped him a few paces down. The old man
turned hopefully — but he really didn't think he was
saved and that was reflected in his eyes.

The soldier said, 'Maybe tomorrow, uncle.'

The old man looked at him with a very kindly
expression of forgiveness as well as understanding and
resignation.

'Tomorrow will be too late,' he said.

He turned down the bank and walked across and up to
the opposite side into the trees where the silent shadows
of the black-clad Khmer Rouge waited. We never saw the
old man again.

Awful instances of human despair became commonplace in
those few days of April 1979. There were so many potential
refugees that the Thai soldiers sometimes co-operated with
the Khmer Rouge soldiers to escort them back over the
border. One long column halted in a Thai village while
some bogged vehicles at the head of the wretched collection
of displaced humanity were moved.

One man had two sons about four and six years old.
While the column halted, he begged some of the Thai
villagers to take his sons. But the Thais didn't say
anything.

At last the Cambodian man told his sons to stay there

— the Thai villagers were around the group — and he hurried off as the column moved on.

But the two little boys, realising their father had gone, burst into tears and ran after him. It was a very sad scene.

Some of the Khmer Rouge soldiers were girls and very young boys. Davis estimated their ages at no more than twelve or fourteen.

They appeared to handle their weapons like veterans.

On the same day that the old man with the monkey had been forced to return over the border, Davis and Korean cameraman Kim Dong Kyu followed a Thai military jeep that was obviously going on a mission in a hurry.

It was late in the afternoon and the sun was almost setting. Suddenly, we saw four Khmer Rouge soldiers on the road.

This was a time when the sight of the Khmer Rouge instilled instant fear in all. These unknown madmen who killed, killed, killed . . .

But they had actually crossed over to defect. There was little sympathy from the Thais. After all, these were not civilian refugees like the kindly old man with the monkey.

The border stream was about a hundred and fifty metres away, and the Thai soldiers trained their jeep-mounted machine gun on them and ordered them back into Kampuchea.

They went, the fourth Khmer Rouge soldier hanging back. The newsmen turned to go back to their car when they heard a shout.

We looked back to see the reluctant one running towards us yelling, with his AK47 rifle in his hand. He wasn't threatening, he was obviously terrified.

Davis and Kim stood on the edge of the road by the embankment. The desperate KR soldier threw himself down at their feet, babbling. He said they were going to kill him, and held his rifle up to a Thai soldier to surrender it. The Thai waved it aside and ordered him back across the border. The KR threw his rifle down and pleaded. The Thais said no, and threatened to shoot him.

That had no bloody effect at all. He laughed, cried and said to shoot him then. It would be infinitely better than what was waiting for him across the stream.

The Thais were really pissed off. Maybe they would have shot him if Mr Kim and I hadn't been there. They gestured impatiently towards the jeep, and as the relieved KR made his way up the bank onto the road one of the Thai soldiers cuffed him across the head in frustration.

Christ, the boy loved him for it! This was kid stuff to him. He got into the jeep — flanked by the pissed-off soldiers — and the bugger was smiling, no doubt about that.

Davis had filmed the incident and the rejection of the old man with the monkey earlier that day. He sent it off to NBC News in New York as an item of about two and a half minutes: long by US standards.

Too long, they said, and not hard news. It was rejected. If I had shot that for Visnews, it would have been used in full by a grateful editorial desk.

However, the item finally made it to air. Ten days later another producer cabled Neil to ask if the situation at the border was still the same. It was.

Next day came several telexes from various parts of NBC — CONGRATULATIONS ON A VERY MOVING PIECE. It had been run in full.

Davis was highly regarded by NBC News and was upgraded from correspondent to bureau chief in Bangkok in 1981. But he was continually frustrated by his inability to place pieces of any length and depth on the American network. There were other problems, too. Davis was not an American, and while this was sometimes an advantage in being able to get into countries not particularly friendly to the US, there was a resistance to having non-American staffers on air.

In 1981, Bruce MacDonell, NBC's general manager in Asia, had to break the unwelcome news to Davis, that the network had taken him off the air and withdrawn permission for him to edit his own material. This was probably because of executive reshuffling in New York combined with general network policy on using American newsmen and presenters on air. But Davis continued a gruelling schedule of news-gathering assignments.

An undated letter from NBC News in New York (probably in 1979) from Al Chambers, the director of editorial planning, told Davis how much a piece on a Cambodian boy soldier had been appreciated, and that it was 'one of those times when what was really a pretty obscure story for our audience came vividly to life'.

The letter continued: 'While I am at the typewriter, let me also say that we all believe you are making great progress on your delivery. You know that we had nothing against fast-speaking Aussies as drinking buddies, but for American television your better-paced delivery is making a difference.'

Davis communicated to camera extremely well. He spoke quietly, but his delivery was measured and incisive. During the tenth anniversary of the end of the Vietnam war, when the American networks organised live satellite coverage from Ho Chi Minh City, Davis, who had done some key negotiating with the Hanoi government to set up the coverage, played a support role to US-based reporters and front men.

He was permitted to prepare a series of reports on the tenth anniversary for Channel Seven news in Sydney. Those who saw the pieces remember them as models of television journalism, not only for their concise scripting and pictorial excellence, but because Neil Davis's to-camera pieces were vivid and compelling.

However NBC's policy of using their own correspondents for major foreign news stories restricted Davis's chances of doing on-camera work. Davis chafed against this situation constantly. Bruce MacDonell remembers he would devise assignments that only he could cover: 'He would say that he had arranged to get into North Vietnam, but "they will only let me in".'

MacDonell would back him from Tokyo, even though he suspected Davis had engineered his exclusive deal through his extensive Vietnamese contacts.

'I would say to New York, "Do you want the story or don't you?" And they would say, "Can't you get someone else in?"

'I wouldn't even bother, because I knew no one else could get in.'

The complete switch from film to videotape in the post-Vietnam-war era also eroded Davis's enjoyment of his work. The quintessential loner now had to work with a soundman linked to him by cables and leads. Davis's soundman was Bill Latch, a big curly-headed American who had originally come to Bangkok as a missionary. He had been attracted to journalism after doing some radio work but he did not have much journalistic background.

MacDonell describes Latch as an intellectual. He spoke fluent Thai and had married a Thai. MacDonell remembers that the first time Latch came under fire during the refugee crisis on the Thai-Cambodian border in 1979, 'This nice missionary boy started screaming every kind of obscenity.

'He seemed shocked by the idea that he might come

under fire, and I don't think he ever really understood how dangerous the job really was, whereas Davis the professional was aware that death walked alongside you in those situations. Davis knew there was danger, but knowing that helped keep you alive.'

Latch the gentle rookie and Davis the uncompromising professional journalist managed to get on amiably enough most of the time, but there were strains. Always meticulous in the care and maintenance of his equipment, Davis had reservations about Latch's ability to meet his standards.

MacDonell feels that the last three years of Davis's working life were not particularly fulfilling for him professionally. Paradoxically, during that time he became more widely known publicly than at any time in his life because of the screening of the documentary *Frontline* based on his combat experiences in the Indo-China war. Young Australian film maker David Bradbury hit on the deceptively simple formula of linking contemporary interviews with Davis to key historical and combat footage. He interviewed Davis in Australia and on location in Southeast Asia. Trips to London to track down historical Visnews footage and to the United States to view Pentagon films of the Vietnam war exhausted his limited finances, but the result was a compelling documentary which was nominated for an Academy Award as the best documentary in 1980 and won other major international prizes. It was shown in Britain, Europe, Australia and several times on the PBS network in the United States.

Before *Frontline* was released, Neil Davis was apprehensive about how he would be portrayed. Bradbury's politics were clearly well to the left. He later made documentaries on the Australian Communist journalist Wilfred Burchett (*Public Enemy No. 1*), the political situation in Nicaragua (*Nicaragua: No Pasaran*) and an indictment of the Pinochet dictatorship in Chile (*Hasta Cuano*). Davis, on the other hand, guarded his apolitical stance jealously and had argued passionately with Bradbury over what he considered the young film maker's polarised political views.

It was no mean achievement for Davis to be welcomed

to North Vietnam in the postwar years, when his hosts were well aware of his journalistic activities covering the anti-Communist side during the Indo-China War. He was so often seen in Hanoi after 1980 that the the North Vietnamese premier Pham Van Dong jokingly called him 'our visiting Australian Foreign Minister Mr Davis' at an official reception. The North Vietnamese must have known of Davis's close contacts with the KPNLF, the Son Sann-led coalition of dissident Cambodians opposed to the Heng Samrin Communist Vietnamese regime in Kampuchea.

Davis was therefore mildly alarmed when, during his visit to Hanoi to cover the fifth anniversary of the end of the Indo-China war in April 1980, he was approached by Vietnamese officials carrying a copy of the Communist Party newspaper *Nhan Dan.*

'Your film was very well received in Paris,' they told him in French.

Davis was puzzled. 'What film?'

'*Frontline* — the one of your coverage of the war of liberation. It was shown in Paris, and the review in *Nhan Dan* speaks very highly of it. Obviously you are sympathetic to our cause.'

'Jesus,' Davis thought, 'what's Bradbury *done* to me?'

He had no further feedback until he returned to Bangkok in mid-June 1980. The first letter he opened from his pile of accumulated mail was from the extremely right-wing journal *Soldier Of Fortune*, saying how much they admired the film and asking him whether he would write an article for the magazine!

In fact, Bradbury had done a superb editorial job. Davis had insisted that implied criticism or praise of the Americans in Vietnam would be countered by similar reflections on the Vietnamese Communists and non-Communists. He was even more delighted when a review of *Frontline* in the Australian magazine *Cinema Papers* said the film left unclear 'just whose side Davis is on'.

Oddly enough, by then Davis had taken a committed

political position. Although both sides had practised atrocities and abuses in the Vietnam war, he believed you could
mount forceful arguments supporting the actions and ideology of both the Communist and the non-Communist pro-
tagonists. But the scale of the barbarous behaviour of the
Khmer Rouge under Pol Pot defied imagination, let alone
rational argument.

When the Vietnamese took advantage of the weakened
Kampuchean situation to invade in December 1978, the
defeated Khmer Rouge Communists had to join the various
other anti-Communist Cambodian groups camped near the
Thai border. In 1983 the shared desire to drive the hated
Vietnamese invaders from Cambodian soil forged an unlikely
alliance between the Khmer Rouge and the Khmer People's
National Liberation Front, an anti-Communist group headed
by the respected and patrician Son Sann, a former prime
minister under Prince Sihanouk. Prince Sihanouk himself
led a third faction. This shaky alliance became known as
the Tripartite Coalition.

Davis had close personal ties with the Son Sann faction.
In particular he liked General Dien Del, one of Lon Nol's
more able generals during the Cambodian war from 1970 to
1975. He became an enthusiastic supporter of the KPNLF
and quite clearly breached his own standards of impartiality
in reporting their activities.

Davis now drafted press releases for the KPNLF and
took every opportunity to present their case in a favourable
light. Jim Gerrand, who was also in Thailand between 1979
and 1983 believes that Davis was certainly conscious of
this and had taken a decision that his feelings about the
KPNLF and non-Communist Khmers generally should take
precedence over his press professionalism.

'This meant,' Gerrand says, 'that Neil sought out stories
that showed positive achievements and goals of the KPNLF
and also slanted stories against rival forces like the Khmer
Rouge, the Sihanoukists, and the Vietnamese.

'This was contrary to Neil's former standards and his

411

rigorous conditioning of "little brothers" like me. Yet I did not lose respect for Neil for this.'

Gerrand believed that Davis had changed his priorities and that his detached 'professionalism' was no longer as important as some form of positive political contribution.

'It was not something that stemmed from commitment to a political ideology, but more to personal friends and a Cambodian way of life which he saw to be much more humane and valuable than the brutality of either Hanoi's or Pol Pot's brand of Communism — or for that matter, a return to the erratic dominance of Prince Sihanouk and his flunkies.'

The press corps also took it in good part, and called Davis 'The Minister of Information' for the KPNLF.

Davis brushed away cultural barriers with a quiet smile and a gentle gesture. His identification and love of Cambodia and its people was one of the great passions of his life.

30

The Picture
of Dorian Davis

Foreign correspondents based in Bangkok went to extra-ordinary lengths to find out Neil Davis's correct age. They were goaded into action by Davis himself, who not only maintained excessive secrecy about his quest for eternal youth but taunted his brother correspondents that they could never discover how old he was.

Joe De Rienzo, a correspondent who lived and worked in Bangkok during the 1970s, joined the United States Navy and was briefed by the Foreign Correspondents' Club of Thailand that if his ship ever called into Hobart, Tasmania, he should contact the Registrar of Births, Deaths and Marriages to find out Davis's date of birth.

This was done. De Rienzo even located and rang Davis's sister Barbara in his home town, Sorell, to double-check on Davis's entry into the world on St Valentine's Day, 14 February 1934.

His fiftieth birthday party was held at the FCCT in Bangkok. Davis submitted to being pushed into the club-house in a wheelchair with a plaid rug around his knees, thoughtfully munching on a beautiful red rose that had been presented to him.

A mock trial was held in which Davis was accused of trying to cover up his age. The prosecution case was overwhelming, the chief witnesses being De Rienzo (back in Bangkok working for Agence France Presse) and Gary Burns of Visnews. Davis's defence was judged to be completely inadequate — a stack of congratulatory birthday cards he had written to himself. One read: 'I'll make a deal with you. I'll tell everyone your real age — which is twenty-nine — if you tell everyone what a good bloke I really am.' It was signed, 'Pol Pot'.

Yet the joke was really on everyone else. Davis had effectively beaten time. Not only had the 'Picture of Dorian Davis' remained in the closet ravaged and undiscovered, but Neil Davis had avoided one of the self-defining lessons that come to sportsmen — having to decide when to retire.

The mates whom he left behind in Hobart were conscious of slowing in their thirties and entering middle age in their forties. With pride, some envy and regret, they saw their children running harder and faster than they could. But Davis was never forced into making new self-perceptions. He remained in action. As a foreign correspondent, he had cut himself off from his own ageing. His genes helped, too. No code in his own DNA made his hair fall out, his cheeks cave, puff or line or his waist thicken. The reflection that Davis glimpsed in shop windows and bar mirrors was essentially the image he had first known when he came to think of himself as a man.

Sickness and injury were fought to maintain the fitness that went with being permanently thirty years old. He had forced vitality back into limbs and muscles deadened by poliomyelitis. Hepatitis, malaria and war wounds had been overcome. But not even the Davis willpower could overcome a collapsed disc in his back and he had an extremely risky laminectomy in Bangkok in 1983 in which artificial bone was inserted to reconstitute the damaged disc. Within weeks he was badgering his colleagues to test him on the tennis court and he resumed his punishing jogging regime around Bangkok's Lumpini Park.

He could match the youngest and fittest cameraman the opposition could throw against him. His reflexes were still sharp and his competitive edge, honed on the tennis court and against himself in solitary gruelling runs, kept him in front of the competition.

His youthful image was enhanced by a thick thatch of blond hair. In April 1984 he went on assignment to North Vietnam with Gary Burns to cover the thirtieth anniversary of the fall of Dien Bien Phu. They camped in a concrete bunker in the famous valley, waiting for the anniversary parade. Burns caught sight of Davis's bottle of Vitalis hair oil; personal secrets could not be kept in the intimacy of cramped and shared accommodation.

'What's this, then?' demanded Burns. 'You're using greasy kid stuff on your hair!'

'No, no,' protested Davis. 'Look, it says on the bottle, it's non-greasy.'

Burns maintained you could have greased a tractor with the stuff, and he and the ABC's Geoff Leach purloined it from Davis's kit. Davis went berserk and accused them of stealing it, turned over all their gear and complained to the Vietnamese in charge of the accommodation. Then he thought some of the local urchins might have taken it and he chased a mob of bewildered kids down the hill shouting, 'Where's my Vitalis?'

Burns said the sight of the big Tasmanian running after them waving his arms was absolutely splendid. However, Davis had exposed his sensitivity to the passing of time; there were demons of unease working within him.

So were the demons of pursuit. One night in a Patpong Road bar, Burns saw Davis making a play for a stunningly pretty girl behind the cash register. She was not a bar girl and Davis's chances were judged by his correspondent companions to be slim. With unholy glee, they sabotaged every effort Davis made to speak to the comely cashier.

They left the bar and Davis returned on a pretext. So did

Burns a few seconds later, and read the card that Davis had slipped beside the cash register, and which had not yet been claimed by the girl in question.

His cards were specially printed. 'I THINK I COULD FALL IN LOVE WITH YOU. RING ME ON (telephone number). NEIL'

31

'Jesus! You're Hit!'

Although Neil Davis was essentially a modest man who demurred when people spoke of him as 'a living legend', he was very conscious of his reputation as a highly informed foreign correspondent and cinecameraman, as well as a sportsman, lover and hell-raiser. The farm boy from Sorell, Tasmania, had made it to the big league. His opinions were sought and respected by his peers. His accumulated knowledge of Asian and world affairs — much of it based on personal contact with the principal politicians and players concerned — was scholarly and impressive.

Some of those leading players sought out Davis's advice as a friend and longtime student of their countries' affairs. He had come to the region in 1964. He had not only come to know many of Asia's future politicians and statesmen but had enjoyed their friendship and confidences before, during and after the pinnacle of their careers. When he covered the assassination of Benigno Aquino in Manila, he knew him and he knew the family.

During the Vietnam war, Davis had had personal contact with key figures in the South Vietnamese administration, both political and military. Sometimes this knowledge would enable him to be onto a story first or to guess correctly a sequence of events and be on hand to record it. But he did not take advantage of this closeness with principal personalities of the region to abuse trust and confidence.

Some of these people would explain a certain situation to me and express their hopes and doubts, knowing that I would respect their confidence. They, in return, were able to have my viewpoint, given as a friend with an increasing knowledge of their own countries — but given as a friend rather than as a calculating journalist.

Despite this easy, instinctive empathy with Asian people, Davis was not a transcultural figure. He did not wrap himself in loose cloth and adorn his arms with jingling bracelets, nor did he proclaim the mind-enlarging and soul-cleansing benefits of local religions. He travelled as an Australian and a lot of Sorell and Hobart went with him. He was intellectually engaged and at ease with Southeast Asia, and in a way the area had educated him. He was unlikely ever to live anywhere else, yet he was always recognisably and self-consciously an Australian abroad.

Neil Davis was in something of a personal bind. The key to involving himself in the politics and major stories in the Asian region was his job as a roving correspondent and cameraman. His compulsive drive for fitness ensured he had the physical capacity, but he was bone-weary of the routine. He was sick of chasing fire engines, and to arrive back in Bangkok after a gruelling two-week assignment in Manila and get orders to be in Dacca within twenty-four hours was becoming a terrible grind.

Davis liked covering stories that required him to display exceptional physical endurance and a cool calculation of the odds in tumultuous actions, to draw on a network of well-placed informants and to make perceptive interpretations dependent on a long and sympathetic understanding of other cultures. He took pride in breaking spectacular stories that made headlines and led news bulletins around the world, as he did when he exposed the murderous proclivities of the insane mercenary 'Colonel Callan' in Angola in 1976.

But he was also aware that any journalist who was often

in places of international turmoil was likely to come across the marvellous, brutal or bizarre. His special skill was to overcome the temptation to grab quick, sensational head-lines — with stories such as ritual cannibalism in the Cambodian army — and to present his stories with better data and sharper interpretation.

When Neil Davis came to Sydney in July 1985 (he had been sent to cover a visit to Canberra by American Secretary of State George Shultz), he and I began planning the detailed structure of his biography we had been working on for some months at a distance. On Saturday morning 20 July, he came with me to watch my ten-year-old son play a game of soccer on Sydney's North Shore. As we stood in the brilliant Australian winter sunshine beside the playing field, with the shrill shouts of small boys echoing back from the surrounding gum trees, I started to ask him what he planned to do. I got as far as, 'Mate, what are you . . .' and he intuitively knew what I was going to say, although we had not been talking about his plans for the future.

'I don't know mate, I don't know,' he said. 'More of the same, I suppose.'

The usual Davis curtain had come down; I was prying too close to the inner man. But I had known him a long while, and I persisted. 'No, come off it. You're over fifty and you're getting bored shitless running after ambulances. Surely you must have some plans. What about freelancing? That would allow you to live in Asia, and pick and choose your own assignments. You could do more writing, and perhaps some documentary work.'

He said he could not afford to go freelancing — not yet. Perhaps another three years on his present salary — and there had been other offers. The Australian Broadcasting Corporation wanted him as a roving Asian correspondent but the money simply couldn't compare with what he was getting from NBC.

I learned later that he had not been on 'American money' for very long. Davis never pushed for salary and conditions, and Bruce MacDonell told me that when he took over NBC's news operation in Asia in 1980, he had been appalled to find that Neil was on a retainer of about $US20 000 a year. NBC staff correspondents were earning more than three times that amount.

MacDonell realised that this was an accident of bureaucracy rather than a comment on the value of Neil's work. He called the vice-president of NBC News in New York, and said, 'I'm firing Davis.'

The vice-president said, 'But why? He did such a great job for us in Vietnam at the end there, and you want to fire him?'

'I'm not going to have anyone working for me who makes so little money. And obviously you think nothing of him if you only pay him a pittance.'

The vice-president asked MacDonell how much Davis was getting.

'I told him and he was shocked. Davis's salary was tripled overnight.'

But despite the frustrations of being moved about the region and the world as a journalistic pawn in the Great Television News Game, Neil Davis had no real alternatives in mind. The Old Fox could not and would not retire to the lair. Yet because of the documentary film *Frontline*, and the prospect of his biography, he was forced into self-analysis. He had seen his own image in *Frontline* and now he had to consider who he was and what he had done. Through his expertise in reporting news, he had himself become news.

During his brief Sydney visit in July 1985, I hijacked him away from telephones and the expected summons from MacDonell in Tokyo to be on the next plane out, to a bush hut two hours' drive north from Sydney. The country boy from Nala did not find it strange to be cooking over an open fire, lighting pressure lamps and drawing water for billy tea from a galvanised iron tank. For the past few months he had been sending me tapes while on assignment in Hiroshima, Manila, and from his Bangkok base. Now we drafted a proposed structure of his life story, and tape-recorded more key incidents.

I asked him about an ending for the book, and he said he thought it should be his involvement with the satellite coverage of the tenth anniversary of the end of the Vietnam war in Ho Chi Minh City, where he had filmed the victorious Tank No 843 smashing down the gates of Independence Palace on 30 April 1975. It was an event that could empha-sise a triumph in a reporter's life.

This seemed a sensible suggestion, but as we sat beside the campfire, having forsaken the traditional billy tea for red wine to keep the chill of the winter's night at bay, I had a strong feeling that this would not be the end; that there would be another, which had not yet been revealed. I had no portent of his death, but felt that the tenth anniversary of the fall of Saigon was not the logical end of Neil Davis's career or his biography. I also knew that, like certain bomber pilots in Britain during World War II, Davis had acquired an addiction for the sharp realities of a life of action. Given the choice, he would always volunteer for another tour. Retirement was out of the question.

Of course a sense of instinct doesn't stop a well-aimed bullet . . . you can always be killed — unluckily killed.

That night in the hut, the man who had faced the prospect of sudden death in combat was strangely nervous, out in the Australian bush where no conceivable threat existed. Something tapped on the corrugated iron roof, and tapped again. The combat cameraman sat bolt upright in his sleep-ing bag and said, 'Jesus! What was that?'

To humour him, I turned out and walked around the back of the hut. I didn't think there were any possums about and the noise had been caused by the branch of a small tree, stirred by a night breeze, brushing against the roof. I cupped my hands and made ghostly hoo-hooing noises. Davis was not amused.

He was even less enchanted by being locked away with a non-smoker. After forty-eight hours, the heaviest smoker of other people's cigarettes the world has ever known turned to me in a burst of irration.

'God, Bowden! Why aren't you a smoker?'

'You're hooked, boy, you're hooked!'

'No, I'm not . . . but why the *hell* aren't you a smoker?'

Our session in the bush sparked many memories. He brought his twenty-one work diaries with him. Every day of his working life from 1964, carefully noted in his tidy, cramped handwriting, was recorded in them. They were a godsend for a biographer. There were records of where he had been, whom he had interviewed, details of the stories he covered (complete with their despatch details) including his daily expenses. But the diaries held no personal thoughts or intimate details. They were essentially practical records and a helpful guide to Davis's remarkable memory for the cassettes of reminiscences he had already begun to send me.

There was a curious valedictory quality to the last tapes he sent. He spoke about parallels people had made between himself and Damien Parer, the great Australian cinecameraman and correspondent of World War II.

Comparisons are not my cup of tea, but I suppose in many ways Damien Parer and myself are similar characters. I've read about him, and I've seen the great black-and-white newsreel thirty-five millimetre films he took — and of course he was killed.

Damien resisted the American offers for a long time, as I did. I believe our reasons coincide. He found it far less rewarding professionally when he sold out to the almighty dollar.

Perhaps that's not it exactly — I think he thought it was an avenue to project his coverages to a larger worldwide audience. That's only partly true. In the USA, the coverages are shown to a bigger audience, but they are edited back far more harshly and often not shown at all.

The savagely cut film loses the feeling you were trying to convey — even through a news item. Such truncated film is, in my view, a greater loss than not having it shown at all.

I feel I understand Parer reasonably well without having met him. I believe he couldn't adequately convey what his sense of loss was, after having joined an American newsreel company. That's why I stayed so long with Visnews. My coverage was shown, cut at length, worldwide. But it's a sort of anonymous outlet, with your items included in a syndicated package deal.

Davis stopped the tape briefly at this point to collect his thoughts, and then his soft, distinctive voice went on.

But comparing cameramen is like comparing boxers of different eras. Runners can be measured with a stopwatch; boxers can't. That's no way to measure capabilities, anyway. It's the way you approach the job.

I've seen some of Parer's combat film, and I have the same reaction as most people have . . . that he was crazy. But he was crazy in his own way, and aren't we all?

I know that behind my back I have been called Suicide Davis, or Death-Wish Davis. But I consider myself a methodical man, generally a cautious person. I calculate the odds and the risk involved in getting a good photograph or good film — I've always done that. Sometimes they are very minor risks, it doesn't always have to be war. And then I face the situation with my eyes wide open.

423

By the beginning of September 1985 Davis was tired, mentally and physically. He had not taken a proper break in years, and was about to. After leaving Bangkok he intended to spend some weeks in Vanuatu just lolling about on beaches, fly to New Zealand to see the family of a Cambodian friend killed during the war, then come back to Australia for a time. In Sydney, he intended to do some more work on his biography.

The last entry in his diary on 8 September reads:

> Run in Lumpini — one lap in 12 minutes 38 seconds (halfway in 6 minutes 7 seconds). Sedate — necessarily so!
> Still 2 kg overweight at 76 kg. Should be making 74 kg, better at 73.

Before he went on holiday, Davis had a pleasant reunion to look forward to. He had just heard that his faithful driver during the war years in Cambodia, An Veng, had made it over the border to a Thai refugee camp with one of his sons. Neil was very fond of the old man, and had only recently learned he had survived the Pol Pot purges. He planned to sponsor him as a migrant to Australia.

Early on the morning of Monday 9 September, Davis's soundman Bill Latch was taking his daughter to school when he noticed tanks in the streets. Thailand was about to experience another coup d'état — something that veteran correspondents regarded as part of the cycle of life in Bangkok, like the wet and dry seasons. Thai coups were generally bloodless, although there had been exceptions. They were essentially military affairs, because Thailand had a military government headed by Prime Minister (General) Prem Tinsulanonda.

Latch headed for the office to telex Bruce MacDonell, NBC's Asian general manager in Tokyo.

PRO BRUCE

JUST A MILD ALERT THERE MAY BE SOME STRANGE THINGS

HAPPENING HERE. TANKS ARE STATIONED AT STRATEGIC AREAS OF CITY. THERE HAS BEEN NONO ANNOUNCEMENTS YET BUT WE ARE STANDING BY. IT MAY BE ANOTHER THAI COUP AND AM CHECKING. PREM IS IN JAKARTA.

CHEERS, BILL.

MacDonell keyed back immediately.

G'MORNING BILL . . . BRUCE HERE. DIDN'T THEY HAVE THIS YEAR'S COUP A COUPLE OF WEEKS AGO???

Latch replied:

NO, THAT WAS THAI ARMED FORCES DAY.

OH . . . WELL GUESS YOU'D BETTER COVER. IS NEIL THERE?

NO . . . I WAS JUST ABOUT TO CALL HIM.

I'LL DO IT. I NEED TO TALK TO HIM ABOUT SOMETHING ELSE ANYWAY.

MAYBE YOU'D BETTER GET THINGS READY TO GO OVER THERE. SORRY TO BORE YOU GUYS WITH THIS. BUT YOU NEVER KNOW . . . ONE OF THESE YEARS IT MIGHT EVEN GET SERIOUS.

NO PROBLEM . . . BI.

BI.

It was a casual, almost mocking appointment with death worked out by friends linked by the capacity and demands of instant communications. MacDonell, an experienced newsman, was not overly excited by the news, but he appreciated the early tip-off on what could develop into a major story. He phoned Davis and, with some apologies, put paid to his plans for a relaxed day.

In Bangkok, Davis and Latch filmed military activity in the streets and made arrangements to have the early footage shipped out to Hong Kong to be sent to New York by satellite. It was a measure of events that day that Bangkok's international airport was still operating normally.

When news came in that some shooting had broken out in Bangkok, MacDonell realised that this might be a Thai coup with a difference. He rang NBC's office manager Kusuma to stress that the early tapes must be hand-carried to Hong Kong, not consigned as freight through customs, or they would not make the satellite feed in time for NBC's major news bulletins.

'About forty-five minutes later,' MacDonell said, 'I realised from the tone of Kusuma's latest telex that the videotapes hadn't been shipped.'

Davis had given his own instructions to Kusuma.

'I was just furious,' MacDonell recalled. 'This wasn't the first time Neil had changed something that clearly did not need changing. I sat down at my typewriter to punch out a blistering rocket to Neil.'

NBC NEWS
BANGKOK

PRO DAVIS

DAMMIT NEIL I SAID I WANTED THE STUFF PIGEONED. IF IT GOES BY SHIPPER WE'LL NEVER GET IT OUT OF CUSTOMS. WHEN I SAY I WANT IT ONE WAY THAT'S HOW I WANT IT. I'M GETTING A BIT TURNED OFF BY YOUR ANTICS ... PIGEON IT!!!!!!!!

YOUR ONCE PAL
MACDONELL

DO I OWE YOU ANYTHING ELSE???
BEST
MACDONELL

Tearing the page angrily out of his typewriter, he headed towards the telex machine.

MacDonell says, 'My secretary came in, giggling — which is a Japanese reaction sometimes to extreme stress or emotion — and said, "Neil's dead ... Neil's dead."'

In Sydney, on that same morning, I began work on Neil's biography, exploring his attitudes to fate and death. As Davis and Latch, Gary Burns and his Thai soundman Daeng

Chou Ping (Julie) Yen and Neil Davis were married in Taiwan on 29 January 1977.

Returning to Bangkok on 22 June 1981, after seven days solitary confinement in an Iraqi prison, Davis found this sign hanging outside the Grand Prix bar — the journalists' watering hole — in Patpong Road. *Bill Latch*

(Left) Another attempted Thai coup d'état. Tanks in the street outside the First Division radio station in Phitsanuloke Road. (Right) Soundman Bill Latch and Neil Davis wait to film any action moments before tanks and machine guns opened fire.

(Left) Even the Thai soldiers seem relaxed. Attempted, or the occasional successful, coup d'états in Bangkok are usually fairly bloodless affairs. (Right) Firing breaks out, and the newsmen try to take cover. A spray of shrapnel kills Davis almost instantly. The gross nature of his injuries leave a ghastly blood trail as his friend Gary Burns drags him along the pavement away from the action.

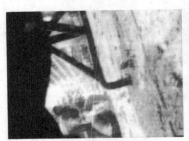 

(Left) For a few seconds the silhouette of Davis's head is framed in his own lens, as his still-rolling camera tilts crazily on its side. It films not only Burns dragging him away, but the tanks still firing seemingly at the trapped newsmen. Davis has actually filmed his own death. (Right) Davis lies dead in a Bangkok street. The mortally wounded Latch can be seen in the background, supporting himself on his hand and elbow as he tries to crawl to safety.

Kariah tried to take cover behind a telephone junction box from tank and machine-gun fire being directed over their heads into the army radio station behind them in Phitsanuloke Road, Bangkok, I was spooling through Davis's recorded tapes for the quotes I wanted.

> *I wasn't afraid of being killed, but I really didn't want to be wounded and lie out there with a gut full of shrapnel — I'd seen a lot of wounded soldiers die like that, and I didn't care for it at all.*

In Bangkok, Neil Davis was seconds away from being 'unluckily killed'. The manner of his death would be spectacular.

Despite its heroic overtones, the deaths of Davis and his sound man Bill Latch were futile, and as MacDonell put it, 'You can be the world's greatest Pollyanna, but you cannot read one decent thing that came out of his death. There was no reason for it happening. *Nothing.*'

Until the firing broke out, Davis's adrenalin was not even faintly stirring. His sixth sense was sleeping. Not even the appalling red socks he had taken to wearing on all occasions brought him luck this time. One of his many nicknames was 'Mean Samnang' — Cambodian for the Lucky One. But not that day.

The four newsmen huddled behind the all-too-small metal telephone junction box outside the disputed radio station, while the ground shuddered beneath them and shrapnel sprayed indiscriminately. The noise was stunning. It seemed hardly possible to think. Burns, who was protected by the bodies of Latch on one side and Davis on the other, put out his arm to draw Davis further in behind the junction box. He noticed blood on Davis's arm.

'Jesus! You're hit!'

'No, no, I'm all right, I'm all right.'

They were not Davis's last words, but death was only seconds away. A withering burst of fire was directed into the wall directly behind them, spewing out thousands of steel fragments.

There was just time for Davis's brain to register that he had been mortally struck. The Thai death certificate said: LACERATION OF THE HEART, LUNGS, SPLEEN, KIDNEY AND BLOOD VESSELS IN THE STOMACH CAUSING EXCESSIVE BLOOD LOSS . . .

Through the crash of the explosions, Burns heard his last words. They were not exclamation and expletive, but monumental irritation as he registered the futility of it all. 'Oh . . . shit!'

Postscript

The death of Neil Davis had a profound impact on the immediate destinies of two of his closest colleagues and friends.

Gary Burns decided to resign from Visnews as a news cameraman.

'It wasn't a question of being frightened. I had to sit beside Neil's body for what seemed an eternity before the firing stopped and I could organise transport to try and get him to hospital.

'As I sat there watching him bleed into the gutter of that Bangkok street, Thai photographers tried to lift up the sheets of newspaper I had covered him with, to try and take pictures of his frightful wounds.

'I thought of all the tremendous things he had done in his life, which had culminated in such an inglorious death. At that moment I decided that I was not going to die like that.'

As Davis himself had said in Vientiane in 1971 on hearing of the deaths of three correspondent friends in a helicopter crash: 'Suddenly I feel mortal'. Gary Burns had been a protégé of Davis's, and they had shared assignments in Asia, the Middle East and Africa for a decade.

Burns and his family left almost immediately for Australia, to find another job.

Bruce MacDonell, NBC News's general manager for Asia, also resigned his position.

'I guess a whole piece of my life has gone with Neil dead. He was fun, he was a friend, he was a delight to talk to and deal with.

'It wasn't NBC's fault. Part of the reason why I left was that NBC to me was becoming like a house where your parents died, or a spouse. It was haunted. I thought about him all the time.'

MacDonell said he really thought Davis would die in bed, that he had survived the really dangerous times.

'I think that's what really affected people so much, particularly correspondents who had known him for a long while.

'Every game has to have its untouchables, and he was the untouchable.'

Epilogue

Committee for the Safety
of Foreign Correspondents in Cambodia

AFFILIATED WITH THE A. F. C. V.

ROOM 25, HOTEL LE ROYAL, TEL. 2-3969
PHNOM-PENH, CAMBODIA

August 5, 1970

MEMO TO FOREIGN CORRESPONDENTS TRAVELING BY ROAD

The following suggested rules have been offered by colleagues:

1. Never choose a jeep, or any vehicle that can be mistaken for a military vehicle, for travel by road in an insecure area. If you are mistaken for a military target you may not even have the chance of being captured alive. Choose civilian vehicles.

2. Be sure your car has sufficient gasoline and oil for the trip. Be sure you have a spare tire, a jack that works, and a spare fan belt. A breakdown in a contested area can be dangerous and is a risk you can minimize.

3. Take a Cambodian-speaking guide with you. Almost no villagers and few troops along the road can speak French with enough fluency to advise you of the situation.

4. Tell someone where you intend to go before you leave and what time you intend to return.

5. Perhaps the most basic rule when traveling in doubtful or contested areas is to repeatedly stop oncoming traffic and ask for information concerning road security.

6. When in a doubtful area if there is no oncoming traffic pull over and wait until someone comes along. If at the same time you see no one walking on the road or in adjoining fields you should leave the area immediately.

7. Watch houses as you drive. If you see them closed and shuttered and do not observe any normal activity you are probably in a dangerous area.

8. Regularly stop at military posts along the road and discuss the latest developments with the officer in command. He may not be entirely informed, but the evidence you accumulate in this way may allow you to form a composite picture of the true situation.

9. Road guards who tell you there are troops 'x' number of kilometers ahead are not reliable. The question is whether security exists along the road between the two points. If no Cambodians are traversing these areas by cycle or on foot, it is certainly unsafe for you.

10. The Viet Cong and Pathet Lao frequently lay a tree branch or spray of leaves on the road surface as a signal to drivers. This signal means you should slow down, that there is danger ahead. If you decide you have to go through, the proper conduct is to slow down. If it is a large obstacle, stop. The Viet Cong and Pathet Lao frequently want to inspect vehicles from the cover along the road without showing themselves, to make sure they are not military vehicles. If no one appears after you have waited at the roadblock five minutes, sound the horn once. If no one appears still, get out and remove the obstacle, moving slowly and making sure it is not booby-trapped. This rule applies to infrequently-traveled roads where there is no military action going on.

11. There is no point in attempting to run Viet Cong and Pathet Lao roadblocks unless you are absolutely certain what lies ahead. The roadblocks are put up for a reason. There is something ahead that those who put up the roadblock do not want you to see, such as troops crossing the road, placing of booby-traps, etc. While speed is an asset on an open road as a precaution against being ambushed, running through a visible roadblock is asking for trouble.

12. Stay alert at all times. Observe the behavior of the people you see. If you get into a tight situation, keep cool.

Index

INDEX